LIFE AND CHARACTER

OF THE

REV. SYLVESTER JUDD.

Eng.ᵈ by J. Mahou

In much love,
Your Son. Sylvester.

Printed by R. Andrews

LIFE AND CHARACTER

REV. SYLVESTER JUDD.

Compiled by

ARETHUSA HALL

KENNIKAT PRESS
Port Washington, N. Y./London

KENNIKAT PRESS SCHOLARLY REPRINTS

Dr. Ralph Adams Brown, Senior Editor

Series on
LITERARY AMERICA IN THE NINETEENTH CENTURY

Under the General Editorial Supervision of
Dr. Walter Harding
University Professor, State University of New York

LIFE AND CHARACTER OF THE REV. SYLVESTER JUDD

First published in 1854
Reissued in 1971 by Kennikat Press
Library of Congress Catalog Card No: 72-122655
ISBN 0-8046-1303-6

Manufactured by Taylor Publishing Company   Dallas, Texas

In the composition of this work, the design has been to make it, as far as possible, an *autobiography*. Not only the existence of abundant material for this purpose, but the desire that Mr. Judd should be made the exponent of himself, led to the adoption of this course.

In making selections from sermons, lectures, letters, and private pages, that would fill volumes, such have been chosen as were thought best fitted, by their playful touches and varied lights, to present him as he was, going in and out in daily life; to delineate in their true shades the multiform and shifting phases of his character, both as to individual prominence and collective harmony; to exhibit the governing principle of his being, in all relations, public and private; and, especially, to show how an earnest seeker after truth and right sped on his way, and with what persevering self-reliance and brave conscientiousness the battle of life may be fought.

If, with this intention, the extracts given shall be deemed too ample, the explanation must be found in the perhaps partial feeling of one who has watched with fond interest his every variety of development, from the first opening of his eyes in infancy to their final close on earthly light,— that the rich mass of manuscript matter left behind was too good to be lost.

The life of Mr. Judd consisted rather in inward progressions than in outward changes, and of course furnishes little variety as a story of incident. But, to those who feel that a range at large in the field of thought is of greater worth than a transition from one physical locality to another, that high and noble principles are more honorable than conspicuous stations, and that wealth of soul far outweighs the richest material products, it will not be found wanting in interest and attractiveness.

Those who have known Mr. Judd only as an author will readily perceive, that this was by no means the most distinctive form in which he put forth his powers; but that the *author* was lost in the *man*, at the same time, as has been truly remarked by another, that "the author was intensely the expression of the man."

As to the plan chosen, it was found quite impracticable to introduce, with that prominence which seemed their due, the important details of his general views and modes of action into the current history of his life, without getting bewildered in mazy, labyrinthian episodes, the graceful escape from which would have been difficult to the writer, and the impression produced upon the reader confused and unsatisfactory. Should it seem that by this method something of repetition occurs, or that any thing is lost as to the general unity and harmonious blending of the whole, it is believed that amends will more than be found in the increased clearness secured, and the greater justice done to salient points.

The compiler — for to authorship there is little ground of claim — has not aimed to pronounce an eulogium on the subject of this history, or to enter into any analysis or critical review of his literary productions. She has sought only, in a simple, truthful manner, to sketch a life and character, which — with a most intimate knowledge of the one, and a perfect understanding of the idiosyncracies of the other — have impressed upon her own heart the deepest love, the most profound reverence; and the preparation of which, by leading her to live over again the past in intimate communion, has served, in some degree, to beguile the deep feeling of loss occasioned by the temporary interruption of sensible communication.

ARETHUSA HALL.

BROOKLYN, N. Y., July 4, 1854.

b*

CONTENTS.

CHAPTER VII.   PAGE

CHAPTER VIII.

CHAPTER IX.

CHAPTER X.

CHAPTER XI.

CHAPTER XII.

CHAPTER XIII.

CHAPTER XIV.

LIFE AND CHARACTER.

LIFE AND CHARACTER.

CHAPTER I.

PARENTAGE AND CHILDHOOD.

WESTHAMPTON.

SYLVESTER JUDD, the third of that name, was born in Westhampton, Mass., July 23, 1813. This is a small town in Hampshire County, about ten miles west of Connecticut River, and one of the four designated, according to the principal points of compass, by the name of Hampton. There is no part of it that can very well aspire to the appellation of village; although its one church, one or two stores, and a few dwelling-houses, sparsely clustered around, form a point of general centralization. It is strictly an agricultural town, and its inhabitants are mostly farmers. The surface of its ground is very much broken, and diversified with abrupt, rocky hills, covered with a variety of forest-trees, thus forming much beautiful scenery of richly wooded hill and shady dell, varied here and there with green pastures and cultivated fields, in the midst of which stand

1

the owner's residence and its appendages, expressive
of neatness and taste, industry, good calculation,
and thrift, or otherwise, as the case may be. The
soil in general is poor, rather penuriously rewarding
the toil of the husbandman. Many of the young
men go abroad to seek their fortune; and, in some
instances, roads from one part of the town to another,
once well travelled, are now closed, and whole farms
given up to pasturage.

The inhabitants are, in general, industrious and
frugal in their habits; and many of them have, by
prudence and economy, amassed what in such small
country towns are considered very comfortable little
fortunes. They are, in the main, moral in their characters, regular church-goers on the sabbath, and a
good degree of religious feeling prevails among them.

Among the first settlers of the place, about the
time of our National Revolution, were several heads
of families, well educated and refined for those days,
and, if not of the highest order of old-school gen-
tility, certainly well nigh approaching it.

First and foremost among these, and, — in the
good old-fashioned times when reverence for age and
station had not become an obsolete virtue, — looked
up to by all the young, as well as their seniors, with
great deference, was the *minister*, the Rev. Enoch
Hale, the first, and, in those more stable days, for half
a century the only pastor of the church. His wife
was a kind-hearted, motherly woman, lady-like in
manners, and exercising a good deal of taste in personal appearance and household arrangements. The
influence of the good parson and his lady on the

society of the settlement, in its nascent state, was by no means small, and its favorable effects have been traceable ever since. All of their own large family of sons and daughters received a good degree of general culture. Two of the sons, Hon. Nathan Hale, long and well known as the able editor of the "Boston Daily Advertiser," and the late Dr. Enoch Hale, of Boston, a highly respectable physician, were educated for the liberal professions.

Dr. Hooker, son of the Rev. John Hooker, of Northampton, for many years the only physician of Westhampton, and now sustaining a beautiful green old age of almost ninety years, must be mentioned as the head of another influential family.

Many other worthy names might be noticed, were this the place. The temptation is strong to linger a little upon this retired rural retreat, and its quiet, friendly people. But it must suffice to add, that, under the early impetus given to the general tone of things, the mass of the succeeding generations grew up with a very good appreciation of learning and intelligence, and, if not with high refinement, at least with an entire absence of vulgarity. Private schools of a high order have been sustained from time to time; and, according to its population, the town has furnished our colleges with a large number of students, who in due time have held honorable places in the learned professions.

THE PATERNAL GRANDFATHER.

Holding a prominent place among the first settlers of Westhampton, was Sylvester Judd, senior, the paternal grandfather of the subject of this history. He was a son of the Rev. Jonathan Judd, of Southampton, the first clergyman of that place, and for sixty years pastor over the same people. Like all clergymen's sons of that day, he enjoyed better opportunities for education and general development than were usual. In due course of time, he began to clear and improve some wild land, purchased by his father in a part of the township near the borders of Southampton; he erected a dwelling-house; he married a wife having peculiarities which are often termed *odd*, and which left their impress in some degree on the son and grandson with whom this narrative has to do; and, while yet a British subject, set up for himself. Bears were often heard in the cornfield near by; and the young mother shuddered for fear in the absence of her husband, and took care to secure her children safely within doors.

This pioneer in a then new country sympathized fully in the interests of the Revolution, but did not engage in active service farther than in buying and forwarding provisions for the army, or something of that sort. He was one of the members of the first Convention for framing a Constitution for Massachusetts in 1779.

Though large and stately in person, he was a man of very little physical strength, and never applied his own hands much to labor. He was the careful overseer of his business and hired men, and engaged pretty largely in buying and selling cattle, sheep, swine, and so forth, for market. Success attended his efforts; and in a short time we find him, in part-

nership with Dr. Hooker before mentioned, the joint
proprietor of a store in the centre of Westhampton,
and afterwards of one also in the adjoining town of
Norwich. He possessed a good deal of shrewdness
in turning a shilling to a pound, a trait for which the
immediate inheritors of his name were not particularly distinguished. A little extra capital soon enabled
him to put up an addition to his house, making it a
square, hip-roofed mansion, commodious, and, in those
days, rather imposing. Large trees stood in the ample yard around; and the whole place had a pleasant,
inviting aspect, suggestive of circumstances quite
above board.

He was the first Justice of the Peace of the town,
and, in those days when titles were less common and
more distinguishing than now, was always known
as 'Squire Judd. For many years he represented
Westhampton in the General Court at Boston, and
served often on committees for laying out roads, and
in other like capacities. He was a man of firm integrity and deep religious principle. A good deal of
the old-school gentleman, he was deferential to the
minister, courteous to woman, and, as known in his
later years, a merry-hearted old man, good company
for the young as well as the old.

As his children, one after another, established
households of their own, the old family mansion was
the favorite place of resort and re-union. *Thanksgiving* was the great holiday festival of the year.
On this day, all the children with husbands and
wives, and grandchildren great and small, gathered
around the paternal board. Great indeed was the

good cheer. Every thing which the farm or the *store* afforded was laid under contribution. The festivity was prefaced with a rich mug of *flip*, and genuine New England cider formed the beverage of the meal. It seemed to be almost a conscientious principle with some to make on this day a thankoffering upon the festal board of every article of food with which the God of harvests had blessed their store.

When the long-continued repast was over, the large old family Bible was brought forward. Its leaves

"The sire turns o'er, wi' patriarchal grace,"

and then, in sonorous voice,

"The saint, the father, and the husband prays."

If more space than seems appropriate is given to these delineations, the apology must be found partly in the desire to perpetuate a knowledge of the good old New England character, habits, and *homes*, which is so fast being lost in the impermanence and railroad whirl of the present day, and partly in the reflection from the mind and writings of the younger Sylvester Judd of that love of nature and primitive simplicity which were in a measure induced by these very scenes.

THE PARENTS.

Sylvester Judd, the second, at the age of thirteen, and having enjoyed only such means of education as the common school then furnished, was placed as a clerk in his father's store. After remaining in that employment about two years, weary of its confinement, and with true boyish restlessness and desire to see something of the world, for about six months he took up his abode in Boston. A part of this time he served as clerk in a store. Fortunately, at his boarding place, he fell in with some persons of intelligence, whose influence was to stimulate his own mind to an appreciation of knowledge and a determination for its attainment. At length, satisfied with his experiment, he was quite willing to return to his former station in Westhampton.

But a new life was begun. The great object now was mental progress. Whatever spare money he could get was invested in books, and all the leisure moments intervening between the calls of customers were devoted to their perusal. Yet these ill sufficed to gratify the thirst for knowledge that had now sprung up in his mind. There was no other way but to encroach upon the hours due to sleep; and for many successive years it was a common thing for the young man to sit up until twelve, one, and two o'clock, poring over his books. For about six weeks only, he received some aid in his studies from the Rev. Mr. Hale, who at that time was in the habit of taking young men into his family, and fitting them for college, or otherwise attending to their education. But with this slight assistance, and under all the hindrances he had to encounter, he mastered the Latin language sufficiently to read Virgil, progressed far enough in Greek to understand the New Testament in the original, obtained a very thorough knowledge of French as a *written* language, and gained some considerable acquaintance with Spanish. He went through a full course of the higher mathematics, penetrated deeply into history and political economy, and made himself quite extensively acquainted with polite literature, — a noble example of the practicability and value of self-teaching.

Soon after he had attained the age of twenty-one, the senior partners retired. A new firm was established by their sons, whose places of business were respectively Northampton, Norwich, and Westhampton; the younger Mr. Judd remaining at the latter place.

About this time, he was married to Miss Apphia Hall, daughter of Aaron Hall, of Norwich, a young lady of much native sensibility and refinement, and of high appreciation of general culture.

THE MATERNAL GRANDFATHER.

Her father, at the time the Revolutionary War began, was in his Freshman year at Harvard College. But the college was broken up, its members scattered, and this young student was forced to exchange the quiet halls of Cambridge for a life in camps. He was in the service, the greater part of the time acting as officer's clerk, until the close of the war. And in after-days, in a good old age, it was his delight to repeat again and again stories of those times that tried men's souls to the listening ears of wondering grandchildren. His early pursuits left a fondness for information, and till his latest days he was much given to general reading. From the great depreciation of the paper currency with which the soldiers of the Revolution were paid, he realized nothing of consequence for his long services and the disappointment of his early hopes and prospects. After following the profession of a schoolmaster for many years, he finally, with limited means, entered upon a farmer's life in the town of Norwich, then in its early settlement. His small, poor farm never afforded him any thing more than a bare living. He was a man highly respected and influential in the town. As Justice of the Peace, he always bore the appellation of 'Squire Hall, and for years served as representative of the town in the General Court. He was a man of high-toned honesty, of great conscientiousness, and of strongly developed sense of justice.

HOME AND CHILDHOOD OF THE BOY.

In a few years after his marriage, the young country trader built for himself a commodious house, opposite his little store, and near the meeting-house. He planted an orchard, and took pains to engraft fine fruit ; and, a thing never done in the town before, set out in the yard around his house shade-trees, and sent to a distance for shrubbery, flowering plants, and vines.

Though born in a house a few rods distant, here the third Sylvester Judd, whose life and character it is the particular aim of these pages to delineate, had his home during his child-life. Here was a portion of the face of nature with which he first became familiar ; and here did he receive his first impressions of the mystery called death, by the removal from the household of a little brother. Here he conned his first book-lessons at the common school; here took his first religious impressions, and received Calvinistic instructions at the sabbath school. In mature years he writes of these teachings: "I cannot forget those days. I well remember the benevolent countenances of my teachers, and the solemnity with which they told their young pupils that we were sinners, and must be born again, or we could not go to heaven. I recollect, too, the mingled look of still unsatisfied curiosity, and unanalyzed yet real disappointment, which came over the more thoughtful of my class, whose minds were just beginning to unfold themselves to the intense impressions of religious things." Here he learned the Assembly's Catechism; and, at the close of the afternoon sermon, took part in the public catechizing, the children being "arranged in the broad aisle, the boys on one side, and the girls on the other, with the minister in the pulpit at the head, and the elderly people occupying the neighboring pews."* Here was the "Noon House, — a small building near the school-house, where several elderly men and women went (on sabbath noons), and ate their dinner, and had a prayer." His father's house was also open on sabbath noons for as many as it would contain of the people living too remote from church to go to their homes in the interval of service. Here the venerable old grandfather and grandmother, in an old-fashioned chaise, followed by a young aunt and

* "Margaret."

other members of the family in a small wagon, were seen driving up in early hour for church service, as regularly as the sabbath came, from his farm two or three miles distant. And in the father's parlor at noon were gathered the grandparents and particular friends and relatives of the family, where they partook of a cold collation of " nutcakes and cheese," and other articles of food that could be prepared beforehand; for there, in those times, as little was done on the sabbath between sun and sun as possible, — " snuffed snuff;" smoked pipes; " talked of the weather, births, deaths, health, sickness," and so forth.

The sabbath was at this time observed, in this quiet country town, very much after the manner of the Puritan sabbath, so graphically described by Miss Sedgwick in " Hope Leslie." At these sabbath-noon gatherings, every face wore a serious aspect; and if, as often happened, the muscles of the elders were relaxed by the outbreaking wit, or rather drollery, of an old aunt, and her antagonist a gentleman of about the same age, it would be accompanied by " a half-deprecating, half-laughing " expression, which seemed to say, " She is so droll, that a body must laugh, though it be sabbath-day."

The young Sylvester was the second child and son of the family; and then followed three brothers and a sister, all born at the " new house," as it was called in distinction from the one where the two eldest first saw the light. As a child, he was quick to learn, and careful to learn correctly. He joined in plays and active sports, but was always distanced in these pastimes by his older and next younger brother. He manifested an amiable disposition, was gentle in manners, and evinced a tendency for getting into sympathy with others. He was distinguished for conscientiousness; and the impression of those then about him is, that he was never known to utter an untruth. Whether, at this early age, there was discernible in him any marked susceptibility to nature's influences, is not known; neither were there remarked striking characteristics of any kind.

The following expressions from his own pen, in after-years, may serve as a hint of his own remembered impressions: "The child has sometimes aspirations that tower high, thoughts that reach far, fears that sink low. We can all remember such moments in our history. How much of eternity has come over that boy's mind, who has cast his fishing-line into the waters of our silently flowing Connecticut! I do not say his reflections may not be dissipated by the first dip of his float; but an impression has planted itself in his heart, which will influence him for ever." And again: "I had from my earliest days thought much of God, and very often did I retire to pour out my soul in secret to him."

For a few years after marriage, the father prospered very well in his pecuniary affairs; but, after the coming on of the war with England in 1812, his small business was very much embarrassed, and at length well nigh closed. After a time, he partially resumed his operations; but no good degree of prosperity attended his exertions. He was not naturally fitted for mercantile transactions, and never

entered into them with any great degree of enthusiasm. As time passed on, his love of study quite
overbalanced his willingness to submit to the drud-
gery of exchanging pins, tape, and snuff, for a few
eggs and paper-rags; of measuring off calico and
ribbons for their value in butter and cheese; or
drawing molasses, rum, or brandy, for waiting customers. For in those days, the country store was
an *omnium gatherum* of all sorts of merchandise, "a
motley array of dry and fancy goods, crockery, hard-
ware, groceries, drugs, and medicines."

REMOVAL TO NORTHAMPTON.

A younger brother of his, Hophni Judd, Esq.,
had been educated for the profession of law, and had
established himself in Northampton. Here, in connection with the Hon. Isaac C. Bates, he had become
a proprietor and editor of the "Hampshire Gazette,"
an old respectable newspaper, the first, and then the
only one, in the county. But, unhappily for sorrowing friends, this promising young man, with
bright professional prospects, and on the eve of con-
summating his fond visions of domestic bliss, two or
three years previous to the time above referred to,
had fallen a prey to slowly-consuming pulmonary
disease.

It was now determined, in 1822, that the Westhampton brother should quit his ill-remunerating
and distasteful occupation there, remove to Northampton, and become sole proprietor and editor of the
paper with which the deceased brother had been con-

nected. It was not, indeed, without some degree of painful feeling that he decided to leave the house which he had built, with its flourishing young shade-trees, shrubs, and flowers, and the promise of fruit from the orchard, which he had taken pains to plant, and the ground around, that had received the foot-prints of one of his little boys that had passed away from sight. His children were, of course, too young to share in these feelings. To them, change, and the prospect of being where there was more chance for amusements, was very pleasant. Of this period of his life, before the change of residence to North-ampton, the younger Sylvester wrote, at a later time, that the memory of it was merely as "a pleasing dream."

But the now aged grandfather, left solitary in his farm-mansion by the transition to the spirit-world of his life-partner, and seven out of his eleven children, and the marriage of the remainder, had, the year previous, given up his old home, and come to reside with this, his only son. A widowed daughter now came to administer to the wants of the declining parent, so that the house was not left desolate; neither did it go into the hands of strangers, but for many years afterwards was the fond place of gathering on Thanksgiving and other times for children and grandchildren.

CHAPTER II.

NORTHAMPTON.

THE spring of 1822, then, finds the boy Sylvester, in the ninth year of his age, transferred from his native place to the adjoining town of Northampton. The village which bears this name, and in which his father now came to reside, is justly celebrated as one of the most beautiful spots in all New England. Its streets are embowered with wide-spreading, venerable elms; it has an abundance of shrubbery, many well-kept gardens and tastefully laid out grounds; in its environs are inviting foot-rambles and pleasant rides; here is Round Hill, with its wood-crowned summit and green-nested residences, looking out afar upon a beautiful panorama of green fields and rich meadows, of neat little villages with their church spires and public buildings; and stretching off in the distance, with the irregular peaks of Holyoke and Tom in the foreground, is the far extending perspective of mountains, with dark cloud-shadows and bright sunlight upon their sides, now reposing in dignity, and anon chasing each other with flying footsteps; here, too, is the well-shaded venerable old burial-ground, where sleep the forefathers of the village.   All these elements conspire to render the place most lovely and attractive.

Amid these charming scenes, Sylvester passed the period of boyhood.   A deep impression was made by them upon his mind and heart.   A sensibility to the beautiful was developed.   Deep religious emotions also often stirred his young spirit.   The account given by himself of some of the religious experiences of his boyhood is as follows : —

" Religion, which as a subject of thought often engaged my attention, and as a subject of feeling deeply interested my heart, was a mystery to me.   It was a fundamental article of my belief, that I could not become religious until I was made so by an extraneous and special operation.   Still I earnestly longed for the ' one thing needful.'   I can but allude to the irrepressible desire, the cravings of my heart, for a full participation in the religious feeling.   But the influences of my creed came over my spirit like an autumnal frost, and sealed up the fountains of emotion.   Abused Nature did not always remain silent under her injuries.   She poured her complaints into my ear with a voice that I should not have disregarded.   But the prejudice of education rendered these monitions powerless upon my reason and convictions.   I supposed myself totally depraved ; and thus was my earlier youth passed without being permitted to indulge in its proper sensibilities.

"The works of God were all perverted to me. They were dispossessed of their highest, their religious beauty. When I fished by the river-side, when I rambled in the woods, when my fancy led me to a favorite hill-top that overhangs as lovely a landscape as our continent embraces, I thought this world was beautiful; I thought it beneficent in its uses; I felt that there was a unison between the scene around me and my own heart. But then I knew that my own nature was cursed, and that the earth had been cursed; and I supposed that this harmony was depraved, or at least that there was nothing desirable about it; and I did not allow myself to cherish it as much as I wished, nor with that delight which it has since afforded me. I used to repine almost, that I had not lived with Adam in Paradise, when the earth was *really* beautiful, and man's nature could properly sympathize with its charms. I used to hope that I might live to see the millennium, when this double curse would be removed, and men would be restored to the true enjoyment of nature. I looked up to the stars at night: I supposed that they had not been cursed. While my imagination would be revelling in the idea of their number and distances, my heart would throw itself abroad, and mingle somewhat in spirituality with the infinite God who made them; I felt something of humility, something of adoration, something of love; but I had not been converted. Of course my feelings were not religion. There could be no right harmony between my heart and the unsullied glories of God's handywork, which thronged the firmament."

2*

HIS BOYHOOD-SCHOOLS.

On coming to Northampton, Sylvester at first attended a private school taught by a lady. Here he distinguished himself for quickness of perception, and facility in acquiring knowledge. He then went awhile to the old Hawley Grammar School of the place. Nothing is known of his doings here, save what may be inferred from a passage in a Lyceum Lecture, which, after attaining manhood, he delivered in Northampton. He says: " Many of us were taught our rudiments in the old Grammar School-house, whose square roof and low walls, with its broken windows and loosened clapboards, still survive to kindle our recollections. There was little study, but an iron discipline. Instead of instruction for the mind were the ferule and switch for the hand and the back. There were school-hating and truant-loving. For philosophical experiments, the combined skill of the school was employed in constructing a fire of green logs, and keeping it active during the day. Perhaps there were better things than these. But these things were. I wish, indeed, I could allude to that old building, with a better tribute to its memory."

In 1824 he was allowed to accompany some young ladies, relatives of his, to Westfield Academy, then under the care of the Rev. Emerson Davis. He was a member of this celebrated institution for only one or two terms, but long enough to attract the notice and win the approbation of the principal, little

boy as he then was, in the midst of young men fitting for college. The kind, good preceptor is remembered to have said, that there was great pleasure in
giving young Judd instruction or correcting any mistake in his recitations, because he never had to repeat
it a second time — it was always remembered. While
here, he commenced the study of Latin, and made his
first attempts at elocution and composition-writing.
His first written production was submitted to the
examination of one of the young ladies under whose
care he was, before being handed to his teacher. It
was quite creditably written, but very short. On her
asking why he did not write more, he very naïvely
replied, "because he was afraid he should not have
any thing left to say in the next one." He did so
well in elocution, always recollecting to observe suggestions previously made, that, at the annual public
exhibition, he had one or two parts assigned to him.
He was at that time a bright, pleasant-looking boy,
gentle in his manners, and very obliging in his disposition. He became quite a *pet* with the young
ladies of the school, much older than himself, who
used to gather around, and make him the subject of
their caresses.

On returning to Northampton, he attended a private school taught by Mr. Charles Walker, from
whom he received a copy of the " Lights and Shadows of Scottish Life," inscribed as "a reward for
attention to study and correct deportment."

In the summer of 1825, we find him at a private
school under the care of Mr. Robert A. Coffin, who
presented him a like testimonial of good scholarship

and deportment. He continued at this school for two or three years; and the efforts at composition, at this period, are the earliest productions of his pen which he preserved. They are very respectable for a boy of his age, but exhibit no particular saliency of thought or fertility of imagination. They contain many indications of moral and religious sensibility. One is entitled, "The Advantages of Early Piety."

A REVIVAL, AND HIS CONVERSION.

In 1826, there occurred in Northampton what is termed a revival of religion, under the ministrations of the Rev. Mark Tucker, accompanied with its usual powerful appeals, and multiplied religious meetings. The mind of the boy being naturally susceptible to religious impressions, and even before this time having been exercised with solicitude about his own spiritual welfare, he very naturally threw himself into the current of strong feeling which was abroad. Without much inward conflict or mental distress, as it is believed, he soon found peace in the hope that his eternal salvation was made secure. Of this experience he writes : " At length a revival came, that long wished-for occurrence. Into its scenes of stirring interest and solemn devotion I entered, with that enthusiasm which the subject was adapted to enlist, and which my own nature prompted. I found that which I sought. I was happy in the free exercise of a new heart, and was satisfied in my election being secured." Zealous in imparting to others the great benefits which he felt he had attained, this young disciple immediately entered upon the ministerial office, so far as laboring and praying for the conversion of his companions was concerned. He, with others, often held meetings in a barn, where, mounted on a barrel's head, he would put forth earnest appeals to his playmates to forsake sin, and enter the pathway of eternal life. There was in his prayers an unction which moved the hearts of those even of maturer age. He did not at this time unite with the church, though the Rev. Mr. Tucker regarded him as his spiritual child.

INTERRUPTION IN STUDY, AND EXPERIENCE AS A CLERK.

He remained at school, continuing to make good progress in his studies, and acting quite consistently with the Christian character. He would have been glad to press steadily on, and fit himself for college. But he was interrupted in this course. This was a severe trial, and for a number of months he was quite unsettled and unharmonized. Nervous irritability developed itself; and, from being the happy, kind-hearted boy, he became at times unamiable, morose, and filled with disquiet. He talked a great deal about going to sea, and his friends feared that in desperation he would yield to his impulse in that direction. His darling wish was to pursue his studies, and it was a bitter thing to give it up. He passed some months with his grandfather in Westhampton, and at length became in a degree reconciled to the disappointment.

In the spring of 1829, determining to try what he could do in the mercantile line, he went to Greenfield to serve as clerk in the store of an uncle. Not succeeding very well in a business for which he had little tact or inclination, he remained about a year, and returned home, where for some months he made himself useful to his father in keeping books and settling accounts. His spirit had in a measure resumed its natural quietness: at least, he had done much towards patiently submitting to the inevitable. While at Greenfield, he had access to a circulating library, from whose shelves he drew largely. A considerable portion of the books read at this time were novels, though a respectable minority of them were on solid subjects. He wrote a brief review of all he read; and, from the dates attached, it is found that in six months he perused, and noticed on paper, more or less at large, forty volumes. No prospect of permanent employment offering itself at home, he embraced an opportunity of trying what he could do as a dry-goods clerk in Hartford. He went now not only with a willingness to devote himself to the business, but with a determination to make most earnest efforts to succeed. The result of this experiment, and his feelings attending it, may be seen from the following letter: —

"HARTFORD, Oct. 14, 1830.

" Dear Father, — My own great, unceasing, and, as I had supposed, *well-directed* exertions have proved useless. After I had been here three weeks, W. asked Mr. —— if it were probable I should stay with him. He said it would be determined soon, and mentioned wherein he thought I failed. Four weeks have elapsed since then, during which time I have been doubly diligent, and fondly hoped I was pleasing my employer. Monday morning last, Mr. —— said to me, without any previous warning, 'Sylvester, I do not think you will answer our purpose.' After a little explanation, I asked if it were *determined* that I should not stay. He replied, 'Yes.' If a bolt from heaven had struck me to the earth, I could not have been more startled.

"Thus, father, am I again thrown out of employment, and my dreams of future happiness, connected with Hartford and my present circumstances, blasted in a moment. But that is not the worst. An indelible stigma is fixed upon my character, at least so far as concerns my capacity of remaining a merchant's clerk. I know not what to do.

"New York is so near that I have a good mind to go down and get aboard ship in some capacity or other, and sail for distant climes, where neither the queries of *present* friends, the inquiries of *present* relations, nor the sneers of *present* enemies, will trouble me more. But still I say, 'New England, with all thy faults, I love thee well.' I do not *mean* to visit Northampton again, at least until I can give a better account of myself than at present.

"There is still another thought that deeply affects me, especially when I consider its consequences either way. Had I known half as much of myself years ago as I *think* I do now, instead of handling the yard-stick, I might now be treading my way, at least to *some* distinction in the paths of literature and science. Still I hope it is not now too late to appeal to the heart of a father. I recollect reading not many years since, in the diary of a person, — [and here it may be added, the son quotes from the father,] — an expression to this effect: ' I ought to have been sent to college, a place by far best calculated to develop the natural propensities of my mind.' If I know any thing of myself, I think I can say without self-flattery, that such is my own case, using the present for the past time. Do I appeal in vain, when I ask, in short, that I may have a *liberal education?* "

KNOWS NOT WHICH WAY TO TURN.

Disappointed, chagrined, despairing, — to use his own words in writing of it afterwards, — he *knew not which way to turn.* The desire of his heart, years before, had been for a student's life. He had sacrificed this wish, and striven earnestly to succeed in the business which seemed most feasible. His best efforts had proved fruitless, unavailing; and, as he thought, the failure had left its stamp of disgrace upon him. He made a trip to New York, and for a few days sought to dissipate his troubled feelings by learning what he could of interest of this great, busy city. In a short time, his mind getting somewhat accustomed to the disappointment, he returned home.

The chief obstacle in the way of his pursuing a liberal course of study was the want of means on the part of his father to sustain him in it. As has before been shown, the business of the father at Westhampton had not been profitable. On coming to Northampton, he had met with good success as editor of the "Hampshire Gazette." It was a business in which he was interested, and for which he was fitted. The paper improved in his hands; it was sought and appreciated for the amount of valuable and highly instructive matter it contained. In a short time, his subscribers more than doubled. But he was never the man to press his debtors to pay their dues, if they were not disposed to come forward voluntarily and do so; and the net income was not large. In addition to the want of means, the father had very little confidence in any thing the professions had to offer, with the exception of the ministry; and possibly, biassed by his own experience, he was a little wedded to the idea that self-teaching was more valuable than any other; and the best way, after all, was for a man to make himself.

The question involved too much to allow of a decision at once, though it is evident there was a leaning towards the affirmative. It was at length settled, that Sylvester should pass the coming winter at his grandfather's in Westhampton, and attend a private school taught by Dr. Wheeler of that place; at the same time giving some assistance as clerk in the little store where his father used to be, and which was now in the hands of a kinsman. Even this arrangement for the winter, with the uncertainty of its being prolonged beyond a few months, was joy indeed to his heart. He resumed his studies with great zest. His compositions at this time

evince quite an enlarged sphere of thought. To
some of the follies and gossip of the school-circle,
he applied the wholesome caustic of a little satire.
Elocution also received some of his attention, and
he joined a class in a singing school, and underwent
a drilling in the rudiments of music. But, his ear
being a little at fault, he never met with much success in his efforts at singing, although he had a great
fondness for it.

This residence for a few months in the place of
his birth, and in circumstances so pleasant to him,
together with frequent visits previously, and attendance upon the Thanksgiving family gatherings at
the home of his childhood, where now the venerable
old grandfather dwelt, added to the remembrances
and associations of his young years, formed a strong
tie to the place, which ever retained its hold upon
him. At about this date, he writes to a cousin, " I
always loved Westhampton, its hills and dales, its
woods, fields, and gurgling brooks, yes, and its inhabitants too ! " And ten years afterwards, writing to
another cousin who was also a school-fellow of his at
this time, he says : " All my youth centres in Westhampton. Northampton is nothing to me : I seem
never to have *lived* there. In Westhampton I did
live. I could die there. Its hills, its meagreness, its
people, all have an interest for me."

In the spring of 1831, Sylvester returned to
Northampton, still perplexed as to what course he
was to take. There was no school in town of the
kind he needed to fit him for college. But Hopkins
Academy at Hadley was only about three miles dis-

tant; the walk back and forth would serve as a good physical balance for the requisite exercise of mind; and he could thus board at home, and save all expense, except that of tuition. His mind also was now fully made up, if he could go through the required preparation, to devote himself to the sacred ministry; thus meeting his father's views on that point.

It was therefore at length settled, that he should enter Hopkins Academy, and pursue his studies as far as the advantages of the institution would admit; leaving it for time to decide whether a college-course was to follow at the end of that period.

CHAPTER III.

PREPARATION FOR COLLEGE, AND COLLEGE LIFE.

HOPKINS ACADEMY.

On the first of June, 1831, therefore, our young friend became a member of Hopkins Academy, boarding at home, and taking a walk of six miles every day in his journey to and from school. But a light heart made willing footsteps. The gently flowing Connecticut he crossed; through the rich meadows of corn and grain he passed; birds in the apple-trees and old elms cheered him on; and the broad Hadley-street, lined with its thick-set ancient trees, afforded him shade and smooth walking at the close of his trip.

He was happy now in the entire abandonment of all his energies to his favorite pursuits. The intricacies of Greek and Latin, and the knotty problems of mathematics, were no stumbling-block to him. He never seemed to study hard, or to make any particular exertion to learn his lessons, and yet he always had them. He was fond of writing, and it seemed to cost him no effort. His compositions at this period are quite full, and on a variety of subjects connected with the times and circumstances, among which were the Military Spirit and the Evils of War. His sense of the injustice done to Poland showed itself in a lament for its fate. All his pieces discover more than a common range of thought, and are marked by religious fervor. Moral subjects, and especially those of reform, attracted his attention. His increase of knowledge all seemed turned to moral purposes. In one piece he thus apostrophizes : " *Charity*, heavenly messenger! thy look tells us how holy seraphs are. A garland encircles thy forehead radiant with gems more white than Ceylon's pearls, more brilliant than Brazilian diamonds. Thy blue eyes are modest as is the firmament above our heads. Thy countenance is lighted up with a smile benignant as those who bore the welcome news, — ' glad tidings.' "

In his second year at Hadley, something of a poetic element was developed in his nature. He tried his pen a little at rhyme and blank verse, in original pieces, translations, and parodies. But, while many of these were very well sustained, there was then no evidence of his possessing great poetical talent. The annexed lines, showing his sense of the pecuniary embarrassments which hindered the gratification of his wishes, occur in an address to Poverty : —

> " Thou potent one, in strongest chains
> Who bind'st me filled with woes and pains,
> Do break the rivet, set me free.
> As birds once held by wires, with glee
> Shoot forth, when loosed, and know not where
> To stop, for theirs is all the air,
> So let me go. No good, I'm sure
> To hold me thus. It will not cure
> My restlessness, however tight
> Thou fitt'st these manacles.
> . . . .

> Good sir, loose, loose your hold.
> Where science leads, I wish to go,
> And soon to reach Fame's temple too;
> Where mind's choice pleasures grow,
> I wish to tread, and there to sow
> The seeds of influence and esteem.
> Regard not these as airy dream,
> But say, God speed thee in thy way.
> . . . .
> Cease clenching thus, lie down to rest,
> Thy bed I'll smooth like linnet's nest.
> . . . .
> Again, I say, let go thy hold,
> Or I will be as thou art, bold.
> Thou leerest like a demon lost:
> By Jove! but thou shalt learn the cost.
> I yet will burst my fetters strong,
> And bind them where they best belong.
> I'll break thy iron teeth, thy jaw
> I'll cleave with steely point, thy maw
> Hot stones shall fill."

At the exhibition which closed his academic course, he was honored with the valedictory address, which he gave in the form of a poem; and, at three or four of the previous quarterly exhibitions, he spoke original pieces. He also delivered an Astronomical Lecture before the Lyceum of the town. Some part of the time he was at the academy, he was president of its Literary Society.

On quitting Hopkins Academy, he writes: "The school is done. The thousand tender ties which have been binding my heart to others for more than a year, have now been cut off; and my heart, thus set adrift, feels desolate. The road which I have trod so often, and always with pleasure, must now be walked by other steps than mine. I leave Hadley with many regrets. Her citizens have always treated me with that civil attention which has made a deep impression on my mind. Their respect is not the hypocritical respect of necessity, but that resulting from kindness of heart, and a habit of attentive courtesy."

RELIGIOUS EXPERIENCE.

As has already been stated, in 1826, at the age of thirteen, Sylvester shared in the interests of a revival of religion in Northampton, and found happiness in the hope that his own eternal salvation was secured. He had always been susceptible to religious impressions, and now he had experienced the great change which he had been taught to believe necessary. The boy's mind was at peace ; and he went on for a year or two, quietly endeavoring to perform what he considered Christian duties, and happy in the thought that he was indeed a child of God. At length, disappointment in pursuing his studies came, together with some other trials and crosses of his natural temperament. He became irritated and depressed. His religion, which was then probably more an impulse than a principle, was not found sufficient for the emergency. Wrong feeling brought self-distrust, and self-distrust again re-acted in wrong feeling. He became lost, blinded and unhappy in his religious course, and was well-nigh inclined to give it all up.

But when the hope of a student's life was revived, with it returned decidedly religious feelings, and the determination to make the ministry his profession. Soon after he commenced attending Hopkins Academy, he made a public profession of religion, by uniting himself to the Calvinistic church in North-ampton, then under the care of the Rev. I. S. Spencer. There was another revival at this time, and into its interests he entered with renewed fervor. Partaking largely of the then existing revival-spirit, he was urged on with a zeal not always according to knowledge. The prevailing idea of his mind was, that all were divided into two classes, — the converted and the impenitent; and that the latter, without the change termed conversion, were for ever hopelessly lost. He had received the belief, also, that their salvation, or the responsibility of their eternal perdition, rested, in a great measure, upon the faith-ful labors of the truly converted. Burning with the desire that all might be saved, and filled with horror at the thought of the eternal misery of any soul, he, with other young converts of the time, labored, in season and out of season, for the conversion of the impenitent, and for the arousing of old professing Christians, who, it seemed to them, were dead to the tremendous realities of their obligations. At the academy, frequent prayer-meetings were held; and many were the admonitions and appeals to his un-converted fellow-students. In company with another young man, he even went so far as to go forth on a sort of missionary tour to the adjoining towns, to hold meetings, and urge sinners to repentance.

ENTERING COLLEGE.

In August, 1832, a little more than a year from the time he entered Hopkins Academy, Sylvester finished the studies preparatory for college. His father could promise only a part of the means requisite for a college-course; but, with some encouragement of aid from other friends, the hope of gaining something by teaching or some other business in vacations, and the opportunity of availing himself of a public scholarship, he entered Yale College in the September following. In a letter to a friend, a short time previous, with reference to the pecuniary embarrassments by which he was environed, he says: " I shall probably go *coarsely* dressed, but do not be ashamed of me. I *must economize.*" The last scene in which he engaged, previously to his departure, was assisting at the obsequies of his revered and aged grandfather, at the old home in Westhampton. Of this event he writes to his brother J. W.: " Our endeared grandsire, the virtuous citizen, the man of integrity, the firm Christian, is no more. His counsels will never again greet our ears, or his living example lead us to purity of life and morals. But he, being dead, may yet speak to us. What a noble pattern for imitation! May his descendants look at it, revere and follow it! His path, we can but think, has been the path to heaven; and there, we trust, he now rests in the bosom of his God.

" We, too, must die; and, when we die, may a

light like his proceed from our graves to guide posterity in the path of virtue and religion! May we be gathered to our fathers, as he will be, attended by the blessings of all around us! Oh that his mantle, as he is borne on angels' wings to heaven, may descend and envelop us!"

And now we see this young man, after his many struggles and disappointments, at last ensconced within the walls of one of our oldest and most honored universities, the dream of his early youth accomplished, the highest wish of his maturer years realized, the path to literary fruition stretching out gloriously before him. He felt that his cup was now full to overflowing, and his grateful heart poured itself forth in lively acknowledgments to the Author of all good. A deep sense of his responsibility to others also attended him.

On finding himself settled in college, he writes in his Journal, Sept. 27, 1832 : —

"On Tuesday last, I was examined, and admitted Freshman here. I have begun a new life. It has its morning, noon, and evening, its hopes and disappointments, its joys and sorrows; its dangers from heedlessness, its dangers from extreme care; its path to glory, and its path to infamy. It presents allurements to ambition, and often pampers envy. The spirit of emulation and unholy rivalry is a deep, gulfy stream, which lies along the path of this life, in which thousands are wrecked. I shall need the instructions of tutors and professors to guide me in the path of science, but especially shall I need the counsels of Infinite Wisdom to direct my way to heaven. How shall I begin? A good beginning seems to offer a successful, beneficial, and happy progression, and a triumphant termination. As a man, I must be honorable; as a student, industrious; as a classmate, courteous and kind; and, more than all, as a Christian, I must be gentle in spirit, exemplary in conduct, chaste in conversation, and ready in every good word and work. Oh for grace to obey the commandments of my Saviour, to cultivate his spirit, and love him with all my heart!"

Some extracts from letters written during his college-life will form the best history of this period. Those which immediately follow will exhibit his religious position on entering college.

FRESHMAN YEAR.

To his Cousin, G. L.

"Yale College, Oct. 29, 1832.

"The multifarious duties of college-life so eat up time, that there is scarcely a vestige of him left, in which to mingle our feelings with those of absent friends, by the medium of letter-writing. As you may well suppose, time so occupied flies swiftly. I have been here now almost six weeks; but, in the retrospection, these dwindle to a moment. They seem like a swift-winged dream.

"Our class has increased to one hundred. About one third are professors. Of the remainder, some are moral, some profane, and some openly vicious. How interesting would be the sight, if all these could be reclaimed from sin to holiness! How noble the work for the Christian, while here, to be engaged not only in fitting himself for greater usefulness, but also in winning these talented youth to espouse the cause of Christ, and consecrate all their talents to him! You will see how responsible a person becomes, who is placed in contact with minds which are to exert a vast influence on society, for the influence he exerts on them. Such is my situation. And may God grant that I shall fulfil the every iota of my responsibility!

"It is not necessary that I give you the particulars of a Freshman's initiation. Suffice it to say, that we had smoking, breaking windows, stealing keys, calling before mock-tutors, and so forth. These a Freshman must endure, and with the more grace the better; for resistance seems almost vain.

"We board in commons; that is, some hundred or hundred and fifty students eat on the lower floor of a building, partitioned into rooms, connected by doors. Our fare is good, but we have noise and confusion without end. While the blessing is being asked at one table, there will be rapping, ringing bells, and hollowing for 'Waiter, waiter,' at another. This mixture of noise and sacred things is sometimes too great for my risibles, so that I am obliged to laugh in spite of myself.

"Permit me to inquire how nearly assimilated you are to the purity of heaven. The true answer to this question determines your advance heavenward. It seems to me that we are apt to labor under a mistake of this kind; to wit, we look upon a Christian, and consider him to be going so fast towards heaven, as he advances in life; and, when he dies, we say he has got to heaven. But, if assimilation of character be the test of a man's nearness to the heavenly world, it follows, that if you and I are less watchful, prayerful, and godly than we were eighteen months ago, we are farther from heaven; and that, if we continue in this cold state, we shall never reach it, or, at least, we shall come to a much lower seat there than if we had died then."

To his Sister-in-law, E. W. J.

"Dec. 3, 1832.

"Now when I write to those in whom I feel an interest arising from a relation like yours and mine, I do not wish to give them, as I am sure they would not wish to receive, the fag-end of a multiplicity of thoughts; but wish, as mother says, to wash up, put on a clean cap, take my knitting-work, sit down in the old rocking-chair, and visit, sociably and freely.

"'The sacred affection,' ha! Really, E., I thought you were a matron, settled down in life, and that you had forgotten the airy things that maidens and poets dream. If you are not so, you must at least consider us students as on the Alps of wisdom, and looking down on the thunderings and lightnings of that 'sacred affection' with a sort of sovereign indifference, free from their dangers ourselves, yet rather pleased to see their effect upon others."

The home-circle was remembered by him with the keenest interest; and to it, jointly or individually,

4

were frequent communications addressed. The annexed letter discloses also how fondly he was kept in mind by the different members of the family: —

" Dec. 15, 1832.

" Ever-remembered Parents, Brothers and Sisters, —'Tis a rainy and gloomy evening. The noise that is ever kept up in and about college has ceased. I am comfortably seated by my stove in the act of writing. My chum is reading by my side. This afternoon I received two boxes of good things from home, and have just had the pleasure of eating my cake and cheese with my friend, Mr. P. and my room-mate, Mr. J. Thus you see we have had our Thanksgiving; although a little out of time, yet not out of spirit. We cut the cake with our penknives, and drank toasts on water. These articles came like water to a thirsty traveller. On opening the box, I was sensibly reminded of the care you all take of me. First came the apples; then mother's care in the form of curtains, carpet, cake, and so forth, which I well knew A. assisted in the preparation of. Then came H——i's bag of pop-corn, butter-nuts, and the choice apples the little ones had taken pains to mark their names on, and send to me. I put P——n's apple to my lips, and thought P——n shall have a kiss, and kissed the apple in place of her rosy lips.

" I received this afternoon, from Mrs. L., a mother in Israel, the unexpected offer of my board without remuneration. This was too acceptable and generous to be refused. So you see my cup of temporal felicity is full. The clouds that have darkened my future prospect seem, at least for the present, to have rolled away. Have I merited this? Indeed not. It is His high prerogative to give, though merit shows no claim.

"My studies, too, are not of a nature to weary the spirit with constant tediousness and difficulty. Devotion to them may be called a recreation rather than a task. To Him who is distilling upon me the gentle dews of peace and prosperity, and not pouring out upon me storms of perplexity, disappointment, and misery, be the glory. I say these things because I have seen some under the iron grasp of poverty, ready to despair, with no prospect of relief; and others vexed at and baffled by algebraic problems, or Latin and Greek abstruseness, ready to throw their books to the four winds.

"The college-bell wakes us at six in the morning, when we hurry on our clothes, wash in a hurry, and hurry to the chapel for prayers ; some buttoning their vests, some tying their handkerchiefs, and all with the sleepy scales scarcely loosened from their eyes. This is too much a formality, I fear, in which religion is too solemnly mocked, but by which it is known that all the students are up, and ready for recitation, which immediately ensues.

"The package of letters I received yesterday. Take care, H——i, that your 'iron-shod sled' don't run away with you. I am afraid that, some Saturday afternoon, it will start off to slide down hill, and take you with it, when you had better be at home.

"P——n will soon learn to write her own letters ;

then she can tell her absent brother what she wishes, without employing an amanuensis. (Look in the dictionary.) I am afraid that I shall not go home in the vacation to get your 'hundred kisses.' Keep your temper sweet as your lips, and then your kisses will be sweet indeed. You had better study your books, P——n, than to make dolls, for your dolls will be spoilt or lost; but what you learn will never be lost. I hope soon to see a neat little letter in your own handwriting. It is now after ten; and, as I suppose you are in bed, so I will be. Good night.

"Your kindnesses, my mother, have ever been reiterated, and too often upon my ingratitude. But I can be ungrateful no more. If your children, or your child, have ever caused you hours of anxiety and silent sorrow, may hours of brightest hope and unclouded joy, on their account, be yours now and evermore!"

A few months after entering college, he inscribed in his journal, the following—

"CONSECRATION."

"Fully sensible of my weakness, sinfulness, and proneness to wander, in full view of the temptations from the world, the flesh, and the devil; aware of the great obligations this act imposes upon me, yet knowing that our blessed Captain requires the entire soul, the supreme affection, and whole devotion of all his followers, not only as the strict demand of duty, but as the happy enjoyment of privilege, and trusting in Him who strengthens the weak, makes holy the sinful, and who gives grace to resist in the hour of temptation, and with much prayer for direction and support, I now make this solemn consecration :—

" I consecrate myself, my time, my talents, my influence, my thoughts, my property, my knowledge, and my all, to God and his service. Be my witness, Holy Father, thou my Saviour, thou my Sanctifier, angels, spirits of the pit, myself.

" I consecrate myself as soul and body, the one to devise, and the other to act, till death dissolves their mutual connection; and then my spirit, wherever in the universe of God its existence may continue, and its service be required. I consecrate my time, to fill up each year, month, week, day, hour, and moment, with some act performed that shall bear the impress, Holiness to the Lord ; — my talents, to give them a decidedly religious culture, and to exert them in the cause of truth and holiness, and in opposition to error and irreligion, wherever seen and however found ; — my influence, to extend its sphere as much as possible ; to have it so decided that all may know that it is for God, at all times and under all circumstances ; to never draw it away for fear of reproach or unpopularity, with whomsoever I may be ; and to make it as wholly for the cause of truth and religion as possible ; — my thoughts, to keep the current of them constantly directed to subjects which directly or indirectly promote his glory, to watch them, and check at once all aberrations, and to give them for food, not the allurements of ambitious or envious contemplations, or lustful scenes, or scenes

4*

of worldly pleasure, but the rich feast of heavenly
and divine things ; — my property, to use what little
I now have, in securing an education for the gospel
ministry, and, should more ever be my portion,
to use none of it for superfluous or rich articles of
dress or household equipage, for the dainties or lux-
uries of food, or for any unnecessary gratification ;
but to make a wise distribution of it among objects
of benevolence, whether the poor and distressed
directly about me, or the dark and benighted souls
all over the world ; reserving so much as a wise
regard to the interests of my immediate dependents
may require ; — my knowledge, when I know sinners are pressing to ruin, to endeavor to bring them
to repentance ; when I know Christians are cold and
worldly, to endeavor to warm their hearts, wake
them to duty, and give them an impulse heavenward ; when I know the result of any measures will
be prejudicial to the interests of religion, acting
always discreetly and carefully, to point out the evil,
and attempt its stay, and to increase my knowledge
by every possible means, in things that have a bearing on the destiny of man, the glory of God, or the
salvation of the world ; — and I consecrate my all
— help, Lord — can I do it ? Have I counted the
cost ? Will my after-life bear witness to a consecration entire, and never disregarded or broken ? How
weak I am ! Help me, dear Saviour, not only to
write, but to keep this last, and each particular, of my
setting apart myself to thy service : yes, I do it — I
make a dedication of my ALL. Henceforth, fare thee
well, vain world ! Welcome, Cross ! I'll take thee

up, and bear thee through strifes, through sneers, though death be my portion. Come, Spirit of heaven! come, take up thine abode in my heart. I would make room for thee there. I would cherish thee as the apple of my eye, suffering nothing to grieve thee, or cause thee to leave me. Begone, Pride, Anger, Envy, Selfishness, with all your train! the blest Spirit comes — make room. Thou Holy Dove! come, and rest on me. I would be meek as thou, as innocent, as pure.

"This act of consecration is to be in force to-day, to-morrow, next year, while I live, in death, and after death — *to all eternity.* I henceforth, in whatever I have not heretofore, stand before the world a *Christian;* a stranger and sojourner here; as one who is not of this world, but as one whose heart and treasure are laid up in heaven; and I will await the hour of death with a calm resignation, following the example and doing the will of my Saviour, till he calls me away, to give me my crown of everlasting glory.

"Resolving to read this considerately and prayerfully, at least once a week, and praying the Lord to enable me to keep it, or, if it be not entire, one more entire, I subscribe my heart and name to it.

"S. JUDD, JR.

"YALE COLLEGE, Jan. 26, 1833."

To his YOUNGER BROTHER, H——L,
Who was residing at the old place in Westhampton.

"YALE COLLEGE, Jan. 23, 1833.

. . . "But you have no one to call you up in the morning. No, that voice you used to hear is hushed;

that inquisitiveness to see that all was right, no longer
makes you particular; that peevishness, as you used
to think it, troubles you no more.   He sleeps in the
dust.   But shall we not let his example live, and
influence us day by day?   His precepts were good,
his carefulness praiseworthy; and shall we not regulate some of our actions thereby?   Oh! he is dead;
I can hardly realize it.   And shall I never see him,
or meet his welcome smile, or shake his aged hand
again?   This reflection starts the big tear, and I can
but weep as I think of it.   The grave covers the
mortal remains of our dear grandfather; but his
name and virtues will never be obliterated from our
memory; and his spirit, we trust, dwells with his
Maker above."

Further on, under the same date, he shows his
sense of the insufficiency of knowledge alone to give
the happiness he sought.

"Would you enter upon the vast field of human
learning, the farther you advance, the wider it spreads
out before you.   You are climbing a mountain whose
height is endless.   Peak on peak will arise on your
view.   One surmounted, another is before you.   There
is no end.

"I would not discourage human learning.   But
the subject is so vast, investigation is attended with
so much uncertainty, and one is so obliged to thread
his way through clashing theories and conflicting
opinions, that I would say to one who can content
himself with a farmer's life, and with such knowledge as is *indispensable* to our happiness, particularly
that of the Bible, in the hope of one day seeing that

which is secret brought to light, — to such a one, I would say, be contented.

"Let me tell you, dear brother, from experience, advancement in learning of itself does not make me happy. I am no more satisfied now than when I first entered Hadley Academy. And were it not that one day, I hope, by what I now learn, to spread farther the news of His salvation whom above all others I love, I would quit college to-day.

"Riches, favor, worldly honors, human learning, are like the fabled Syrens, in whose embrace we revel, and are delighted awhile; but, if they do not destroy our souls, they soon leave them to disquietude, desolation, and misery. But there is divine learning which *satisfies* the soul, and will satisfy for ever."

To his Sister-in-law, E. W. J.

In which appear his efforts, even then, to solve the problem of the salvation of children.

"Yale College, Jan. 28, 1833.

" 'Tis in *social* prayer-meetings we knit the bonds of brother or sister-hood more closely. 'Tis there we catch a mutual flame that burns along the road. 'Tis there we begin and cement a union that shall never end.

" I can assure Miss G. that I am not studying for the *Baptist* or for any other *denominational* ministry, but for the *Christian* ministry.

" I am sorry you have so little faith in children's conversions. This much seems to be true, that, when they are able to understand the nature of conversion, they can be truly converted, and will endure to the end. But, when they are not able to *understand the nature* of it, how can they *experience* conversion? And on what principle of the Bible or common sense will they be damned?

" I think that, if children can understand conversion, they can also be made to know what it *costs* to be a Christian. The world and its charms, and its emptiness too, also the treacherousness of their hearts, should be set before them, and likewise the heavenly world and its charms and its fulness, and hell and its misery. And if they can understand this subject fully, surely they can choose which they will, and *persevere* in the choice. The evil is here. Children, by nature and education, are taught to feel, that to look pretty, to dress well, to excel companions, to be gay and happy in the world, and so forth, are the chief end of man. Just alter this state of things, bring down eternal things to their understanding and feelings, let a *child* know that a few short years set us afloat on the ocean of eternity, and all things earthly will pass away, — I say, let them know and feel these things, let parents, teachers, and guardians constantly teach, and live themselves, in view of these things, and I think there is but little danger of children's 'taking in the bewitching world' as they grow older; for they learn to set a true estimate upon it."

To his Young Sister, A.

"Yale College, Feb. 8, 1833.

. . . . " I would ask, as a far more important question, what proficiency you are making in the school of Christ? The lessons which he teaches are not like those of arithmetic and grammar, which affect the head only; but are lessons in humility, meekness, faith, holy love, and holy zeal, and affect the heart and life. You have not been long in this school, but long enough to have made great advancement in the divine knowledge which it teaches. Persons, after attending this school awhile, are very apt to grow weary, to be remiss in their attendance, and not half get their lessons. Oh, how cruel it is that we should slight our blessed School-master so, who has been at infinite pains to establish a school, the only object of which is to make us wise for our own present and eternal happiness!

"You will recollect that the teachings of the Bible fit us not only for a heaven hereafter, but for a heaven here on earth. If all people would be meek and lowly in heart, gentle in disposition, patient in tribulation, ready to forgive, mild in temper, ready to assist others, of truly polite manners, courteous and obliging, do you not think the world would be a heaven begun? Let us aim at cultivating these inestimable graces, these dispositions of mind, which assimilate ours to the character of angels; which make us like our blessed Saviour. We should never be fretful, impatient, or overbearing, though a brother or sister, a father or mother, or any one, should request of us to do, or should themselves do, any thing which crosses our own convenience or pleasure. Christ never was, and we never should be. We have but few years at most to live, and soon the attractions of the scenes of time will be lost in the awful grandeur of the scenes of eternity."

To his Sister-in-law, E. W. J.

"Yale College, April 4, 1833.

"This is a misty, gloomy night; but such, you know, is the very element of revery and contempla-tion. Dark clouds hang over the face of the hea-vens. The moon and stars are gone: their faint light can scarce show the late traveller his path. This reminds me of the veil that extends between us and eternal things. Oh, if it could be withdrawn, what glories, what beauties, what soul-enrapturing scenes, would burst upon the view! The ineffable glory of the Son of God, clothed in loveliness and compassion to the humble believer, but in wrath and terror to the guilty sinner, would be revealed. The New Jerusalem, with its golden streets, its gates of pearl, would appear adorned with a beauty and mag-nificence, which fancy with all her powers can never reach.

"Since I was with you, I have read my Bible more, and felt more, as I have turned leaf after leaf, that the Almighty Jehovah was speaking. With the eye of spiritual discernment, I have been enabled to discover the application of various promises, and have applied them. This has given me strength and boldness in prayer, and implicit reliance on the good-ness and mercy of God, and lit up in my soul a flame of holy love. Often in secret on my knees in prayer, I have felt a holy transport, a sweet peace, that I would not exchange for the wealth of Indies, for the sceptre of empire; blissful prelude, I trust, of the time when no sin shall embitter our enjoyments, and 'not a wave of trouble roll across my peaceful breast.'"

Finding it very difficult, with the greatest economy in all respects, to obtain the means of defraying his expenses at college, Sylvester decided to pursue the regular studies by himself at home, the last half of his Freshman year. During this time, a conflict began to arise, with considerable violence, between his reason and his received faith. In trying to reconcile the former to the latter, sceptical feelings were evolved which greatly distressed him, and from which he shrunk back with horror.

To A. H.

"Northampton, June 23, 1833.

"You are a very watchful Mentor, and I am sorry that your Telemachus is not so docile as he might, and perhaps ought to be. You are a very discreet adviser, hold a gentle rein; but he is apt to feel the bit, and knows that *entire obedience alone* will secure gentle treatment.

"I take my station daily by the north chamber window. Here I sit and muse in my own solitude, annoyed by no bell, no tutor's call, or fear of the black mark. Here I become wrapt in the story of Helen and Priam, laugh at the fun of Horace or am half enticed by his sensuality, or plunge into the depths of Euclid. Love! how strange a thing it is! As you remarked going to B., it rules the world.

Yes, little naked Cupid, with his bow and arrow, effects a mightier conquest than all the crested myriads of ancient times, or all the artillery of modern days. We see this abundantly substantiated in our classic reading. I speak, of course, as one who stands upon an eminence, and gazes upon the busy world below; wonders, remarks, but keeps himself aloof. What a sight you have daily to gaze upon! Why, any one, but you and I, would feel that he was on enchanted ground, and would tread lightly. But you and I, so wise, so experienced, look on in cold indifference. If I don't get me engaged first, I want you to select for me the most suitable of your heaven-born pupils. The wife makes the man. If you make the wife, you may make me. So don't despair yet."

To his College Chum.

"Northampton, Aug. 12, 1833.

"Dear Friend I. — How do you do? How are you enjoying yourself these long summer days? I doubt not you will say my days are passing gaily and happily. But there must be quite a contrast between the present and last winter, when we used to hang the old blankets round the stove. The sun, I think, must 'bate in, all in a fury,' as a Paddy says, to your chamber. And this reminds me how pleasantly I am situated. I enjoy the luxury of a large chamber, with windows on two sides, through which the air circulates freely, and shade-trees all around. And more, you must be hauled out of bed, *nolens volens,* at five. I sleep as long as I please. You must be hurried off to recitation at the precise hour, be subject to a tutor's intrusion into your room, &c. &c.; all which things I am happily rid of. I go where I please, study when I please, get my lesson perfect as I please, and am altogether my own man. But I have had a hard summer. The first part of it was passing most happily, when I got poisoned. God only knows how. It affected me terribly. The sickness, in consequence, broke up all my plans and resolutions, broke up my studies, and too much of my religious devotion. I am not systematic in any thing ; and all things, of course, are at loose ends. The disease still, in a diminished degree, hangs about me. I know not that I shall ever get wholly rid of it. But the Great Disposer of all events will, I doubt not, glorify himself in me.

" I have many esteemed friends here. But they are not just the ones to say every thing to, and go everywhere with. I was made indeed for society. But there are few, I think, who can make more agreeable companionship with solitude than myself. So you need not suppose my solitary hours are woful ones.

" I have a little garden, where I spend some of my morning hours. I find an occasional ride very pleasant. My prospects for unalloyed earthly felicity were never brighter than at the commencement of the summer, and my hours seemed winged with enjoyment ; but that saucy poison got hold of me, and made terrible havoc. *Religion* can solace me in my sorrows, can heal the wounds which disappointment has made, and make me my happy self again; and to her I would fain apply. . . .

"If, — and you see I but repeat what I have often said, — if, I say, the things which are commonly believed by Christians with reference to heaven and hell are *true, immutable truths,* what exertion can be too great, what self-denial too severe, what agony too intense? Who would pronounce a man a fanatic for being all excited to pull a sleepy neighbor from a burning house? And who will sneer at and denounce those who manifest a *little* zeal at most, in saving poor blinded mortals from the fires of an interminable hell? Let Christians be reasonable men. Let them tear their creed to tatters, scatter their Bible to the four winds, call hell a delusion, and heaven a lie, or else act up to their belief. What! exchange the everlasting crown of glory for fame's fading laurels, and the felicities of eternity for the fleeting joys of time! Oh, is it not madness? Who will do it? Will you? Will I? Or will we see others do it, and be as indifferent as when we see a woman peddle her eggs for snuff? But I will not amplify. I was only *thinking* of what strange material man is made, — man, who boasts of his reason, his sense, his forecast; who prides himself on acting according to the dictates of his reason, and yet plays the fool most egregiously."

SOPHOMORE YEAR.

Again at college, and entered on Sophomore year, he thus writes —

To his Mother.

"Yale College, Nov. 7, 1838.

. . . . "I received to-day a prettily bound Virgil, English edition, bearing this : —

'SYLVESTER JUDD,

'Ob operam Latine scribendo feliciter novatam, hoc volumen Virgilii opera complectum, adjudicaverunt examinatores Berkleiani.

'Quod testor,   'Jeremias Day.'

"If never before, now at least, I know what it is to be pressed for time. Every hour is demanded long before it comes. If the days were double their length, they would all be occupied. But, though my thoughts are so much confined here, they occasionally creep out of their shell, and look towards home. Blessings are doubly prized when lost ; and home is doubly dear when absent. However, I am happily situated here, more so than last year.

"I was a little surprised not to receive a special token of remembrance from the dear brothers and sisters at home, when I received the box ; as I expected a letter from each of them. Hope they have not forgotten their absent brother, and will write soon. Thanksgiving is coming on soon. I should rejoice to be at home, but shall content myself here. . . .

"Do write me as often as you can. Sensible how great the task is, your letters are the more valuable.

"Your ever affectionate, though perhaps you think too fitful and unstable, son,

"Sylvester."

5*

"Yale College, Dec. 5, 1833.

"My dear Mother, — Your 'token' was received yesterday. I am highly rejoiced at receiving the gift, but still more so in the thought that my mother is devoted to my interest and happiness. The contents of the box remind me of Thanksgiving seasons at home; the cake especially, which is like that you always make on such occasions. Hard study, like hard work, makes one hungry: mother may suppose, then, of course, that it is very pleasant to resort to a little *buttery*, as indeed it is. . . . But H——i and P——n, what has become of them? Have they forgotten me? I looked the papers all over carefully twice, but could find no 'From P——n,' 'From H——i,' and was quite disappointed. Was H——i off playing with the boys, or P——n with the girls? I do not understand what it means, and would like to have the matter explained. I have been expecting letters from the little ones for a long time; but none have come. Has P——n forgotten that she promised to write me 'certain, true'? . . . .

"Neither death nor severe sickness has come nigh us. But can we always live? Who shall be taken first? Is it a brother or a sister, or one of our dear parents? Is it I? But I can say, though I walk through the dark valley, yet will I not fear."

The winter vacation of this year he spent in Hartford, where was going forward a general 'revival of religion.' Throwing himself into its interests, and nerving himself to meet its doctrines, he succeeded in throwing off, for a while, the sceptical tendency which had come over him, and returned to college full of the revival-spirit.

To his Brother H——l.

"Yale College, Feb. 2, 1834.

.... "You are not called to the joys and privileges of the children of God, without also being called to partake of their trials and labors. You must work; you must fight. The Christian's life is a warfare; his whole life is the scene of action. . . . .

"You have come into the kingdom at an auspicious moment. The great wheels of revolution, moral, political, and religious, are beginning to move. In the church, erroneous doctrines, false views, antiquated prejudices, that have rested with a mountain's weight on all its energies, are beginning to be torn away. .... I could ask you a great many questions about particulars and individuals; but they are summed up in this: How is religion in H.?"

To his Sister A.

"Yale College, March 20, 1834.

.... "There can be no doubt about the *duty* of talking personally, on the subject of religion, to your companions. But how shall you do it? Take proper times, be discreet, be mild, and, above all, show a spirit overflowing with love for their souls. You must be in the *habit* of conversing with them, not only saying something to-day, while there is excitement, but at all times. In order that your words may take effect, your whole life and actions must correspond to what you say."

To his Mother.

"Yale College, March 8, 1834.

"Dear Mother, — I am informed that the Lord is graciously reviving his work in Northampton. I need not say that this excites in me great joy and thankfulness; and has stirred me up to greater importunity of prayer, that the influences of the Spirit may be felt throughout the whole town; and particularly that my friends, those connected by the nearest earthly ties, may become subjects of the work. . . . I hardly know what to say with respect to little brother and sister, H——i and P——n. They are not too young to become Christians, decided Christians. . . . Ministers rarely preach to children. School-teachers are not apt to be faithful. . . . My vacation commences the last week in April. I look forward to its recurrence with interest, as the time when I shall meet again with those I love, and when I shall be able to throw in my little strength to aid the cause of religion in Northampton."

To his Brother, C. P.

(Same date.)

"Dear Brother, — Permit me to say, that the speculations, philosophical, metaphysical, rational, or whatever they may be, of your last letter, have nothing to do with the great subject before us. The object of my last to you was *to incite you, by motives and arguments, to enter with your whole soul into the work of saving souls.* It was not my aim to discard philosophy or Franklin. None can have a greater respect for one or the other, in their *proper places,*

than I have. I regard Franklin as one of the greatest men of his times. In unsophisticated common
sense, in wisdom and shrewd insight into men and
things, he had few equals. He is the boast of his
country, and will be the pride of posterity. But
' there is no other name given under heaven, whereby
men can be saved, but the name of Jesus.' Take
care that you do not wrap yourself in your subtle
abstractions about the nature of things, without
making a proper use of things as they are. It may
prove the winding-sheet of your soul."

To his Brother, H——l.

"Yale College, July 2, 1834.

. . . . "This is a term which is always noted for
its want of a high tone of religious feeling. Still
I believe there are some who feel for the cause of
Zion, and are willing to pray and labor for her
upbuilding. There is a general apathy in the city
and in all this region. . . .

"Mr. —— is, in many respects, to be esteemed;
but his manners, in respect to gentleness, suavity,
and his disposition in respect to opinionativeness, I
think might be improved. He reminds me of myself. He is a complete picture of a Judd. I derive
a double lesson from it: 1. I learn the folly of
expecting perfection here below; 2. I learn how
my own actions appear in the sight of others. Take
these improvements of the subject, so far as they are
applicable, to yourself. It gets to be second nature
with some people to be positive and overbearing.

This makes them appear conceited and haughty. But I'll not enlarge on a disagreeable subject. . . .

"How do you succeed in your studies? Is the walk pleasant? Do you get acquainted with the citizens of Hadley? A thousand pleasing and varied recollections spring into my mind at the thought of Hadley. The year and little more, that I spent there, was certainly the most happily passed of any in my life. I began my course there, just after a long series of disappointments and vexations. It was a course, too, on which my heart had long been set, and one just suited to the bent of my mind. My daily companions were of the most agreeable sort; and, though now scattered and far distant, their remembrance is pleasant. I presume there is no danger that you will not study enough. But you may grow proud, and lose your spirituality. Here is great danger. Take care."

To HIS MOTHER.

"YALE COLLEGE, July 24, 1834

. . . . "Need I ask if your bosom is filled with pity, sympathy, and love for the poor black man? Truly he needs all this. He needs more. He needs that we stoop and raise him to the high moral and religious character which we ourselves have attained. . . . The religious state of things in college and the city is not so favorable as last term. My own current of feeling has been more interrupted and changeable than then. Still it is good to love and serve our Master in heaven. We are determined to advance his cause in our hearts and around us. My natural

temperament, you know, mother, is ardent, and subject to change. This occasions me some trouble. I
fear sometimes going too far in too exclusive devotion to one object. I am sorry that there should be
any decline of religious feeling in Northampton. It
need not be. We can *always* feel."

To his Sister A.

(Same date.)

. . . . " Calculate not too strongly on obtaining *happiness* by any change of circumstances in your future
life ; for instance, going away to school, and the like.
I do most solemnly assure you, that you will be disappointed. I have wished a hundred times, within
two years, that I was living again in the sunny
scenes of my childhood. But considerations of *duty*
will not suffer me to *harbor* such feelings, and they
make me contented where I am."

The sentiment of the last paragraph was no doubt
occasioned by the religious difficulties in his own
mind ; from which he had suffered with increase
of knowledge, and which had returned upon him
after the early part of this year. Yet he had revealed
them to no one, and had made up his mind to press
forward in all the duties his professed faith demanded.
With this came the torturing feeling that he was
playing the hypocrite. Then, in his zeal to act up
consistently with what he considered the implied
claims of the Calvinistic system, he was considered
by some of his class-mates as officious, as going too
far ; and thus he became somewhat unpopular, and

experienced additional trouble. He was at times tempted to give up the whole matter of going on through college, especially as his pecuniary embarrassments were so great.

JUNIOR YEAR.

But still he persevered; and, to get money for helping to pay his expenses, he passed the winter of his Junior year in teaching at Middletown, Conn., at the same time keeping up with his class. Soon after his establishment here, he writes —

To his Father and Mother.

"MIDDLETOWN, Dec. 13, 1834.

"You will feel somewhat interested to know how I get along in my new situation. Every thing has gone well, so far. . . . The number of my scholars this week has been thirty; their ages from twenty-two to fourteen. I teach every thing, as a matter of course in schools of this character. A tolerable acquaintance with most of the branches pursued enables me to pay sufficient attention to my classes, without taking up much of my time out of school, so that I have most of my mornings and evenings to pursue my college-studies. I *hope* to be able to prepare myself in what will be absolutely necessary for the college-examination next spring.

"I do, I must own, feel quite weary, after having kept my tongue going in asking questions, explaining, remarking, and so forth, for three hours on the stretch, with scarce a moment's intermission. But

Mrs. W. furnishes me with a first-rate dish of tea; and after supper I feel quite refreshed, and prepared for study."

To his Cousin, G. L.

"Yale College, April 5, 1835.

" Dear Cousin, — I own I have neglected you. Great pressure of duties will be a sufficient apology. I returned from Middletown last week, where I passed my winter much more pleasantly than I could have anticipated in so laborious an avocation.

" But I come to other subjects. We are enjoying a most delightful revival of religion. Professors are very humble and prayerful; sinners are being converted almost daily, and great solemnity is on the minds of those who are still impenitent. The work is attended with little excitement; but, like the still water, *'tis very deep*. The whole aspect of things, in and about college, is changed. . . .

" We shall probably meet in a few weeks, when I can communicate with you on a thousand subjects, about which I have no time to write now; — am *pressed* with studies and other duties."

During Junior year, his mind was ill at ease as to the theological basis of his religion; yet he shut up his troubles within his own breast. He became more than usually reserved, and correspondence with his friends was less frequent.

SENIOR YEAR.

Just entered upon his last, his senior year in college, still secretly troubled and unsettled as to his creed, and sensible of the unaccountable appearances in himself to which it occasionally led, he thus writes —

To his Mother.

"YALE COLLEGE, Oct. 24, 1835.

"My dear Mother, — I suppose that you have been expecting a letter from me these several days. But I have not had, neither have I now, any news of particular interest to communicate. College has become rather an old story. I will only say that I find myself more agreeably situated this year than in previous years. . . .

"When I think what I have passed through, I am sure no consideration would induce me to enter Freshman again. Still the ordeal is most necessary, and highly salutary in every point of view. Some never learn to control themselves, until they have been absolutely controlled by others. A man in college learns his proper station, and loses those notions, both of inferiority and superiority, which he may previously have indulged. It is not an unpleasant reflection that I am so near through my college-course, or, at least, that I am so near through the fatigues of college-life; for there is something in the prospect before me, at which I shrink back. I must be soon thrown upon my own resources, must take stations of responsibility, must be looked up to

as a counsellor and guide, and must be bereft of that
support, protection, and guidance, which a young
man in college, under his own father's roof, so constantly receives. Reflections of this sort make me
most wish that time would stop awhile, and let me
stay where I am; for, just now, every thing goes
pleasantly as I could wish, and more so than I ever
expect again in this world. I find, mother, that I
am getting into rather a loose reverie, and will return
to matter-of-fact things. . . . .

"Talked with C. P. about temperance. He, of
course, goes the full length. It may be that benevolence demands that a man should entirely abstain
from invigorating drinks; but, if it does, it also demands that we dress in sheepskins, in order to send
the surplus money of our clothing to the heathen. . .

"The religious appearances in college at present
are very favorable; more so than usual at the commencement of the first term."

To his SISTER-IN-LAW, E. W. J.

"YALE COLLEGE, Nov. 15, 1835.

"Dear Sister E. — When I contemplate writing
you, I feel that I must unlock the secret chambers
of my soul, and present to you a transcript of what
passes therein. This I *cannot do*. It would do you
no good, nor will it benefit me. Every one possesses
his own secrets, which he keeps concealed in his own
bosom, revealing them to no mortal eye, and only
waiting till the light of the judgment-day shall beam
in upon them. It is well that a veil is hung over
the hearts of all. For, if it were not so, who could

be happy, even in the presence of his dearest friends? We should distrust every one, and the tranquillity of society would be at an end. There is perhaps nothing peculiar in my case. My nerves are nicely strung, and I may feel more keenly than some. I know I am more apt to express what is going on within. I felt deeply and sadly, the morning I left Northampton; partly because I was going away from those I loved, and was about to leave them in the enjoyment of so much happiness which I could not stay to be a sharer in; partly because I had incurred the censure of those whose good opinion I so much valued; partly for other reasons, of which I will not trouble you with a recital. You thought, and so did mother, that I was *odd*. If I did thus act, it was only to divert myself under the pressure of reflections that were every day weighing me to the earth. These did not originate, as you perhaps conjectured, in ————. No, it was something else. Nothing in particular, — partly of a religious nature.

"We are occupied, this year, with a variety of agreeable pursuits; and time passes so rapidly and so smoothly, that I should hardly note its lapse. I have been here more than six weeks. It seems but a moment. I could almost wish that senior year might last for ever."

About the same time, he writes his brother H——l:
"You recollect, perhaps, that I appeared rather low-spirited during some parts of the vacation. This had nothing to do with ————, but was a *religious affair*."

To his Sister A.

"Yale College, April 10, 1836.

. . . . " You are very happy at home, receiving the instructions of your father, helping your mother, comforting the poorly brother H——l, and enjoying the thousand little delights of the family circle. P——n, too, has some one to sleep with. Poor little thing! how cold she was! How lonely and sad — like a dove without its mate!

"I presume, dear sister, that your *feelings* are right; but the *expression* should be right also. Your countenance should be lighted up with the sympathizing emotions of the heart. It is of little use that your internal emotions are right, while the external expression is of an opposite character. Be cautious and attentive on this subject, and recollect there is great danger of deceiving yourself, from the fact that you know a great deal better how you *feel*, than how you *appear*.

" *Make bosom-friends of our own family.* If they are not to be trusted, who are? If they cannot sympathize with you, who can? Be friendly to all. Make friends of few, and confidants of still less. Be a friend to yourself. Stand erect in your own independence; but never refuse to associate with others because you *fear* them. This is servility. Yes, 'open your soul;' but take care, in the first place, *who looks in;* and, in the second, *what you expose.* Never expose a weak spot; but rather make show of your strength, if you have any. You need not expect to live through life on *sentiment:* intellect

6*

and reason must sooner or later be called into action. The perplexing scenes of active life will soon demand your energies. 'Tis pleasant to indulge our reveries, but it is too often a dangerous practice. Toil, sorrow, and disappointment are before us. Habits of reverie do not train up the mind for the stern conflict; they do not prepare it for the grief and pain that are liable to overwhelm us."

To his Mother.

"Yale College, June 6, 1836.

"My dear Mother, — If I have omitted too long to write you, you must ascribe it to the thousand little occasions of delay that are constantly occurring. My visit at H. was, of course, very pleasant, and more especially as I found myself in the midst of many of our dear family. I do not know how great an occasion there may have been for offering burnt-offerings; but I am sure our meeting was a very happy one. When I read the letter from W., I felt for a few minutes quite 'homesick.' By a longer absence, I suppose, I am preparing myself for a greater felicity when I do go home. I am pleasantly situated this summer; board with Miss C., spend about two hours a day, attending to recitations. I enjoy very much the polished and literary society of New Haven. The ladies are said to be very beautiful. . . . .

"My shirts suit exactly. I know you love to have your children *suited*, and take indefatigable pains to accomplish the end. I am only sorry that they are so difficult at times to please. Perhaps their nicety is owing to their education: it may be they have inherited some of it. . . .

"H——l was in doubt where to enter college: I gave it as my opinion decidedly, that he had better go to Amherst. C. P. intends to enter here. I am sure I do not wish to have three brothers of us graduate at one college. If three of us graduate, I know it will add to our gratification, and also our usefulness, to do so at different colleges. For my own part, I should not wish to be a class-mate with a brother. It does not seem to work well."

To his Sister-in-law, E. W. J.

"Yale College, July 6, 1836.

"Dear Sister, — I have this day, this hour, finished my college-course. I need not, and I could not if I should attempt it, describe to you my emotions. 'Tis certainly a pleasant thought, that fatigue and hard study are over, at least for the present. But this is a small consideration. The questions recur, What have I accomplished? How am I able to meet the responsibilities that now rest upon me? Am I better? I am perhaps a little wiser; but am I *better?* I dare not answer. 'Tis painful to part with class-mates. Our examinations were closed yesterday. To-day we have listened to a poem and a farewell address, — both interesting, affecting. Our class is now dispersing for six weeks. We come together again at Commencement, and receive our diplomas. I, of course, shall remain here until after Commencement. I have been extremely busy for the last six weeks, as you may suppose. I am

obliged to spend about three hours a day in Miss
C.'s school, and have been quite busy with my own
regular studies.

"A. spoke of your visit (home), which I am sure
I quite envied you. When I received a line from
W., saying that you were going, I felt for a moment quite homesick ; but I am soon to be separated still further from the friends I love, and must
extinguish in my heart the struggling emotions I
cannot control. A man's friends are always more
lenient and partial than the world at large."

And now the college-life, so ardently desired, so
fondly anticipated, comes to a close. Like all happiness in prospect, this had failed to be to the eager
student all that he expected. Not that he did not enjoy much ; not that the mines of literature and science
did not yield him rich rewards for his toil ; but, like
the wise man, he found, that in some respects " he
that increaseth knowledge increaseth sorrow."

He pursued the regular course of study with great
avidity, and held a distinguished rank for scholarship
and talent among his class-mates. He was made a
member of the Phi Beta Kappa Society ; and, in his
Sophomore year, he received the Berkelian prize for
Latin composition, and also the prize for English
composition. He again received the prize for English composition in his Junior year. At the Junior
Exhibition, as well as at his Commencement, the
part assigned to him was an English oration ; a part
there, as elsewhere, reckoned a most honorable distinction.

To reduce his expenses as much as possible, besides spending part of his Freshman year studying at home, he sometimes kept bachelor's hall, and boarded himself; and made his journeys, in vacation, on foot. He taught, more or less, in schools in New Haven. A kind, Christian lady, Mrs. Lee, of New Haven, for a term or more, invited him to the hospitalities of her house. Yet all this was not sufficient to meet his bills; and, with his father's security, he was obliged to get a loan for the balance.

And thus, with great effort, much self-denial and economy, a large share of embarrassment, and some mortification, added to his heavy and unlooked-for inward struggles, did he make his way through college.

CHAPTER IV.

CHANGE IN THEOLOGICAL VIEW.

———

RECAPITULATORY.

In nothing is the high value in which Mr. Judd held religious truth so strongly seen, as in the discriminating care with which he suffered himself to adopt new opinions, and the fears he entertained, through a long period, lest, in changing his religious views, he should hazard every thing most valuable in this life and the next. A person of less delicate sensibility to the worth of truth and religion would, long before the inward conflict had been so far protracted, have gone over to the other side, and boldly announced his change of position.

Possessing naturally an inquiring mind, and having from his earliest years been influenced by his father to think for himself, he could not receive upon trust any truths, doctrines, or dogmas whatever, that might be presented to him, without an examination of the evidences for himself. He had, in early years, been puzzled in reconciling some of the doctrines of that system of religious faith under which he had been educated. As his mind matured, and his sphere of thought enlarged, his difficulties and embarrassments of this kind increased; so that the happiness, even of his first year in college, was marred by doubts and perplexities arising from this source.

In this year, he thus writes in his Journal: "I had half resolved to go away, abandon all I know, and become a sailor on the seas, or an inhabitant of the wilderness. For what? To seek for happiness I have lost? No: that, I fear, is *for ever* gone. But to rid my friends of what must be a canker to *their* joys."

Religion was all in all with him, permeating the inmost recesses of his soul. His natural sensibility to its influences was very great; and, under the power of the teachings and measures to which he had been subjected, he had yielded himself, heart and life, to what he supposed its claims. Love to God reigned in his spirit; delight in his works penetrated his whole being. Co-extensive with these were love to his fellow-men, and a burning desire that they might be saved from the miseries of the impenitent in the world to come. Having received from the cradle the idea that all come into the world in a state of depravity, naturally hating God and goodness, and loving sin and all unholiness, and of course needing an entire and necessarily an instaneous conversion to save them from irremediable and eternal destruction, — in true consistency with this creed, as has already been shown, he threw all his energies of mind and body into the work of saving the souls of the unconverted.

In this spirit, from the time at which he dated his own conversion, he began to labor; and, with the same zeal for the salvation of his fellow-men, he entered college. How earnestly he labored and prayed for the conversion of his fellow-students; with what untiring energy he sought for a continued revival of religion among them, and in other places in which he was interested, may be seen from the preceding chapter. Almost racked with efforts for the promotion of this all-absorbing object, and at the same time tormented with doubts as to the truth of the system according to which he was acting, his nervous susceptibility increased, a quickened self-consciousness was induced, his general health suffered, and he sank at times into deep despondency. But, faithful to the natural instincts of his heart, he labored on, imparting nothing of this inward conflict to his friends, from an unwillingness to give them pain; and was deterred from making known the doubts forced upon his mind, to his instructors or fellow-students, lest the cry of heresy should burst forth upon him, in answer to his honest inquiries and conscientious scruples.

Thus, that college-life, to which he had looked forward with such longing desires and such joyous expectations, passed on. And thus unhappy, unharmonized, and at times on the very verge of scepticism, yearning for sympathy, and yet not free to impart his mental anguish to any one, he closed his collegiate course.

TEMPLETON.

In the autumn of the same year, 1836, in order to obtain the means of liquidating the debts he had incurred for his education, and of providing means for the further prosecution of his studies, — after having, through some misunderstanding, met with a severe disappointment in regard to a situation as teacher in Westfield Academy, — he took charge of a private school in Templeton, Mass.   There, for the first time, he began to have intercourse with that denomination of Christians termed Unitarians, and came to understand more fully their distin- ·guishing views.   Previously, he had been very little acquainted with Unitarian works or Unitarian preach- ing ; but he now perceived that the deductions of his own unbiassed mind, and the conclusions towards which he found it verging, were much in harmony with those received by this body of Christians.

New troubles now were let in upon his afflicted spirit.   Difficulties were rife between the Calvinistic and Unitarian societies.   He was under the patronage of the former, and was supposed by them to be committed to their interests.   His own heartfelt convictions sided with the latter, and all his sympa- thies were tending in that direction.

To increase the embarrassment of his situation, he had many family relatives in this place.   He thus writes —

To his Brother J. W.

"Templeton, Jan. 13, 1837.

"About half of our friends are Unitarians, and the other half Orthodox.   This is the only thing that is disagreeable ; yet they treat me kindly.   Still the Unitarians cannot be very friendly towards the

7

school.   These religious divisions are paltry things, and engender strife and wicked feelings enough to sink the whole church to perdition."

To his Sister-in-law.

" Templeton, Feb. 29, 1837.

" My feelings have been so multifarious, I could not give you an intelligible history of them.   They have been so vacillating, that you would hardly be able to recognize their identity from one moment to another.   More than this, I do not wish to disclose all my heart.   Such feelings ! I should tremble to pen them, and you would be pained to read them. You know too well my disposition.   You know too well how my thoughts are apt to play their pranks, for me to recapitulate.   I seek for no relief, no improvement, until I have ' shuffled off this mortal coil.'

" I suppose you have been made acquainted with the state of society in Templeton.   I have been employed by the Orthodox party ; but, alas for me ! I am too liberal.

" I am getting to be a very poor correspondent. My heart is as warm with affection for my friends, as the most enthusiastic could wish ; but I am not always in a mood to converse with them.   I am obliged often, from fear of wounding their sensibilities, to restrain my words.   I would not be odd, and I know I am not original.   There are recesses in *every one's* heart, where he loves sometimes to retire and shut out the world.   Perhaps I visit these too often, and tarry too long, till familiarity has made seclusion sweet; and the world has less strong hold upon my interests. All this is possible."

About the time of leaving college, he was invited to fill a Professorship in Miami College, Ohio. In reference to this, he thus writes —

To his Brother J. W.

"Templeton, March 24, 1837.

"I am desirous to explain a little relative to my declining the offer to go to the West. I did not come to my decision, without the most deliberate and prayerful consideration; and the disappointment to my friends could not have exceeded the pain in my own feelings. The amount of my objection to taking the proposed situation may be contained in a word : I was not willing to be placed under those restrictions in religious thought and feeling which would necessarily be imposed upon me in the contemplated circumstances.

"Too long has the world groaned under the bondage of superstition, intolerance, and bigotry. I am not going to enter upon a crusade against mankind; but I cannot, I dare not, lend my influence to bind more closely the yoke; neither am I willing to yield myself to its thraldom. God made man, made you, made me, made all men, for high and noble ends. He made us in his own image, to reflect his own glory before the eyes of the universe. A spiritual nature was given us, by which to mount up, as on eagles' wings, to an elevated existence, to an assimilation with the Deity. We dash in pieces our heavenly image; we sink from our high estate; we become the slaves of one another. Yes, man is the most abject slave of his fellow-man. He dare not think for himself; he dare not speak or act for himself; and, more than this, becomes the slave of himself. An unnatural sense of right and wrong causes him to tremble at his own footsteps, and startle at his own breath. Delusions, that settle like the pall of death upon the soul, have come down from many generations. Their antiquity gives them authority, and the assumed sanction of Deity begets for them reverence. None dare question their truth; or, if he doubt, he is condemned if he speak. I boast of no superior penetration; but there are some things so plain, that he who runs may read. I can claim no superior boldness; but, if I have not courage enough to attack the absurdities of others, I am sure I have too much obstinacy to be led by their perversions. . . . Away with faint-heartedness! Let the cry of heresy come. Let persecution come. Only let *truth*, God's own truth, prevail. I anticipate the day when truth shall ride forth, conquering and to conquer. I cannot say when; I only pray for nerve and resolution to urge on the chariot-wheels. I cannot rest. The Lord has been leading me by ways that I thought not of. He has sorely tried me, to see if I would trust him. I hope he will make me a fit instrument for accomplishing his work. I do not seek independence of action for its own sake. No, no. It is always easier to float with the current. But alas! 'twas 'floating me down to dark despair.'

"These considerations have long been pressing

upon me: at times they have made me wretched. Convictions were overwhelming me; but I would not yield to them, and then came the struggle. I thought of what my friends would think, and then came a deeper agony. O yes, that I must disappoint the expectations of my dearest friends, — this has been my bitterest anguish. But God has sustained me in my resolutions, and I trust he will aid me in the execution. Feeling and thinking thus, you see I could not become connected with an Old School Presbyterian College in Ohio. May I never repent my decision!"

What was to be done? It was misery to live so. It was more: he felt it to be moral dishonesty. To go on as he had done, he felt to be hypocrisy; to avow his true position, a step for which also he did not feel prepared, was to break up his school. Much, therefore, as he needed the pecuniary aid which it might afford, he resigned the situation, and returned to Northampton in the spring of 1837, disappointed, disheartened, broken down almost, under the difficulties of his situation.

THE GREAT CRISIS.

A great, an inevitable crisis he saw approaching. The ranks of Calvinism, in which he had been quite conspicuous, he must now desert, and go over to the enemy. The connection existing between the associations of his earlier years and his present state must be destroyed. A change of religious sentiment was then, even more than now, looked upon almost as the Hindoo regards a loss of caste. From his church, if not for excommunication, he had to look for severe censure. Among the friends of his youth, he might expect marked coolness. His own family he knew would be greatly grieved, and would feel in him their fondest expectations disappointed. The dearest ties of his heart must be sundered. In short, he felt that he would be looked upon by all as weak-minded, an apostate from the true faith, an outcast almost from the hopes of heaven. He thus utters himself in his Journal: —

"May 6, 1837.

"Go to the Unitarian Church. Oh! 'tis misery to think of it. It is an *open* step, which I have not yet taken. Truth, thy way is a thorny one. . . . . Walked out in the evening. In Nature's temple I love to worship, whose dome is the sky, whose pillars are the mountains.

"'Had rather see me in my grave.' I ask not your pity; I ask not your charity even: only do not grieve. But the emotion, — this unmans me. One tear weighs more than a folio of arguments."

"June 24.

"My spirits are gone, my vigor, my ambition. What will raise me, I know not. The future is one black atmosphere of night. Its heavy darkness is reflected upon the present."

The conflict with himself, endured so long unshared, had so channelled itself even into his physical being, that he was now almost prostrated in body as well as in mind; and, in this condition, no doubt he took exaggerated views of the trials of his situation, and suffered a keener anguish than he otherwise would. His family friends knew something of the change in his views, but were not aware of the extent to which they were about to lead. He dreaded the full *dénouement* to them and to the world. Moaning around the house, he would go, with hardly life enough to drag himself up and down stairs, sometimes humming in heart-piercing tones, " Oh, where shall rest be found ? " or " Hast thou not *one* blessing for me, O my Father ? " He would say he envied the cartman in the street, the blacksmith at his forge, the shoemaker, anybody whose life was so private that he could enjoy his own opinions in obscurity and peace. If he could be any thing but a clergyman, or could so modify his views, that, with any degree of consistency, he could preach in the denomination in which he had been educated, it would be a relief. But no, it would not do. He must go through the ordeal, and abide its scathings. He must be true to his own conscience, his own convictions of duty, let come what would of earthly loss or reproach.

As an exposé of his position, and a history of the change which had come over him, he about this time prepared, for the private use of his father's family, a manuscript, which he entitled " Cardiagraphy." It is dated Northampton, June, 1837; and, twelve years later, he writes a friend, in relation to it, " On none of the points have my views undergone any change." Extracts from this will put the whole matter in a truer light than can be thrown upon it in any other way. He introduces the subject as follows: —

"CARDIAGRAPHY.

"I write to relieve myself in expressing my feelings, and to gratify my father's family, who may wish to know me better.

"The sketch will be a medley, because, in the ceaseless tide of feeling, it is impossible to detain it sufficiently long to give a connected account.

"Some parts may seem to contradict others; not but that I am as nearly a unity as it is possible for a human being to be, but because there are shadings of thought and feeling, for which there are no corresponding niceties of words. Hence, language may be at variance, where the heart harmonizes. . . . .

"I seem to be changed. In some respects I am; but in a higher sense, I am not. So far as relates to the fundamental point of all religion, — that which ought to be the great end of energy, intellectual and physical; that which antedates and supersedes creeds, formularies, communions, schools; that which is immutable amidst all other changes, to wit, the happiness of man and the glory of God, — I declare I am conscious in myself of no change. Men have always differed, in all ages, as to the *means*, that is, as to the best mode of belief and action, by which this end can be secured. The same man, at different periods of his life, embraces different views.

"The circumstances of men, from education,

temperament, government, location, are perpetually changing; and it can hardly be supposed, that the same creed, *explained in the same way*, will be best adapted to all. As one, advancing in the study of man, becomes more acquainted with the nature of his race, his views of the means alluded to will undergo some modification. But as it regards the great end before him, God's glory and man's happiness, the good man will never change his views. This will be his pole-star, by which he will guide his course for ever, though compelled to tack and veer as storms and currents sway.

"From these considerations, I can better answer the question, have I changed? I can only reply, that if ever I had this great end in view, if ever I was actuated by the high motive of doing good to man, and glorifying my God, I am now. From my earliest years, I have been susceptible of impressions relative to the glory of Him who made the universe, and who seeks its happiness, and relative to the happiness of my fellow-beings. And now that my mind and heart are more mature; now that I can more fully appreciate the worth of happiness, and can more clearly conceive of it in its highest, noblest, purest and most imperishable exercise, — I am conscious of no diminution of this susceptibility, but would hope that its strength is increased, its action is more decided, and its discriminations are more delicate.

"Will you, my friends, call me changed, — sadly, dangerously, greatly changed?

"In regard to other particulars, do I love God? Do I delight in his service? I can only say, if ever

I experienced these feelings, I do now. These are the holiest and most delightful emotions that can fill our hearts; and why should I neglect or repress them? But you will say my course of religious action is changed. That is true to a certain extent. But you must be aware that courses of religious action have almost infinitely varied in all ages and all parts of the religious world. There is no identity here; and it is unreasonable to fix upon *one* course as the only test of religious character.

"Yet, while I am thus conscious in myself of no alteration in respect to the fundamental motive of action and the chief point of character, I am too well aware that you possibly, and the world certainly, will consider me greatly changed.

"I allude frequently to consciousness, and, as I think, with truth; though I might infer, from what some of you have said, that the evidence derived from this source was not to be depended upon. But I am not mistaken when I affirm, that it is a primary, incontrovertible, unequivocal source of evidence. It is the sense by which we take cognizance of the world within, as by the other senses we become acquainted with the world without. These, as the eye and ear, sometimes deceive us. Nor is it surprising; for the external world is limitless in its extent, and infinite in the variety of its objects. Still, we rely most implicitly upon these senses, and never allow ourselves to be contradicted when we have them for a witness. Now, consciousness is the eye of the soul; and the soul, as a sphere of vision, is circumscribed in its extent and in its objects. The soul is one, though presenting a variety of aspects. By carefully looking within, we may soon survey the whole ground of observation; and whatever we thus see, we are sure exists. If we are conscious we love or hate, are envious or liberal, are angry or pacific, are pained or pleased, we are sure we have these feelings; nor could all the counter-testimony in the world shake our conviction. It is, indeed, true that consciousness sometimes deceives us; but the aberrations of this sense may be corrected as easily, and I think much more easily than those of the other senses, by the aid of the judgment and by further examination.

"By the necessities of my nature, then, I am compelled to rely upon my consciousness. In so doing, I aim to act with the Christian philosopher; who, discovering in the laws of his nature the laws of God, makes it his high purpose, in all things, to obey them. He who knowingly transgresses the laws of his nature, rebels against God. You will see, then, that that religion, that doctrine, that proposition of any sort, which contradicts my consciousness, must be contradictory to the laws of my nature, contradictory to reason, contradictory to God. It opposes all true religion, for that is founded in God; it is impious, it is absurd. It is not 'mysterious' and 'incomprehensible:' it is absolutely false. I cannot estimate the wickedness of the man who freely embraces it; and will only add, that, though it may present many attractions, its 'house will be found in the way of hell, going down to the chambers of death.'

"To speak more immediately of my present religious sentiments. I am emerging, or rather have emerged, from the abyss of doubt and universal scepticism. I was infidel to what? To the great points of Calvinism. But Calvinism, it was said, was most assuredly the religion of the Bible; and God was the author of the Bible and of that religion. Here, then, was the struggle. The prejudices of my education, the sermons I continually heard, the authority of the multitude, of the learned, of antiquity, the menace of everlasting perdition that hung over a spirit of doubt, had infused into me a *nature*, so to speak, which must accord with Calvinism. Soon another nature, my earlier, original nature, began to rise within me. It asserted its claims to supremacy in my heart. It uttered its stern notes of remonstrance and reprehension at my self-immolation on the altar of prescription. I listened to its voice, and felt that it was the voice of reason and conscience. But I dared not think for myself freely. I dared not act independently. Still the strife continued. 'Tis painful now to think of it, and still more painful would it be to give you the details of days and weeks and months of agonized conflict. At last, however, I did yield. My original nature conquered its foe. But it was not at first a victory of subjugation, but seemingly of utter extermination. In losing Calvinism, I seemed to have lost my Bible, my religion, my God. But an unseen hand was guiding me. The Spirit of the true God was upon me. I was led to examine my Bible, to see *what* it contained. I found my God there.

I was led to look upon the works of his creation, the heavens, the earth; and I found him there. My God, my Bible, my religion, were returned to me; and I was happy. I record this with the most profound gratitude to Him who is the author of all light, truth, and blessedness.

"This course of doubt was commenced with intensity four years ago, and was protracted, with alternating influences, through three years or more. Doubt seemed to have settled as a disease upon me. It was a canker-worm at my heart. My best affections were withering to their root. Nor am I still entirely free of its effects; and indeed I can hardly expect ever to be, so long as I am invested with my frail mortality.

"I have not spoken, nor will it be embraced in my present design to speak, of all the causes, secondary and remote, that may have led me to doubt. Some of them were trifling, others of serious character. It was enough to find myself in the eddies of scepticism, and it is enough that I have been enabled to escape from the apparently inevitable destruction.

"When I was spending my college-vacations at home, you knew that I was not happy. There was more than one cause for this. Some of them you might have understood. But you probably did not imagine, that one great cause of my despondency was to be attributed to religious doubts and anxieties. A combination of causes pressed me to the earth, and my spirits were prostrated in the silent agony of my heart. You called me *oad*. But I was only odd to divert myself. I could not be regular. I

8

could not have acted out myself, for that would have
been the bitterness of death to you all.   I loved
your happiness; therefore I did not tell you my
miseries; for I knew that you could neither sympathize with, nor relieve me.   How much would you
have been overwhelmed with anguish, had I declared
to you the deep darkness, the gloomy disquietudes,
the damning doubts of my own crushed heart!

"I hoped, though my hopes were often dim as
night, — yet I hoped continually that the day of my
illumination would come, and joyfully anticipated
the hour when I could tell you all I knew and all I
felt.   I thought you would rejoice to see the wanderer return to his father's house.   Why should you
be disconsolate, if he seems in some points to differ
from you?   In the wide region of, to him, untra-
versed thought through which he has been obliged
to range, with attention painfully yet intensely directed to every object that met his vision, are you
surprised if he has learned something new?

"Your happiness has always been near my heart.
Forgive me, if in any thing I have made you grieve.
I have always been keenly sensitive.   I know I have
not disciplined my sensibilities as I ought.   I am
too easily irritated by trivial circumstances.   The
bitterest trial, and indeed there can be none bitterer,
is to witness and excite the solicitudes of my friends.
I do not wish to be forgotten; but I wish, rather
than to be remembered with sorrow, to be cast into
your oblivion.   Though all my friends should choose
to abandon me, I should still feel that I can rest,
with all the calmness of love and felicity of hope,

upon the bosom of my God.   Heaven's mercy, like the canopy of the skies, is a limitless expanse; and, though I should not see you in body, and might not commune with you in spirit, I should still feel that you were somewhere sheltered beneath it.   But I must turn to other topics.

" The doctrine of original sin is the substructure of Calvinism, and, indeed, of the popular Orthodoxy of the day.   It is the foundation of most of the other objectionable doctrines that have agitated the church, such as infant-damnation, limited atonement, irresistible grace, inability, and so forth.   And it seems strange to me, that men should have protected and cherished a monster, against whose true offspring they are so implacable.   This doctrine, in its proper interpretation, is this, — that from Adam has been transmitted, through all generations of men, a sinful or depraved moral nature; and that the distinguishing property of this nature, in respect to God, is to hate God, to rebel against him, and to seek to dethrone him.   We are told these are the *first*, spontaneous, natural feelings of our hearts; that they are increasing so long as the object is before them, — enduring as long as we endure; that they become invigorated by exercise, more depraved by mutual contact with men, maddened by opposition, desperate by defeat; till at last, gathered together under the eye of Him whom they naturally hate, they burst out into the full blaze of hell for ever. There is another form of the doctrine, which, while it denies the hereditary defilement, still affirms that the first and all the subsequent exercises of the soul

are sinful, and only sinful. I could have no choice
between the doctrines. You may say that this is not
a fair statement of the doctrine, — that you are not
conscious of embracing such a doctrine. I fear,
truly, that too many are not aware of the absurdities
of their own creed. But I believe this is the doctrine of native defilement, in its naked, unpruned,
uncompromised truth. A consistent Calvinist must
admit this doctrine, and all the consequences that
legitimately flow from it. I do not wonder that reason revolts and conscience frowns at such a principle
in religion. I do not wonder that the Calvinistic
church, in all periods of its existence, and the Presbyterian and Congregational churches now are convulsed by it. I wonder rather that men dare not
re-assert their proper dignity, and rend asunder the
manacles of superstition and darkness that enchain
them. I wonder, too, how Christianity, with such
an incubus upon its energies, should ever have
achieved its gigantic triumphs. On this latter point,
the truth is, Christianity is adapted to human nature ;
and men practically act according to their nature,
though their speculative theology may be contrary
to it.

"When God looked down upon the works of
his creation, the heavens, the earth, man, all living
creatures, he pronounced them *good*. I now look
upon the sun and moon and stars, and find them
adapted to good. I look upon the earth, and find it
adapted to good : even its hurricanes, its earthquakes,
its ocean-storms, are all for good. I find the beasts,
the birds, the insects, all for good. I look upon

man in his physical frame, and find all adapted to good. The eye is pleased with light, the ear with sound, the smell with odors; all senses have their appropriate objects; which objects, if rightly used, promote and are essential to our highest sensual happiness. I look upon the intellectual system, and find it adapted to good. It is surrounded by its appropriate objects, by which it is ever won to action, and with which it is ever delightfully engaged. So far, all conspires to good, and to the highest happiness of man and the glory of God. I next turn my eye to what has been called the *chef-d'œuvre* of the Almighty, and the crowning glory of the human race, — the soul of man. What a hideous spectacle am I *taught* to behold! The vision of horror flashes out in one word: it *hates*, hates God, hates all that is good. I see no adaptation to good, but only to evil and utter woe. I can hardly say that it was made to love; for it seems to be formed only to hate and be wretched. But what are its objects? What shall it love, if it can? — and God commands it to love. Shall it love God, the loveliest of all beings? It looks at him, and hates with a perfect hatred. Shall it love man? But men hate one another, and with undying energies strive to crush one another in the dust. Shall it love that which hates itself? Shall it love the external world and the brute creation? But these are all made for good, and to please God, and it must hate them too. Do you say it may be indifferent to all things? No, that cannot be. All our senses must *be active* in reference to their appropriate objects, either for pain or pleasure, for

8*

love or hatred. The soul of man must act; it does act. It needs religion, but religion it hates. Men must live together in society; but the quenchless fires of hatred burn and blacken their souls. Man's *intellect* looks through universal nature, and discovers beauty, uniformity, design, — in all things a God, and is pleased with the discovery. But his *soul,* with malicious envy, looks at the scene, and recoils in bitter hatred. How can it escape its wretchedness? Can it love its hatred, and be happy? But man was made to love the lovely, and he cannot be happy while he loves the hateful. Besides, if he can be happy in loving the hateful, he would love his fellow-haters, and men would form alliances with the fiends of the pit, and, in their mutual happiness, would plant a new paradise in the regions of hell; and then 'blasphemies ascending to Heaven' would be the requiem of their malignity.

"But who makes the soul of man? God. Human agency is concerned in the structure of the body; but God alone makes the soul. And God commands the soul of man to love himself. What conclusions do the premises of Calvinism drive us to about our God! I cannot sketch them: the thought is blasphemous. I must be an atheist, and reject them; an idiot or a madman, and admit them.

"Unbiassed man, in his active emotions, must love the lovely, and hate the hateful; or love the hateful, and hate the lovely.

"Look into your own hearts, my friends, and tell me, do you find there dark despair, malignant hatred, insatiable envy, bitter cursings? There can be no half-way course. Whenever your feelings have been enlisted, it was either to love or to hate. Do you say that you loved the mercy, and hated the justice, of God? You may have feared punishment; but to fear punishment, and to hate God, are two very different things. Besides, if you had really felt that you deserved punishment, you would not hate God for punishing you. If you really felt that you did not deserve punishment, you could not have feared that you would have been punished. And more, if you had contemplated his character calmly and fully, you must have realized, that, if he was just to punish, he was as merciful to forgive; and even more so, from the fact that he still continued to you the means of grace. How could you, then, have hated him? Do you say that you still continued in sins, and therefore hated God? You were either happy in your sins, or you were not. If you were, you could not have hated God; for no man can be exercising feelings of hatred towards God, and at the same time be happy in any thing. If you were not, if your sins were a loathing to you, you were in the very state to receive pardon from God; and how could you then have hated him? If you were thoughtless about God, I have nothing say. For the man who never thinks of God, knows not whether he hates or loves him. But you say you spontaneously hated God. Back again upon all the horrors of original sin! Is it true that man's nature, *before actual sin,* is adapted to hate his God? Alas! alas! What infatuation possesses the human mind! How has man mistaken himself! How has he mistaken his

God! O delusion, doubly damned, that causes our creed to give the lie to our consciousness, and makes the soul dig in *itself* its hell, and then lie down in its own suffering!

"But I turn from this gloomy prospect. I would escape from these dark ages of a deceived and deceiving theology. Truth and Love, twin angels of a better dispensation, are calling me away to their own bright home. 'God made man in his own image.' This declaration is reaffirmed by Daniel, Solomon, St. Paul, and St. James. The last says, 'Men are made after the similitude of God.' To discredit our Bibles is to deny our God. To be ignorant of ourselves is to enter upon the broad way of all error and all delusion. To know ourselves, and not act according to our natures, is supreme folly and unhappiness. To know ourselves, and yet willingly debase our natures, is rebellion against our Maker, and justly exposes us to his wrath. God has made us, and not we ourselves; and to speak freely of ourselves implies neither presumption, self-conceit, nor pride.

"My soul looks upward to its God; it sees his perfections; it loves and is happy. It looks upon its fellow-beings, it sees in them the image of its God; it loves and is happy. It looks over the face of nature, it sees everywhere the manifestations of its God; it loves and is happy. The soul craves a pure, a godlike religion. It finds such in the Bible, and knows the Bible is divine, and rejoices in its possession. It looks upon Jesus Christ, and, seeing in him the counterpart of its God, rejoices to find its God 'manifest in the flesh;' and that, amidst the many infirmities of our being, its aspirings after conformity to its God are assisted by a sensible exemplar. My soul seeks happiness, and finds it, where alone it is to be found, in the fulness of my God. Man, discovering in himself the image of his God, learns the true idea of his own dignity. I abhor slavery in all its forms ; that of the body and of the intellect, but chiefly that of the soul. Confidence is the great bond of society, and I learn the true grounds of it. *Man is to be trusted.* Religion is the soul loving its God. I learn, then, in whatever clime and by whatever name this feeling is exercised, there to join the communion of my own heart. Religion does not consist in ' going to meeting,' or in any formal exercises. It is the soul communing with its God. I would strive, then, to make the ' world my temple, and life itself one act of devotion.'

" These views and feelings, my dear friends, — and I have not told you half, — I delight to cherish. I am *fixed* in them. I cannot give them up. They are part of my being. They are within me and of me. They are inwrought into the fibre of my soul. I am *conscious* of them. I shall rejoice to live for them, and I would gladly die for them.

" If they are not founded in truth, then there is no religion, no God, no soul. The world is an enigma. We ourselves are a wild chaos of absurdities. All things are the sport of a malignant chance. There is no truth. We are in a whirl of illusions. But this cannot be.

" Liberty, light, love, — this is my motto. With

regard to liberty, all men are free to act, so far as they do not interrupt the lawful action of others; and the lawful action of all men is that which produces universal happiness. Men may think within the bounds of truth. Universal truth and universal human happiness perfectly agree. In determining the question, What is truth? this may be the test, its adaptation to promote happiness. That is not truth which impairs the glory of God, and takes from human happiness.

"With regard to light, all knowledge is useful. The objects of knowledge are the things which God has made. All philosophy, all science, all learning, are to be prized as we would prize the things of God. All knowledge is the handmaid of religion, and it is religion that gives knowledge its chief value. All truth harmonizes.

"Reason is the great instrument of knowledge, the great instrument of truth. Reason is sacred. It may no more be trifled with or abused, its dictates may no more be slighted or contemned, than truth itself, or God himself. Reason is the arbiter of the soul. It judges upon what is presented in nature and in the Bible, and declares to us the truth. Reason guides us to the throne of God. There the heart holds sweet intercourse; there ˌthe will submits in lowliness; there the intellect receives new treasures of knowledge. God has made nature, he has made the Bible. Truth is immutable. It is the same in nature and in revelation. Who will, then, impiously dissever the Bible from nature, — revealed religion from natural religion? God speaks, and reason is the echoing of his voice. He creates, and reason is the mirror of his omnipotence. He is the author of truth, and reason is its revelation. Who will be indifferent to reason? Who will slight his God? Who will trample down reason? Who will prescribe his God?

" I would yield my heart cheerfully to the dictates of reason. I cannot, I dare not demur. I reject Calvinism because it opposes my consciousness, my reason, nature, and the Bible. In following an unbiassed reason, I feel that I please my God. My soul bursts from its prison-house ; it walks forth, buoyant with freedom ; it treads upward towards its God.

" Love, ' love is the fulfilling of the law.' ' God is love.' ' He that loveth is born of God.' To love is godlike. To love is to be happy. We should love all men, because there is something lovely in man. We should love God supremely, because he is infinitely lovely. I should love all men, and all men should love me. This would make a heaven of earth, as it is the heaven of heaven. If I have not loved others, it is because I have not known them. If they have not loved me, I would fain hope it is because they have not known me. Love is the cincture of heaven, and the golden chain that may raise earth to the skies.

" To love is the prerogative of the soul ; 'tis its commanding excellence. It is its free, native, blissful exercise. But, according to Calvinism, the soul naturally hates. It cannot love its God. It cannot love the human race. O creed, full of all abominations !

" Unitarianism, — I am too well aware of the odor in which this name is held. But I have learned not to fear names. A hard lesson has this been to me. There is only one name which I almost reverence, and towards which I am perhaps too strongly pre-possessed. That is Truth. Whatever bears this name has a passport to my heart.

" But what does the name Unitarianism wear upon its face so revolting? It relates primarily and solely to the Unity of God. In this sense, with the Jews of old, we are all Unitarians. But you are something more. You are both Unitarians and Trinita-rians. It is possible to believe too much as well as too little. Men constantly vibrate between credulity and scepticism. You believe that God is one, and that he is three. But you will say, that you do not mean that he is in the same sense one that he is three, or three that he is one. You believe in a Trinity. I should go farther, and aver that we have good evidence of a quaternity and a quinquenity in the Godhead. If you will read carefully the account of angels in the Pentateuch, and of wisdom in the Proverbs, you will find all the attributes of the Almighty ascribed to them.

" With regard to the Holy Spirit, he is either the one Great God of the universe, or he is a being distinct from him. If you think he is one and the same, so far you are Unitarians. If he is dis-tinct, it must be in one of three ways: he is either greater, equal to, or less than God. If greater, then God has a superior, which cannot be; if equal, then there are two Gods, which cannot be ; if less, we have an inferior Divinity, which cannot be.

" Christ also is the one great God of the universe, or a being distinct from him. If you think him one and the same, then you are Unitarians. But the Trinitarians say that he is in *some respects* distinct from God, yet that he is truly God. Now, in whatever respects, properties, attributes, qualities, or any thing you choose, he is distinct, he must differ in one of three ways. He is either greater, equal to, or less than God. But either of these cannot be. Therefore, in whatever sense he is in the least degree distinct from God, he is not God. But the New Testament everywhere speaks of him as a distinct being, — as a person by himself ; and so I believe he truly is : but I cannot believe he is the one great God of the universe, indivisible, incommunicable. Whatever and whoever differs from God differs, in a strict, metaphysical sense, infinitely. You say we do not understand the connection between our mind and body. True ; but we do fully understand this, that our mind is not our body, nor our body our mind. The very idea of connection implies a difference in the things connected.

" Let me appeal to your own experience. When you direct your petitions to God and to Christ in the same prayer, do they seem to you as one and the same ? Do you regard them both as the one Infinite Jehovah ? When you pray to Christ alone, or when you think of him by himself, do you think of him as the Infinite God ? Do you worship Christ, having the clear idea of him as God ? If you do not, and he be really the great God of the universe, you are guilty of the habitual sin of degrading God, and you degrade him infinitely; for, as we have before seen, whatever differs from God differs infinitely. You say an infinite being must die to make an atonement for sin? I will only ask, could God suffer? could God die?

"Yet Christ is a great, a glorious being. There is no other like him. He is 'the brightness of God's glory, the express image of his person.' He is truly, I do not say in a literal sense, 'God with us.' He is 'God manifest in the flesh.' He is our Redeemer from sin. He is the 'Captain of our salvation.' He is 'the High Priest of the new covenant.' We may love him, because in him dwells the perfection of excellence. We may imitate him, because he is like God. I wish only to preach Christ. For me to live is Christ. In the days of my doubt, I had almost given up Christ. My soul wandered over the tumultuous waters of scepticism, and could find no rest for the sole of its foot. It has now returned to the ark of its everlasting rest.

"If the rejection of the obnoxious and essential points of Calvinism necessarily involves Unitarianism, you cannot imagine that I should hesitate which of the two to choose. If to desire the greatest happiness of the universe, and the highest glory of God; if to see the wisdom and goodness of God displayed in *all* his works; if to take elevated views of his noblest work, man; if to believe and love the revelation which God has made of himself to man; if to unite the philosopher and the Christian, and make them harmoniously subserve the same chief end; if to desire to see the image of God, wherever prostrate, raised, — wherever bright, made still more radiant; if, in a word, to desire to see man illuminated in his darkness, purified from his sins, delivered from the dominion of his Adversary, elevated from his degradation, and to see him loving and being loved, ascending towards his God, unfolding his large capacities for the bliss and holiness of the skies; rising, in the full vigor of his strength, in the intensity of his longings, upward and upward, till earth and heaven shall meet in rapturous unison; and the souls of men and angels, and the Spirit of the living God, shall flow together in one infinite, changeless heart of love; — I say, if this is to be a Unitarian, then I am one. And I rejoice in the ineffable glory which God, by such a character, is pleased to confer upon us, unworthy worms of the dust.

"If Unitarianism looks coldly upon man, and with indifference upon its God; if it locks itself up in the shadowy recesses of selfishness; if it indulges no lofty aspirings, no holy desires; if it has no sympathies, no heart, no head; if it be a negative insensibility in respect to the great, the godlike, and the good, though it may abjure Calvinism, I am *not* a Unitarian.

"Death I do not fear. The thought has sometimes been oppressive; but now the shadows have all melted away in the clear light of faith and hope. I have some dread of the *physicalities* of dying, — nothing more. I *have had* a desire to die, that I

might escape the miseries of existence. In the lap
of the grave I would gladly have pillowed my aching
head, my burdened heart. Thoughtworn, careworn,
I would gladly have relieved my crazed brain anywhere. I used to sing, or rather groan out, you
know, 'There shall the wicked cease from troubling,
there shall the weary be at rest.' I felt it all to my
inmost soul. I have few such feelings now. I look
forward to death with calmness, yet with some exhila-
ration. Death is only the vestibule of heaven. Its
threshold may be easily crossed. Our bodies are
the furnace of the soul, from which it will issue at
death, defecated and polished, to mingle in communion with the Holy and the Infinite. *Where* the
disengaged spirit goes to, we cannot tell. 'Tis
enough to know it goes to its God; that it lives in
his life, is beatified in his bliss, is glorious in his
glory. Why should we, then, fear to die? Jesus
Christ has dissipated the gloom of the grave. There
is no terror there. I would reverberate that outbreaking of ecstasy and triumph, 'O death! where is
thy sting? O grave! where is thy victory?' I thank
my God, who giveth me the victory through my Lord
Jesus Christ.

"What is hell? To be without God is hell. To
have any other society than that of the holy is hell.
To have your natures undeveloped to the spiritual is
hell. To be assimulated to the earth, till the soul
becomes materialized by the gross contact, is hell.
Any thing that is not heaven, holiness, God, to beings
born with such natures and such susceptibilities as
we have, is hell; 'tis the 'gnawing worm,' the

' quenchless fire.' There *may be* direct inflictions of punishment ; but this is not necessary to make a hell for us. God, in this world, generally punishes men by leaving them to the fruit of their own doings. In the next world, it will be hell enough to be un-spiritualized, unholy, unglorified.

" I am happy in my religious views ; but there are thoughts associated with them which make me very wretched. My heart is like the landscape over which the shadows pass, blend, break away, and mingle again. My indiscretions are a permanent source of unhappiness. My irritability makes others unhappy, and, of course, reacts upon myself. The anxieties of my friends awaken concern in my own heart.

" I have told you something of my wanderings. I have unfolded to you something of my *heart*. This is my *Cardiagraphy*. I have not told you every thing. I could not. You would not wish to know. There are chambers which may never be opened. I shall throw the keys away. I say I rejoice in my religious thoughts. Joy, of course, with me, must be a qualified term. I rejoice with trembling. I am at a period in life when young men are apt to look with a cloudy eye. The shadows of my dark night are not yet all dispersed. I feel sometimes as if I had reached but the twilight of a brighter day. When moral diseases have once settled upon the mind, it is with difficulty they can be cured. To doubt was my disease. Its effects, as I have said before, are still experienced. Yet I will not despond. I must be nerved for every conflict. My eyes, I am

9*

sure, have seen the salvation of the Lord, and I will try to go on my way in peace. I reflect with the deepest interest on many events of my life; nor can I ever forget them. You may be disappointed in me; may even regret that the expense and pains of a college-education have been bestowed. But I beg of you to forbear such thoughts. I would hope that I am a wiser and a better man. I would hope that I am fitted for more usefulness in the world. I love my friends, and always shall. If, as again a wanderer, I am compelled to leave the communion of their hearts, my heart will return perhaps more fully to the bosom of its God, where I know your hearts are, and where our hearts shall meet to be for ever blessed together.

" I have been looking over what I have penned. I am afraid you will think I have expressed myself too strongly; but I feel deeply. I have written hastily, because feelings never sit for their portraits. You have sometimes chided me because I have kept myself concealed. You will not blame me, then, for turning aside the veil, even though you witness what you might wish had no existence. As a member of the family, I wish to be not coldly but warmly known. Yet transparency we may rather deprecate, except when 'tis permeated by truth and beauty.

" I feel that I am an infant in knowledge, a novice in attainment. But I am determined, ' forgetting the things that are behind, to press on towards the mark ' of truth, holiness, spirituality, perfection in God. No, I cannot rest. I feel a Spirit stirring me up to holy purposes, to high accomplishments. The courses of religious action, as before alluded to, are various. You will not care what name I bear, provided I am only engaged in removing the sin and earthliness of man, that he may reflect, in unobscured lustre, the full-orbed glory of his God."

The above extracts, with their intensity of feeling, and somewhat incoherency of expression, form a good portrait of the mind of Mr. Judd at this time. About the same date he writes —

To A. H.

"I am at home, doing nothing. I have no disposition to write anybody, or say any thing. There is no topic on which I can speak freely. The present is perplexing and disagreeable; the future is shrouded in uncertainty and gloom. My mental and moral powers are under a perfect paralysis. Take, if you please, this scrawl, not of my thoughts, for I have none; not of my feelings, for the 'mire and dirt' of those troubled waters I would not put upon paper. I would ask to be remembered to my friends, if I were what I might be; but such a thing as I am, how can I care to be held in remembrance?"

Here he was now a young man, just entering upon his twenty-fifth year. He had received those advantages of a public education which had been the hope of his early years, — the ardent wish of his more mature youth. With all the enthusiasm of his nature, he had entered upon them as preparatory to the profession of a Calvinistic minister. With him went the expectations of family and friends, and of the church with which he was connected, that he would become a zealous and distinguished clergyman of the Calvinistic faith. But, compelled in conscience to sever himself from the religious denomination of his fathers, he now found himself, so far as the associations and many of the affections of his former life were concerned, stranded upon an unknown shore, half crazed by the tumultuous buffetings from which he had just escaped, and fainting with weakness from the conflict he had endured.

Not possessing a very firm physical organization, but with affections deep and strong, and keenly alive to blame or reproach, it was hard for him to withdraw the veil, and abide the shock of a disclosure, with all its attendant consequences. His whole being, physical and mental, reeled under it. This change in theological views, involving the costliest sacrifices of the heart, put him to the strongest test that a man can be called upon to endure, that duty, principle, truth, were with him paramount to every thing else.

His father was a man of much liberality of feeling. He had always encouraged freedom of opinion, and had therefore not much to say condemnatory of the position in which his son now found himself by the honest exercise of this freedom. But it is true, that to many of his family friends, this was a sore trial. He had, as they thought, embraced error which might be fatal to his own soul; and he was to become a teacher of this error to others.

On perusing this "Cardiagraphy," however, this

baring of his conscientious, loving spirit to their view, they were completely disarmed. They could utter no word of opposition to the stand he took, when they beheld the fearful but honest strife that had so long been warring within him. They even stood back in reverence before the integrity of feeling evinced, the costly sacrifices he was ready to make to his sense of truth, and the general purity of soul revealed. And from those nearest him, he from this time experienced no interruption in the current of kindly sympathy and love.

Taken all together, this summer of 1837 was to Mr. Judd a period of such almost annihilating suffering, that his friends sometimes feared as to the final result. Its scathing influence he very sensibly felt for several succeeding years, and from its paralyzing effects upon his nervous system he indeed never recovered.

CHAPTER V.

LIFE AT THE DIVINITY SCHOOL.

FIRST YEAR AT HARVARD.

On entering upon his theological studies, Mr. Judd was embarrassed by the same pecuniary difficulties with which he had all along been forced to contend. There was indeed the additional perplexity arising from being severed, denominationally, from all his old Christian friends, from whom otherwise he might have hoped to obtain easy loans until he should be able to refund the sums furnished. But now he certainly could not expect from them any facilities in aiding him to become what they considered a preacher of error. His father had already furnished him all the means in his power. To the Unitarian body, with which he now found himself most closely allied in views and feelings, he was an entire stranger. But, as knowledge of his change of opinions spread abroad, he did not have to wait long for the kindest attentions from those of that communion with whom he came in contact. He naturally wished to make Harvard the *alma mater* of his theological course. Here he availed himself partly of a fund for the benefit of divinity students, and partly of the liberality of Mr. Edmund Dwight, of Boston, a gentleman who was in the habit of loaning money to students there, without interest, to be returned or not, according to convenience. So, with the most strict economical arrangements, he entered the Divinity School of Harvard University, at the commencement of the academic year in 1837.

Here now he found himself a member of venerable old Harvard, the reputed hot-bed of what he himself had once regarded as heretical opinions ; in the midst of strangers to his former faith ; an alien from the household of Calvinism ; in the exercise of new habits of thought, and in all respects surrounded by new scenes and associations. Boston, the seat of refinement and literature, was of easy access ; Bunker Hill and Dorchester Heights, the thrilling scenes of whose history had traced their imagery on his boyhood's imagination, were not far off ; Mount Auburn, the ' city of the silent,' was near at hand ; and nature, in her highest forms of beauty and cultivation, was all around. He was settled in a religious faith, which, to him, was the truth of God. All his doubts and scepticism were dispersed, the struggles with his early creed over, the dreaded ordeal of development past, and his stand taken in a new course. With his escape from those tormenting disquietudes, and with the free and full unbosoming to his friends of what had so long been shut up in his own soul, forming a sort of cold barrier between him and those closest to his heart, returned the gentle tenderness of his childhood-days, and an openness of communication quite in opposition to his natural reserve. He felt his spirit in harmony with itself, with heaven and with earth. Love, in its highest sense, was the element in which he floated.

But was he now completely happy? No. The health of his physical nature being impaired, his nervous system, like the strings of a wind-harp, was tremblingly alive to every gentle breeze or rude blast that might sweep over it. Next to the presence of God in his soul, the greatest want of his nature was *human sympathy*. Partly in consequence of his own idiosyncracies of character, and in part from the religious struggle which was going on in his mind, he went through college without any *bosom* friend among his fellow-students. On going to Cambridge, he felt that —

> " His soul had been
> Alone on a wide, wide sea;
> So lonely 'twas, that God himself
> Scarce seemed there to be."

His spirit yearned for sympathy, for companionship in all its ·recesses, in all its weaknesses. He felt how poor a thing was human weakness to contend with strength. His experiences had been varied, intricate, entangled. He himself found it difficult to trace the clew of light through the labyrinth of darkness in which he had wandered; much more so, in his enervated condition, to give an intelligible, consistent trace of it to any one else. He was too vulnerable on all points of greatest interest to him, to bear the shock of a misunderstanding, or a shortcoming to his needs. Yet he was not sufficient to himself. He needed the tender support of a strong mind that had itself *suffered* as he had, that had gone down to the silent abyss of unutterable sorrow, that knew all its devious ramifications, and that understood how to remove the garment of sadness so gently, that the change would be known only by the refreshment which succeeded. With him were longings for the infinite, the unattained. These he found satisfied in a good degree in his God and his religion; but as to human participators, where should he find them? He descended into the depths of the loneliness of his own spirit; he sounded its profoundest recesses, and drew up thence fountains of knowledge which enabled him ever after to discover the standpoint of suffering souls, and to get into a real sympathy with their griefs.

Yet the sunlight of joy gilded the tops of rocks that rose above these troubled waters. Some parts of his many-sided nature were more than satisfied. He found delight in mental investigations. He did find much sympathy and congeniality. And on he went, manfully yet sorrowfully, with a brave, though sinking heart.

The Unitarians he thought had too little fervor in their religion. He was instrumental in establishing private meetings for prayer among his fellow-students, and was distinguished among them for readiness to bear his part, and for the nearness with which he seemed to approach their common Lord, and pour forth his supplications. In his Journal, Feb. 23, 1838, he writes of them, "These are delightful seasons. We seem to get each night a little nearer to heaven."

In his second year, under the title of "Familiar

Sketches," he communicated to the "Christian Register" a series of letters addressed to his friend W——n, upon the change in his religious views, which were soon, at the request of the American Unitarian Association, under the title of "A Young Man's Account of his Conversion from Calvinism," published by that body as Tract No. 128. He commences thus: —

"Dear W——n, — You desire of me some account of myself, — of what I am, what I think, what I feel;" and then goes on to state, in the main, what has already been given in the preceding chapter on his change of theological views. He speaks more at large of what he considers the difficulties of the system of Calvinism, its practical effects, its opposition to the Bible and to the analogy of nature, the fear of Unitarianism, the objections raised against it, and the arguments for the creed of the Genevan. "The doctrine of the Trinity," he says, "which is regarded as the great point of division between the Calvinists and Unitarians, was secondary in the order and the interest of my inquiries."

In the third letter, he writes: "I have given you a summary account of some of the results of my inquiries. These may appear, at first glance, to be simple, natural, and easily reached. The process, however, is not instantaneous, or unattended with difficulties. Our religious investigations have this peculiarity, that at every step they are thronged with considerations of momentous and changeless consequences. In philosophy we may digress in our inquiries, diversify our experiments, revolutionize our theories, without the apprehension of affecting seriously the welfare of society, or of giving a new determination to our immortal destiny. In religion it is not so. A consistent religious course is of supreme value to every man in this life. But in the next — who can measure the tide of consequences that flows on through eternity? We tremble at every thought, decision, act, lest we impart some slight bias to the nicely adjusted sequence of events, by which, in the progress of ages, instead of being elevated to the happiness we desire, we shall become involved in inextricable misery."

Speaking of the metaphysical subtilties in which on a certain occasion he found himself involved, he says: "I might have persisted in these perplexing abstractions, I cannot say how long, when my thoughts were diverted by the entrance of a little girl, who came tripping in with the freedom and glee of youth. She was in the incipient development of her primitive being. She had not experienced, so far as I know, a change from what was her original nature. I called her attention, and read to her the verse, 'Blessed are the pure in heart,' and so forth, and asked her if she thought it was good in God to bless only those who had pure hearts. 'Oh!' said she, 'I wish my heart to be always pure.' Then she added, with a look between a smile and a thought, such as you sometimes see pass over the face of a child, 'I should not be happy in heaven with God, if I had a wicked heart.' All the world may not perceive the bearing of this slight occurrence. You will understand me when I say it was a hint, a blessed hint, to better things."

Farther on, he says: "There is one thing which engages my attention much : it is the *naturalness* of the religion of Evangelical Unitarians. Religion with them does not appear, as we sometimes witness, an exotic transplanted to an uncongenial soil, to be cultivated by artificial appliances ; but as something which has sprung up in the native mould of the heart. It is warm, free, constant. It is not active for a time, and then chilled by the intervention of worldliness. It is not assumed for a sabbath, a meeting, or an accidental emergency ; but interests itself in the various circumstances of life, and expresses itself on every fitting occasion. It mingles with the recollections of childhood, and with the scenes of youth. God has ever been to it a Father, the Holy Spirit a Sanctifier, and Christ a Saviour.

"Evangelical Unitarianism does justice to human nature. This is its peculiar excellence. Christ did not come to create a new race of beings on the earth, but to develop, bring out, elevate, and re-establish the existing race in its original purity. Unitarianism recognizes in all men the priceless ' pearl ' of the ' kingdom ; ' and it would raise them up into the full light of truth, and the rich joys of holiness. It is teaching the great doctrines of humanity, which shall subvert and utterly demolish, throughout the world, every system of oppression and degradation, religious, moral, and political. It is teaching the sublime and godlike lesson of the worth of the universal human heart."

The reader may already have remarked a change in Mr. Judd's general style of writing, from the time he first found repose in his new views. These were attended with a perfect mellowness of feeling, a full and easy flow of thought, an elevation and richness of expression: they seemed, in a sense, to produce the full flowering of his being. As a whole, his Cambridge correspondence is in quite striking contrast with that of New Haven.

Copious extracts from letters written while he was in the Divinity School will form the principal material of this chapter. A greater space is afforded to his miscellaneous correspondence of this period than would otherwise be, because it so fully unfolds the *general* elements of his character.

His first communication home is addressed —

To his Mother.

"Cambridge Theological Seminary, Aug. 27, 1837.

"My dear Mother, — You see I am on the heretic's ground. Strange as it may seem to myself, unanticipated as it has been by you, it is nevertheless true that I am here."

"*Aug. 30, Commencement-day.* — A great assembly as usual; a multitude of venerable men and learned men. It seemed like standing in the shades of Old England's aristocracy. But, alas! I *lost my dinner*. Contrary to the custom in New Haven and Amherst, those who are only A. B.'s are not invited to dine with the Faculty. . . .

"I shall room alone. It will cost more, but I can study more. Every thing, you know, is to be sacri-

10*

ficed to study. Shall have no one to irritate me by
paltry disturbances. So I may be as calm as the
wood-sheltered lake.

"I feel that, in coming here, I have bid a sort of
everlasting farewell to most of my old Orthodox
friends, so that I have not the solace of communion
with the absent. Still, I do not love them the less,
but truth the better."

To A. H.

" CAMBRIDGE THEOLOGICAL SEMINARY, Sept. 7, 1837.

"I suppose you are prepared for every thing; and
it is unnecessary to allude to my own feelings on
finding myself in this new, this strange, this forbidden situation. Yet I am almost surprised to realize
that I am here. It seems sometimes like a dream,
from which I shall soon awake. And the past, the
past! Where is it? How has it flown? Either
that or this *must* be a dream. How changed are all
things around me, and before me in the future! I
seem to have experienced a sort of metempsychosis.
But the past was real. It lingers, dilates, kindles in
my thoughts, as does the vision of his home-valley
to the distant traveller.

"I shall touch briefly upon the present. The
associations of this whole region are of a most interesting character. New England had its origin
here. This is the land of our ancestors.

"The subject-matter of your notes, of our frequent
conversations, and indeed of my whole life, for these
many months, is of such a nature that I rather avoid
entering upon it fully. It borders, some would

think, too much on the sentimental. It certainly is incorporated with those deep emotions which have no language, which will not bear a calm retrospection, and such as we rather tremble to feel, than are ready to communicate. There are abysses of feeling which we know nothing about till we are plunged into them. I shudder as I look back upon the past. Man knows not the heart. It is a thing of mysteries. It is the mystery of mysteries. Its full capabilities it will take an eternity to reveal. To feel is my nature. It is my thought, my act. I have always felt. But *such occasions* as the last eight months have environed me with, I have not always been subject to. Every object was an emotion, and every feeling a pang. Man frowned me from his presence. Nature, my mother nature, chided my sorrowing. Self was a dashing sea. But this is all past, for ever past; I mean the occasions, not exactly the feeling. This throws its currents over me when I would gladly rest in solitude and distance.

"This summer has been most eventful to me, both in feeling and act. Old relations have been broken up, and new ones assumed. I cannot forget the past. It embraces too great a portion of myself. I would not. The very anguish of my feelings begets a sort of pleasing delirium. Besides, at present, I have nothing to feel about; and, were it not for the past, I know not but that my heart would turn to marble. I am lonely here. I am not much acquainted even with the students yet. I have not found *my man*. Hope a good Providence will send him soon. Where is *she?* Where is the 'well of

waters' by which I can stand 'at the time of evening when the daughters of men come out to draw
water'? This perhaps will seem to you idle and
unworthy of me. I dismiss the topic. If we stand
still, I have heard it said, the world will come round
to us.

"The events of the summer seem to have no
regular *éclaircissement*. They are a labyrinth from
which I escaped, not by a proper egress, but by a
flight out at the top. . . . I must commence life again.
Religiously I have; so I must in other things. But
my poor nature seems almost wrecked, and almost
without the power of resuscitation. I feel sometimes
as if I were sinking into old age. Perhaps this is
only the exhaustion of over-action. My life in its
vigor may return."

To his Mother.

"Cambridge Theological Seminary, Sept. 7, 1837.

"It makes a stranger feel much more lonely
to be with a multitude who all know each other.
This is the loneliness of the multitude, which is
much worse than the loneliness of solitude. In the
latter case, we are never alone; for we can commune
with ourselves and our God. And we can hold converse with nature, who is never engaged, but always
solicits our acquaintance by innumerable attractions.
We need never *fear* to make the acquaintance of
nature. Man sometimes deceives us; nature, never.
Man grows tired of our company: nature is ever
presenting new fascinations in order that we may
stay. I do not know but you will think I am sick

of men. I am in some respects, but I love nature more. She is my companion, my study, my delight. She reveals a God.

" *Sept.* 8. — I was interrupted in my reverie yesterday by the bell. Perhaps it is well for me that my thoughts are brought back, I was going to say, to real life. But my own reveries are as much real life to me as any thing else; so that, whether I am in the world or out of the world, I am in my proper life. As I hinted in my last letter, our seminary is retired. This is favorable to study, and especially to theological study; which always flourishes better in·the grove than in the city. Indeed, it sometimes seems to me almost impossible for a man to cultivate a perfect religious character in the city, where the earth and the sky are paved out and walled out from his view.

" I find myself in the midst of an aristocracy of literature, wealth, and family, — in my proper element, I suppose father will say. There is the aristocracy of the lower orders, and the aristocracy of the higher. Who would fillip a copper for the difference? Man is aspiring. That is his glory. If he were not so, he would be of the brute. The world would stagnate. Give each man all the influence he can get, and we shall all have our proper influence. The scholar looks down upon the farmer, the farmer upon the shoemaker, the shoemaker upon the chimney-sweep. All, in my estimation, are good enough. 'Tis folly to be proud, 'tis misery to envy. Where shall *I* stand ? An egotistical, but a very proper question, — where I can, of course. I have none to raise me; and, I am sure, I wish for none to pull me down. It was no more intended that there should be a perfect level of influence, than that there should be a dead level of thought. And to desire influence for the good of men and the glory of God, is a most religious motive.

"You must be very busy in fitting C. P. off. Let not my affairs hurry you. I am afraid, I know indeed, you exert yourself too much for your children. If they all prove such heretics as I have, I do not know but you will be discouraged. But we shall ever be grateful.

"*Sept.* 10. — We had a most excellent sermon this morning from Prof. Ware. It was Orthodox enough for any one. All that Unitarians need is to adhere to their principles, and acquire some of the *spirit* of the Orthodox."

TO HIS COUSIN G. L.

"CAMBRIDGE THEOLOGICAL SEMINARY, Sept. 9, 1837.

"Dear Cousin, — I wish, in the outset of this letter, to allude to my neglect of correspondence. You may have thought it very strange. It was strange. My apology is to be found in my history. You have some conception of what that has been for the last two or three years. Religious considerations, of a new and peculiar nature, have been pressing with such weight upon my mind, that I could not write. I have often wished to write you. I have more than once taken up my pen, but have thrown it down in despair. I could not disclose to you the subject about which my thoughts were most anxiously engaged. I was entering upon an untried world. Objects around me were indistinct, and yet of overwhelming importance. I could not write about them. I could only think and feel. When I write to a confidential friend, I wish to, I must, write from the heart. But where our thoughts become involved, forbidden, strange, we must not pen them.

" I have been struggling these many years with the difficulties of Orthodoxy. 'Tis no new thing. Long before I went to college, I was often in doubt. You can guess something of my ups and downs. But why did I not tell you something of the matter? Alas! I could not. I said nothing, as you know, to our own family. It was the secret, the corroding, burning secret of my own heart. Perhaps my reserve was not quite reasonable. Yet I did disclose myself as soon as I could. Perfect conviction and settled determination on a change of such vast moment are not the work of a day. My last act, previously to an unreserved declaration, was to read my Bible from Genesis to the Apocalypse. With the whole word of God, as I thought, on my side, I felt ready to meet the world.

" You have noticed some peculiarities in my conduct. But you, as well as others, mistook their occasion. It was religious doubts that hung about me like mill-stones, and haunted me like spectres of midnight. To free myself of these, I sought every kind of diversion. I was willing to talk about the ladies, to laugh with my fellows, to ramble in the fields, or any thing else.

" I have always loved religion, and I think I do

not love it the less now. I have always rejoiced to see it promoted, whether by revival, preaching, conversation, or any way. I think my solicitude on this point has not subsided. It is the *doctrines* of your faith that have troubled me. It is on the *theory* of religion that my mind has gradually been undergoing a change, till it has finally settled on its present views. During my last year in college, my mind was not *decided*, as it is now; still, I had light enough, if you will excuse the language, to make 'darkness visible' around me."

Under date of Cambridge Theological Seminary, Sept. 13, 1837, after describing Bunker Hill Monument, and the extensive, varied, and beautiful view from its top, Mr. Judd thus writes —

To his Mother.

" The reflection involuntarily arises, how man and nature have conspired to render this world beautiful. Why need men deem the world cursed? Why need they deem themselves cursed, whom God has made so beautiful? If men would take half the pains to improve their own natures that they do to cultivate the world around them, then indeed would the 'wilderness blossom as the rose.' But man seeks the outer. The inner is suffered to go to waste.

" The reflection occurs, too, how changed since the poor Indian paddled his canoe in these waters, and hunted here in an unbroken forest! Two centuries have witnessed a change in man's external condition, the like of which the world has never seen. May the next two centuries see as great a change in his moral aspects! But the poor Indians, where are they now?

" I must leave the scene, and descend the monument. I admire the monument, I love the patriotism that designed it. But there is, after all, something so exclusive, so *cruel* in patriotism, that we are half disposed to condemn the whole thing. It makes us love our own country to the sacrifice of every other. It has always filled the world with blood. Yet I am sure you will not wish to be introduced so coldly to the sentiments of the Revolution, or to those deep feelings that naturally arise as you stand by the graves of the martyrs of Liberty.

"Thoughts of blood, agony, and death, make the heart curdle. There is a sublimity about a battle-field, beyond any thing else that this world realizes as sublime. The hosts of men, the gorgeous trappings, the mortal conflict, the ending of time, the beginning of eternity, — these raise the feelings to an unsurpassed elevation, yet one that I would like to experience. Yes, much as I hate war, if a fight *must* occur, I would like to witness it. But may such an event never happen! War is a most unnatural, inhuman system. I am a peace-man, ultra as need be. I am withal so great a *coward* that the consistency of my principles will probably never be hazarded.

" *Sept.* 14. — Last evening, I and two of my classmates were at tea at Prof. Ware's, jun. We were agreeably entertained. Mrs. W., who is an English lady, is a charming woman. She thinks

11

that, if the Orthodox and Unitarians *knew* each other better, there would be much more charity and harmony of feeling among the two denominations. They are strangely ignorant of each other's true excellencies. But I sometimes almost despair of their ever being cordial towards each other, until they get to heaven together. Perhaps our differences here are designed to fit us for greater unity there. Still, the case is very bad. I must hope and labor for better things.

"I board in commons. Have good bread and good butter, which, you know, are the essentials of good living. I shall expect a parcel of letters when the bundle comes. May I not have one from my mother?   "Her son, affectionately."

Postscript in the Same.

"Dear Sis. A., — How do you get along without some one to plague you? Does not this want make life seem dull? Does C. P. fret any? Does P——n mind? . . . . Have you received letters from R., or written to her? What do you fill your paper with when you write her? Have you a thousand girlish indescribables to pour out into her bosom? You will probably have more before the world has done with you; so you need not be in haste."

To his Mother.

"Cambridge Theological Seminary, Sept. 16, 1837.

"My dear Mother, — It is Saturday night. My thoughts revert from present scenes to those I have left behind. It is the hour of rest and reflection with you at home. I wish I could be there to participate in your sympathies and thoughts. You may fancy this language sounds strangely from *me*, from one who never seemed ready to share in the happiness of others, or to communicate his own. Truly I have been too much an *isolated* being — with you, but not of you. This is partly the fault of my nature, partly the fault of circumstances. No one who has not been through the untried states that I have for the last three years can realize the unavoidable *necessity* there is imposed for being alone, thinking alone, sympathizing alone. A *habit* of seclusion in this way is contracted, which it is not easy to abandon. The stars and the twilight, the dim moon and the lonely walk, that were the solitary man's companions, he comes to love, and he continues to love, even when he might return to the haunts of men. He pours out his heart into the ear of nature, and he would listen to her responses. She becomes at once his confidant and his oracle. Still, men should not be forgotten, nor could I be indifferent to them.

"Such a state of mind is the occasion of irritability. The interruptions from those immediately about him, which a man feels whose thoughts are away, will always make him fretful. This disposition is not excusable, although it may in some respects be palliated. . . .

"But I would let these things pass. It is to be hoped, that time, regular occupation, the society of those who are not opposed to cherished views and kindred influences, will assuage the waters of this troubled sea.

"I wish, then, that I could be at home to-night. I am tired of strange faces. In walking over half Boston the other day, I met no one whom I had ever seen before. I anticipated that I should fall in with some familiar countenance; but not one passed me. In Cambridge, to be sure, I am becoming somewhat acquainted with *faces;* but the order, in such a case, is from the face to the heart, and it takes some time to understand the latter.

"*Sept.* 19. — I wonder that I do not receive any letter from home. It is now three weeks since I left Northampton, and I am impatient at your silence. I go to the post-office three and four times a day, but no letter from any source. This silence of my friends, added to the natural loneliness of my situation here, makes me feel doubly solitary. No familiar faces, no familiar voices, no familiar words. This, you may imagine, makes me strongly anxious to hear from you.

"*Sept.* 20. — Yesterday I was informed of means by which my expenses here will be principally met. A benevolent gentleman in Boston gave one of the students, who has this year left the seminary, one hundred dollars a year, which he might either regard as a gratuity, or repay whenever he preferred to do it. He is now settled, and is going to reimburse the one hundred a year. Prof. Palfrey says that I may have the same, in the same way. He says the donor is rich, does not want his money, only wishes that it may be doing some good. I can receive it with or without becoming obligatory for it. I, of course, shall choose to repay it whenever I can. So you see my anxieties are nearly at an end. This sum, in addition to the hundred and twenty-five or hundred and fifty dollars which I shall receive from the funds of the institution, in common with all the members, will nearly cover all my expenses.

"So I may go on my way as blithe as a bird. The Unitarians, *it is said*, do not oblige any one to preach their creed, even though they assist him."

To his Father.

"Theological Seminary, Sept. 22, 1837.

" With regard to stories about your withdrawing aid, and so forth. When I thought of going to Cambridge, I was obliged to look about for means. I stated to my Unitarian friends that you had assisted me to the *extent of your ability*, during my college-course, and that I could not think of applying to my Orthodox friends. I always said that you rather favored free investigation, and that I esteemed it fortunate for myself, that my own mind had not been biassed by parental prejudices. Of opposition from our family I have not complained. I have some-times alluded to passing remarks of my Orthodox friends at large, that I 'was an infidel,' and worse things than that.

"I can readily see how stories are exaggerated· Unitarians in times past have been somewhat perse-cuted. They are *expecting* that every one who leaves Orthodoxy will meet with the same treatment, and construe the intimations of a wounded, disappointed feeling, such as would be perfectly natural to my Orthodox friends, into open opposition. The world

11*

will talk. I am getting used to it. It affects me that my dear friends at home should be implicated."

To HIS FATHER.

" CAMBRIDGE THEOLOGICAL SEMINARY, Oct. 21, 1837.

" Dear Father, — You will gather from my letters to the family, something of what I have interested myself in, as a stranger in these parts. Every place in all this region is full of high ·interest. Last Saturday I strolled all over Boston, with an epitome of its ancient history in my hand, for a guide-book. . . . . I went over the city as a sort of antiquarian. You allude to the library. 'Tis vast. We are surprised at the *great size* of many of the old books. Such were manifestly made for *the few.* Books for *the many* must be *small.* The small size of books in our day evinces a great change in the spirit of the age, in reference to the diffusion and levelling of knowledge. As one casts his eye through the immense alcoves of the library, all stored with books, the very *titles* of many of which are more than he will be able to read or remember, he is apt to feel saddened at the thought of misspent hours, and of the brevity of life itself. But there may be a mistake here. Our best knowledge does not come from books, nor even from the world around us. It comes from *ourselves.* Still I should like to pass my life with such a library in my reach."

To A. H.

" CAMBRIDGE THEOLOGICAL SEMINARY, Oct. 28, 1837.

. . . . " Friendship, yes ; but I am troubled with

my old difficulty, — reserve, concealment, *un*-com-municativeness. Shall I, can I, be free of it? What, with you? Yes, with you. You have *other friends.* They possess your heart. How can I allow myself to be introduced into mixed company? But I am too bad with you, — too bad with myself. I have been thrown into tortures because I would not say any thing; and yet I have suffered in the after-thought, when I did communicate. . . . Yet in all things you must still allow me to hesitate, to check myself, to caution you, &c. &c. Can the Ethiopian, &c. . . . I hate to be obliged, *to a friend,* to reconcile all things. How can I recapitulate the ecstasies of bliss and pain, the entanglements, the self-destruc-tions of those days! I am impatient, vexed, so full of repining that I can hardly write. I could curse my fate. But this is not a right state of mind: I will pray for equanimity and submission. . . .

" I wander about, dying, wasting an inch a day in my own solitude. Come, Friendship, from earth, from heaven, come! I will rush to thine embrace."

TO THE SAME.

" *Nov.* 3. — Twenty-four years of my life are passed, and I have not been myself yet. What might have been, if, and if, and if, I cannot now say. Here I am, helpless as a new-born babe; without vigor, without courage; unsupported; seeking sym-pathy, but finding none; seeking aid which is every-where refused. Yet I am not altogether so. I have another self; a busy, every-day self, — all which the world knows or cares about. Still I am in a sense so ; a sense that oppresses me with its weight, and comes over my spirit at times in the full tide of its reality.   I am too boundless in my desires : nothing fills them.   The world itself cannot satisfy me."

To his Brother H——l.

"Cambridge Theological Seminary, Jan. 13, 1838.

"It is not well to neglect our friends.   I confess I have done it.   But now, since all personal crises are passed, and the world knows me as I am, I hope I shall make amends for my many omissions, and enter with my original freedom into the society of those I respect and love.   If there be any wish on your part to know me better, surely I am ready to remove all barriers to such information.   I am willing to appear upon the confessional at any hour.

"Tell C. P. I think I shall board myself this term. My situation in Cambridge is, in the main, quite to my mind.   My external circumstances were never better adjusted for my happiness.   The pursuits of the seminary are congenial with my taste ; the spirit, with my feelings."

To his Cousin G. L.

"Cambridge Theological Seminary, Jan. 16, 1838.

"My excuses for not writing and confiding my thoughts to my friends, you remark upon with considerable severity.   I will only allude to one thing by way of reply, or in farther extenuation of my conduct.   When one is in a state of doubt, he does not know what the result will be.   In his revolutions of thought, he may come back to the old ground.   Of course, he will not wish to disquiet his friends by intimations of what is indefinite and uncertain in his own mind.

"As to my reading the Scriptures, I wished to represent to you simply, that, as a consummation, I reperused the whole, more clearly to understand the connections, bearings, and spirit of portion in relation to portion, and of each portion relative to the whole. The Bible *is* the standard. It must not bend to our reason, and our reason need not *bend* to it; for they perfectly *harmonize*. This is the beauty and delightfulness of our condition. The revelations of the Divine Will, in the Scriptures, in Nature, in the human heart, are all perfectly coincident. They are mutual supporters and illustrators of the same glorious truths. . . .

"Our 'orbits' may be different, but I pray to God that they may be 'harmonious.' I wish to do good. My whole heart and soul, I speak without boasting, are more than ever bound up in that great end. I believe the time is coming when *Christians*, Trinitarians or Unitarians, will see eye to eye, and will learn to love each other more, and will feel that they have only one Master to serve, one world to save, and one heaven to gain. *Christianity*, in its true development and legitimate action, is what we want, not '*ans*' or '*isms*.' I wish I could introduce you to some of our students. I am confident you would admire the manifestations of the genuine Christian character, however you might deplore their theological errors. . . .

"I am as happily situated at Cambridge as I can

expect to be anywhere. The pursuits of theology were ever most congenial with my feelings; and our daily tasks are only such as give us a pleasant employment, without fatigue in the application. Our students are those in whose intercourse, social and religious, I pass many delightful hours. The society of Cambridge offers many attractions to such as are disposed to visit. My habits are rather reclusive. My occasional calls are exceedingly pleasant."

To his Mother.

"Cambridge Theological Seminary, March 15, 1838.

"My dear Mother, — The package of letters from home came to my hands last evening. I need not express to you the pleasure I feel in receiving the kind memorials of so many of our family. It concerns me to know that your numerous debilities are aggravated by a new affliction. I doubt not that it is a satisfaction to yourself to be assured that your 'absent children' are sharing a degree of temporal felicity, which is not always universally diffused through so large a family. For this, how much are we indebted to the instruction, example, and prayers of our ever-devoted mother! Long may she live! Long may we be blessed with her blessings!

"My last letter was rather long. You see I have now taken a still larger sheet, and perhaps your patience will be frightened even before it is exhausted. When I purchased, last vacation, these mammoth sheets, father wondered what I should do with them. Possibly he did not imagine, that he should be set to the task of reading over the whole of one closely written. If the substance of the epistle were equal to its length, there might be a compensation for reading. But, alas! I cannot promise that. . . .

"I need not say that it is my strong desire that H——i should never appear in *regimentals* again. A military spirit should rather be repressed than fostered in children."

"*April* 10. — By a comparison of dates, you will see that some days have elapsed since I last wrote. During the interval, I have been variously engaged. Monday I called on Dr. Channing. He is a man of small proportions, very indifferent in his appearance. There is nothing in his face, his eye, or his head, that indicates the great mind which reigns within. He is now quite indisposed, — cannot talk with his friends very long at a time. Yet, from what he did say, it was evident that his soul was full of great thoughts, great plans of progress, reformation, and Christianization. He dwells not with common men or common Christians. He aspires to something higher, holier, purer. He feels a deep interest in the young men of the seminary. He teaches us to attempt and hope for greater things than the world has yet seen. Liberty and Christian love seem to be the ruling principles of his heart.

"Yesterday I walked alone to Mount Auburn, that place of beauty and death, of melancholy and delight. All my evening walks have been gladdened by an unclouded moon. When I come out of Boston unaccompanied by any human being, it is pleasant thus, at midnight, to look upon the silvery light, and breathe in the quiet air. . . .

"How many times has this '*I want*' of your children been repeated! When shall it end? Truly, I suppose you do not wish it to end, while you have the means to supply it? But it would be pleasant to us to return, in some feeble measure, the ten thousand favors we have received from our dear parents. May God bless them with his infinite fulness!"

To A. H.

"CAMBRIDGE THEOLOGICAL SEMINARY, June 3, 1838.

"I seem to myself to be quite impatient of writing. There is the vexation of waiting months for a reply to emotions that burn in the heart. Then there is the trouble of not being precisely understood, and all that sort of thing. Yet I must write, and write I will. Only these despairing circumstances do almost persuade me not to assume my pen.

"I have been very busy. The German I have commenced, and must give it some study. I have taxed myself to read some French every day, also to prosecute some miscellaneous readings. Last week was Anniversary-week, and we were called into Boston every day. Spring, too, has burst upon us in all its beauty and attractiveness. This has called me much from my room.

"But the under-current has been ever flowing. Yet few know it, and fewer care for it. It is only when my external self, my known being, staggers and reels, that I fear some observer will detect the hidden cause. 'Tis strange how I, that is, one like myself, catch the sympathies of longing hearts. . . . There is now and then a person in this world 'charged;' and you have but to touch them, and the fire of their souls is at once emitted.

"You will not think but that other and higher thoughts engage my attention. With you alone do I take the liberty of writing freely."

"*June* 29. — You manifestly *dabbled* when you wrote. But that is sometimes excusable. The mood — ay, yes, *the mood* — 'tis that gives us inspiration. When that is off, to write is like the nightmare. . . . We are strange creatures. For the good we have, we are thankless. For the good we lose, we absolutely rebel. 'Total depravity,' — well, so be it. Heart *is* every thing, with or without husband or child. With, — perhaps 'tis more than every thing. There are hearts in heaven. We are apt to think of Christ only religiously. But did it ever occur to you (I am serious) that he sympathized with our affection's heart? He was tempted like as we are, was he not? Yet without sin. Ay, there is the rub, — *without sin.* Our hearts *do* make us sin.

"Aim at the stars, you say. What if, in a dark night, I catch a glow-worm? . . . Elevated society has its drawbacks. I love sometimes to escape to the low, home-spun realities of common life. Its rudeness only provokes an agreeable humor. In it you expect nothing, and never run any risk of disappointment."

12

SECOND YEAR AT HARVARD.

To A. H.

"CAMBRIDGE THEOLOGICAL SEMINARY, Sept. 7, 1838.

"I am on the rack to-day. I pace my room, 'poke' my hair, seek the diversion of classmates. Let me not write then. Let me wait till I can be more calm. The impressions of the present moment make me somewhat tumultuous, somewhat irregular. . . . . Let us despair. 'Tis well. Then we shall be ready to leave this world, to plume our wings to an upward flight to the realms of everlasting fruition. . . .

"Dr. W. pleased me very much. How pleasant is it to meet, in his own home, such a man, whom you have known as Dr. W. on Depravity, or Dr. W. in controversy with Dr. T.! The man at home, — how much better than the man abroad; or, I should say, how much more he comes to your heart!

"I am tolerably unhappy. Yet I should be happy. Am lonely, while many are around me. Yet I would not be without this heart of mine. . . . But I leave it and all, — leave hope, and take to sighing. No, let me turn to a petrifaction. Write soon to   Your wearied, aching brother,

"SYLVESTER."

To ——.

"CAMBRIDGE THEOLOGICAL SEMINARY, Sept. 15, 1838.

"If the muse has departed, does not her haunt still remain? Sunsetting still comes to you, and midnight and the stars. The bay is still there, with its many islands, like the repose of thought, amidst the eddyings of everlasting being ; and the ocean, with its fathomless heart of poetry. . . .

"An oppressiveness had settled on my spirits, for the dissipation of which, I hasted to seek the influences of my friend, confident, nurse, Nature. . . .

"I love sometimes to utter myself; and the communion of congenial hearts, — that rare water-spring in this desert-world, — is dearer to me than all things else this side of eternity. God bless you and love you, as my Lamb says. So prays sincerely your friend."

To the Same.

"Nov. 5, 1838.

"Yet why do I write ? What impulses summon my pen to an unfamiliar and almost forbidden duty ? I have disciplined myself these years to silence ; still, silence is my agony. Yet our very agonies, thus cherished till they become a part of our existence, seem sweet unto us. But — buts, yets, dashes — they are the cliffs and chasms that intersect the path of us mountain-wanderers. How much better, then, to keep in the smooth plains below ! To the heart is allowed no free utterance. It is awed by its own aspirations ; it is exhausted by its own struggles ; and more — it dare not trust its loved emotions with a mocking world. Is this right ?

"I write compactly ; for I know, that, if I once commence, I shall have much to say, and still leave all unsaid. How can we bring our souls within the compass of three pages of a letter-sheet ? And, besides, what if I should never take the letter from my room ? Is there no pleasure in a sort of auto-correspondence ?

"The study of character has been the habit, and I might say delight, of my life. An irrepressible longing for sympathy first led me to the observation, which has received a fresh stimulus from the demands of my profession. I have accustomed myself to scale the heights of character, to fathom its depths. The result of this has been, that there is much of genuine sentiment in the world, so we can but detect it. Some persons possess one point of excellence, some another ; some many points, some few. So we can meet one with whom we sympathize on all points, how would our souls rush together, like sister-angels ! The three indispensable elements of the perfect character are intellect, sentiment, virtue, — these in their broadest and most embracing significance.

"And by virtue I do not refer to the cant of sect, or the abstractions of philosophy, but to all moral excellence, to religion in its highest exercise, to morality in its holiest practice. These qualities, blended, relieved, sustained, matured, constitute a character which we gaze upon with loving admiration ; to which we bow with a delightful reverence ; and which if we can unfold to our own embrace, and call in any measure our own, we feel like participants of the heavenly joys. The actual of this ideal we sometimes see in the world. But too often the excess or deficiency of some one quality deforms and obscures the whole. Frequently, when those qualities combine in equal degrees, they are not elevated ; and, when they are elevated, they are not equal. Intellect palsies sentiment, and sentiment is the foe to virtue, and virtue sometimes rises to that bigot-excess which looks with contempt alike upon intellect and sentiment. And then, more often, the lustre of truly noble and consistent characters is dimmed by some one of those innumerable petty faults which are grouped under what we call disposition and temperament, such as vanity, selfishness, petulance, nervousness, idiosyncracies of all sorts. This topic is exhaustless ; but I leave it."

To his Cousin G. L.

"Northampton, Feb. 15, 1839.

"I left Cambridge in the latter part of November. My health was not good. I suppose I had indulged in too close attention to books, without sufficiently regarding diet and exercise. My nervous system became most painfully deranged. My system has somewhat recovered its tone, which I attribute, in a good measure, to the course of protracted and vigorous exercise which I pursue every day. I am beginning to be sensible, what I have hitherto, in a great measure, been indifferent about, that exercise is very essential to the student. In college, my health was good without exercise. So I was lulled into the fatal notion that it would always be. . . . I did not think of giving a dissertation on physical regimen. I have only stated a bit of experience. To me it has been of some service. If you can make use of it, you are welcome to the knowledge.

12*

The clergy are all sick and dying. What is the disease?"

To Mrs. E. H.

"Divinity School, March 18, 1839.

"I often act impulsively. A disposition to speak out the emotion of the moment overleaps the perhaps proper barriers of conventional decorum. But more than this, and higher too, as some think, — a love of sympathy is irrepressible with me. This passion, which plants itself in all hearts, seems to have especially luxuriated in my own. Specifically and immeasurably have I looked for *religious* sympathy. Always, I say, but not so much now as in some previous years. Yet I can find but few who know what it is to have struggled and wept. Life and thought, with most, seem to have been a pleasant current."

To his Brother H——l.

"April 1, 1839, Cambridge.

"Dear Brother, — What shall I say to you? What shall I say of myself? Separated, but not estranged; absent, but not forgetful, we should still commune as the spirit prompteth. Have we been long silent? It is our mistake and necessity, more than our purpose and crime. We love communion; and none but an imperious occasion could or should interrupt it.

"You have sometimes complained of the crookedness of conventional life. True, there is much wrong. The spirit struggles to break from untoward environments; rather does it struggle to subdue them to itself, — a noble conquest, never half-achieved. Then do we moralize and weep. These things are disciplinary, and serve the highest good of the soul. Therefore do not murmur. Be true thyself, and all things shall be true about thee. Perhaps, after all, there is not so much that is false as we imagine. No one man is so bad as we conceive. We suffer from an optical illusion. In contemplating the multitude, the little bad that each man possesses is presented to us in the aggregate of the whole, and our judgments become severe as our aversion is intense. All the vices of society should not be visited upon one man. Give each his due. Make individual man more your study. He is natural; society is artificial. He is true; society is false. Society is the masquerade of humanity. Under each mask you will detect the true man, and be satisfied. Study, then, the individual man. You will find in each the same uneasiness, the same craving, the same aspiration, in a measure, which you may have thought peculiar to yourself. Humanity, — that is, what is common to all men, what each man possesses, — is a vast and rich field of observation. Look beyond the adventitious, the trappings and tinsel which all despise as much as you do, and you will discover much to delight, much to profit and content you. Dissatisfaction with man is not well. It bodes no good. It impairs the energies of reform. It embitters the soul. It frustrates the ends of human existence.

"Excuse this homily. It does us good to reflect;

to check the course of our thinking, and compare ourselves with others, — compare our prevailing speculations with man as he is.

"Your health, we all hope, will soon be established. Be patient. Let few things irritate you. Don't overdo. Health is a more valuable acquisition than property, wives, any good except truth. Bow submissively to the Infinite Will.

"I have been to walk to-day to Mount Auburn. A delightful day, delightful spot, delightful company, delightful time. 'Tis well to dip into society. You will sometimes bring up pearls even from mud, diamonds from sand. The world is rich in hearts, heads. Fear not. Man was not made to be feared, but to be loved. Love will draw all hearts after you.

"Let me have a letter from you soon. Speak all. Repress no feeling. Dark thoughts become light when brought into sunshine.

"I am quite well, and life is pleasurable.

"Your brother most affectionately."

To ——.

"DIVINITY COLLEGE, CAMBRIDGE, April 2, 1839.

"The impressions of such a day as yesterday are too decided to be lost in a few changes of the dial-plate. Yet I cannot recount them, — shall not attempt it. Mount Auburn, the spirit's home, the answering nature to what we cherish in our own hearts with so intense a love; the dear, sweet spot that kindles emotion but to tranquillize it, and awakens thought but to sanctify it; the receptacle of the dead, and yet the life of the living; its deep, solemn, silent, melancholy shades; its evergreens, so like immortality, — its leafless trees, so like death; Mount Auburn — my very thoughts die out in utterance. Let me be silent; let me sit still and *feel*. The soul would lie down in the repose of a solemn contemplation and an earnest listening. The shade and the sunlight, the dell and the slope, the verdure and the searedness, come over us with a refreshing, subduing influence.

" The emotion of such an hour, — is it not one, indivisible ? Does it admit of definition or analysis ? Subtile, how can we seize it ! Vast, how can we confine it ! Yet real is it as our own life, deep as our own eternity.

" I would die among my own kindred ; but I wish to be buried in Mount Auburn. If an ancient fancy were true, that the spirit delights to revisit the place of our sepulture, mine should come to a place so sweet, so lovely. It should hardly miss its heaven for it.

" We were speaking of a sense of unworthiness before God. Did you allude to the subject because you thought I cherished too much assurance ? Yet I am persuaded, I cannot doubt, — except in those moments when we seem insanely to doubt of every thing, — 'He that loveth is born of God;' and nothing can disturb that conviction. 'Tis to me as my own life.

" We grovel too much. We take our flight beneath the clouds, and become immersed in their shadows and drippings. If we would but mount above them, we should see these gloomy masses permeated and transparent with the light of the all-enlightening sun. As we approach that luminary, we become light ourselves, and all things glow with light about us. To an inhabitant of the sun, there is not a dark spot on the face of the universe.

" Truth is light, love is light, God is light. Truth, Love, God — O my soul! By what art thou surrounded! To what canst thou attain! How glorious may be thy life! Yet how dost thou fold thy wings, make feet of thy hands and claws of thy feet, and crawl about in the dark caverns, the slimy pits, of this nether world! Arouse, O angel within me! Shake from thy pinions the dusty coatings of earth. Start thee on thy celestial flight. Falter not, till thou shalt rest, serene, secure, and blest, in the highest heaven of truth, love, and God."

To his Sister P——n.

"CAMBRIDGE, April 6, 1839.

" How does my young sister do? Is she happy, and making all happy with whom she has intercourse? Make the most of your youth. It will soon be past, and no earnest wishes can recall it. Your young years are given you to be happy in and to be good in. Be both. Be good, and you will be happy.

" How is your grammar? Have you learned how to dispose of the infinitive mode? Your parsing lessons seem uncommonly perplexing to you. But practice makes perfect. The nominative case will not, by and by, skulk behind the objective, and the adverbs get hid among the adjectives, where you cannot find them. They love to play bo-peep awhile; but they will grow tired of it before long. And then the rules are so apt to slip away. You must tie a string to them, and hang them up, each one on its own nail. You sometimes put two or three on one nail, or else one on another's nail, and, when you come to take them down, you find you are using the wrong one.

"I suppose, now I am gone, that knob of hair gets posted up on the back side of your head, like a hump on a camel's back. I am sorry you wish to be an old woman so soon. You will be glad enough, by and by, to go back to the short hair or braided ringlets of your girlhood."

To A. H.

"CAMBRIDGE, April 6, 1839.

"In the progress of the heart, we have a thousand casual, incipient, stray thoughts and feelings, such perhaps as should never be expressed, but which, when expressed, are exceedingly liable to be misunderstood. They possess no meaning that you can explain, no end or aim that you would acknowledge. Yet stir they within us, and it pleases to give them utterance to a trusty ear. Beyond this, we cannot allow them to be spoken, even to our best friends. These feelings have no consistent character. They are one thing to-day, and another to-morrow. They vary with persons, places. How unsafe, then, to unfold them to the world! There is a key, indeed, that explains the whole; but who has it?"

To his Mother.

" Cambridge, April 6, 1839.

" Dear Mother, — I am in the way of writing letters this morning ; and although, according to the strict rules of epistolary ethics, I can hardly feel that I am in your debt, yet am I constrained to give you also a word.

" In the first place, with regard to my health, it has never been better than during the past week. I know, when we speak of health, we refer to a permanent state of the system ; but I am very grateful for a week's soundness and stability. It is an augury of good to come. I walk from six to eight miles a day, and purpose that nothing shall interfere with the habit. Our hold on health is not sure. While life is ours, may we live well, then shall we die safely."

To his Cousin G. L.

" Divinity School, Cambridge, April 9, 1839.

" A letter from A. speaks of a revival of religion in the Mount Holyoke Seminary, and adds that cousin T. has been particularly interested. Can any one rejoice more than I do, that your sister has come at last to the enjoyment of her true life ? Can any one appreciate, more than I, the value of that change by which the soul unfolds itself to divine influences, and becomes a partaker of the ' divine nature ' ? Truly this is the end of our being. For this does the soul aspire. Any thing short of this is a check upon our nature. We wander about like lost sheep, straying from the fold of the divine Shepherd. We find no green pastures, no still waters. God addresses us, 'Return, O wanderers, return, and ye shall find rest unto your souls.' Do we thus return, do we go back to our Father's house, are we reinstated in a Father's love, — what a heaven is ours!

"A revival of religion, while it appeals to the deepest susceptibilities of the human mind, has something unnatural about it. It makes religion too much a matter of times and seasons, of places and positions, of formularies and plans. It generates something of a false, superficial, temporizing piety. And yet I suppose great deference is due to the spirit of the times. If this demands what are generally known as revivals, it will have them, and you will find it difficult to convert men in any other way. This spirit does not prevail equally in all denominations. Which has the advantage, I will not judge. It is a curious fact, that Methodists are rarely converted, except in camp-meetings. So each denomination has its *modus operandi*. This is somewhat natural and scriptural, somewhat unnatural and unscriptural. Who shall strike the balance?"

To ———.

"Divinity School, April 10, 1839.

"This meeting of friends, it is the feast-day of the soul. All mortal joys do minister to a noble friendship. Such communion shall the stars nightly bless. If it be less intense, it possesses fewer alloys than love. If it does not transport like love, it suffers less from jealousy. It is more divine than love, — such love as is rife in the world, — because the lat-

13

ter often originates in the inferior passions, while the former springs, pure, ingenuous, angelic, from the heart of the soul. I believe your sex is favored as regards friendship. There is but little of the genuine emotion in ours. The habits of men are too commercial and restrained, too bustling and noisy, too ambitious and repellant, for the cultivation of those nice sensibilities on which a true friendship rests. Women are the bonds of society, and the conserving principle in human intercourse. Their secular aspirations never lead them to isolation, either the isolation of solitude or the isolation of superiority. Their susceptibilities are so ardent, that, if raised into elevated positions, like waves of the sea, they soon melt into the common mass around them. Men are like mountains, bold, icy, moveless, that woo the winds and worship the stars, but frown an eternal defiance at each other. Yet does man turn to woman for those resources of sympathy and love, without which he must die. I cannot say, indeed, but there is something generous, chivalric at least, in a man's declining intercourse with his fellow-man, that he may offer an undivided confidence to woman. Still I wish, for my own happiness at least, that we were more disposed to cultivate the friendly relations.

"Is there no friend for me ? Is there no Damon to my Pythias ? It is a notion which I humor myself in indulging, that there is, somewhere in the world, somebody *just like me*, whose modes of thought, habits of philosophizing, intellectual and religious training and discipline, whose aspirations, hopes, doubts, whose idiosyncracies and eccentricities, are the counterpart of my own. You smile at this; and so do I, and call it all a dream. Yet we live to dream. But to come to what is realizable. I hope to encounter some one who will be as much to me as I expect ever to be to any one. More than this, I cannot ask. Can you direct me to such a one; one who, while he retains the distinctive peculiarities of his own person, will be so much like me as to welcome me to the full communion of his heart? I am growing very egotistical and prosy."

"*April* 14, *Sunday*. — 'Welcome, sweet day of rest,' — day that shines on millions of our race with a refreshing light: my eyes rejoice in thy dawning, my heart awakes to worship and to praise. Yet do sad reflections press upon my spirits. With what a discordant note are the voices of men sent up to the eternal Ear! Are not these voices impeded on their way by so much of strife and collision? and do they not die away, mid-heaven? Angels might close their ears to such music as ours. As we have one common Father, so can we never have one common worship?

"And then, in its own character, how deficient is the worship of Christendom! What does it lack? So far as the answer can be given in one word, I should say *heartiness*. It needs an earnest soul, an active spirituality, an intense humility. We do not require a new soul, but the thorough agitation of the old one. Revivals and sermons, the representations of heaven and hell, all of which do but affect the soul outwardly, as I may say, are not so much required ; but quiet, retirement, introversion, solemn self-questionings, thorough self-explorations.   We hear much of the worth of the soul, and that worth is usually measured out to us in terms of duration, or in estimates of pleasure and pain ; while few seem to imagine that the soul is valuable for *what it is in itself.* But what is it in itself? How few know! How few trouble themselves to inquire! How little do our public ministrations teach! We occupy ourselves with gazing into eternity, and wishing we were there, as if eternity were not within us. Love in the soul is heaven there. Good thoughts are angels. Good fancies are golden streets and gates of pearls. Christ attends us with all the sympathies of an elder and a divine Brother's love. God, the eternal Spirit, is about us and over us ; that unreplenished light which no night-shadows immerse, no clouds obscure. He who loveth is immortal. What wait we for more ? Simply that this body, that invests us like a drapery of mist, may dissolve and melt away. So shall we come to the undimmed visions of eternal glories.

"I look for no millennium, for no extension of Christ's kingdom, for no progress in ethics, for no substantial advance in the common principles of morality, till men shall come to realize that *they have souls*. I love preaching, I love the sabbath. But these must be so improved as to restore man to himself, or their highest efficacy will not be secured. When I grow tired of hoping, then I sing, —

> 'Thine earthly sabbaths, Lord, I love ;
> But there's a nobler rest above.' "

"*April* 18. — Dr. Follen gave his last lecture on Atheism yesterday evening. The Theistical problem, is it not vast? Are we not confounded when we would tell what God is; what Nature is? Is Pantheism a system unnaturally unnatural? Do we not discover Pantheistic tendencies working in all minds? The Infinite One, εἰς καὶ πᾶν. The tendency of philosophy is to generalize, *ad infinitum*, which is, to reduce all things to the one. This result can only be prevented by the instinctive repulsion of our nature. Reason tends to unity; spontaneity, to variety. Reason seeks for resemblances: spontaneity forces us to acknowledge differences. And then our religion does sometimes lead us to the confession of universal absorption, — God in us, and we in God. Our hours of reverie also do carry us away from our individuality. We follow in the track of some principle, — existence, extension, life, heat, — pursuing our course through men, trees, the earth, sun and stars, till we have made the compass of universal being. We discover an inexorable oneness binding together all objects and creations. We begin to lose ourselves in the vast conflux of existences to an indistinguishable identity; and then, for fear of an irretrievable perdition, to be sure that any individuality remains, I pinch my hand, get up and walk, feel proud, any thing, that I may return to my identity, and rescue myself from the horrible sensation of being swallowed up in the infinite abyss of the One!"

"*April* 21. — Can we reach the friendship we long for? And how does it dissolve in our hands

13*

like snow-flakes, when we have grasped it! It is not strange that we grow jealous of that which we prize most highly. It is not strange that we return with a melancholy repugnance to that life of loneliness and heart-aching, from which the voice of love and friendship has once summoned us, — a condition rendered doubly caustic from the recollection of intervening felicities."

"*April 23.* — The intensity of an emotion is sometimes the direct means of its relief. Our heaviest wretchednesses do sometimes, of very grief, like children, cry themselves to sleep. Eternal Silence! on thy bosom let me rest. Breathe upon me, O breath of Silence! that this tumultuous heart may be subdued into a calm slumber."

To his Brother H——I.

"Divinity School, Cambridge, April 28, 1839.

"My dear Brother, — You are our youngest brother, and, as such, must ever claim a peculiar share in our solicitudes and love. Have we at any time been arbitrary, or exacting, or capricious, yet do we not love you the less. You have now left your father's house, and entered upon your apprenticeship to the business of life. You are thrown into circumstances of increased responsibility and multiplied dangers. Of what concern is it that you *set out* well! Listen, then, to a brother's counsel, which he gives from the love he bears you, and also from some experience of the necessities of your new situation.

"Be faithful. In all duties that come under your charge, execute them to their fullest demand. Slight

nothing. Slur over nothing. Be always ' on hand.'
Let it make no difference whether your employers
are present or absent; but do every thing well, and
equally well at all times.

"Be honest. I am told that some merchants and
booksellers are not so honest as they should be.
This is very wrong, 'tis very wicked. Cultivate the
principle of honesty, that you may be scrupulous in
all things. Do not allow yourself to be influenced by
the loose example of any whom you may see doing
wrong. Always give the half-cent when it is due.
Give a fair account of all the goods you dispose of.
Take no advantage of the ignorance of others, but
rather enlighten them. Disdain all low tricks of
trade. Be in all things open, frank, fair, as you
wish others to be with you.

"You are, indeed, partly in the employ of your
brother; but you must not expect indulgence on that
account. You must consider that in all *business-
relations*, he will treat with you as with any other
clerk; that he will be as strict in his requisitions,
and as severe in his reproofs.

"Be very careful in the choice of your companions. There are many unprincipled men and boys
in the city. Never associate, not for an hour, with
one whose character is in any degree suspicious. If
any one is profane, or uses vulgar or profane language, or if he would tempt you, in the least, to any
vice or dissipation, shun him as you would a viper.
Break off all intercourse with him. There are young
men, in the city, of good and estimable characters,
whose acquaintance you may seek, and by whose

society you may be profited. But it is not best, at first, to have too many acquaintances. Make your acquaintance slowly. Reserve your time for other things. Read as much as you can. Do you not have many leisure-moments which could be devoted to reading? You are surrounded by books. Can you not make much use of this privilege? Every bookseller should be acquainted with the character of the books he sells. Spend your evenings in reading. Do not read many novels, but take more substantial books, such as history, biography, travels. By and by, you will come to relish poetry, philosophy, metaphysics, &c.

"Above all things, my dear brother, cultivate your religious character. Daily read a portion of the Scriptures. Daily lift your heart in prayer to your heavenly Father. Seek his guidance and protection. Make him the object of your supreme affections. He will listen to your prayers. He will surround you with his influences. He will preserve you in the hour of temptation.

"Be regular in your attendance at church on Sundays. Do not trifle away the Lord's day, as some young men are disposed to do. Occupy its leisure hours in meditation, or in reading books of a devotional character, or such as tend to cultivate your moral and intellectual nature.

"Strive in all things to be a *man*, a *good man*. Do not regard the low standard of character that may prevail around you. Embrace high and noble principles. Be disinterested, be self-denying. Do not think that the great object of life is to make money, but rather to elevate and purify your own character, that you may be a blessing to the world. Let all with whom you associate feel that you are a young man of principle; that you cannot stoop to vice, or be drawn aside by error.

"Be kind. Love all men. Make your brothers, your sisters, all with whom you associate, happy by your presence.

"That you may be and become all such as we wish and counsel, is the earnest prayer of

Your Brother."

To ———.

" DIVINITY SCHOOL, June 14, 1839.

"If you observe the dates — but what are dates? The soul knows no dates. Successions are they of sun-risings, meal-taking, heart-aches. They do interfere with the unbroken oneness of the soul's being. Yet, in time, according to the laws of succession, the soul does vary, revolve. Week rolls upon week, and the heart pours along its floods evermore. I have seized my pen; but the ink, that comes flowing from my inkstand, glimmers and is quenched in the utter despair of my heart, of my life. Felt you ever so, when the wildest impulses of your nature tempted and urged you to an act, which a still stronger impulse would not suffer to be done? Rosalie [Allston's painting], Corinne, and then the vile admixtures, the obstinate interference of this mechanical world, the imperiousness of expediency, the impudence of discretion, and then my own faltering, tameless nature.

. . . . "I do not forget your doctrine, that a direct expression of sympathy is not always needed or desirable, objectively or subjectively. But the oppressiveness of sympathy may be as caustic and restless as the agony of our subjective emotions, and equally demands our utterance. The greatest evils of life are not always so much the pain received into our own breasts, as the sufferings we inflict, either in the way of cause or occasion, upon others. Nor is a consciousness of rectitude on our part always sufficient to prevent the ingress and corrosion of this reflex agony.

"The language of sympathy is brief and direct: indeed it is not so much a language as an action; and its power lies, not so much in utterance as in silence. Those nights when the sleepless heart struggles with a wearied body, how bad they are! The eye, shut from objects which the light of day brings to its relief, fastens with a wild intensity and aching minuteness on those scenes which have interested the heart."

To A. H.

"CAMBRIDGE, June 27, 1839.

"A philosophical tranquillity, if it were attainable, is perhaps at all times our most desirable condition. At least, it is natural for us to grow averse to those things which have flattered and lured the soul into a perpetual disappointment and pain. As to myself, I can say nothing. 'The end of man were an action, not a thought, though it were the noblest.' Let us, then, 'do that which lies next us.' So we bestir ourselves, we may set agoing the mists that crowd heavily upon us, and they shall all roll away into the infinite void."

To his Brother H——L.

"Divinity School, Cambridge, June 29, 1839.

"The anti-war question has been pretty thoroughly discussed in the seminary; and we are perhaps surprised to find that our whole school, with scarcely an individual exception, sustains the position, that all war, offensive and defensive, is inconsistent with the spirit of Christianity. This is a result, which, as I am aware, has not been reached in any other seminary, literary or theological, in the country. It is in no way of boasting, when I intimate that Unitarianism is most peculiarly fitted for such a conclusion. Its idea of the worth of man, as man, and its faith in the indestructible principles of human virtue, render such a decision comparatively easy. We see that the man is too valuable to be shot down for the capricious and 'honorable' ends of government. And we believe too, that, if a right course is pursued, all disputes which agitate nations may be settled by appeals to the exalted sentiments of the soul. I would insinuate nothing, in this connection, against other denominations. I believe that all, *in some way or other,* will eventually arrive at the same results. I only claim for ourselves a little vantage-ground. As regards non-resistance, there are some questions connected with it which some of us find it difficult to settle. However, our only inquiry is, What would Christ do? What does he in all strictness require of us? The testing fires of a life-struggle are before us, and will prove the genuineness of our resolves. . . .

"Suppose you should say, you could not conscientiously serve in the militia. Then would they not thrust you through an iron door, and feed you on bread and water? Yet these same iron doors have been sometimes an heaven's vestibule; and bread and water, angels' food. Be courageous in thine own purposes. Stick fast to thy position, and the world will come round to you. You cannot go round to it. The race is moving. Make a Christianly and true life of the present. Here lies our hope. The world has ever needed a regeneration, — never more than now. Thy own true life shall be the spirit that bloweth where it listeth, and makes roses in the desert, a new creation from surrounding death.

"I shall be glad to know of your progress. But, if you cannot write, still live, and all men shall be your epistle unto me. — Your Brother, in much love, hope, and consolation."

To ———.

"DIVINITY SCHOOL, July 6, 1839.

"I know not how it is, but a slight misunderstanding sometimes affects me more than the most serious differences. In the latter case, the hope of reconciliation leaves us, and the soul summons all its powers of endurance. In the former we are balanced in suspense, which is the most intolerable of all conditions.

"There are but few in whom the intellectual and sentimental developments are equal and perfect. When there is a consistent harmony of these somewhat antagonistic qualities, then is our admiration and love more especially interested. In the general, we see but parts of men in men. The great lump, humanity, is sliced and divided, the portions distributed. To some is given an eighth, to some a quarter, while some get only a paring. To attain our ends, we — that is, those in whom the perfect humanity resides — are obliged to make the circuit of society; and even then the result comes to us so disproportioned and disjointed as to half-disgust and weary us. If we are so fortunate as to find our Rosalie's face, we must set it upon the body of the hag in 'Gil Blas,' and place the whole upright on Jeremiah's foot. *Eh! bien!* It seems like a wild-goose chase to hope ever to realize our aims. Why aim, then?

"Furthermore, it always seems selfish and unfair to make use of a man for a particular purpose, and then dismiss him in favor of another, who happens to meet our next want. I recollect a lady, whom I asked to sing, once said to me, 'You don't care for me, but only for my singing.' Well, she insinuated a truth. I then thought I would never ask a lady to please me by her musical powers again; I would seek all enjoyments in myself, my infinite self, and retire there for all sympathy. Sometimes a lady's whole being is her singing. But this lady had another self. 'Care for *me*,' she said. That 'Me,' — what did it comprehend? What would it have?

14

This illustrates the more general matter of sympathy in its various conditions and exercise. . . . Yet we cannot well live without it; and, if we cannot find it in wholes, we must take it in parts.

"About the time I dropped my pen at the bottom of the preceding page, the dinner-bell rang, and the 'keen demands of appetite' urged me to another duty. This eating, — is it not a pleasant thing? Your gastronomer, — is he not the true philosopher? This three times a day, table-gathering and beef-eating, butter-spreading and tea-drinking, and friendly chat, and free laugh, makes one wonderfully content with life. It satisfies a most important and importunate part of our nature. Why not centre all life in that? Why trouble one's self about the philosophers? All men have their eating susceptibility; and you will not find it necessary to go out of ———— to get company. Did you ever look into a swine-fold? 'So I can but get meal-mixture enough,' says the hog-philosopher, 'and mud-mixture for a siesta, I am content.' 'Amen!' says the hog-moralizer, who sees no end but the butcher's knife and the salt-barrel. 'Amen!' adds the hog-sentimentalist, who settles his fair proportions still deeper in the heterogeneous compound that forms at once his bath and his bed. 'Amen!' respond all the little piglings, who scamper at their feet's end up and down the straw and the mire. 'Amen!' shall we not all say? This is the genuine gastrosophy; and, since life is allowed to be pretty essentially connected with the stomach, we must believe that the true eating is the true *sophia*. *Eh!*

bien! again. Soups and puddings make us qualm-
ish and fretful. The end *is* not reached. So plates
and spoons urge us to our immortality. I would
soar, but I am clogged. Shall I to my bed and
sleep?"

"*July* 9. — I recollect what you said about parting with Rosalie in a crowd. When we make our
adieus to those we love, no eyes should see us but
silence and the stars. There are times when we
shrink from any thing like participation of feeling
and interest. Such are our parting hours. We can't
bear the stupid and half-sympathetic gaze, the wonders why, the curious inquiries, of the vulgar. Besides, those are most self-moments. We would not
be distracted. We seek an absorbing concentra-
tion.

"I have learned now, what I could never reconcile
or understand before, what the true malignity of sin
is. It is not that I was born with a defiled nature,
but that, differently constituted, I do sin. I sin
with angels, not with devils; and this afflicts me
with a prostration of soul, with an utter self-humi-
liation and condemnation.

"Our earliest impressions of the stars make them
the abiding-place, and, as one may say, the observatory, of the Divinity; nor does a corrected philosophy
of our maturer years wholly dissipate this illusion. . . .

"My ideal of the religious mind, and the model
according to which I would shape my affections, is
not so much Jeremiah as it is John. I seek rather
the loving than the weeping mood. Standard writers
and types for me are such men as Fenelon, Cud-

worth, Law, Thomas Smith, Bishop Hall, Howe, and others of a similar taste.

"Five years ago, under the elm-trees and deep midnight of New Haven, I struggled and questioned, and doubts beat upon me like a storm of fire. All men seemed to leave me then. . . .

"But how shall I put this into readable and hold-togetherable shape? I can think of no other way but to run a thread through the backs of the sheets, and so tie them fast. What, too, if they should get displaced in your hands? I am such a consistent piece of mechanism myself, that the least mismanagement of that sort would utterly confound you. So I go to work. The student has turned seamster, or, rather, I am the man seamstering. But you would have chuckled. What a bother! The first point is to thread one's needle. I am not altogether inexperienced, yet is it a perpetual vexation. However, I succeeded after a due trial. Then I clapped my thimble, — a good one it is, my mother gave it to me, — on the proper digital. Then, by a due force, I pushed the resolute needle through the quire of paper, have tied the ends of the thread together, and so am a consistent man. Consistency, thou art a jewel.

"Oh for a wife, — a great-souled, worth-appreciating wife, — to put on my buttons, and stitch my manuscripts! Shall I never find such a one?"

On a vacation at Northampton, Mr. Judd thus notes, in his Journal, an account of retracing his old Hadley walk : —

"July 29, 1839.

"Up Bridge-street were the old familiar houses, sidewalks, roads, fences, gateways. That old, weather-worn barn looked towards me, and would receive one look of recognizance. The boys, — not my own boyhood's boys, they are scattered, and for ever, — new youngsters, coming out upon the same grass, to play and hope and die, like their predecessors. Onward I went, through the narrow foot-path, in the wide street. The great elms are its guardians still. The old gate-keeper still draws up the tinkling gate. The bridge, — I looked through its windows northward. The river issues from green hills, wood-land. On it flows, and Nature retinues it with a thousand shadowy trees, and meadowbanks. It opens in the embrace of a green, shrubby island, imparts a lingering kiss, and flows on for ever. I would plunge into its stream, and be borne onward too.

"Then the expanded meadows, the corn and grass, the same dusty road, the same tree too, under which, a weary, satchelled school-boy, I had rested. I turned now, and most mechanically leaned against its trunk, for the sake of auld lang syne.

"Returning, the moon was out. Southerly it lighted and hid the heavens. There were clouds, and Lyra and Cassiopœia, and, in the dim horizon, the Bear and thin clouds. Misty the air. Mount Holyoke shone purely, like a bank of milk-white mist. Angels might have wrought their drapery from it. And the moon shone upon the Connecticut, as I looked through the bridge southerly upon it.

14*

The water was trembling in light. The dark, shaded banks enclosed it like a gem. From the high heavens I fancied it looked earth's night-jewelry. Walked the thoughtful quickly on. The burying-ground, — its white monuments stood up like the sheeted dead, new-risen from their graves ; and its black monuments, like the wasted skeletons of a hundred years. As he hurried by, these dead seemed to move. They joined in dance over the hillocks, in the dim moonlight, the black and the white, under funereal pines and elms, with tall, gaunt weeds that grew there. They danced noiselessly, as the dead must dance. They danced to no music ; for they needed none, save the silent wind. He quickened his pace, and this dance of the dead grew more hurried and more involved. When he was well past, and looked back, the dance was stopped, and the moveless stones stretched their grizzly necks to gaze at the passer. He was soon hid by a turn in the street, not frightened ; for he felt that such communion was most fitting to his spirit."

THIRD YEAR AT HARVARD.

To his Mother.

"Divinity School, Sept. 12, 1839.

"This term we begin to write sermons, and next term shall preach, not abroad, but in the College Church. The duties of my profession, — responsible, arduous, solemn, — begin to come upon me, no longer as a prospective imagining, but as a home-pressing reality. May I have strength, courage, faith, holiness, for the great work ! "

To ———.

" DIVINITY SCHOOL, Sept. 19, 1839.

" I feel, every day of my life, I need *encouraging*. I stumble at a straw. I sink with a feather's weight upon me. How is it that on some points I am all self-trust, and on others all outward repose ? How do the giant and the child blend so together in our little framework ? Why should not the giant sustain the child ?

" I am, if your doctrine be true, an angel *fallen* from the bright haven of his earlier home, who now, with a palpitating heart and broken wing, is dragging himself wearily through morass and mist, in search of what he has lost.

" I have made some most astonishing resolutions for this term, — that I will not sigh or complain once. Why should I not be a man, and have done with effeminacy and nonsense ? "

" *Oct.* 28. — Have you considered the value of autobiographical writing, in general ? There is a positive pleasure attending that species of composition, because the subject is at once interesting and familiar. It is a revelation of *the life*, while much else that we write is a speculation, or a doubt, or a social necessity ; it improves the habit of self-observation ; it subserves the memory ; it is a convenient index to the events of our life ; it is a source of pleasure to our friends, or to the *one friend* whom we might favor with the perusal of it.

But the capital advantage, as I conceive, lies in this, — the aid it affords in the solution of the problem of man, — of what I am, of what you are. All the data are before you, and a skilful combination of the figures will enable you to approximate the result. Influences are traced up to their source, and onward to their issues. Doubts that have once perplexed us find, in the present retrospection, an easy resolution, and are carried upward to the vast Unknown before us, and aid us to calculate its uncertainties, and throw some light into its mysterious depths. You learn what you are destined for, by perceiving what you have lived for. In observing what you might have been, you decide what you can be. This retrospection will correct a thousand mistakes into which the enthusiasm, the vanity, or the ignorance of youth may have involved you; and you will find your present position the more secure, just in proportion to this subtraction of errors. A multitude of questions in the philosophy of mind and of opinion will receive some light from such an investigation. It will conduct you to a more definite understanding of the place you hold in society, in the world, in the universe. By what limits *are* we connected to the Infinite? How does a general or a special Providence *actually* touch the soul, and circumscribe human actions? To these questions it will render some satisfaction. But I need not enlarge. The great questions, 'What am I, and why am I?' would become somewhat disentangled by a careful review of one's life. And is not this compensation enough for such a labor?"

" *Nov.* 1, *half-past ten, evening.* — Our prayer-meeting continued to this moment. Conversation took a deep, searching, and exceedingly interesting character. Our prayers were most earnest. Our souls seemed very near heaven. We melted into love and holiness. God was most especially present. Our hearts were softened, cheered, — all holiest purposes quickened. To God, my God, my Father, commend I my soul this night. Holiest One, I am thine, for ever thine."

To ———.

" *Nov.* 15. — I have just come from our prayer-meeting. A good time it was. We pray as the spirit moveth, and each brother breathes out the deep things of his heart. God seems especially nigh to us at these moments. The Holy Spirit visits us with his especial influences. Were you ever one of a social praying circle? How precious they are!"

" *Nov.* 25. — It rains this morning, rains fitfully, windily, darkly. My spirits droop like the wing of a bird. To be alone, shut up in my chamber, is oppressive. And yet not always so. Sometimes I like to be alone when darkness and storms pervade the world without. But this morning I seem predisposed to an indefinable dejection. The influences of last evening hang heavily upon me. Last evening was one of deep and thoughtful interest. The ordination-services affected me more than I can describe. What I must soon encounter, with its responsible duties and its momentous issues, was

impressed with a painful vividness.   'Who is sufficient for these things?'   O my God! be thou my
help, my supporter."

"*Dec.* — The low murmurings of the soul are all
that is heard. We listen, but perceive no voice, only
an indistinct moaning. From the depths sound up
evermore that inarticulate wail. Is it the smothered
pantings of the soul? Is it the lament of some other
spirit incarnated and incarcerated in our own? Is
it a cry heard only in heaven, and one which will at
last find its fulfilment there? O Earth, Earth!
wherefore are we cast upon thy dark borders? Wherefore is the longing soul tantalized by thy shows!
Wherefore thy racks and troubles? Yet I love thee,
Earth. From thy womb sprang I into light. On
thy bosom have I been nurtured. Thy flowers are
beautiful. Thy heavens are glorious. By thy probation am I purified for my coming destiny. Through
thee, as a vestibule, I pass into brighter worlds.
Hush, then, this tumult of the heart! Let me patiently bear and suffer, and wait, that I may at last
triumph and enjoy.   Let me be a child, and submit
to that chastening which for the present seemeth not
grievous, but which will terminate in exceeding
joy.

"All things sadden me.   Mr. —— coming in, and
talking about 'these views,' makes me sad. Philosophy, theology, poetry, make me sad. Coleridge,
and Ripley, and Norton make me sad. My Father's
presence with me now makes me sad. The snow,
my rose-plant, the cold moon, produce the same
effect. The past, the present, and the future, life

and no life, what I am and what I have been, the
letters of my friends, pain in my head and in my
heart, — all, all deepen that one feeling. Now do
not attempt to thread these things all on one string.
You cannot do it. You cannot detect a common
point of harmony. Possibly none such exists. Such
a mood likes sometimes to utter itself without point
and without coherence. It has its own idiom, and
adopts its own language." . . .

To his Brother J. W.

"NORTHAMPTON, Jan. 15, 1840.

" Those who suffer from the conduct of other men
should guard themselves against indulging an undue
severity of judgment respecting such as have injured
them. A case of this sort affords the finest opportunity for the exercise and for the cultivation of that
first of Christian virtues, — charity. I think we are
too apt to *wrong* those who have done us an injury.
The wasting, bewildering, chilling effect of mercantile reverses, is to my mind a greater evil than the
mere loss of property. The latter may be remedied.
The former is too apt to penetrate the character, and
constitute a permanent feature of the life. It becomes us to consider that there is a higher than
property, and that the peace and repose of the soul
are infinitely better than the rescue of debts, or even
than the flush of business.

" Your boy is doing admirably. He and his uncle
go out to slide every morning. It would please you
to see him fagging up the hill, with a red face,
panting breath, his feet pressing with a short, quick,

divergent step, into the snowy path; his arms swing-
ing up and down like a young bird on the ice. He
is on the sled; and hurrah! down he goes! His sled
shies off into a snowbank, and over he goes. Up
he jumps, spitting out the snow from his mouth,
pushing up his cap which has fallen over his eyes,
with — 'Well now that's too bad, I declare, uncle
Ves.' He drags the sled up the hill again, and prepares for another overturn."

To A. H.

"NORTHAMPTON, Jan. 17, 1840.

"A. complains that you are too philosophical, that
is, I suppose cool, unimpassioned, cautious. This, I
agree, is well. We come to it at last, whether we
will or no, find, after all, plants and pebbles are about
as good as any thing else. What signifies a perpetual
stretch of the mind? Let us come back into our
own little world, and amuse ourselves with such toys
as we can find there. It is curious to see one and
another reaching the point of *bursting*, and longing
to *pour over* somebody. If this disposition can be
gratified, well. If not, do not let us consume with
regret. Our resources, which in youth we deem
ample enough for the whole world, are apt enough
to get squandered; and, when it is too late, we mourn
over the desertion and emptiness of our hearts. Yet
experience avails little for the newcomer on the
stage, and the same round will be run over and over
again. The repose of religion is the only secure rest
for the soul.

"I am now upon my last vacation. The ensuing

term will soon be gone, and then — may God be my helper and guide."

"Divinity School, Cambridge, March 5, 1840.

" I am not insensible to what you say about the unsatisfactoriness of metaphysical studies. In all the horrors of their perplexities, my own mind has been involved. Perhaps you will think my own feelings are somewhat sectarian. But I am persuaded that any system of theology which is sustained merely on metaphysical grounds must ever prove unsatisfactory. And I am also convinced, from thorough experience and a most faithful observation, that the popular orthodox doctrines are sustained in that way ; and I have found my only relief in the simple views of Unitarianism.

" I would not have you abandon your idea of preaching. *Time* will settle all your difficulties. There is truth enough somewhere in the world ; and, by waiting, you will find it. For my own part, the other professions have not the least relish for me, unless, indeed, it may be teaching. The religion of the New Testament, simple, unsystematized, unglossed, will afford ample scope for your talents and your piety."

To his Mother.

"Divinity School, Cambridge, March 8, 1840.

" My dear Mother, — I write you once more from a room, to which, on account of its quiet and convenience, I am very much attached ; and from scenes

15

to which I am always happy to return. Some degree of thoughtfulness attends the reflection that my last vacation is over. These seasons of interval from study have always been anticipated with delight ; and the time spent with my family and friends has never failed to afford an abundance of profitable enjoyment. My subsequent life must be one of uninterrupted devotion to the duties of my profession. Yet I cannot doubt, that, if these duties are entered upon with proper motives, and a just reliance on Him from whom comes all our strength, they will ever be attended with that degree of satisfaction and pleasure, which, aside from any higher consideration, shall be a full compensation for their fatigue."

To his Brother C. P.

"Divinity School, Cambridge, May 16, 1840.

"Dear Brother C. P., — Your letters of March 21 and May 2 are before me. So many letters at once seem like a sort of ' run upon the bank ; ' but I believe I can meet my dues, though I cannot always pay gold and silver. I can let you have more *paper*, which perhaps, in this case, will do as well. I am glad you are in so good a mood ; and, as laughing is healthful, I shall not suffer much from disease while I can have letters from you. 'Tis well to have the dulness and torpidity of study broken up once in a while. I wish I was at home to be merry with you. How comes on the fishing ? Did you have any glorious nibbles ? By the way, I shall not soon forget how you looked on your back, flinging up heels and hands, convulsed with laughter, when I fell into the water."

"Divinity School, Cambridge, May 17, 1840.

"It is only for those we love that we feel justified in growing uneasy. *Apparent* coldness, attended with a *real* interest, in our friends, seems to be sometimes necessary; yet it is one of the most disagreeable states into which we can be thrown; and, if excused by the circumstances of the case, it is perhaps to be regarded as a sort of *martyrdom to principle,* and not to be set down as a result of caprice or selfishness. However, when it can be avoided, it should be. There are real cold shadows enough to fall upon the pathway of life, without throwing a screen before the little fire that does burn. In all these things, however, I have been as great a sinner as any one; and, while I suggest a proper course for another, I would endeavor to reform myself."

On finishing his theological studies, he thus writes in his Journal: —

"*Cambridge, July* 17, 1840. — My studies are over, my profession acquired, my work before me. My bodily health at least is good, my energy vigorous. My heart, O my heart! is it fully sanctified yet? Am I humble? Life — am I prepared for it, and *its?* Heaven — am I thither tending, and thither taking men's souls? Nine years ago, the first of June, found me commencing my studies at Hadley Academy. Three years — how quickly passed!

The choicest, best part of my life, how gone! What have they carried me through? No matter now. I am a better and a calmer man. I have few agitations, know few griefs. Could name one or two things, but they are trifles. I enter the theatre of the world to act my part. What shall I accomplish? With what object link myself, to what idea give an impulse? Christ, I am thine, wholly thine. Sanctify me to thyself; make me wise for thy sake; make me energetic for thy sake; make me influential for thy sake.

"A Unitarian — never more one; never more opposed to what is opposed to it. Another name for Christianity. Shall it not be carried forward in the world to a universal triumph? Yet am I no sectarian, no party man. Care little for names, &c. &c.

"Give me thy blessing, O my Father in heaven! as I enter upon the work of my life. How can I be strong without thee? How can I but utterly fail without thee? Make thy good Spirit my everlasting guide."

CHAPTER VI.

SETTLEMENT AND RESIDENCE AT AUGUSTA.

————

SETTLEMENT.

On the 6th of July, 1840, a few weeks before closing his course at the Divinity School, Mr. Judd made an engagement to supply the pulpit of the Unitarian Church in Augusta, Maine, for a period of six weeks. To meet this engagement, on the evening of July 24, he took passage from Boston. In his Journal he writes, " Out of the harbor we passed through a multitude of islands, and plunged into the eternal sea and its eternal swell." The next morning, " made the mouth of the Kennebec, under a bright sky," among " a parcel of rocky, barren islands, and woody shores near at hand ; the waters dashing and breaking, and scattering their spray wild and beautiful." The sail up these new waters he found " charming."

His first sermon in Augusta was preached on the morning of the 26th of July. In the evening, he walked out upon the hill back of his boarding-house, west of the town, where his attention was attracted to the "east bank of the river, a broad, green slope," he says, " swelling into the horizon, divided into green plots, sprinkled with neat white houses, and,

15*

withal, some public buildings, constituting a very pleasant picture."

True to his filial duty and affection, the first letter known to be written from this place was addressed —

To his Mother.

"Augusta, Me., July 27, 1840.

"My dear Mother,— A new date commences a new life. It is now Monday morning, the morning after I have taken the first step in that new life. Here I am, away in a novel part of the world, surrounded by strange faces. I have rooms assigned me at one of the hotels, — a quiet and retired place, fine room, amply furnished within, and ample in its view without.

"Yesterday I discharged the regular pulpit duties. How I *succeeded*, it is hardly worth while to inquire. If any good is done, I shall be glad. I can say but little about the people yet. Those whom I have seen are very intelligent and serious men. They begin to urge my staying with them."

Under the same date, he writes his brother H——i: "Yesterday, for the first time, I entered upon the regular discharge of the duties of my profession, saving half a day that I preached last Sunday in Boston. What strength of character, what purity of heart, what love for souls, what faith in God, is requisite for him who undertakes to become a preacher of the gospel! May I be thoroughly furnished as a good soldier of the cross. I enter upon my public duties with very considerable resolution and hope."

Mr. Judd's health, which was so much impaired when he went to Cambridge, was now as fully confirmed as it could be while yet a weakened nervous system held it at its mercy. On finishing his studies at the Divinity School, and entering upon his professional duties, he strove manfully to leave the trials of his lot behind, to "let the dead past bury its dead," and to labor and feel only in the "living present;" but, do the best he could, the dark clouds of the past would at times project themselves over the sunlight of his present, and shade with melancholy his otherwise happy prospects.

During this first week of his stay in Augusta, he received the most courteous attentions by way of calls, hospitable entertainments, rides, walks, and the like ; but, nevertheless, something of this sombre spirit would come upon him. He thus writes in his Journal : —

"*July* 30. — Augusta, as I may have told fifty people, is a very pretty place. But I am somehow un-homed here. The books on my table look uneasy. Webster's Dictionary, my Bible, the inkstand and wafer-box, seem to be strangers, and are looking up to me for sympathy. Well, ye shall have it. . . . I went to the post-office. The clerk shook his head as I entered ; but I felt as if I could castigate somebody."

Again: "*Aug.* 1. — I stood out upon the piazza that shelves out from my room, paced it up and down, and my mind set to revolving some old, forbidden thoughts of faith and virtue and spirituality, and some others not perhaps wholly spiritual. Then came out Mrs. —— and some little girls, and I was back again to the world, talked of my getting wet this afternoon, of my nearly getting immersed yesterday afternoon, &c., &c. This diverts me, but does not relieve me."

After hearing but four sermons from Mr. Judd, two members of the parish committee called upon him to ascertain whether he would consent to stand as a candidate. He had had some thought of passing the coming winter at Mobile, Alabama; and, moreover, he could not easily reconcile himself to the idea of what *then seemed* to him being so far off from his past circle of acquaintance and associations. His mind was a good deal excited about the matter. He asks, "What is duty, what is duty?" The next morning, he says, "I went out of the village upon the highlands north, up, up, over granite ledges, through the woods. Was so happy! Could have died. We are always ready to die when we are happy."

He speaks of attending a small, pleasant party at Mr. ——'s, August 7, and humorously says: "Discussed for the forty-eleventh time the beauties of Augusta. Strong coffee saved me the trouble of going to sleep, and set me into a horrible fantasy."

During the time of his engagement at Augusta, he visited Deerfield, Mass., and sought to get a release from an engagement he had made to preach there the next September, but did not succeed.

Under date August 24, at Augusta, he writes, "Feel about as blue to-day as I know well how to get along with. Some new things, some old things reviving, or sending up their ghosts. The society had a test-meeting last night ; agree to like me, if they can raise money enough."

"*Aug.* 26. — Received the formal vote of the society to become their pastor, which I shall say ' yes ' to for a year. May God help ! I am weak. I am cowardly. Nerve me for this difficult work. How can I glorify thee ? How can I save souls ? "

On the 31st of August, he left Augusta to fulfil the claims which the Unitarian Church in Deerfield had upon him for four sabbaths in September. The impression he made here was so favorable, that the church wished very much to retain him as their pastor. He enjoyed much pleasant social inter-course, and many delightful rural rambles. He visited the sick and afflicted ; thus making, as he said, his " first essays at the clinical practice." He spent many days at Northampton, and made one of a family gathering, of which he was always so glad to be a member. He went to Westhampton, and, with his cousin G. L. and a brother, visited the grandfather's old mansion, then in the hands of strangers, his father's former residence there, the old store, the orchard, the large black walnut planted by his father when he was a little boy, and feelingly marked the changes in all. He thus comments : " Men's faces change, their hearts not much." He was glad to avail himself of the opportunity of seeing all his family friends in the vicinity. He felt him-self very much drawn to Deerfield by the many manifestations of kind regard on the part of the people, as well as by its proximity to the circle of his home-friends. Yet, while enjoying so much in various ways during these four weeks, so much of old, depressing feelings still hung about him, that he represents himself, at one time, as feeling "so much between an exclamation and an interrogation," that he hardly knew how he did feel. The evening before his first preaching in Deerfield, he writes, —

"$7\frac{1}{2}$ *o'clock.* — Heaven prepare me to do good to-morrow ! May some word be fitly spoken !

"Heaven bless my poor heart !

"Some female voices in the room below are singing Greenville, and the sound calls me back to this world and man ; a fact I stop to record. Sing on, sing on."

"9 *o'clock.* — I hear some one praying in the room underneath me. It comes upon me, a penetrating, gentle influence, and I feel as if I could pray too. . . . No ink in the stand. Bothers me to get enough to write with. So I will stop. Have enough to say, this poor self of mine longs for vent.

"*Sept.* 15. — Made some calls. This parochializing hard rather for such a temper as mine. This *diffusing* of such a solitary, anchoritish kind of fellow is queer business. May the Lord bless me therein ! It *is* an effort, but how much more agreeable than I could anticipate ! How, in imparting happiness, are our own souls blessed ! . . . But I, too, need some ministering. Who will come in to speak to me, to pray with me, to love me ? "

He writes to his father, Sept. 16 : — " I have made nearly a dozen visits ; not, however, to the rich and the great, but among the sick and afflicted.

This parochial clinicism is new business to me, and that for which I feel most unfitted. All the habits of my life, all the tendencies of my nature, shrink from such duties. The sick-room, the bedside, the anguish of disease, the alarm of friends, I am not fitted to encounter. But it must be done. May I have aid from on high!"

On the 30th of September, he is again at Augusta, under which date he writes: "My friends in Deerfield clung to me to the last. Their interest in me, too, too kind. I cannot forget them. Had I known their feelings at an earlier period, then I should have been happy to stay with them. As it is, my engagements, both in heart and in honor, are here."

Thursday, October 1, Mr. Judd received ordination as pastor of the church and society known as the East Parish in Augusta. All the Maine Unitarian clergymen were present; and, in the evening, the Maine Convention of Unitarian Ministers was held, and a sermon preached by the Rev. Mr. Hedge, of Bangor.

Of these services, Mr. Judd says: "All the feelings that have crowded into this occasion, I could not describe, nor shall I attempt it. A most animating as well as solemn time. New vows are upon me, a new life before me. Who is sufficient for these things?"

His first sermon, after becoming a pastor, was preached October 4, from the text, "Woe is unto me, if I preach not the gospel." The next day he writes to his mother: —

"I have received ordination for the gospel minis-

try, and am in the midst of the scenes of my professional labors. Say what any one will of forms, this
induction into office, according to the usages of our
church, is no light business, to the candidate at
least, I assure you. Its immediate impressions, its
prospective reflections, are of the gravest character.
Pray for me, that I may be found faithful."

Immediately after settlement, Mr. Judd set about
organizing a Sunday-school, and establishing teachers' meetings ; in which effort he was heartily seconded
by children, parents, and teachers. He also, the
first week after his ordination, began to employ his
afternoons in visiting among his people. They
seemed quite aroused, and, as he writes, "strongly
animated for every good word and work." The
ladies presented him a gown and white cravats for
the pulpit, in which, from that time, he always officiated on the sabbath. He writes of this to his
mother : "You would hardly know me, expanded
by so many folds of black silk." His arrangements
for board were most agreeable. His room was pleasant, and he was surrounded with every thing that
could minister to his comfort and convenience.

Thus was he happily settled with the prospect in
his professional life, stretching out full of hope and
promise for the future. His heart was in the great
work to which he had looked forward through his
long course of preparation, and in which he felt
ready to labor, body and soul, so long as he should
remain a tenant of earth. Yet, even now, "stifled
breathings from the smothered deep of the dead
would move from their long sleep ; " and, in the

dejection of his spirits, he often felt that "the grave would be sweet unto him." Yet these feelings he endeavored to keep hushed in his own bosom; and probably no one among his people once dreamed of the heavy weight of past sorrows which lay entombed in his heart.

About this time, he had an invitation from the church in Deerfield to settle with them, when the year for which he had engaged at Augusta should have expired. But he thought it would be injurious to his church in Augusta to announce at that time that he would leave them at the end of a year, and therefore declined the Deerfield invitation.

On the 26th of November, he preached his first Thanksgiving sermon. With associations natural to the occasion, he writes in his Journal, that he wished he was at home with his dear mother. He writes to her, Nov. 30: "I thought of you Thanksgiving-day, and should have been most happy to be with you. I had to make Thanksgiving for others; that is to say, I preached a sermon, and tried to direct the hearts of my people in the proper way for such an occasion. I have a great deal of visiting to do. I have made between one hundred and fifty and two hundred calls. And this is hard work among a strange people. My duties are arduous, but not painful. I wish some of my good family friends were here, or at least within speaking distance. I shall not see you before summer. May God bless you, and keep you and all of us till then and for ever! . . . "Your loving Son."

Mr. Judd thus writes —

16

To A. H.

"Augusta, Dec. 14, 1840.

"What do you think of me? Well, chide me, do an if you will. But I cannot write you. I am mere matter of fact; and, as such, I might as well roll a mountain up hill as to write you. Can you understand this? Will you, then, excuse me? I have always been accustomed to write you in a different strain; and now, to commence on this, 'tis impossible. Might as well keep up a correspondence with an enemy as with a friend, when our feelings change. Not changed towards you, but towards the world; towards much that once interested me. When I came to Augusta, it was in a belligerent attitude. I was determined to make war upon myself. How I have succeeded, — but no more of that. Some occasional tamperings with, and yieldings to, the enemy perhaps. But, on the whole, I have held my way pretty well. My common, every-day life, what do you care to know about it? 'Tis pleasant, active, various, and useful, I hope." . . .

During this initiatory period of strangership, Mr. Judd's thoughts, as was very natural, often turned to his home-friends. He again writes —

To his Mother.

"Augusta, Dec. 28, 1840.

"My dear Mother, — I was delighted and surprised to get your last letter. It was so long and so kind. It seemed like a renewal of your youth. I should have rejoiced to be at home with you Thanksgiving-day; and if it were not for being obliged to make Thanksgiving for others, in the way of preaching sermons, I should hope I might enjoy many more of those seasons with you. As it is, I hardly know when I shall be at home Thanksgiving-day again.

"This morning, I feel somewhat, to use a cant-term of the profession, *Mondayish.* This is said to be the minister's sabbath. It may be a day of rest: it is also a day of ennui and uneasy idleness.

"I shall hope for a letter from you soon, though I know my mother does not forget her children, even when she cannot write them."

Under the same date, he writes —

To his Sister-in-law E. W. J.

"I wish you, in the most *un*dignified manner possible, would just drop in and see me this afternoon. To-day is Monday, when it is allowed to the minister to be a little free, a little unclerical; and I'll engage you should not be awed by any stiffness on my part. Indeed, I should be very glad of the chance to break out a little, I am obliged to be so precise and formal. I occupy a delightful room, with the river, old Kennebec, flowing just behind me, not four rods from our house. I have married no one yet, but expect to officiate in that service this week. I thought of A. day before yesterday. I went out to slide with a little boy; a member of the family, about as old as he. I remembered how he and uncle 'Conspicuous' slid down Round Hill, last winter. Alas! we never shall again. A kiss for the boy, and unfailing love for yourselves."

As Monday was Mr. Judd's letter-writing day, here is still another epistle, having the same date: —

To G. L.

"My dear Cousin, — I acknowledge my remissness, if that will go any way towards excusing it; and, for the rest, appeal to your charitable consideration of my position, my engagements, labors, &c., &c. Settlement is not being settled after all. It is a perpetual move and fluctuancy. Our hours are not our own, our thoughts are not our own. We are obligated to the church, to God. I find enough to do, and my heart is in what I do. My labors are constant, but not arduous; they are fatiguing at times, but not wearing. I am in good health, never better; and good health is as good as faith. Visiting, ministerial decorum, funerals, marriages, &c., &c., are full of matter to talk about among the *initiated*, and, great or little as they may be in themselves, are full of difficulties. Society here, I am told, is quite animated during the session of the Legislature, which meets next week. But, whatever goes on, it is all the same to me. I have my duties, and the world its pleasures. If we touch these last, we are too apt to be contaminated by them. If we could correct, elevate, and sanctify them, happy should we be.

"W. is dead. Merciful God! to what are we coming? Make us ready.

"I board in a fine family, and am surrounded by all needful comforts. Heaven make me grateful, active, and holy! . . . .

" Hurrah for Harrison! Do give me leave, in this little by-place in my sheet, to say it. A minister must not be a politician, you know. Add to this, that a majority of my people are Democrats, and you will see I don't get a chance to express myself very often."

1841.

The remainder of the history embraced in this chapter will be arranged under the successive years of the period. The design is to give the general current of Mr. Judd's pastoral life, which, indeed, is, in the main, of so even a tenor as to furnish few external incidents of striking interest. As in the other parts of the work, large drafts will be made upon his own writings. His Journal has the following entry at the opening of this year : —

" *Jan.* 1, 1841. — Have been wished a happy new year ; hope it may prove so. I wish all men a happy new year."

To his mother he says, Jan. 18 : —

" The first of January I was called to marry a couple. I trembled, I assure you, — more than they did, I guess. But I shall get used to it, I suppose."

Again, in Journal, Jan. 23, he writes : —

" Good Saturday night. The sublime Sunday is near. How I love thy tabernacles, O Lord! I do love them. I lose myself ; or, rather, myself is all-absorbed and taken up into infinity."

16*

FROM A JOURNAL-LIKE LETTER TO A. H.

"AUGUSTA, Jan. 25, 1841.

" I am getting to like my situation here more and
more. Give me good friends, and I should be
happy in Spitzbergen. This morning (Monday) I
dawdle and putter about. Have but little to do, and
feel like doing less. Have a great many calls to
make. I am often reminded of the dilemma of the
young clergyman, who said he frequently did not
ask for the babies where they had some, and did
ask for them where they had none. However, I
shall get acquainted by and by."

" *Jan.* 28. — Wrote sermons to-day ; ate breakfast
and dinner and supper. We sometimes do such
things here."

" *Feb.* 2. — Attended the funeral of Judge F.
to-day. God prepare us to die ! I sometimes feel
I should not haggle long with Death, if he should
be disposed to take me."

About this time, Mr. Judd entered into a matri-
monial engagement with Miss Jane E. Williams,
daughter of Hon. Reuel Williams, of Augusta. Mr.
Williams was one of the original founders and liberal patrons of the Unitarian Church in Augusta ;
and, from his first ministrations in the place, Mr.
Judd had been in the habit of visiting in a friendly
way in this family.

This was a great epoch in Mr. Judd's interior
life. As is evident from the general tone of his
previous inner history, union of soul, sympathy of
spirit, love and affection in general, was to his nature

the greatest want, next to the favor of Heaven. But, tempest-tossed as he had been through so long a period, and still keenly suffering at times from the depressing effects of what he had endured, a solace like that arising from such an alliance of heart with his heart was peculiarly required, and particularly suited to his present needs.

In the interval between his engagement and marriage, he went on fulfilling his ministerial duties with more devoted energy, with deeper love for his whole flock, with larger desires for their highest happiness. In the month of June, he took a rural walk with the children of his parish; the first of that series which he ever after annually kept up. At this time, they passed through a favorite little place known as "Happy Valley," and onward to the tomb owned by Mr. Williams, and to the high bluff near by on the eastern bank of the Kennebec, commanding a pleasant view.

On the 4th of July, he preached a sermon entitled "The Beautiful Zion," the design of which was, in a plain and simple manner, to set forth to his people the prominent objects at which they, as a Christian church, should aim, and the purposes for which he, as a Christian minister, should labor. This discourse he printed at his own expense, and distributed to each family of his congregation for their study and consideration.

Warmly interested in the religious state of a brother, he writes to him, July 27 : —

"I hope you will model yourself after Christ, and not after creeds or professors of religion. Make the

New Testament your study. Imbibe the full spirit of Christ. Conform to all his precepts. Let it be your constant prayer that you may be a *Christ*-ian indeed."

In a familiar way, he thus gives an account of the publication of his bans, to A. H., August 9 : —

" We were published yesterday. 'Rev. Sylvester Judd, jun., and Miss Jane E. Williams, intend marriage.' People seemed glad their minister intends marriage ; just as if they had not known it for six months. But there it is in the box, to satisfy the law, and, as is usual in such cases, particularly dissatisfying to the parties concerned."

On the evening of Aug. 31, 1841, Mr. Judd was married. The morning after, he set off with his wife, to introduce her to the family gathering at his father's home. And here he passed three or four weeks in the beloved family circle, and found pleasure in revisiting the haunts of his childhood, — the old familiar scenes, the spots, in some instances, where the dark waters of sorrow had overwhelmed his soul. And not one of the least pleasures of this occasion was a ride to Springfield, in company with his wife, for the purpose of refunding to Mr. Dwight the money of which he had been so kind as to give him the use in facilitating his theological studies. The means of discharging this obligation had been secured by the most rigid economy in the use of his salary. But the delight experienced in now cancelling the last debt for his education was more than a recompense for the self-denial.

To his brother C. P., lamenting his absence from the home-circle at this time, he says : " You are at a great distance. We are widely separated. The same good God cares for us all. The religion of Christ is *blessed* everywhere. The virtue of our own hearts will suffice for us as well in South Carolina as in Maine. The same Heaven will unite us all."

In remembrance of this visit, he, a month or two afterwards, writes a brother: "I shall long remember our sweet, happy visit at home. May we have many such ! "

Shortly after returning to Augusta, Mr. Judd was established at housekeeping on the east side of the river, in the midst of a very large and pleasant circle of new family connections, besides the agreeable society of his own particular people. He now felt himself fairly *settled*, in the fullest import of the word, and ready to enter, with singleness of purpose and integrity of spirit, upon the labors of that profession which had been his early desire, and in reference to which he had devoted so many years of untiring study.

He writes in his Journal, Oct. 1 : "A year since my ordination ! What a year ! How interesting its events, how solemn its issues ! Have I been faithful to my people ? I have given myself to them, have recognized no interest separate from my profession. God bless me and them ! "

His congregation slowly increased; church meetings were kept up; sabbath-school teachers' meetings were pleasantly sustained; the sabbath-school itself flourished; and he found himself very happy in discharging the duties of his office. With leisure for self-collection, he cast about for subjects which he deemed of first importance to present to the consideration of his people. Among these, the evils of war and intemperance had their place. In regard to war, it will be remembered, that, as long before as when he was a member of Hopkins Academy, its opposition to the principles of the Prince of Peace attracted his notice, and formed the theme of one or two compositions. Nov. 8, 1841, he writes a brother: "I am sorry you must train. The militia is a horrible system; barbarous as ten heathenisms; utterly antichristian. So I view it. Can a Christian be a fighter, a killer of his own flesh and blood? What think you of that?" On Thanksgiving-day, this year, he writes his mother of his thoughts of her, and of his wish to be at home; and hoped the time would come when all the members of the family could be there at that festival.

1842.

At the commencement of the year 1842, Mr. Judd formed the plan of delivering in his church, once a month, on sabbath evenings, a lecture on some moral subject of general importance. The first of this series was delivered to a crowded audience. The subject was "Washingtonianism," a form of operation in favor of temperance, in which he was very much interested. The second lecture of the course was upon "Popular Amusements in connection with Morals and Religion," which was also given to a very full house.

The theme of the third lecture was "A Moral

Review of the Revolutionary War; or some of the Evils of that Event considered." The aim of the discourse was to make the evils of the Revolutionary War, which he acknowledged to be the holiest war on record, an argument to the minds of his hearers for the renunciation of all war. The Legislature of the State was in session; and many of its members were among his audience. In detailing the *evils* attending the contest, he was understood by many to reflect upon *Washington* and other *fathers* of the Revolution. Some members of the Legislature were so angry as to leave the house while he was speaking, and the most of them were seriously offended. Mr. Judd, in common with the other clergymen of Augusta and Hallowell, as was customary at every session, had been requested this winter to officiate in turn as chaplain of both houses. So high was the state of excited feeling among the members, that the first official business they did, on meeting the next morning, was to pass and transmit to Mr. Judd an order of dismissal. His own people, however, stood by him, and even adhered to him the closer for this unwarrantable attempt to interfere with his liberty in the pastoral office.

The excitement produced by this discourse, and its consequences, were altogether surprising to Mr. Judd. He wrote it, not as a politician, but as a Christian, and from the conscientious conviction in his own mind that *all* war is wrong. He felt that his position in the matter was wholly misunderstood; that few, if any, whom this sermon displeased, looked at the subject from his *point of view*.

He therefore felt it important to publish the discourse, that all who heard him might have the opportunity of a calm, deliberate perusal, and thus the better judge of its true spirit; and that, so far as rumors went abroad respecting it, the public might have an opportunity to judge of his true position. This he did, adding copious notes, and giving a long list of references as authority for his statements. The whole was prefaced by an Introduction, addressed *" To all who love the Lord Jesus Christ, and would be obedient to his heavenly mission."* He commences by saying, " The writer of the following discourse is a minister of the gospel; of that gospel which was ushered into the world with glad tidings of peace, and left to the world with a promise of peace; of that gospel whose soul and life, whose doctrine and practice, are peace among men." He goes on to say, " He believes, that, if Christ himself were now on the earth, he would never, for any pretext, reason, or motive whatever, engage in war. . . . . It is his single desire, in this discourse, by unfolding the evils of war, to disseminate the love and the observances of peace. He would make the evils of the Revolutionary War, be they more or less, an argument to the mind of his hearers for the renunciation of all war. He would dispel the illusion of war, by entering its most sacred retreats, and showing that an essential evil cleaves to the system, and that immoralities are inborn in its purest sources.

" He protests that he has no wish to reflect upon the fathers of the Revolution; as noble a race of

men as the earth affords, *in every other capacity,*
but who, in their war-capacity, — and among them
he enumerates his own ancestry, — the facts developed in this discourse serve to indicate, were not
proof against that gorgon-face which turns every
thing it looks upon into another nature.

" In the conduct of the discourse, he has confined
himself chiefly to facts ; facts which are a matter of
historical record ; facts, which, in the copiousness
of the references, are open to every one's revision.
If there be any sentiments in the discourse, they are
the sentiments of facts ; if there be any argument
in the discourse, it is the argument of facts ; if there
be any crimination, it is the crimination of facts ; if
any strictures, they are the strictures of facts ; if any
libel, it is the libel of facts. He took the facts as
he found them, — too stubborn things to be winked
out of sight ; and he presented them as he found
them, hoping that the facts, and the *facts alone,*
would have weight with his hearers. . . .

" He freely allows to all concerned to regard the
war in what light they please. He claims the same
right for himself. He does not ask his readers to
adopt his point of view. He conceives, that, if they
will only stand in it but for a moment, they will confess the writer is not to be wholly condemned. . . .

" The writer is supposed to have been actuated
by hostile feelings to the Revolutionary War in
particular ; which is so far from being the fact, that,
if there is any war for which he may be supposed to
cherish friendly feelings, it is that war. But he
looks upon war in the abstract, — upon all war, —

17

as antichristian and demoralizing. When contemplating the subject of peace or war as one of the
series of his monthly lectures, it was a matter of
comparative indifference to him how he treated it, —
that is, whether by discussing its general principles,
or exhibiting its characteristic details, — provided
only he could secure this effect among his hearers ;
a love of peace, and an aversion to war. Finally, in
casting about over a field ample enough for volumes
of discourses, he thought he would select the American Revolution as that with which both himself
and his hearers were most familiar. . . . He threw
off the facts to his hearers in such language as first
suggested itself. If there be any thing in *the
writer's own expression* calculated unnecessarily to
wound long-cherished sensibilities, or to retard in
any degree the object he has in view, no one can
regret it more than himself. . . . He does not deny
there were causes for a *separation* from Great Britain ;
for rebellion against the government, if you please.
He only submits if there were causes for a *war* with
that country. . . . He does not conceive we are to
attribute the freedom, independence, prosperity, and
ease we now enjoy as American citizens to the war,
so much as to those elements of liberty which God
has implanted in the human breast, and which are
stimulated into action by a just view of man, and of
his relations to society ; elements which are enduring
as the soul, and will survive when armies and battle-
fields are forgotten for ever. He does not conceive
that our liberties depend upon a point of polished
iron, but upon the deep-seated purposes of liberty,

habitually cherished and rightly exercised in the soul itself. We are free, not because our fathers exchanged shots with British soldiers, but because we *would be free*. Independence is of the soul, not of nitre, sulphur, and charcoal."

The discourse and explanations being published, and an opportunity thus given leisurely to examine the grounds taken by Mr. Judd, it was found to be not so great a bugbear as was supposed; and the excitement soon died away.

The American Peace Society passed a "resolve of sympathy with the Rev. Mr. Judd, in the persecution he had suffered, of admiration for his courage, and of approval of the great object of the sermon as correct and Christian." He received many letters of sympathy, mingled with congratulations, for the stand he had taken in the cause of peace ; and the press, to a considerable extent, espoused his cause, and condemned the course of the Legislature in dismissing him from office for the utterance of his own honest opinions, in his own church, and to. his own people, while they had nothing of which to complain in the discharge of his official duties to them.

The subject of re-appointment, as one of the chaplains, came up at the next session, and caused considerable debate. Several members claimed, in effect, " that the clergyman alluded to should not be punished for opinions expressed, not in the House, in the way of his duty, but among his own people, and in his own desk." One member "regarded the act of the last year as intolerant;" another "thought the address did not contain such charges as were alleged, or could be sustained ; " another, still, " did not want to hear prayers from such a source. He believed that the sentiments of Mr. Judd came from his heart. They came from a heart desperately wicked, and the Scriptures teach us that the prayers of the wicked are an abomination *before the sight of the Lord.*" The matter was finally evaded by appointing a committee for inviting clergymen to officiate; and Mr. Judd was omitted.

Near the commencement of this year, Mr. Judd began meeting a class of young ladies for literary improvement. He held social meetings, at private houses, for the general improvement of his congregation. He also established a sort of parish levee for pastor and people, to be held once a month.

There was this year a general excitement, on the subject of religion, among several denominations of the town, in which some of Mr. Judd's people shared.

It had always been a great desire of his heart, that the barriers of sect should be broken down; that Christians of different name should become acquainted with each other, should mingle their sympathies on common ground, and thus learn to love one another ; and now, in the earnest hope of effecting this object, he addressed the following proposal, for a union-meeting of the several denominations of Christians in the town of Augusta, to each of the clergymen : —

" Rev. ——   " AUGUSTA, April 9, 1842.

"Dear Sir, — In view of the religious interest which pervades so deeply all classes of the people, it seems desirable that there should be a better understanding among the several varieties of Christians.

"I propose, therefore, that a union-meeting of all denominations be held, at some convenient time and place ; say at Dr. T.'s church, as that is most commodious ; perhaps on Wednesday evening, April 20th : the several congregations to be represented in their several ministers, and the several ministers to be represented in their several congregations.

"The action of the meeting shall consist in a mutual confession of sin ; mutual forgiveness and reconciliation ; mutual prayer for the blessing of God ; exhortations to kindness and brotherly love ; persuasives to holiness ; in endeavors to promote harmony of feeling in the midst of variety in doctrines and forms ; to enlarge the rights of conscience ; to stay the progress of infidelity ; to add to the reverence of our common religion ; to compose the discords that mar the beauty of our Zion ; and things similar and tantamount. The aim and object of the meeting shall be the destruction of sin, the triumphs of the gospel, and the taking of some steps towards the ushering in of the millennial days.

"It might be well, perhaps, that the ministers should conduct the exercises of the occasion.

"Topics that might serve for consideration, or be made subjects of remark, and form a basis in this movement of harmony, are such as the following : —

"The necessity of reconciliation as a means of securing the blessing of God, — Matt. v. 23, 24; The beauty of holiness; The harmony of heaven; Agreeing to disagree; Love the chiefest of the graces; Our points of harmony numerous and important; The preciousness of the gospel; Attachment to Christ; How much better our motives are than they seem; The evil of sin; — and such like topics as may seem best adapted to secure the ends of the meeting.

"Such a meeting, it seems to me, would be, or might be made, one of the happiest our town or the church of Christ has seen for many a day, and would tend essentially to the advancement of the Redeemer's kingdom. With great regards, I subscribe myself your Christian Brother,

"SYLVESTER JUDD, JR."

In reference to this, he afterwards expressed himself as follows: "This proposal only contemplates a single meeting, for a single evening; a one hour's union and conciliation of the scattered members of the Christian body about their common Head and Master, Christ; a solitary conjunction, in the interval of ages, with the great central Orb of the lights of the world, whose several circuits are so diverse, antagonistical, discordant; a momentary realization, here on the earth, of that heaven we hope so soon to enter, and whose level we must so soon be compelled to take."

It was expected, that the several congregations, while each retained its peculiarities of doctrine, form, and practice, would retire from the meeting with kinder feelings, readier sympathies, and a more consonant zeal in the great work to which all are devoted.

This proposal was concurred in by the ministers of the Episcopal, the Universalist, and the Free-will Baptist churches: but the Calvinistic and Methodist declined; the Baptist did not fully respond to the call; the Roman Catholic clergyman was out of town; and, much to the grief of Mr. Judd, and the disappointment of his hopes, the proposed plan for fostering Christian intercourse between those taking the same gospel for their standard, and journeying on in the hope of enjoying the same heaven through eternity, entirely failed.

Ever feeling that the spirit of human brotherhood was one of the first importance, and, on the contrary, that war was one of the greatest hindrances to national prosperity, his Thanksgiving sermon this year was on "Peace as a Means of retaining our National Blessings."

In his usual Thanksgiving letter to his mother, he says, "A., in her letter to P——n, gives you an account of our Thanksgiving. It is less joyous to me, because I must preach; and at such times, too, I am wont to select topics that please neither me nor my hearers best, but such as I consider most necessary. Then, too, I get so tired. When I came home from church, I could hardly sit in my chair for very weariness."

1843.

In the spring of 1843, Mr. Judd entered upon his first effectual labors of authorship, so far as the *manual* execution was concerned. He found it difficult, however, to secure the necessary leisure for this purpose, while at the same time attending to his numerous ministerial, parochial, and other duties ; and it was by great industry that he made much progress in it. So much was he engaged in his literary efforts this year, that correspondence with friends was much less frequent than was his wont. To his brother H——i he writes, under date, —

"AUGUSTA, April 9, 1843.

"Press towards the mark. Be temperate in all things, — eating, drinking, feeling, acting. 'Make haste slowly' is an old maxim. Our country presents a certain uniform level of distinction, wealth, and so forth. No one can rise to advantage, except his ground be most secure. A merchant's life is an honorable and a useful one. But read much, think much, acquire a reputation for sound judgment more than for summary despatch. Integrity is respected, disinterestedness esteemed. I say nothing of those who by artifice and show gain popularity. Their fall is generally sudden, as their rise is unworthy. Honesty of purpose, purity of motive, soundness of understanding, will alone endure in the long-run. Be above the 'tricks of trade,' condescend not to low artifice, despair not of humanity, love all, and serve God. Be not too much immersed in politics. I was moved to say a few words to you, my dear

brother, and shall be glad to know of your views
and feelings and plans. Your interest and happiness
are near my heart."

In allusion to his studies in ornithology, to which
he was led with reference to the literary work on
which he was engaged, is the following letter —

To his Father.

"July 4, 1843.

"We have been giving some attention to birds,
that C. P. will tell you about. One is astonished at
the variety of birds, and the extent of his own
ignorance regarding them. I find the common people know nothing about them. The farmers and
woodsmen can't give me the name, even a common
name, for the most familiar species. For years, the
birds, the same birds, have been flying, singing all
about them; and they have made no distinctions,
laid up no observations. Boys and girls don't know
the yellowbird or goldfinch. The robin, I believe,
all know, and but little more. All know it by sight;
yet few are acquainted with its sweet, soft, long-
continued warble. I have heard it deep in the
woods, and about our house, by the hour together."

He passed some weeks in Northampton about this
time, and visited Westhampton, and also Norwich,
the former residence of his maternal grandfather,
seeking some hints for the romance he had on hand.

The extracts that follow are from a letter written
to one of his church, on the removal of a sister
from this life : —

To Miss S. F.

" It has pleased God, in his own time and in his
own way, to take her to himself. *To take her to
himself,* I say. You know somewhat my views of
death ; you know my own hopes of the departed
believer. I have endeavored in various ways to
unfold what seems to be the great gospel doctrine
of our relation to the future world. This is a
fundamental idea, — that the good Father of all receives to, and cherishes in, his own bosom the souls
of all his children. Christ said he was going to the
Father, whence he came ; and he tells his disciples,
that, where he is, there shall they be also. I believe
that we enter upon a new condition of existence ;
that we assume new bodies like unto Christ's glorified body. Hence, as I have often had occasion to
say, there is no death to the believer. What we
call death is only entering the door of a higher and
better life. It is the bridge that carries us across to
fairer lands, to more propitious skies.

" But these thoughts are familiar to you ; and I
cannot doubt, in this hour of darkness and bereavement, you look to the serene, unfading Light in the
heavens which disease shall never blight, nor death
destroy. Already, in repeated instances, has your
heart been called — to mourn, shall I say ? To
weep ? to be distressed ? Yes, if you please. But
has it not been called also to heaven ? Has not
your eye been raised to the world of spirits ? Have
not voices been sent to you from Jesus, to summon
your own faith and affections to the abodes of the

blest? If the light that has shone about your earthly path be extinguished, does it not glow more brightly in the world to which you go?

"May the blessing of Him who was ever ready to sympathize with the distressed, comfort the mourning, and sustain the dying, be and abide with you continually! With sincere regards and prayers for your peace, I am yours."

1844.

Jan. 1, 1844, began with Mr. Judd by his receiving from the ladies of his congregation a valuable cloak, and sundry other articles of convenience. On the 8th of this month, he received official notice of his election to act as chaplain at the State House. Having pressed on, as best he might, in the composition of "Margaret," this spring found him advanced to Part III. In April he set out many trees about the house of his father-in-law, which he occupied, in Myrtle-street, doing much of the work with his own hands. In the front part of the yard he planted quite a thicket, by grouping together young trees of many different sorts, as they are often found in their native woods.

The ensuing May, after attending the religious anniversaries at Boston, he spent a few weeks in the city of New York, and examined carefully all the objects of nature and of art in and about this great metropolis; taking with him, as sole companion on his excursions, the same little nephew in whose down-hill sliding sports he participated a few years before. He passed up the Hudson to Albany, highly enjoying the beautiful scenery upon its banks, and from that city pursued his way homeward, through the grandeur of Berkshire highlands, to Springfield.

In June, after his return to Augusta, we find him taking the sabbath-school children to " Happy Valley," to lecture them on ornithology. And, for the August following, he planned a rural festival for sabbath-school scholars, teachers, and parents, to be held among the pines of " Malta Hill," an eminence on the eastern side of the Kennebec, and there delivered a sermon, full of beauty, on " The Church in the Woods." Finding none enough at leisure, or sufficiently enthusiastic in regard to the happy influences of such a rural, social gathering, to afford him much aid in the preparations, — pressed as he was in his own literary and other labors, and naturally having very little power of physical endurance, he went to the woods nearly alone, and worked hard in making the appearance of the spot as attractive as he could.

This year, having become somewhat widely known as an engaging speaker, he received many invitations to give public addresses.

In order to indulge his natural fondness for mechanical operations, and, at the same time, furnish the little articles of convenience that it would afford, he fixed up a sort of carpenter's shop in his barn, obtained tools, and from time to time disposed of some of his hours of exercise there. He also cultivated, with some assistance, quite a garden.

His relations to his people went on pleasantly,

and his various other pursuits and interests did not call off his attention from the great objects of his profession.

In September of this year, his first child was born. Something of his impressions, on entering upon this new relation, will be found in another chapter. In November following, the twin, ideal child, " Margaret," was matured for birth into the literary world. With reference to its completion, he thus writes : —

To A. H.

"Nov. 24, 1844.

" I finished my book last Friday. I have written on it till my hand is stiff, my eyes are sore, and my back aches. It has taken every leisure moment. I have not written a line to father, mother, brother, or sister, these months. I was resolved to finish that, before I did any thing else."

1845.

Since the first rise of Washingtonianism, Mr. Judd had been actively engaged in its objects. As time passed on, its method of operating on the principles of moral suasion had seemed to fail, and interest in it had declined. His faith in it, however, had not abated, neither was his interest in temperance diminished. And, in the beginning of 1845, he preached to his people, and afterwards published, a " Discourse touching the Causes and Remedies of Intemperance." He finds the failure

18

of the Washingtonian movement to arise from this, that it was rather an impulse than a principle, a sentiment rather than sound faith; and reiterated his belief, that light, love, and God's spirit, would be availing. A great deal of excitement about temperance arose in the place; and in all the movements respecting it he was concerned, but constantly adhered to his original principle, that the *spirit of love* might be made more effectual in removing the evil than the penalties of law. He held conversations with intemperate men, entered into sympathy with them, sought to understand their difficulties in the way of reform, and encouraged their efforts for regaining lost respectability.

The jail he frequently visited, and endeavored to exert humanizing influences upon its inmates, and to elevate their aspirations to virtue and honor. He inquired into the state of their families, and, as far as he was able, sent necessaries to such of them as were suffering.

On Christmas eve of this year, his church was, for the first time, opened for religious exercises, — a practice ever after continued. The necessary aid in trimming the church not forthcoming, he went forward himself, and obtained the evergreens for the purpose.

After many delays in publishing, in August "Margaret" was fairly out of press, and ready to make her *début* in the world. From various causes, Mr. Judd was disappointed in his hope to keep himself concealed as the author of the book. He now appeared before his people in a new aspect, and there became attached to him a degree of personal publicity, which he did not intend or wish.

He had, for some time, been desirous of a more commodious study than the house he occupied afforded, and one more favorably situated as to prospect and the inflowing of nature's influences. He wished for a larger extent of ground, such as should give opportunity, in addition to a garden, for fruit and shade trees, for shrubbery, lawn, and walks; and, in the spring of this year, he began to look about for such a building lot as would afford scope for the realization of his wishes. He obtained a copy of Downing's " Cottage Residences; " and from this work, which he examined with great pleasure and interest, he received most valuable suggestions, which aided him in maturing a plan of such a house as would satisfy his taste and convenience.

But, with his small salary, he had no means of his own, wherewith to carry this project into execution. In this juncture, his father-in-law gave him a commodious lot, adjacent to his own homestead, a site Mr. Judd particularly admired, and furnished him funds to the estimated amount of the cost of the buildings he had planned.

His correspondence this year was, in consequence of his increasing engagements, quite limited.

1846.

The beginning of 1846 finds Mr. Judd devoting his leisure to the writing of "Philo." In February he became a member of the Sons of Temperance.

The basis of this association being such as he could
fully sympathize in, to its interests he devoted much
of his time.   In March he was appointed by the
town one of the committee on common schools, the
interests of which had received much of his attention.

As the spring opened, he began to be very much
engaged in preparations for the building of his
house, the superintendence of which, the preparation
of the grounds, setting out trees, and so forth,
engrossed much of his time for the following summer and autumn.   In July of this year, however, he
found time to prepare an address, which he delivered
before the Sons of Temperance in Waterville.

On the 21st of November, he removed to his new
home.   His first thought, after getting well settled,
was to have a consecration of its freshness to his
people.   A general invitation was publicly given to
every member of his congregation to visit him on
Thanksgiving evening.   The verandas and every
window of the cottage being illuminated, a beautifully attractive and welcome aspect was presented to
his people as they approached.   On entering, they
found the study — which was the largest apartment,
and the room of reception — adorned with evergreens, and, in the midst, their loving pastor, with
deep and tender emotion beaming from his countenance.   In another room was spread a sumptuous
repast, furnished by the guests themselves.

In the latter part of the evening, Mr. Judd gathered all to the study, and there, with a trembling
voice, and feelings almost too strong for control,

spoke to his people in a most familiar and heart-felt manner. He acknowledged that his cares in the erection of the edifice had beguiled him somewhat from his attentions to them. He begged their pardon for any neglect, but at the same time assured them, that the labor had been in part for them; that that study was for the better preparation of spiritual food for them; that theirs it was for familiar resort to their pastor at any time; that the verandas were for them to sit under, the walks to promenade in at their pleasure, and the arbors for their children to sport in. He told them he felt that all these comforts would tend to make him more entirely theirs. And, in conclusion, he baptized his new domicile, as consecrated to them, under the name of Christ Church Parsonage, and then closed the evening with fervent prayer for himself and them in their mutual relations.

1847.

The first month of this new year, Mr. Judd, still anxious for a pleasant intercourse among different denominations, invited all the clergymen of the town, with their wives, to meet each other sociably at his house. Quite a number accepted the invitation; but, from various causes, the circle was not so complete as he had hoped. The example was followed in one or two instances, and then non-intercourse again ensued. He had, in various ways, sought to maintain agreeable ministerial intercourse; but, not meeting with those results for which his own heart yearned, he made no more marked efforts for its attainment. In the summer of this year, however, he was gladdened by the union of all the sabbath schools in town, in a floral procession, on the Fourth of July. This affected him so deeply that he made the value of such a union, and the happy consequences flowing therefrom, the subject of a discourse the next sabbath.

During this year, his duties as one of the school committee occupied a great deal of his time and thoughts. He examined teachers, made frequent visits to schools, talked with scholars and teachers, if any difficulties existed, tried to obviate them, and sought to stir up parents to a greater interest in the education of their children. He wrote several annual reports of the committee, in which the state of the schools was set forth with a degree of plainness and satire quite forcible and amusing.

Temperance continued largely to occupy his attention. He met with the Sons of Temperance in Augusta, and delivered an address before an association of that name in Unity. At Bangor he gave a lecture before its Lyceum, and in Hallowell delivered an address at the county meeting for Cattle Show and Fair. He preached occasionally at the Poor-house, and at the Hospital for the Insane; he attended once a fortnight, as was always his habit, the Utilitarian Society, an industrial association of ladies of his parish. In August he met with other clergymen at Belfast, for the ordination of the Rev. Mr. Niles; and, a few days afterwards, was called to the same place, to preach a funeral sermon on the death of him whom he had just assisted to install as a minister of the gospel.

" Philo " was farther prosecuted in the first part of this year. In the month of June his second daughter was born. In August he commenced the revision of " Margaret " for a new edition.

The war with Mexico, which was going on this year, so totally opposed to Mr. Judd's principles in general, and to his sense of right in this case in particular, took a deep hold of his feelings, and entered largely into his public ministrations. And, when the annual Thanksgiving occurred, so fully was his mind impressed with the horrors of this war, and its attendant train of evils, —

> " Cross battering cross on heights of Monterey;
> ——————————— the rupturing
> Of ties that should all nations interlace;
> The thrusting in of ages right in front
> Of progress, long step backward of all good," —

that he could not summon his feelings to utter the voice of joy and thanksgiving on that day before his people. In his prayer, unaffected contrition in behalf of the nation fell from his lips, and deprecations of justly-merited national punishment found an earnest voice. On rising at the usual time for sermon, he opened the Bible at the Lamentations of Jeremiah ; and then, with paleness of face and trembling voice, he uttered with deep pathos the moanings of the old prophet over the sins and desolations of his beloved country, and then dismissed the congregation.

Some, even of his own people, regarded the services merely as a very good joke ; some were almost offended that he gave them no better treat on that day of their rejoicing. The newspapers very extensively told the story; and, in their comments, some approved, and others regarded it as oddity, affectation, or desire for notoriety. But few understood just how the matter lay in his own mind, and what moral necessity there was in his own bosom, *forcing* him to give the tone he did to the services of the day. He also omitted to read the Governor's proclamation, because he thought it contained an unauthorized prescription to clergymen as to what they should preach in their own pulpits.

What leisure he could find amid the many other engagements of this year was spent in exploring the neighboring woods for trees suited to carry out his plan for the embellishment of his grounds, and in transplanting them to their appointed places. Almost every variety of forest-tree in the vicinity was laid under contribution for this purpose; and he sent to his father to procure him *seeds* of such as were not found about him, on which he wished to experiment by way of cultivation.

1848.

In 1848, Mr. Judd's invitations to lecture abroad before lyceums and other societies very much increased; and compliance with them added to the multifarious labors he had already on hand. The Fourth of July, he delivered an address before the common-school celebration at Gardiner. In August he addressed the literary societies of Waterville

College on the subject, " Christ and the Scholar, or what Christianity is to the Scholar."

The bereavement suffered by a favorite aunt on the removal of her only remaining child, a daughter, in the spring-time of life, called forth the following letter of condolence : —

To Mrs. S. J. H.

"Augusta, Feb. 28, 1848.

" My dear Aunt, — I have learned with great concern of the death of S. Such an event, while it may sometimes have been present to your imagination, could not, I am sure, at so early a period, have been anticipated. Your cup of sorrow, already full, must now, indeed, overflow. W., in the flower of his youth, was snatched from you ; and now your only remaining child has followed. I can just remember being present at your marriage. I can remember then, a very little boy, riding with you and uncle H. to Northampton. I remember seeing Governor Strong, who called me to his garden, and gave me some peaches.

" But these things are past ; they hover as shadows among the dreams of my childhood. Eventful, indeed, has been your experience since those days. Time has hastened swiftly by : you are now motherless, and you weep by the graves of the past. Your own sunshine has been flecked by many a cloud.

" God help and comfort you ! Though you walk through a valley of shadows, may you be enabled to trust in Him with whom are the issues of our days ! God have us all in his keeping, even until our appointed time shall come !

                    " Your ever-affectionate nephew."

In the trial and condemnation of Dr. Coolidge for murder, which took place in Augusta in March, he took a keen interest; and it was the occasion of developing more fully his views on capital punishment and the treatment of prisoners. He visited the condemned man in his cell, and strove to impart such support as he might in the awful moment of condemnation. The sabbath which followed the rendering of the verdict, he preached a most touching discourse from the text, "Let the sighing of the prisoner come before thee; according to the greatness of thy power, preserve thou those that are appointed to die." In various ways, as far as was in his power, he sought to minister to the moral and religious welfare of the wretched man, until he was transferred to the State's prison.

In the beginning of this year, "Philo" was again prosecuted with a good deal of assiduity, and was completed for the press in March.

About the same time, Mr. Judd learned, with great pleasure, of the illustration of "Margaret" in a series of outline sketches by Mr. Darley, of New York, and, through the kindness of the artist, was favored with the loan of the portfolio containing them. These, of course, he examined with avidity, and found great satisfaction in seeing his own ideals delineated with so much force, and, in general, with such truth to his own conceptions. This was a stimulus and encouragement to the further prosecution of his literary labors. He also looked forward with impatient desire to the publication of these sketches.

Mr. Judd had been aiming steadily, from his first settlement in Augusta, to bring his whole congregation up to the true standard of spiritual life. It had grieved him that so few joined in the communion, and that there was so great neglect, on the part of parents, to bring their children to baptism. About this time, however, he commenced a course of labor with reference to these subjects more exclusive and systematic. He directed his attention more particularly, at first, to the latter ordinance. He talked about it with individuals personally, and alluded to it often from the pulpit. He was successful in moving the hearts of parents in this matter, and of many adults who had not received baptism; and the sabbath of June 11 he appointed for the administration of the ordinance to all such in the congregation as were willing to come forward for the purpose. On this day, he made a strong appeal upon the subject to his hearers; and then, with fearful heart, lest many of his beloved ones should still withhold themselves or their children, he invited all who had not received baptism to present themselves. As he saw heads of families, one after another, stepping into the aisles, and drawing near the altar with their groups of children, and some adults coming forth alone, his heart was almost too deeply moved to utter its burden of joy and thanks, and implore appropriate blessings on those about to receive the seal of oneness with the visible church, and, as he hoped, with the great church, invisible and catholic, throughout heaven and earth. And, when he descended from the pulpit to the baptismal basin, and proceeded to baptize " in the name of the Father, and of the Son, and of the Holy Ghost," — in some instances, first a parent and then the children, and, last of all, his own little ones, the weight of his emotions almost overpowered him, and his voice well nigh failed in pronouncing the many-times-repeated formula. Mr. Judd felt that a good work was begun, and rejoiced in this evidence that his labors had not been in vain.

The year before, the Universalist Society united with the Unitarian, at their church, in the celebration of Christmas-eve ; and, this year, Mr. Judd's church, agreeably to an arrangement then made, and reciprocating the service, joined them in their observance of the evening.

1849.

In April of the following year, 1849, the two churches above referred to united in several social religious meetings, at their respective places of worship, which they found both interesting and profitable.

The following letter Mr. Judd addressed to a young lady of his church : —

"CHRIST CHURCH PARSONAGE, May 10, 1849.

"Dear J., — I cannot say how deeply, how solemnly, how gladly, your note of a few days since affected me. ·Your heart seemed to be speaking to me, and my own heart was touched. How I live amongst my people, and yet seem to know but little of them ! Yet I do know a great deal of them, more than they think I do. The trouble is, they do not all speak so freely to me as you do (in your note). They say they are afraid of me, and all that. You try to be good, I know you do; you seek for a conformity with what is divine, pure, and beautiful: may you be aided in all your exertions! What is good is beautiful, and a tender sensibility to the beautiful is one method of becoming good.

"You have trials too. You seem to me too young, too innocent, too fortunate, for trials. That shadows should fall on *your* path, that so soon you should begin to think of mysteries, and be wetted with tears, is what I should not anticipate. But so it is, so it too often is. God preserve you in all you have to endure! Cast your cares upon him, for he careth for you. I have my trials too, my sorrows, my unavailing woes. You and I, and all of us, need a divine strength, — need the infinite love of the infinite Father.

"I do not think it well to dwell too much on our sins. I would repent of them, I would view them in their just wickedness, I would pray God to forgive them; but to have them perpetually near, to have them fill the imagination, and to tyrannize over the memory, is not well. Rather turn to what is elevating, cheerful, hopeful. We should be like travellers, rather advancing towards the bright hills, than stopping to reflect on the obstacles we have met.

"Yet bear your cross bravely, it must be borne; every day it reappears, Jesus' cross, he bore it for you; bear it for your own soul and for the world. It will grow lighter; by and by it will sit your

19

shoulders well; gradually it will change its shape and its office, and then it will become a crown.

"All sweetness, peace, and holy serenity, be yours, through Jesus, the blessed One! — so prays

"Your affectionate friend and pastor,

"Sylvester Judd."

In his regular ministrations, Mr. Judd gave his people a sermon in July, entitled "The Communion for Sinners." In this, he takes the position, that Christ lived, labored, and died, for the cleansing, the purgation, of the human race; that the blood of Christ stands for his life, and his life is his inward, vital energy, the yearnings of his spirit, the profundity of his benevolence; and this is shed, poured out, lavished, for the remission of sin.

He therefore said, "To-day, so I think, to-day, if any of you have regrets for the past, agitation for the present, and pious purposes for the future; to-day, if any one of you would be cleansed by the blood, quickened by the life, of Christ; to-day, if you would be gathered into the circle of the divine sympathies, of which Christ is the centre, — if you would enter the communion of the church universal, of which Christ is the head, — you may partake."

For three or four years after settlement at Augusta, Mr. Judd regularly, every year, paid a visit to the paternal home. But at length the pressure of engagements, and the economy he found it necessary to practise, rendered his visits there less frequent. But, in the summer of this year, he made a journey thither.

While absent, he wrote as follows —

"Dear Mother, — It has rained every day but one since I left Augusta; though, on the whole, there has been much good weather. The grass is fine, and the world of vegetation is coming out in great glory. What beauty there is in this valley of the Connecticut, and particularly in this portion of it! So deep, so rich, so magnificent, a beauty, I never beheld. It seems more like our ideas of the tropical regions. When I walk out, I seem not to be walking, but *wading*, in the midst of beauty, with seas of it about me, and waves of it rising above me. The shrubbery here, the gardens, the shade-trees, the walks, are unsurpassed. I am amidst the scenes of my youth; and there are many changes. The change is great in the material world: it is greater in the human world. My early friends are all gone, elderly people that I used to know are dead, and those whom I meet 'know not Joseph.'

"I have been into the graveyard. There are the old familiar names; there are recalled the old familiar faces; there, in that silence, is clustered much of what was once life to me. Amidst the beauty of which I speak, and under the shadows of those grand old elms, seem to me to move unseen spirits; and they are pervaded with the recollection of a past generation."

1850.

In the beginning of the year 1850, Mr. Judd was called to experience a new and tender sorrow, in the sundering of one link in the chain which had so long, unbroken, bound together the home-circle of his youth. His strong family attachments have been somewhat developed in the previous pages. And now one of his brothers must be taken from his sensible communion. On hearing the tidings of immediate danger, he hastened on to have one more interview; and, if it must be so, to soothe and sustain the parting spirit. But he was too late. An unconscious, insensible form was all that remained, over which, with all the susceptibility of childhood, his sobs and tears gushed forth. He, however, restrained his emotions sufficiently to perform, with tender love, the funeral offices of his dear brother.

Soon after his return to Augusta from these solemn obsequies, he preached a fraternal sermon, touching in its pathos, on "The Affection of Brothers," from the text, "And Joseph lifted up his eyes, and saw his brother Benjamin, his mother's son, and said, Is this your younger brother, of whom ye spake unto me? And he made haste; for his bowels did yearn upon his brother, and he sought where to weep."

In May, 1850, he gave a sabbath discourse in his church on "The True Dignity of Politics," from the text, "The Lord shall be for a spirit of judgment to him that sitteth in judgment." The Legislature of the State then being in session, a large number of its members were present.

The next day, he received, by the appropriate hands, the appended communication: —

"State of Maine, House of Representatives,
May 2, 1850.

" *Ordered,* that a committee be raised to wait on
Rev. Mr. Judd, and request for publication a copy
of his sermon delivered last evening, at Christ
Church, on 'The True Dignity of Politics.'"

On his complying with this request, by order of
the House a thousand copies of the sermon were
printed for the use of the Legislature.

On the Fourth of July of this year, Mr. Judd
delivered an oration on "Heroism," in the Court
House Square, Augusta, before the fire-clubs of
Augusta, Hallowell, Gardiner, and Pittston, which
was published by request of the audience.

In the early part of the year, "Philo," after a
delay in publication of two years from the time of
completion, was finally issued from the press.

During this interval between the finishing and
publishing of "Philo," securing the time for it no
one knows when, Mr. Judd had brought far towards
maturity another work, entitled "Richard Edney."
This book was brought out the same year, soon after
"Philo."

To a young boy of his flock, absent at school,
whose mind was led to a particular consideration of
religious subjects, he addressed the letter below: —

"Augusta, May 6, 1850.

"Dear A., — I am very glad to hear, that you are
attentive to those interests which are of the highest
consequence to every human being, even your moral
and spiritual culture.   What is it to be a Christian?
The word Christian comes from the word Christ,

19*

and signifies one who is like Christ, or who loves
Christ, and is willing to be a disciple of Christ.
What is it to be like Christ? It is to endeavor to
feel as he felt, and to do as he did. Christ is our
example, and we are to walk in his steps. We must
endeavor to do good, to cultivate a right temper and
disposition. 'If ye love one another,' the Bible
says, 'all men shall know ye are my disciples.'
'The fruits of the spirit are love, joy, peace, meekness, temperance,' and the like. If you would know
whether you are a Christian, you must ask yourself
if you have these fruits. Again, the Bible says,
'He that loveth is born of God, and knoweth God.'
If you would know whether you are born again, you
must ask yourself if you have Christian love. Do
you love God and your neighbor? Do you try to
love all men? Are you willing to do good to those
that hate you, and can you pray for those that de-
spitefully use you? If so, then you are a child of
God, and a disciple of Christ.

"I hope and pray that you may be led in the
right way. Avoid that which is evil, and cleave to
that which is good. Let your light shine among
your companions and in your school. When you
are engaged in plays and sports, even then remember that you are God's child, and that you may do
no wrong. Let no bad word escape your lips, and
no wicked feeling arise in your heart. Trust in
God, and he shall keep thee. Read your Bible, particularly the New Testament, and see what Christ
says, and what Christ would have you do. The best
sermon that was ever delivered in the world is the

Sermon on the Mount. Study that. Every day, in prayer, ask God to bless you and to keep you.

" I need not say that I am interested for you. All the little ones of my flock are very near my heart.

" That you may be happy and good, and grow up a worthy Christian man, is the earnest prayer and wish of your affectionate

"Friend and Pastor."

An old tradition of the Indians had suggested to Mr. Judd the plan of another work, in a poetical form, the main scene of which was to be laid at the White Hills. That he might carry out this purpose, he felt the necessity of visiting these mountains. He was also very happy to be able to make a little excursion, such as his means had never before allowed him to indulge in.

In August he started with Mrs. Judd, and first fulfilled an appointment to meet his college classmates on the classic ground of his *alma mater*. Then, passing to New York, he luxuriated in the beautiful scenery on the banks of the Hudson, witnessed the fashion and frivolity of Saratoga, kept sabbath in sight of the quiet waters of Lake George, passed over the smooth bosom of Champlain to Burlington, and thence, amid the picturesque views of the Green Mountains, proceeded to the White Hills.

The new work, it is believed, was commenced soon after his return.

1851.

In Mr. Judd's regular sermon, at the commencement of this new year, occur the paragraphs following : —

" How, withal, our years grow shorter ! How what was once as a great, overshadowing expanse dwindles away, until it becomes, like the little cloud, no bigger than a man's hand !

" I feel this myself. I have passed through the long years of childhood, and the less long years of youth, and have reached what may be termed the middle-sized years of middle age ; and see beyond, and feel myself rapidly approaching, the downward series, where our days drop like water from a height, thinning as they fall, till they terminate in the merest thread.

" Yet I sympathize, and will sympathize, with every thing beautiful, every thing good, every thing joyous, every thing useful, in the world ; and to the furtherance and increase of such things I will give what of ability or means God gives me.

" Still, too, I know and feel, and in this I can but share the common sentiment of many who now hear me, that these things must end ; that I am hastening to the final bourne, to death and the judgment. I am sensible, that, even if I should live as many years as I have lived, and repeat the precise number of my months, that the remaining portion of my life will seem to be a very short one. There will not be, either for me or for you, any more long summer days, any more long winter nights.

" Whatever, however, we do, how many of us are sufferers! Many a mute shadow of woe passes by us at these times. Many a phantom of hope and love is recalled on New Year. There are some cold firesides, some desolate chambers. In the night-wind of the year that has just come to its close, you hear many a farewell voice. New mounds rise in our graveyards, new monuments in our memories ! "

January, 1851, found the sabbath school in rather a declining state, both as to numbers and interest. The past superintendent had become discouraged, and he declined further service. No one seemed willing to undertake to carry it on. In this exigency, the pastor, rather than see an institution on which he depended so much go down, went forward, and added the care of this to his other engagements. He declared to his people most earnestly, that, as long as *one* scholar remained, he should stand by and sustain the sabbath school. He therefore performed the duties of superintendent from January until November of this year.

With his people at large, his labors were persistent and systematic in carrying forward what had become his leading idea, that the pale of the church should be so far drawn back as to include the *whole* people, and thus become a bond of union rather than a separating barrier.

With this aim, he this year went quite fully into an explanation of his views. In March he preached upon " The Utility of the Communion," from the text, " What mean ye by this service ? " This he explained, not as necessary to salvation, not as evidence of any marked change in the character of those who partake of it; but, like many other usages adopted by men, as a sign and a memorial.

The next subject in course was the consideration of the question, "What is the Church?" As simple tests of the church, he mentioned, that it is the pillar and stay of the truth; that Christ is its head; that it teaches the method of salvation by Christ. And by these tests he claimed that the Unitarian body is the church, and that all believers in Christ were truly in the church.

This was followed by a discourse, the object of which was to show that all are religiously responsible for the observance of Christ's precepts, he who makes no public profession of religion as well as he who does; and that all are equally privileged and equally bound to obey his command, "Do this in remembrance of me."

Then came a sermon on "Birth Relation to the Church," in which it was shown that we, in Christian lands, are as truly born into the church as into the family or the state; and that it was a false theology which had divorced a part of the community from the Christian church, and forbidden its most prominent means of grace to a large portion.

Again he considered the "Inconsistent Neglect of the Communion," showing how eagerly people would receive other proffered goods and advantages, whatever would minister to their interests; but, when it came to the memorial fitted to make upon their hearts the deepest impression of what is life to their own souls, through a mistaken idea they would turn their back upon it.

In another sermon he dwelt largely upon " Lay Co-operation " in connection with carrying forward the great objects of the gospel.

He gave a sermon expressly to Sunday-school teachers, and one to children, on their relation to these subjects.

In one sermon he took pains to explain what he considered *Unitarianism* to be, and the advantages it claims.   In another, considering Christianity as best adapted to promote the highest interests of the human race, he enforced the duty of spreading it.

In the value of the noted temperance-law of Maine, as a remedy for the evils it was enacted to suppress, Mr. Judd had no confidence.   Before the passage of the law, in June of this year, and while the subject was being agitated, he delivered a discourse bearing upon the matter from the text, " They were not able to resist the *spirit and pow   by which he spake.*"   He maintained that a combination of all the means, motives, and influences by which the human mind and heart can be affected, brought to bear upon the subject, would supersede and exclude the idea of physical force, which, he claimed, ever fails to affect the mind and heart of man ; that men should be treated as rational and intelligent beings, not as brute beasts ; that the former course penetrates and subdues, the latter evokes anger and opposition.

In July, 1851, Mr. Judd was invited by the newly formed Unitarian Church in Brooklyn, L. I.,

where a brother was residing, to supply their desk
for a few sabbaths.   Much of the time, during
his stay of two or three weeks, was spent in the
neighboring city of New York, about which he
moved, exercising his usual habit of keen, philoso-
phic, reflective observation.   Nothing in this great
Babel of contrasts and varieties escaped his remark,
or failed to call forth his thought.   He visited the
opera, and the newly-arrived emigrant-ship; gal-
leries of paintings, and cellars and stalls of old
books ; artists' studios, and shops of glass-stainers ;
looked in upon gorgeous churches, and upon the
wretched abodes of poverty and squalidness.   He
had the pleasure of examining many valuable paintings, and some originals of the old masters, at
private residences.

He joined the Universalist Sunday-schools of New
York in an excursion to Biddle's Grove, and very
much enjoyed the beautiful scenery of the spot, and
the happy influences of the festive gathering.

The change which this little journey and visit
afforded in his usually quiet and studious life was
quite agreeable, though the city offered, in the main,
few attractions to draw him from his peaceful, rural
home.   But he returned with his mind enriched
with many fresh thoughts and new images to subserve his ministerial labors and literary studies.

On his arrival, he found that a beloved sister-in-
law — one most lovely in her character, and but
recently a wife and mother — had, in his absence,
passed from the sphere of earthly communion, in a
manner too sudden to afford opportunity of his learn-

ing her danger. Moved with tender sorrow at this loss, and his mind glowing with the pictured forms he had so lately viewed, he composed, for the following sabbath, a beautiful and consolatory sermon from the words, "And they saw his face as it had been the face of an angel." He spoke of the lovely "Madonna face;" of the place it holds in the heart of the Roman Catholic; of its soothing, prompting influence upon him, and the more than angel-power with which it comes to him. He alluded delicately, but remotely, to the loveliness and Madonna-like serenity of the departed, and to the aureola with which death crowns all the loved and lost; in a touching and soothing manner, he adverted to the blessed influences which the memory of those lost to sight may still exert upon fond ones left behind; and showed how here and there, in many a seemingly desolated dwelling, might be beaming forth upon its occupants, as it were, the face of an angel.

Having always felt, in the highest degree, the advantages of religious and social intercourse, and of rural festivals, from the first plan of a railroad connecting Augusta with other towns in the State, adjacent and remote, Mr. Judd had watched its progress with the keenest interest, in reference to its facilitating these objects. He had conceived the plan of having sabbath-schools of different churches, within such distances as to render it practicable, gathered together once a year in the open air, under forest-shade, for the formation of acquaintance, the exchange of friendly greetings, the inculcation of the idea that all are one in the general church of

20

Christ, and the indulgence of recreation and innocent amusements.

With this end in view, and also that he might
have a rural place of gathering consecrated for the use
of his own sabbath school, he selected a pine-grove
on the "Malta Hill" eminence, the region which
had always been with him a place of favorite resort.
Here he went forward in clearing up the underbrush,
in constructing a rude rostrum for speakers, and cir-
cular seats around for hearers. Ample space was
made for the setting of tables, and for various
amusements. In September of this year, he appointed a meeting, at the spot, of his own sabbath
school and congregation, where he preached a sermon, and dedicated the place under the name of
Greenwood Church.

He consecrated the place to the advancement of
the children in Christian knowledge and practice ;
dedicated it to the love of the beautiful, — the garment with which God clothes his works, and a
vitality with which he inspires his rational offspring.
He recognized it as one of the original temples of
God, and consecrated it to him as a rural sanctuary.
"Adam and Eve," said he, "first worshipped in the
woods, that is, among the trees of the garden. Their
sermons were delivered in the murmur of the brooks
Pison and Havilah. Their organ was the piping of
the winds, their choir was the birds of Paradise."

Mr. Judd was in the way of noticing from time
to time, in an anniversary sermon, his ordination.
The extracts following are from a sermon preached
Oct. 5, 1851, from the text, "We preach Christ,

warning every man and teaching every man in all wisdom, that we may present every man perfect in Christ Jesus : " —

" It is eleven years since I was ordained to the sacred ministry and instituted to the church of Christ in this place. As the times go, this is a long ministry. I have seen changes in every other parish in the city ; in some instances, several. There is not an officiating clergyman in town who was here when I was settled.

" There have been changes in the church ; changes by addition and by removal ; changes, many and sad, by death ; and, what is perhaps sometimes more painful, changes by ingratitude, indifference, vanity, and worldliness of mind. There have been changes wrought simply by time : babes have become youths ; youths have mounted to manhood and womanhood ; wives have become widows ; and children, orphans.

" Amidst all the changes that we might note, in the period of time referred to, I sometimes think, — I know not whether it be a commendation or otherwise, — that *I* have changed as little as anybody. As to my manner of life, and purpose of heart, and principles of truth, I believe no one can accuse me of change. I have differed with persons, perhaps wiser and better than I ; I have not often differed with myself, as I should hope never to with Jesus. I think I am safe in asserting this, — that I have been amongst you such an one as this might be said of, ' You always know where to find him.' The first year of my ministry, as to its general drift and bearing, was a pretty fair index to what the whole has been.   God had thoroughly indoctrinated me in the great truth of Christ and the church, peace, temperance, recreation, human nature, human duty, human destiny, before my settlement; and I have only had occasion to mature, improve upon, and apply these views since.

" By bringing me to Unitarianism, God unsealed my eyes; he led me to a world of truth, before hidden; he flooded my mind with blessed revelations of himself, and Christ, and man; and, unless I were traitor to God, love, and my convictions and conscience, I could not but preach and do as I have.

" It is not my purpose at this moment to speak of personal or local affairs, except to remark that eleven years of labor among a people, if nothing else, at least involves a minister in peculiar, interesting, and solemn relations to them, and, conversely, them to him.   So much church and Christian labor with a people establishes this fact, at least in their history, that they are all bound to the church and to Christianity. Would I have preached and prayed here for eleven years, — would I for one year, for one month, with the consciousness that nine-tenths of the parish were under no sort of obligations to religion, or to Christianity, or to the church, or to the pastor, who in a sense represents all these?   Have I baptized these children; have I followed them onward into youth; have I been throwing, so to say, my parental arms about them, and shedding my parental heart over them; and are they imagining they have nothing to do with religion, or the church, or God, in whose name I have acted, and whose spirit has ever been, or ought even to have been, working through me? Nay, these children are in a sense my children, and mine simply as pastor of Christ Church, and of course they are children of the church. And this obligation, my friends, of at least eleven years' growth as regards many of you, is waxing stronger and stronger every year. No matter who may be pastor of this church, whether I or some other man, you cannot get rid of this obligation, except by a species of unheard of self-excision, by putting yourselves, so to say, out of the world. This obligation is in every sermon you hear, it is in every sabbath that comes over you, it is in the very soil you tread upon. No: to get rid of this highest, most personal, most vital church and Christian obligation, you must become expatriate in your native land, an excommunicant in your native church.

"I have endeavored, and I think you will all bear witness to the sincerity of that endeavor, — I have endeavored, I say, in the language of the text, to preach Christ. Nor do I make boast, but only refer to it as a simple matter of fact, when I express it as my sober belief, that, for the past eleven years, Christ has been more preached in this pulpit than in any other in the city; that more sermons have been formed on a basis of simple reference to Christ, and Christ has gone into the staple of more sermons in this pulpit, than in any other in this city."

In conclusion, he says: "May I not bespeak, on your part, a stronger, more sedulous attention to the great things of which we treat? Have I not fairly laid open to you the matter of the church, the matter of human nature, of human duty? have I not fairly stated the important topics on which from time to time I have discoursed? If ye are wise men, will ye not judge wisely and act wisely?

"This is a sort of anniversary sermon. I ought perhaps to have preached more such. As long as I continue here, I shall intend to preach such. Eleven years! How quickly they have flown! It seems but yesterday; it was a darker autumnal day than this; we were assembled here for the ordination of your new minister. It was a day, to my own heart, full of hope, full too of concern. The years have hasted away, and are hasting. What men, what women, what children, will we be? Shall no new life be kindled, no new altar-fires burn? Shall death, judgment, and eternity hurry on, and we be no better, no purer?

"Is there one of these children, now maturing in my eye and blooming to my thought, whom I cannot, by and by, call my child? There are bereavements in this world, my friends, almost as bitter as those of death.

"And more: will not all these children, these young men, and young women, fulfil my own, as it were the anxious hopes of a parent? will they not give themselves to Jesus? will they not covenant with his church? will they not grow up sons and daughters of righteousness for ever?

"I have been here long enough to see changes, I say; and among them have been the removal of our youths, by marriage, for business, or whatever the cause may have been. Others still are going off.

Will the young man who leaves us, who goes to distant countries, whose home shall be on the wide sea, — will that young man remember us, and the hearts that love him, and the church that prays for him? and will he not suffer the good seed that has been sowing these many years in his soul to spring up to his everlasting life?"

On Christmas occasion, this year, he discoursed on the jubilant element, — the susceptibility of deep, strong joy, — as a primitive and an eternal condition of our nature. He referred to the social element of happiness, and to the sad abuse of festivals and holidays; but maintained the necessity of our natures for something of the kind, and expressed the belief that recreative pleasures, on a large and general scale, are not unfavorable to morality.

On this same Christmas-day, — while he and his household were spending the day from home with family-friends, — quite unknown and unsuspected by him, his people were testifying their kind regard by erecting a Christmas-tree, and loading it with their diverse offerings for himself, his wife, and his little children, and spreading his board with a liberal entertainment. As nightfall came on, and he with his family were expected to come home, they illumined his house, and made ready to receive him. The surprise on his part was complete; and, for a moment, he did not know how to understand it. His heart was deeply touched. After the festivities of the evening were mainly passed, and before the company separated, he poured out his grateful thanks to these kind friends, and expressed the sense of stronger union to his people, and greater security of their co-operation, heart and soul, with him, than he had ever before experienced. It was with him an hour of deep and tender joy.

He wrote as follows to young ladies of his charge, away at school : —

"Augusta, Feb. 7, 1851.

"My dear A., A., and C., — I often think of the absent members of my flock, and am sincerely desirous of your peace, purity, and happiness. I am sometimes solicitous about you, particularly such as are young and inexperienced. I know you have trials, and that you must encounter many disappointments. My wish is that you may have strength to endure all that shall be appointed unto you.

"Allow me to say a few direct words. Be faithful to your studies. Do not misspend your time. Remember that these years of your youth are both fleeting and precious.

"Be faithful to your own tempers and dispositions. Banish envy and prejudice. Do not suffer yourselves to repine, if in any thing others excel you.

"Be faithful to your religious duties. Read the New Testament of our Lord and Saviour Jesus Christ. Do not forget that you are the children of God, and that you ever owe your heavenly Father your supreme love and obedience. Cultivate the habit of prayer. Bear in mind that the Bible is your creed, and the words of Jesus your counsellor and director. Particularly take the Sermon on the Mount ; read that, ponder on its meaning, drink in its spirit, make it your guide and comforter. Remember that you are to reject all human creeds, and to rely on Christ's words alone.

"If you are in darkness, doubt, and despondency, apply to your own hearts the blessed promises of Jesus. If you are weary and heavy-laden, go to him, and he will comfort you. Feel evermore your nearness to God, and repose implicitly on your heavenly Father's love.

"I know you will miss home, and your old friends, and these Augusta streets and houses. But remain patiently and improvingly where you are, and by and by you will be ready to come back again. We shall be glad to see you when you do return.

"I wish each of you, or all of you together, would write me. Receive these few words from the kindness and affection of

"Your Friend and Pastor,

"SYLVESTER JUDD."

"THE PARSONAGE, AUGUSTA, June 22, 1851.

"My dear E., — I was glad to see that you remembered me, and am always glad to know how what St. John calls 'my children' are doing. I wish, above all things, that they may prosper, and be in health.

"Am I to understand, from that programme you were so kind as to send me, that the several young ladies spoke their parts?' What did you say about 'chivalry'?

"There is much that is beautiful in our ideal of that thing. But those gallant knights seem to have been very cruel and bloodthirsty men. One of the

darkest and saddest pages of history is the taking of
Jerusalem by the Crusaders. Have you read Frois-
sart's Chronicles? You will find a good deal on the
times and manners of chivalry in Scott's novels.

"St. John was rejoiced to hear that his children
were 'walking in the truth.' So I hope you are
doing. I trust you cleave to your Bible; that you
feel an interest in Jesus, your blessed Redeemer and
divine Teacher; that you cultivate a spirit of conscientiousness; that you maintain habits of prayer;
that, in all things, you seek to conduct yourself as a
child of God, and a lamb of the flock of Jesus.

"Believe me your affectionate Friend and Pastor,

"SYLVESTER JUDD."

1852.

Mr. Judd's reputation as a lyceum lecturer had
so extended, that in 1852 his applications of this
kind had become very numerous.

But the great, absorbing subject which enlisted all
the energies of his spirit was the interests of the
church, — the advancement of principles relating to
its progress in spirituality, which had been the frequent theme of his discourse. Long and patient
had been his investigations, deep and earnest his
thought; and his conclusions were to his own mind
clear and incontrovertible. With the modesty natural to his character, he had heretofore abstained from
thrusting upon the public at large views peculiar to
himself. In speaking with a friend, he adverted
to his always having kept back in his denomination,

and left it to others to go forward ; "but now," said he, "I am getting to be almost forty years old, and I feel that, if I am ever going to do any thing, I have a right to do it now."

On the birth-relation to the church, he spoke much to his people in public, and conversed with them in private. At meetings with his brethren in the ministry, the question, " *What shall we do with the children?* " had been so often put in the same form, that it had assumed something of the character of a by-word ; and its reiteration, although regarded as an interrogatory of momentous import, had come often to provoke a smile. Yet satisfactory answer came there none.

Touching this general subject, he thus writes —

To Rev. E. E. H.

" Augusta, July 27, 1852.

" Brother H., — For years I have been burying myself, plans, hopes, speculations, in a something I call the church, the true, Christian church. In ' Margaret ' the thing is broadly hinted at ; in ' Philo ' it comes up in another shape ; in ' Richard Edney ' it becomes an assumed fact. It is, of course, ' catholic ; ' it is, of course, ' orthodox ; ' it is *the* church ; it is ' holy and apostolical ; ' and it is, to the core, Unitarian. To these ideas I am gradually bringing my own parish.

" There is no salvation for this world but in Unitarianism, — the one God, the one humanity, the one communion of all souls, the unity in God of science, art, religion, life, earth and heaven, time and eternity. The idea of the Fall of man begot that of the Trinity, the disunity of God. There has been no harmony since; no harmony of states, churches; none of the spiritual and secular element; none of science and religion.

"Believe me everlastingly yours and God's,

"S. JUDD."

Other subjects of prominent interest to his mind were the means for rendering public worship more impressive, and the value of a permanent organization of the churches of the Unitarian denomination.

The Unitarian clergymen in Maine had, very generally, become deeply interested in all these matters. Many of them agreed, that, at the Maine Ministerial Association, which was to be held in Belfast, August 3, 1852, they would remain as long as need be for the full discussion of these subjects, and would not separate until some steps were taken towards the furtherance of these interests. This meeting continued three days, and was one of intense interest to Mr. Judd. It was voted, "That measures be taken to form a permanent organization of the churches of the Unitarian connection in Maine; and that a Convention be called for that object, to be held in Portland in the following September." The draft of a plan of organization was prepared to be submitted to the Convention, which was printed and distributed to the several churches throughout the State. The preparation of a Preamble, or Declaration, setting forth the reasons and principles of the proposed organization, was entrusted to Mr. Judd.

On the sabbath after his return from Belfast, Mr.

Judd laid the whole matter before his people, explaining the reasons and advantages of such an organization, and the many important objects of interest to the church which it was intended to promote. The pathos of his tone and look showed how fully his very soul was fused into the interests of the church of Christ on earth. The hearts of his people were deeply touched. In giving an account of it to the Rev. Mr. P., he says, "One brother moved that the people substantially approve the plan. This was seconded. I asked all, men, women, and children, in favor, to rise. *All rose!* the whole congregation, some strangers. I felt strengthened. These are the times of God's Spirit, — these are all Pentecosts!" So full was his own heart at this unanimous, approving testimony, that his faltering voice scarce sufficed to pronounce the benediction.

He adds, "The more I think of what we have done, the more it seems just and right, timely and auspicious."

In the interval before the meeting of the proposed Convention, Mr. Judd followed up, with his people, his great idea, underlying all his other wishes for improvements in the church, that of bringing *all* his congregation, including children, to believe and feel themselves as of the church.

To one of his church, he wrote : —

"Christ Church Parsonage, Augusta, Aug. 11, 1852.

"Dear ——, You went away so suddenly and unexpectedly, I had no time to see you. Do write, that we may know how you are. Believe, dear ——, that God loves you ; that you are his child, his holy one ; that he will never leave nor forsake you ; that Jesus bears you in his soul, even as a tender lamb.

"I have been very busy indeed since you left. I hoped to get a moment's leisure this summer ; but duty and toil seem to crowd more and more. I spent all of last week with my clerical brethren at Belfast, consulting on matters pertaining to Christ and the church.

"I hope you will write me ; do, a word. Assure me of your remembrance.

"I pray for you, and hope for you ; and be assured of the deepest interest and unfailing intercessions of your Friend and Pastor,

"SYLVESTER JUDD."

In August, he was successful in realizing his long-cherished idea, that, through the facilities afforded by railroads, the sabbath schools of churches in distant towns could be brought together in rural festivals. "Greenwood Church" was put in repair for the occasion ; and a white flag, bearing a cross, waved above the tops of the trees.

The day appointed was fine. The children, with happy faces, gathered in great numbers from several other towns in the State, attended by parents and teachers. Addresses were given, hymns sung, and then for a time the children were dismissed to their various innocent and exhilarating recreations. Refreshments were served, the old renewed their youth in participating in the children's joy, pleasant acquaintances were made, kindly feelings cherished, an enlarged benevolence generated. In meeting again to receive the parting benediction, children were brought forward for baptism, and, in God's own temple, consecrated to his service.

According to appointment, the Convention met in Portland in September. With scarcely an exception, all the Unitarian churches in Maine were represented by pastors and delegates.

The Preamble finally adopted was as follows : —

" We, the Unitarian Church of Maine, ourselves and our posterity, are a church ; a part of the church universal, of the church of God and Christ ; a church congregational, evangelical, apostolic. We are the church, not of creeds, but of the Bible ; not of a sect, but of humanity ; seeking not uniformity of dogma, but communion in the religious life. We embrace in our fellowship all who will be in fellowship with us.

" Locally, and in a limited sense, a collection or society of Christians is a church.

" These Christians, with their families, uniting in regular assembly for religious worship, instruction, growth, and culture, having the ordinances and a pastor, constitute a *parochial* church.

" These Christians, with their families, in any city, town, or precinct of the State, not having the forms and means of regular religious service, and without a pastor, constitute an *unparochial* church.

" In the State of Maine there will therefore be parochial and unparochial churches.

" These several churches, considered as a whole, constitute the Unitarian Church of Maine.

" This church, as auxiliary to the divine purpose

that calls it into being, proposes to create an organization of a permanent character, to meet annually, to be called the Association of the Unitarian Church of Maine, and having a Constitution, which is hereto adjoined.

"The objects of this association are mutual conference, illumination, and strength ; to gather more and more into one the scattered elements of our faith ; to deepen the sympathies that should exist in all parts of a common Zion ; to review the condition of the several churches ; to concert the best methods of propagating gospel truth ; and to adjust ourselves more nearly to the course of events, whereby Divine Providence seems evidently to be ushering in a better and a millennial day to the whole human race."

The Constitution provided, that "any church not calling itself Unitarian, yet sympathizing in the spirit and objects of the association, might be represented in it." Also, that "no ecclesiastical power or authority should ever be assumed by the association, or delegated to it."

Among other officers of the association were six business-committees ; namely, on churches, on Sunday schools, on missions, on charities and reforms, on publications, and on church-art.

It was also provided, that "at each annual meeting there should be a convention-sermon or address ; written reports from the Executive Board and the several business-committees ; a public discussion of matters pertaining to Christian philanthropy and the religious life ; and the administration of the Lord's Supper."

Mr. Judd was appointed one of the Executive Board, and chairman of the committee on churches. He was, of course, deeply gratified in seeing the plans which he and his brethren had formed thus fully consummated.

About the last of September, with his little girl of eight years old for company, he again visited the White Hills. Proceeding across the State to Barnet, Vt., he passed through the pleasant valley of the Connecticut to his beloved Northampton home.

During this visit, he was in a most genial, happy state of feeling ; a boy once more under his father's roof, and by his mother's side. He was interested in noticing every thing about the town. To the annual cattle-show and fair he gave much attention. The various kinds of fruits and garden-vegetables he examined closely, with a view to ascertain the best kinds. He wrote, almost daily, graphic, picture-like letters to his wife, placing before her all that was being said and done.

Oct. 5, he writes : " Yesterday was rainy. We stayed in the house, about the fire, talking, laughing, joking. We boiled chestnuts ; ate pears and peaches ; talked about the reason of using hops in making yeast ; whether P——n said Jenny Lind painted ; the effect of poor land to make Democrats ; whether there was a natural law of reaction in human affairs." He gives minute directions about his affairs at home. His mind seems to have been in an unusually active state. He preached his views of the church here.

Leaving Northampton, he proceeded to New York, where he spent a few days, availing himself of whatever of interest he found there. But of this city he writes to his wife: "It is not agreeable to me. It is a dreadful impersonation of human life; nothing real, nothing common, but a vast hungry shadow of things. To meet so many people whom you never saw, between whom and yourself is such a chasm, — 'tis horrible."

After paying short visits to Philadelphia and Washington, he repaired to Baltimore, to be present at the Unitarian Autumnal Convention, to attend which his people had cheerfully contributed the means. He had hoped to introduce for discussion before the Convention those topics relating to the church which were of so much interest to his own mind. But other matters, previously arranged by the business-committee, occupied nearly the whole session of the Convention. He did, however, at the very last of the meeting, find an opportunity briefly, but eloquently, to indicate his views. He felt disappointed and rather saddened at not being able to secure for these subjects more prominence, but consoled himself with the thought that they were fairly introduced, and that, on the *next* year, they would receive the chief attention. He presented this subject also in sermons in Brooklyn and in Baltimore.

Happy was he in returning to his own people, and, as he wrote while absent, to "what is to me the most beautiful spot on earth, the parsonage."

He now addresses himself in great earnestness to the realization of his wishes among his own people, — the bringing of *all*, parents and children, to consider themselves as part and parcel of the church of Christ, and to express this conviction by receiving the symbols of his death in communion with each other. He meets the children to talk with them about the meaning of the Lord's Supper, and the fitness of their joining in it. He meets the adults of his congregation at private houses again and again ; and they familiarly discuss the subject. He draws up, has printed, and circulates among them, the following Declaration, which he proposes shall be signed by every individual under his pastoral charge, by family : —

" CHRIST CHURCH, AUGUSTA, ME.

" Being no longer strangers, but heirs of the covenant confirmed before of God to the fathers, we, the undersigned, pastor and people, parents and children, constituting Christ Church, Augusta, of the Unitarian Church of Maine, of the church universal, express the following : —

" We recognize the church, co-ordinately with the family and the state, as a divine and permanent form of human society.

" We confess to the authority of God's most holy Word, and cherish the dispensation of grace and truth by Jesus Christ, his Son.

" We believe in the unity of theology, religion, and morality, and the harmony of nature and revelation.

" We hold to the Christian ministry, worship, and rites.

" We aim at the highest Christian culture, spiritual birth and growth, and the perfection of our natures.

"We will seek to bring up our children in the nurture and admonition of the Lord.

"We will do good as we have opportunity.

"We will aid in the extension of the kingdom of Christ in the earth.

"So far as in us lies, we will live peaceably with all men.

"It shall be our endeavor to do justly, love mercy, and walk humbly with our God.

"Acknowledging the essential unity of the Christian body, we claim the right of private judgment, and the sanctity of the individual conscience.

"We would live agreeably to the laws of God, and die in the hope of a glorious immortality."

He has several meetings of his people to consider this declaration, the final result of which was, that it received the hearty approval of his people by an almost unanimous vote. He gets ready a blank book to serve as a register of names subscribed to this declaration. He had, for a few months previously, omitted to administer the Communion at the regular period; and the last time the table was spread, when the hour came for this service, his feeling that they were then entirely on a wrong basis was so strong, that he did not administer the emblems. He then said to his people, with the deepest feeling, and in the most solemn manner, in reference to dismissing the congregation and administering the rite to a solitary few, "that he NEVER SHOULD DO IT AGAIN."

But now all the indications among his people are as favorable as he could hope. Some who had always stood aloof from any thing pertaining to the *church,* exclusively, come forward and support his views. He is cheered by the prospect of the consummation of his long-cherished desires. His whole nature seems peculiarily harmonized with itself. His affections go forth to his family friends with even more than wonted tenderness. To his mother he despatches short familiar missives of his daily life, more frequently than usual. To his brother H——i, he writes: " I remember your fraternal kindness when I was in New York. Many years may we all live ; in love, purity, and piety, may our days go by ; may the world be better for our having lived in it ! God keep us in his covenant unto the end ! "

By letter to Rev. Mr. Palfrey of Belfast, Nov. 2, he says : " The question you asked me at Baltimore, ' Shall we not have a meeting of the Ministerial Association ? ' has risen with great force on my mind since I got home. I feel that we have commenced a great work; that we are only at the beginning of things, and of mighty things ; and never more than now did I feel the need of conference with my brethren, and prayer to Almighty God. Curiosity and interest are awake everywhere. There is a waiting for the dawn. The movement in other places hangs somewhat on our lead. There is need of fuller explanations than our association-documents contain.

" More than all, we have hitherto conferred somewhat in the mist, somewhat in doubt. But having taken the decisive step; having, so to say, just landed on the shores of that great country that has been the object of so much toil and anxiety, we are now in a condition for fair and calm deliberation.

"Shall we have a meeting?"

In another letter to the same, Dec. 20, he says: "It has seemed to me, that we, some of us, ought to publish to the world some of our church-principles, views, and plans. There is a spirit of inquiry awake in this vicinity. Yet there is hardly a published word anywhere that can be got hold of. Our own people need to see the thing in print. It is matter to be pondered. Our 'Report' even does not explain itself to anybody. I propose there be published a book of this sort: 'The Church, in a series of Discourses by Clergymen of the Unitarian Church of Maine. Boston: Crosby and Nichols.'

"I am willing to take all the risk of publication; and what I want is, that any of us whose minds have been exercised in this matter should give to the world a discourse upon it. You take up one point, I another, &c., &c. I want we should show a kind of organic, unitary front. I am tired of so much personality. For my own part, I have several discourses I might put in. Have you not preached some sermons that are *just the thing*?

"I repeat, *I take all the risk*."

And again to Mr. P., Dec. 24, he writes: "Into our hands, my dear brother, God has thrown the initiation of the great cause. It must come from Unitarians: it can come from nowhere else.

"Suppose a man does say '*I won't*,' we mustn't

mind it. Suppose one to say, 'I won't consider myself a sinner, or that I have religious responsibilities, or that I ought to lead a spiritual life, ought to love God,' &c. &c., — we go to work, and endeavor to *convince* him of these things. Suppose your child says, 'I won't be your child,' or 'I won't keep the sabbath,' or 'I won't go to school,' you just *assume* these points, and then go ahead.

"We shall find plenty of the 'don't-care' sort of folk. It is our duty to make them care.

"We have the *authority* of God, the Bible, history, reason, common sense; and, if higher is wanted, I know not where to look for it.

"My people at this moment are in an interesting state. The great, the solemn question is now before them, 'Will we be a church, to all intents and purposes?' We have had several meetings. No question can be so searching. There is shaking among the dry bones, I assure you. I never felt that I could preach the gospel as I can now. I never felt what a sword the spirit is as now. I will report results in due time: there are doubts and scruples and hesitancies, of course.

"Would that all our churches could move together in this!

"So I must prepare that volume of discourses without your help. I am sorry.

"We have asserted the church of *all* our churches; the next step is for these churches, that is, *each individual church*, to assert the same of itself. This is essential. But, slow and easy, there is time enough."

He lectures before lyceums at Richmond, Gar
diner, Kennebunk, Portland. He has immediate
engagements for lyceum lectures at Salem and Gloucester, and a large number of similar engagements
for the coming winter.

He engages to preach in Boston the first Thursday Lecture of the year 1853. With great labor, he
condenses, as far as possible, his views on the birthright church into one discourse. He rejoices to
have an opportunity to lay them before a clerical
audience.

1853.

Mr. Judd preaches to his people the first sermon
of the new year, and, as was his wont, reviews the
one just past. He speaks of those who in this
period have passed away from sight, — of those who
may depart the coming year. He notices the great
mortality there has been among his people, and asks,
" Who of us will be missed from these seats on
another New Year's day? Which of you shall I
next be called upon to lay in the grave? Or will it
be you that shall perform the last sad duties to the
cold remains of your pastor? "

The succeeding day, with much fatigue, he com-
pletes his preparation for the Boston Thursday Lecture of the same week. At night he leaves his home,
to be conveniently situated the next morning for
starting at an early hour on his way to meet his
engagements in Boston and the towns near by.

And now, the subject of this history having arrived at the fulness of manhood's years ; his mental and moral powers, if not yet at the acme of their capabilities, at least having reached a high degree of development and maturity, — let us pause in this life-drama, and notice the prominent characteristics which make him, as a man, what he is.

22

CHAPTER VII.

RELATION TO THE MINISTRY.

EARLY POSITION AT AUGUSTA.

THE object of this chapter is to unfold and explain at large many points which have been but cursorily hinted at in the preceding one.

Augusta, the scene of Mr. Judd's ministerial labors, being the capital of Maine, and occupying rather a central position, has always been regarded religiously, as well as in other respects, an important post. The Unitarian church in this place was one of the earliest of that name established in the State. It was at first small, and was sustained principally by a few individuals. Previously to Mr. Judd's settlement there, a number of clergymen had preached for the church, for longer or shorter periods, and one or two had been settled as pastors; but, for various reasons, no one had remained a great length of time.

When Mr. Judd entered into the pastoral relation with this church in 1840, it was still so feeble as to require aid from the American Unitarian Association. But, few in numbers, and somewhat cold in religious feeling, as were the people whose charge he assumed, he entered upon his labors with the warmest desire for the promotion of the highest, the spiritual interests of his whole flock. While he embraced the general principles known as Unitarian or Liberal, he brought into their service all the ardor of feeling, all the desire for spirituality and devotion, of those called Orthodox, in communion with whom his early life had been passed. On his first intercourse with the Unitarian denomination, he felt the coldness of intellect too much predominating over fervor of spirit. And, while he saw full well that this was a natural result of the opposition it had had to contend with, and the controversy in which it had been forced to expend much of its energy, he believed the system itself pregnant with life-giving, spiritual warmth, and felt that the time had come for bringing forth its legitimate fruits of devoted piety.

A high reverence for truth, and a spirit of earnest, religious devotion, two features which had strongly marked his previous course, inspired him at the outset, and formed the basis of his whole career as a Christian minister. The very first sermon he ever wrote, while yet unlicensed to preach, was from the text, " Buy the truth." He had a high sense of the consistency, the sacredness, the imperiousness of truth. He regarded it as the element of the soul. He believed it manifested to us by means of an internal, corresponding ideal, and that a man's own consciousness must therefore be the arbiter as to what is truth. He felt that man's better nature had been much abused and fettered by infusions of error, the tenets of mere sect. He rejoiced to see strugglings for release, and was happy to witness tokens of change.

He sought for and embraced truth in its simplest, most unsophisticated forms. He did not care to make out a formal system of doctrine. He wished no creed but the simple language of the Bible. He took the words of Jesus with childlike trust to his own heart, and gave them out to his people as the guide of their lives, and, if obedient to them, their passport to heaven. Christ was the grand idea that underlay all his preaching. To be Christ-like was the alpha and omega of all his teachings. He presented Christ to his people as the life of their life, the wellspring of their souls ; his cross, the burden of life which all must bear, and which, if borne well, would bring forth flowers and fruit to their souls. His church he caused to be designated as Christ Church. His sermons were practical rather than theoretical. He at once looked to the spiritual needs of his church, and, from the first, began to labor with a systematic bearing upon the growth of his whole congregation in Christ-likeness.

To this end, besides the regular ministrations of the sabbath, he early commenced meeting his people socially at private houses for religious conversation. Baptism and the Lord's Supper he regarded, the one as a seal of Christian birth, the other as a means of growth in Christian graces, — both open to all, and equally binding upon all. At the very beginning of his ministry, it grieved him that so very small a proportion of his hearers seemed to feel the obligations of Christians resting upon them ; that so few

brought their children to baptism ; so few observed
the ordinance appointed in remembrance of himself
by the great Founder of the Christian system, under
which they lived, and the mighty blessings, civil as
well as religious, which it conferred upon them.
One of the first topics of conversation at these religious meetings was Baptism and the Lord's Supper.
Not that he considered these ordinances as possessing
any inherent efficacy ; that the baptismal water or
the eucharistic bread and wine conferred on the
recipients any peculiar sanctity ; but rather that their
tendency was to bring such as observed them to a
fuller sense of the inevitable obligations arising
from their having birth under the Christian dispensation ; obligations equally binding upon all, and
to which they added nothing by complying with
these observances.

In his sermon called "The Beautiful Zion,"
preached within the first year of his settlement,
are found the following passages : —

"The beauty of Zion," he says, "will be enhanced
by the number of those that come to her altars. The
entire mass of the Jewish population frequented the
courts of the Lord, and contributed to the services
of the temple. In the apostolic days, whole families,
children included, joined in the commemoration of
Christ, and participated in the use of the sacred
emblems. The eastern and western churches, in
their prominent divisions, — the Greek, Roman, and
Episcopal, — permit the privileges of the Eucharist
to all who choose to enjoy them. It is an innovation
of Protestantism, I believe, that discriminates access

22*

to the altar. But, says the Psalmist, '*all they in Zion appear before God*.' It is desired and expected that all who love the Lord Jesus Christ should remember him in his death. I know of but one pre-requisite for church-membership ; that is, love to Christ. This may include the young as well as the old, and would shut out no one who aims at a conscientious fulfilment of his religious obligations."

As years passed on, Mr. Judd presented to his people, from time to time, a rich variety of topics, fitted to awaken thought, to expand the intellect, to enlarge the sphere of knowledge, to arouse sensibility to nature's teachings, to administer consolation to the afflicted, to throw a cheering light upon the transition from this to the invisible world, and, more especially, to enlist the affections of the heart in love to God and love to man, and to deepen the spirituality of the soul's life. But, amid all these, and as a means of forwarding all valuable Christian progress, ever and again he returned to the prevalent distinction between the church and the world, which he considered a formidable barrier to the universality of Christian character.

On entering into connection with the people of his charge, he found a covenant which had been the basis of their church-organization. All that was required of those considering themselves peculiarly members of the church was simply writing their names under this covenant. But Mr. Judd did not at all insist on this. He invited to the communion, as it was administered from month to month, all who loved the Lord Jesus ; all who felt interested in the blessings of the gospel, or who were religiously disposed. Yet almost the whole congregation would turn their backs upon this memorial·of their Saviour, and the urgent entreaties of his minister, who, with sinking heart and a despairing sense of the futility of his labors, would descend to break the bread and administer the cup to the scattered few that remained.

At length, as has been seen, many parents became so far aroused as to bring their children to baptism, until nearly all his flock had received this Christian seal. Instead of dismissing the congregation, and making the communion a private service, separate from the other acts of religious worship, it was made a part of the regular afternoon-exercises. This practice was much more consonant to Mr. Judd's feelings than that of sending away, as it were, those to whom he would gladly administer, to the fullest extent, the bread and the water of life. By this means, some few were added to the number of partakers; but, in the main, very little was effected. Many, disliking the constraint and embarrassment it imposed upon them, finally began to absent themselves from church on such occasions. A good deal of dissatisfaction ensued; and so much opposition to the course at last arose, that it was found expedient to abandon it, although a return to the old method was, to use Mr. Judd's own words, "like plunging a dagger into his heart."

THE BIRTHRIGHT CHURCH.

As years elapsed from the time of his settlement, Mr. Judd's mind had, by degrees, become more and more impressed with the idea that the prevailing sentiment as to what constitutes church-membership is erroneous ; and, for the last two or three years of his labors, his attention was mainly centralized to this one point. He wrought out his views into a regular form, which, to his own mind, was consistent and truthful. He felt that they were of vital importance to the welfare of the church, if not, indeed, to its preservation as a distinct organization. He felt, also, that his maturity of years entitled him to speak out, not only to his own people, but to the world at large, the conclusions of his own mind. He presented them in a distinct manner to his congregation ; he brought them out very definitely before the association of the clergymen of his denomination in Maine ; he introduced them to the Autumnal Convention of Unitarians at Baltimore ; he prepared to lay them before a clerical audience in Boston, — all of which has been already stated.

His fundamental position was, that the church, equally with the family and the state, is of divine appointment. Touching this subject, he says, " I would have the church resume the position in human society which God designed it to hold. There are three, and but three, great, eternal, and divine organizations of human beings, — the family, the state, the church. The first organizes the conjugal element ; the second, the political element ; the last, the religious element. The first gives us a home; the second, a country; the third, heaven. The symbol of the first is the fireside; of the second, in ancient parlance, a throne; of the third, the altar. These three are holy, and have their foundation in the unalterable texture and appetency of the human mind. These three, in a true community, exist in harmony; these spheres are respectively different. Over and in and through the whole is one God, universal Sovereign, Legislator, Father. While other things, needful for the moment, rise, perform their office, and pass away, these alone remain.

" In each of these, all men are. To each of them, every human being sustains a fundamental *birth-relation*. We are born into the family, into the state, into the church. We continue in them all, until, by due process, we are disowned from the first, banished from the second, excommunicated from the last. As no man remembers the time when he began to be in the state, so he should never know the time when he *began* to be in the church."

He continues: "God entered into solemn covenant with Abraham, and with his seed for ever, with the special promise, that in him all nations should be blessed. This was the gospel, Paul tells us, preached before unto Abraham. Under that covenant, a church was gathered. This church was a heritage; into it the children were born, in it they were trained up; all it had, it gave them. This church had in its keeping the precious promise of universal blessing, and the great doctrine of the one God. Christ came to fulfil the oath sworn to our

father Abraham, that all nations should be included
in the covenant-blessings of God.   Christ enlarges
and spiritualizes the old covenant.   The same law
of transmission and continuity holds.   Children are
born into the Christian church.   'Of such,' says
Christ, 'is the kingdom of God,' — the new, the
all-comprehensive, and heavenly dispensation.   The
command is, 'Feed my sheep,' 'Feed my lambs.'
Peter says, 'The promise is unto you and to your
children.'   Paul declares the children of believers
are holy.   The new era is inaugurated ; Christianity,
as we call it, becomes an institution, a common-
wealth.   Whatever other changes, there is none in
the fundamental principle, that the church transmits
itself by natural succession, that the lambs follow
the sheep, that children are trained up into that
which their parents are."

Mr. Judd maintained, that baptism in the Christian church, as circumcision in the Jewish, presup-
poses a church-estate ; that it does not introduce
into the church, but is merely the *seal* of the covenant eternally existing between God and his children
and their seed for ever.   And to this view he derives
support from the Cambridge Platform of 1648.

He did not regard Baptism and the Lord's Supper
as the only ordinances of the church.   His own words
on this point are as follows : " The church is not that
which has in its keeping, and observes, the sacraments
of the Lord's Supper and Baptism alone.   These are
ordinances, but not all the ordinances.   Preaching
is an ordinance, public prayer is an ordinance ; and
one ordinance is as sacred as another.   The church

comprehends all the ordinances.   They are all parts
of Christian service, all means of grace alike.   Its
peculiar devotional ordinance is prayer, its peculiar
church-ordinance is singing, its peculiar instructional
ordinance is preaching, its peculiar festal and com-
memorative ordinance is the Lord's Supper.

"The idea of the church implies all these things ;
one as much as another, the whole as well as a
part.   I would root out the notion, that a part of the
church-services are for one set of people, and another
part for another.   In entering the church, I would
have every man enter the whole reality that the
church is.   I would have the masses and the children feel and acknowledge that the whole church is
theirs ; not only its sabbath, and its Bible, and its
singing, but its communion likewise.   I would do
away with the notion, that a different moral, spiritual, or religious responsibility rests upon one more
than upon another.   If it is the duty of one man to
pray, it is the duty of all men to pray.   If it is a sin
for one man to dance, it is a sin for all men to dance.
If it is the duty of one man to partake of the communion, it is the duty of all men."

The object of the church he considered to be
"Christian nurture, regeneration, or the birth of the
spirit, the communication of the life of God and
spirit of Jesus to the soul of man ; and that children
were to *grow up* Christians *in the church,* and not
out of it; that the outward fertilizers, or means of
growth, were the sabbath, prayer, singing, the
preached word, and the communion of the body and
blood of Christ."

These ideas he claims to have been originally implied in the gospel, and practised upon in the early ages of Christianity. Here are his own words again : " The gospel did originally embrace children. Christ, if I may so say, laid the foundations of his kingdom in the heart of childhood. The 'new covenant,' the enlargement of the Abrahamic covenant, threw itself about infancy, and girdled, with its promises, its sanctity, and its beatitudes, the generations as they rose. But something intervened to prevent the progress of Christianity towards its consummation in the ages ; something intervened to suspend the beautiful law of nature and of God, whereby what is most blest and most pure descends from father to son. This hindrance was the doctrine of total depravity, a correlative and offshoot from the dogma of the Trinity ; a monstrosity in human speculation, an unheard-of thing in the history of philosophy, a Upas-tree in the fair field of the evangelical dispensation. Through the monk Augustine, this came ; it got into the Christian church ; it was decreed orthodoxy. Like a dyke it rose, right in the midst of the fairest flow of things the world has ever seen ; like a volcano, it was upheaved in the midst of the most beautiful scheme that ever gladdened the eye of an angel, and distorted every thing, turned currents out of their course, and filled the bed of a pure Christianism with blackened scoria, and all horrid shapes of wild and woful thought.

" The old covenant that comprised children with their parents is broken. The children are born corrupt, of the devil, out of the Christian pale. In a word, as I have said, this dogma unchurched all the children; it flung the generations, as they rose, loose out into the world; it broke the goodly covenant-relation Christ made with his children and his children's children for ever."

And now, he says, "We come to a pause in human affairs, so far as Christianism is concerned. We see the whole church is thrown into a dilemma. Evermore the question presses, 'What shall we do with the children?' 'Water-baptism is regenerative,' the high priests of the new school said. 'Baptize the children, and we shall cure their depravity, renew their natures, and thus recover them to the church.' So things went on for some centuries. After a sort, the children were huddled back, like melancholy lambs, into a fold from which they had been rudely driven.

"Calvin and Luther, still holding firmly by the Trinity and total depravity, yet had the common sense to see that water could not purge the soul; and, while they admitted infant-baptism, they still suffered the infant to be out of the church. They baptized the innocent vagabond, and then let it run wild still. At least, this is the final result of Calvinism, or the older Augustinianism, in America.

"The consequence," he adds, "is, that, in the United States at least, nine-tenths of the people are growing up, in a technical sense, sinners, unchristian, unholy, prayerless, hopeless. The covenant which God made with Abraham, that in him, through Christ, all nations should be blessed, — a covenant with him and his seed after him to all generations, —

is broken ; the promise that these great blessings were to us and our children is falsified ; the cardinal principle that children are of the kingdom of God is set at nought, and the beautiful law of religious perpetuity interrupted for ever. A single thing, a little thing apparently, a short paragraph, a penful of ink, — the doctrine of total depravity, — has done all this."

"What now calls itself the church and Christian is a little knot of people in Christendom, a few scores in what is called a *society*, a few hundreds in our towns, — in no sort of covenant-relation even with their own wives or husbands, fathers or mothers, brothers or sisters, sons or daughters ; a little knot, I say, and all the rest is the world, — Christendom, not gentildom ; not so good as that, but devildom.

" Next, what ?   Invariably, inevitably, this : these few must try salvatory measures on the great multitude of outsiders.   But how many shall be saved ? The elect, says ultra-Calvinism.   We must preach to all, but expect to save only a few, says a more moderate Calvinism.   Do not dispute about these things, says Methodism ; but make a rush, and save as many as you can.   Universalism hushes the whole trouble, and says, Never you mind, all will be saved. Unitarianism, — *horresco referens*, — legitimate descendant of the old-church patriarchs and prophets, of the Messiah and the apostles, — sole heir of a gorgeous and a divine antiquity, — sighs and takes on ; does not know ; tries ; is, like Ephraim, ' a silly dove, without heart : they call to Egypt, they go to Asyria.'

"The great question now is, How shall we get men into the church? The voice of the true church cries even in the false church, Give me back my children. Now, to get people back into the church, Romanism, or the Catholicism of the fourth century, devised the scheme of water-regeneration. This alone saved the church of that time from extinction. So in the English Church, the latent, perhaps, yet really vital, question of all questions is, How shall we get the people into the church? And that sect also baptizes them in."

In New England, Mr. Judd instances the revival-system as a means of replenishing a wasting church. He recognizes the fact, that, in this cause, devout clergymen have labored and worn out health and life, and yet this system is found to be a failure. He shows, by many statistics, that the proportion of church-members at this day, compared with forefathers' time, "has dwindled into a small, and is yearly dwindling into a smaller, minority." "The world," he says, "is every year gaining on the church. Revivals, the grand harvest-seasons of the church, are losing their power. With paper and pencil, one can easily figure out the final issue." He notices the heart-sickness and discouragement of many ministers, — "This having a sacred rite, and having so few to attend it; seeing the multitudes going away; seeking to get them to it; blamed if there be no increase; feeling as if they would abandon the whole thing; coming almost to despise what they tenderly love; shaping a sermon for their object, now this way, now that; some tempted to

demolish the pale and have no church, others painfully struggling to augment its numbers."

And then, in the discourse upon this subject from
which the above summary of his views has been
deduced, he comes to this general conclusion : " I
see no possible escape from these difficulties, but
first to depress the pale wholly out of sight, and then
to bring it up, with a wider sweep, around the whole
worshipping congregation.   I know of no other way
of restoration than that whereby the children of
Christian parents may be included in the Christian
covenant and pale, the system of forms and doctrines,
and the sphere of blessings and responsibilities, in
which their parents are.   I mean, that whatever may
be the highest Christian institutions known to Christendom ; whatever be conceived to be the most sacred
communion and fellowship ; whatever typifies the
highest Christian experience, or points most peculiarly to the supreme relation we hold to God, Christ,
and the moral universe, — that into that, most essentially, most integrally, most fully, the children be
admitted ; and, inasmuch as the church does stand
for the highest Christian institution, and is the most
sacred communion and fellowship, and typifies the
deepest Christian experience, and the supreme relation we sustain to God and Christ and the moral
universe, into that church the children should be
admitted.   More than admitted ; that into it they be
born ; that of it they form a part ; insomuch that
they shall never know the time when they were not
in and of it, any more than they know the time when
they began to be citizens of the state, or when the

first summer morning shed its sweet beams upon
them, or the first sabbath enfolded them in its sanctity and rest. If there be a school of highest Christian discipline, a circle of highest Christian culture,
a theatre of highest Christian action, a place of highest Christian life, peace, enjoyment, I contend that
not only the children, but the great mass of the
community, should be included in it. And such a
school, circle, theatre, place, is the church. I would
take this which we call the church, with all its awful-
ness and beauty, all its beatitudes and obligations,
and not wait to see if I can get here and there a man
into it, but take it and carry it right under the whole
bulk of the rising generation, and endeavor that they
shall all be in it. I would carry it under the yet
unborn generations, and see to it that all share in it
as their birthright."

In carrying out this idea, he adds, " Where the
ground is open, I would cease to gather people in
what are called *societies,* with a peradventure that
by and by they will organize within the society a
coterie called the church, to be by and by increased
by additions from without. I would gather people
in church-estate, and no otherwise, and at once and
for ever. I would gather them and their fami-
milies for the whole blessing that the church is:
they should be committed to the Bible, the sabbath',
the preaching, the communion, alike. If people are
not fit to come together in this way, they are not fit
to come together at all. Religious or Christian
society defines the word *church;* and any man that
is fit to be a member of a Christian society is fit to

23*

be of the church. Any man that is fit to unite in one church-ordinance, be it singing or prayer, is fit to unite in another, even the communion. So that if the question were upon starting a new Unitarian *society*, so called, in any place, the real thing should be the forming of a new Unitarian church.

"I would bring people together with the feeling, that, if they accept one ordinance of the gospel, they are bound to accept the whole; that, if there be a special centre of sanctity, or holy influence and regenerative impression, there, if nowhere else, all are bound to be. If I am a pastor, and the people are my flock, and there be any one place where the grass is greener and the waters clearer than in another, there, by all obligations of the soul and God, am I bound to take them all. If Christ is bread and water, I am bound to give him to all who need salvation.

"As to existing things, I would have our societies, so called, become *churches* as rapidly as possible. I would have a religious society feel that it is a church, and realize at once all the grandeur of its position and vastness of its obligations. I wish all people at once to enter upon all its ordinances, all its privileges, and all its duties. Especially, I wish that *all the children* should be brought at once into their true church-position, and be trained up, now and evermore, in the central sanctity, the holy of holies of the Christian dispensation."

In still more extended furtherance of this idea, Mr. Judd says : "Inasmuch as our country has certain political divisions called States, and these divisions represent a certain amount of available and suggestive unity, I would have all the churches in a State form a general church of the State ; the bond of union and centre of action to be a State Association. . . .

"I believe that if the church would in this way adjust itself, I will not say to the world, but to the community in the midst of which it is ; if it would become the open, free vehicle of divinest Christian ideas to the masses and to the children ; if it would fold in its central sanctity the generations as they rise ; if, instead of reserving to itself, it would give out its most sacred, its heavenly food, and communion and hope, to its own children born into it, — we should witness such a development of spirituality, such an advancement in all Christian virtue, such a progress of the age to millennial glory, as history has never yet recorded. I do say, that on the present church-system the millennium can never come, — never ! It recedes every year."

In a sermon entitled "The Communion for Sinners," he asks, "What is involved in the participation of these emblems ? what in becoming a communicant of the body and blood of Christ ?"

He answers, "Not that a man assents to a creed, not that he can answer a series of theological questions that may be propounded to him, — a clear head for theology and a simple heart for the ordinances being distinct things ; not that the opinions of others are of consequence, that we satisfy everybody or anybody ; nor that participation implies that a man is not a sinner, or that he is regenerated, but that a man should desire to receive whatever the sacrament is fitted to give; that it is not so much a test as an aid of character; that it is the earnest of hope, as well as the reward of attainment; that it does not declare that one is good, but that he would be good; not that he has experienced salvation, but that he is looking forward to it; and that the communion does not offer itself to the confirmed believer exclusively."

He then inquires into the direct and immediate effects of the emblems, and finds it, not miraculous, not mysterious, not possessing any intrinsic efficacy nor any virtue from sacerdotal consecration; but mainly suggestive and associative; as a summary of his life and death; a condensed gospel; a visible token of great invisibilities; silent preachers, an inarticulate utterance of profound truths; as awakening personal questions of salvation by him; as epitomizing the highest truths of the religion of Christ.

He said it was necessarily implied that a man, though a sinner, must have some interest, some earnestness, some faith, some desires to be a better man.

He contended, that, if the sinner may partake of the benefits of the blood of Christ, and find therein cleansing, health, and salvation, he may also participate in the emblem which typifies that blood; if the sinner, however vile, or however gross his depravity, may be urged to come to Christ; then, if the bread and the wine do in any degree aid the approach to Christ, may he be urged to partake of these emblems ; and if the symbols are too holy to be touched by profane hands, how much more should Christ, the eternal substance of this fleeting shadow, be deemed too holy for the approach of sinners !

He regarded the communion as a means of grace, a means of bringing sinners to Jesus, a means which like prayer, like the sabbath, like preaching, God will bless to our redemption and ultimate sanctification.

With such views in regard to Christian nurture and church-relationship, as may well be supposed, Mr. Judd took great interest in the training of children — in the impressions which young minds should receive. Even before he became a pastor or a father, as early as 1838, he could find no better subject for a lyceum lecture in his Northampton home than " Children." As is shown in the previous pages, in the early part of his ministry he commenced bringing them under the gentle teachings and moral influences of nature, in the rural May walks to which he invited them. However much he might be pressed with various labors, on some beautiful morning in the month of May, he would have all the children of his charge — and but too happy if any others would join them — gather around his cottage, from which he would lead them forth to witness the fresh resurrection of nature, to gather wild spring-flowers, and listen to the vernal greeting of the merry wood-birds.

In the same spirit he met the young ladies of his flock, for literary, social, and moral culture. He preached occasional sermons to young men. To impress the fathers and mothers with a sense of their responsibility, he wrote in his own unique manner the sermon, which, after being delivered to his own people, was published in the newspapers under the title of " The Little Coat; " the text being — " His mother made him a little coat." Passing from the letter to the spirit of the subject, he speaks of clothing for the mind and the soul; and endeavors to impress mothers that they should be more solicitous about *such* little coats, than for the fashions of frocks, jackets, or other garments of the body.

" I meet a man in the streets," he says, " literally clothed in rags ; clothed also with manifold tokens of a depraved life.   I ask, Did not his mother, when he was young, make him a little coat ?   When I see a person clothed in humility, entertaining a modest sense of himself and a just estimate of others, unostentatiously attaching himself to great principles, meekly waiting the will of God, reverent of truth, and supple to goodness, I am allowed to conceive, that, when he was young, his mother made for him a little coat. . . .

" These coats last a long time.   Children shall wear them when parents are dead ; they shall wear them in distant lands ; that old family style shall show itself in many places and times.   What sort of clothes are you making for your children ?   Is their vesture wisdom or folly ?   Is it the true beauty of goodness, or a poor imitation from the drapers ? Your words, your acts, go to make up this clothing. Something you did yesterday becomes part of a garment your child must wear many years. . . .

" Young mother, a naked spirit comes to your hands as well as a naked body. You have prepared clothing for the last : shall the first go unendued, picking up what it may wear at haphazard ? Is the body of your child all you have thought about ? It is yours to dress a new, living spirit ; to cut out and make for it celestial attire ; it is yours to give it the robe of immortality. Your older children are even now wearing coats you made for them years ago. Do you like them ? Is it a garment of praise ? Have they a character which you would wish them to wear for ever ? But the child you are dressing for almost the first time, — for whom you are making his first little coat, — what shall he be ? . . . .

" Make the little coat, O mother ! Make it so that it will be no disgrace to him before God or his fellow-men to be seen in it ; so make it that it will be to him a robe of dignity and esteem in the world, and a robe spotless and bright in the kingdom of heaven for ever."

After his ideas as to the birth-relation to the church had been accepted, and in due form concurred in, by all his people, and they had asserted and assumed their responsibility as a Christian church, in a sermon with reference to their new position, he asks : " What then ? Is this the end ? 'Tis only the beginning. Now the great work of life fairly commences, to be continued through time, and perpetuate itself in the endless years of our futurity."

He then began a series of discourses on " Christian Education." In one, he maintained that we think in words. In another, his object was to show the force of the words that children are educated to use, and that become with them familiar, household words, in forming their character intellectually, morally, and religiously. He showed that we become what we are educated to be, and that we may become Christians by being educated to Christianity, according to the wise man, — "Train up a child in the way he should go, and, when he is old, he will not depart from it." He would have children taught forms of words like the following: "God is my Father; I am his child. Christ is my Shepherd; I am his lamb. The church is my company; at its altars I commune. I am a Christian, and am to be like Christ."

In answer to objections made by some of his people to admitting children to the communion, he appealed to that saying of Jesus, "Of such is the kingdom of heaven," and maintained that, if fit for the kingdom of heaven, they were fit for the communion of saints on earth.

UNITARIANISM.

While Mr. Judd, as a Christian minister, ranked himself under the name of Unitarian, he was no sectarian. He was willing to exchange with other professedly Christian ministers who would exchange with him. He was ready — nay, his heart yearned — to be in fellowship with all the good, of whatever name; and he believed the truly good were to be found under every name. How much he longed for Christian intercourse on common ground among ministers of different denominations, — that different sects should unite in love, — has already appeared in the foregoing narrative.　He would, as " Philo " has it, that —

> " The roses white and red of conflict long,
> And vile religious enmities, be tied
> In beautiful bouquets of fellowship."

He believed that different sects would love each other, if they dared to meet in Christian intercourse, and become acquainted.　He had great faith in human nature, and gave due credit to the conscientious convictions of those who differed from him. For religious controversy he had a great distaste ; and in it he never mingled.　He recognized the opposition of other denominations, but opposed their opinions only in self-defence.　The simple gospel was his creed ; and, in his preaching, he loved to dwell upon that which affects the heart rather than that which alone reaches the intellect.

Yet he had definite doctrinal opinions which to him were of inestimable value.　The doctrine of total depravity he considered the fatal root of all religious error.　Difficulty in receiving this was what first shook his faith in Calvinism, and what, at length, became the turning-point in his renouncing that faith.　With that, as a matter of course, fell his belief in the doctrine of the Trinity.　He delighted in the idea of the entire Unity of the Great Supreme, the Lord, God over all, and the unity existing in all his works, which binds all to him, and each to all. In discussing this idea, so glorious to his mind, he

24

would revel in and exhaust the whole vocabulary of unitary words in the language, and still coin others to suit his purpose.

In this light, he gloried in the name Unitarian, and maintained for Unitarianism the highest rank and antiquity.

" As a Unitarian," he says, " I believe in the simple, whole, unqualified truth as it is in Jesus. Unitarianism, as I understand it, is the gospel itself; it is this, I mean, to my own mind; it is this to me, or it is nothing. If I did not suppose Unitarianism to represent the gospel, as it came virginal, verdant, beautiful, from the hands of its God, I should cease to be a Unitarian. Unitarianism is not merely a denial of certain things, nor an affirmation of certain other things : it is the spirit and substance of the gospel itself. It is that, or, to me, nothing."

And again : " I seem to be taking it for granted, that devotion to what we call Unitarianism is a devotion to the truth as it is in Jesus. I do indeed. It is this, or it is nothing, I repeat. It is this, or palsied be this tongue ere it should utter a syllable in its behalf."

A few other passages bearing upon this point deserve a place in this connection : —

" Unitarianism destroys nothing : it restores. It breaks off the withes wherein divine truth is bound, and liberates it. Take Christ away from humanity, and you degrade humanity. Unitarianism, by bringing Christ back from an unnatural and factitious place in the universe, and restoring him to the world as an elder brother, elevates humanity ; and in Christ every one becomes a brother of man and a child of God. . . .

"But why, you ask, care aught about the name, if you only have the thing? I think I do not. Give us the substance of the matter, and perish names, I say. What is the substance of the matter? That the church should fall back on the simple gospel; that it should leave the deserts and fastnesses and briery ways of creeds and denomination, and come into the happy valley of love and evangelical feeling; demolish its idols, its popes, its Calvins, its metaphysics, and return to the sanctuary, the corner-stone of which is Jesus, laid in Jerusalem; the pillars of which extend ' down through all time; the worship of which is in the spirit, and, being so, is one in heaven and one on the earth.'

"What is Unitarianism? It is a system of absolute truth, even as Christianity is. It is not the side of any thing: it is many-sided in itself. It covers the whole of what is, the same as God does. It is not an exigency, or experiment, or device, or temporary want: it is essential, continuous, contemporaneous with rational being, profound as the soul, enduring as the eternity of God, in which its own life is, and its aim is perfected. It is not a cold system: it is warm, genial, vivifying as the Sun of Righteousness, which is its central beam. It is not simply a critical system: it is experimental, operative. While it judges, it produces; and wherein it is most keen and searching, that is but the development of its own purest vitality. It is not simply an intellectual system: it touches the feelings, it thrills all chords of rational sensation; it weeps with Jesus, it energizes with Paul; in the darkest day, its face may be seen to shine like an angel's with Stephen.

"It affirms the unity of the revelations of God in Scripture and in nature. It takes along with itself human reason; it takes along with itself nature; it explains the mission of Christ, — explains it? is it, — the gathering of all things into one, the making of twain one, the reconciliation, the atonement, the propitiation, the communion of saints, the return of the prodigal, faith and repentance, the one body, the one church."

He maintained that the Unitarian church is not a departure from the word of God, but a return to it; that it is orthodox, because it possesses *sound* doctrine, according to reason and scripture; is catholic, as seeing all men one in Christ; apostolic, as having the foundation of the apostles; evangelical, as adhering to the whole scope and spirit of Christianity.

"The doctrines of Unitarianism," he says, "what are they not? Whatever Christ taught, whatever prophet has uttered or martyr died for; whatever truth God from creation has been pouring, from the bright urn of central reality, over the realms of nature, or into the recesses of the soul, — these are its doctrines.

"Unitarianism expresses a great idea, the greatest and profoundest of theological ideas. If there be those who see in it nothing but sectarian partiality and narrowness, I am sorry; I do not. Considered as a name rejected by the multitude, and welcomed by the few, in that sense, perhaps, it is sectarian. But, considered as the name for God's everlasting truth, it is not sectarian. It expresses the highest truth of God, the universe, man.

"But what do I mean by Unitarianism? In what sense do I use the word? In its plain, natural, and strict sense; as expressive of the great unity that God is, that all things are in God; as expressive of this fact, that above the heavens and beneath the foundations of the earth, and through all space and time, God is, God sole and indivisible; that Christ is no part of God or person of the Godhead, but is included in the circumference of the Unity of God. Before there was any Bible or any Adam, or any Christ, God was, one and indivisible; and out of this oneness or Unitarianism of God came the earth and its beauty, Adam and his fleshy nature, Christ and his spiritual nature, man and his immortal nature.

"I mean, then, by the term Unitarianism, that which expresses the spirit in which the Bible was conceived, and the only true method of its interpretation. I mean by it the unity, the harmony of God and man, time and eternity, religion and life, religion and recreation, religion and reason, religion and nature; the unity, the harmony of man and man, nation and nation, things angelic and things terrestrial; or, in the language of the apostle, all things in God.

"I believe that Christ came on this atoning, uni-

24*

fying, unitarianizing errand, to reconcile or make us all at one with God.

"I believe that sin is a departure from God, a breach in the unity that should subsist between the soul and God.

"I believe, that, in proportion as a man becomes, in the highest sense of the word, unitarianized, divinely unitarianized; in proportion as he enters into this harmony, and becomes at one with God; in proportion as he accepts the doctrine and realizes the power of the great Unity, he ceases to sin.

"I believe, furthermore, that the corruptions, errors, wrongs, and woes of the Christian church were owing to the loss of its original Unitarianism.

"There is the unity of the church. I yearn for it, I pray for it. I long to be united to my Methodist brother, and my Episcopal brother, and my Baptist brother, and my Calvinist brother, — my Trinitarian brother, of every name and sort.

"In the unity of God, the unity that Christ prayed for, in the unity that really subsists between all goodness, I feel that I can be, I feel that I ought to be. Heaven speed the time when I shall be! . . .

"Standing on the eminence I now do, I seem to see the narrow horizon of our mortality extending away, and merging in the horizon of immortality. I seem to see, travelling up this steep of the divine Unity, myriads of the human race, on their way to the seats of eternal blessedness, growing out of this unity of heaven and earth; I seem to see heaven encompassing earth, and seeking to irradiate our

pilgrimage, and to breathe into our imperfect life
some of its own loveliness and beauty.

"Clouds lower, and tempest falls, and darkness
gathers; but God is the same, yesterday, to-day, and
for ever: his unitary love and goodness continue on,
and by and by it will shine out as the sun. . . .

"Our circle is wide. It includes all good men
and women under heaven; it loves all whom God
loves; it sends all good men to heaven, without
regard to their speculative notions.

"We, as Unitarians, as Liberal Christians, stand
in the very centre around which, here on the earth,
the great circle of the communion of saints must of
necessity sweep; we are most peculiarly in the
heart of the current of the Holy Spirit, along which,
if I may so say, God is borne, and Christ, and the
holy angels, and all the spirits of the just. . . .

"Standing as we do, so to say, on the infinite
plane of God and the absolute verity of things, we
can, in a sense, see all that God sees, as we approve
all that God approves. Our great and good are
indeed a throng that no man can number. Creed
does not narrow our vision, nor creed limit our
embrace. As Unitarian Christians, we are restricted
neither to country nor age, to color nor condition.
Some of our saints may be found among the Roman-
ists; there are Calvinists whom we recognize as the
children of God; our fellowship reaches as far as
there is a single man on the face of the earth who
fears God and does righteousness. Wherever throbs
one desire for virtue, that we legitimately feel;
wherever arises one prayer for blessing, that legiti-

mately pours on us.   We do not reject a man from
the true church because he believes in total depravity ; we include him rather, because he, in his own
person, is proof that man is not totally depraved.
The martyrs who have died for the truth are our
martyrs ; the heroes who are battling for the right
are our heroes. . . .

"Every virtue that ever flourished beneath the
skies is ours ; every green and sunny spot, sacred to
innocence and repose, is ours ; every great and noble
deed that has blessed mankind is ours ; every deep
and earnest prayer that human lips ever breathed is
ours ; every home where fidelity and piety reign
is ours ; there is no church, no temple, no fane, —
there is no ocean-side, no wooded glade, where the
pulse of man has beaten lovingly, or his thought
dilated sublimely, or his soul aspired divinely, that
is not ours.   And all, too, is Christ's, and Christ is
God's, and we in Christ are in God."

IMPROVEMENTS IN PUBLIC WORSHIP.

Mr. Judd's interest in and approval of an organized association of the churches of the Unitarian
denomination in Maine, have been noticed already.

Another topic which interested him was that of
devising measures for rendering public worship more
impressive.   As a means to this end, he thought a
book might be prepared for church-service, to be
used at the option of the clergymen in the regular
sabbath exercises.   Such a book too, he believed,
would be very useful to small collections of people

wishing a religious service by themselves, not regularly organized into a church, and too feeble to support a clergyman; also to sabbath schools and weekly religious meetings. He considered the materials for such a book rich and abundant in the church-literature of the different denominations of past ages. He would willingly glean from the Roman Catholic church, or any other that furnished prayers and hymns of an elevated, spiritual, and devotional character.

In writing to the Rev. Mr. P. on this subject, he says: " I would suggest that there be a service for the ordination of pastors and deacons, and bishops, if you will. Our deacons ought to be inducted with some little solemnity.

" Also a service for the sea. What quantities of sailors we have in this State! what a seaboard! From Kittery to Calais are thousands, captains, mates, fore-the-mast-men, vessel and all, that ought to have such a book, with a burial service too, for the sea.

" Fast and Thanksgiving are perpetual New England days, both old and of the future: should they not be briefly remembered?

" You would add a page for Christmas. That, at least is our day, shall always be."

Yet the idea of a liturgical service was in his mind quite subordinate, compared with that of the birthright church, or even with church-association. His own words are: " The question of a liturgy is to my own mind a subordinate one. Let us become a church; and, if some liturgical services are desirable, we can have them.   It may be that something of that sort would help the other."

In regard to church-architecture, Mr. Judd felt a great interest.   Taking the ground that it did or *should* symbolize an idea, he maintained that we had no strictly *Christian* architecture; an architecture emblematical of the great leading ideas of Christ's teachings. The Gothic, with its pointed arch and all its upward leadings, he contended, carried the mind all in *one* direction to the great God above, and did not, at the same time, embody the idea of his being brought *at one* with us through Jesus Christ; he our Father, and we his children. He objected that the decorations should be Jewish rather than Christian; showing forth scenes and characters of the patriarchal time, rather than of the time and life of Christ. The great Christian idea of human brotherhood he could not find symbolized, and he disliked the assumption of priestly superiority indicated by the elevation of the minister so far above his people.

He made church-architecture quite a study, collected what works he could find on the subject, and looked forward hopefully to the time when he might have a church built for himself, embodying the true Christian idea, as he understood it.

SUBJECTS OF DISCOURSE, MANNERS, ETC.

Mr. Judd's subjects of discourse were extremely varied, embracing the whole range of human interests. Each was treated in his own original manner, and was eminently suggestive to the minds of others.

The theme most predominant was Christ, on whom he delighted to dwell in every phase of his character and relation to us. The following are some of these themes: "The indwelling Christ; Christ to the believer; The remembrance of Christ; Christ the light of the world; Christ's sympathy with his people; Christ's changing us into his image; Christ passing through the veil; The moral beauty of Christ; Spiritual coming of Christ; Christ the inspiration of Scripture; Christ the hope of the world; Christ the resurrection and the life; Christ our righteousness; Faith in Christ; Christ the rock; Christ the vine; Christ and the scholar; Christ the way, the truth, and the life; Cross of Christ; Christ a mediator; Coming to Christ; Christ and nature." Such are a few among the many subjects of which Christ was the basis.

His sermons upon the great, leading objects he labored for have been often referred to.

An uncommon proportion of his congregation was removed by death. Those occasions led to a large number of discourses on suffering, death, and immortality, which are rich in the sweetest consolation. They illuminate that valley which to so many is dark and fearful, open the portals of eternal life, and, with a glowing faith, reveal the blessedness of those who find a final home in the bosom of their God. From these might well be gleaned a volume rarely adapted to soothe and cheer the sorrowful and mourning heart.

His subjects were often on his mind for months, before he wrote upon them; and, when they were

at length written out, it was with difficulty that his
pen kept pace with the rapidity of his composition.
The clothing of his thoughts seemed to flow in upon
him unbidden.   His subjects so grew upon him, so
stretched out into infinity in their various ramifications, that he often seemed at a loss what to select
from the mass of material lying before him.   There
was a logic in his own mind by which he legitimately
came to his conclusions ; but it was often by jumps
from point to point, natural and easy to him, yet
such that others could not always find the interme-
diate *terra firma* on which to follow him.   He had
an intuitive perception of the separate links of his
chain ; but, from the fact that they were so evident to
his own mind, he could not always point them out,
one by one, to the view of others.   Amid the rapid
flow of thought arising from his comprehensive view,
he could not always wait to assort his ideas in the
most consecutive manner ; and therefore his sermons
may sometimes have left the impression of being a
series of detached thoughts, not very closely related
to each other.

In the illustration of his subjects, he drew largely
from nature and art, from all times and from all
countries, evincing great general knowledge and
reflection, and the most acute observation ; thus
making his pulpit, in an educational point of view,
a rare school for the mental expansion of the young.
Common, daily life he also brought largely under
contribution.   Little incidents of a moral bearing, in
the streets of the city, at the mills, the dam, would
often surprise by their reappearance from the desk,

and lead to the feeling that there "was a chiel amang them takin' notes."

A lady of his church, in writing of him, says: "Very few ministers bring their innermost feelings respecting life and death, and the sorrows of our common lot, so tenderly, and with such simplicity, before their people. I think Mr. Judd had the faculty of entering into everybody's heart, of placing himself in the situation of every mourner, parent, child, brother, sister, or friend; and he seemed to feel just what they felt."

Mr. Judd did not often trust himself to preach without notes. His reflective habits and natural diffidence combined to prevent that ready utterance and self-possession necessary to ensure success in extemporaneous speaking. He therefore very seldom made speeches or took part in discussions at public meetings: he indeed often shrank away to some obscure seat, where he would not be likely to be noticed; and sometimes, when loudly called for, he would not come forward, because he felt he *could* not. As he had very limited opportunity for exchanges, his labor in writing was quite confining.

Mr. Judd's manners in the pulpit were peculiarly modest and humble. He might be seen entering the church with noiseless tread, and passing up the aisle in the most quiet manner, as though he wished nobody to see him. The black robe in which he officiated always draped itself upon him in simple, easy guise, displaying no self-consciousness or ostentation. His face was exceedingly youthful for one of his age; and, in the pulpit, he was often taken for a man of much younger years. His ample forehead and penetrating blue eye gave him a highly intellectual expression; while his fair skin, softened, sandy hair, and delicate small hand, imparted to him a gentle, scholar-like appearance. He so ordered the several parts of church-service, reading the Scriptures, hymns, prayer, and preaching, as to produce a general harmony of the whole. The Scriptures, which he was accustomed to expound as he read along, and the sacred songs, had *meaning* as they fell from his lips. His prayers were usually rather short and informal, poured forth from the present spontaneity of his own spirit. He felt the needs of the hour and the occasion, and ceased when he had uttered the appropriate petitions.

In his elocution, there was a blending of the earnest and the tender. He uttered his words in a subdued tone, but with great distinctness, solemnity, and pathos. He was perfectly absorbed in his subject, and in the duties of the day. Many of his unique expressions would cause a smile to circulate through the congregation, and produce a general rustle in the house; while the deep seriousness of his own tone and look would show, that it was more in sorrow than in mirth he spake, or that simple earnestness in his subject had led to the unexpected juxtaposition of the word or thought. He seldom used much gesture, though occasionally he would throw off a very impressive one.

He often became so pale and trembling from his own emotion, as scarcely to be able to utter the afflictive thoughts that pressed upon his heart. Such an instance was that, when, on first preaching to his people on the birthright church, and enumerating the various expedients of different denominations to get the outsiders into the church, personating his own feelings particularly, he said in tones of grief, "And Unitarianism has folded its hands, and wept." In a sort of despairing anguish, came such expressions as the one quoted a few pages back, "Never, no, never." And, in urging upon his own people the adoption of his views of the birthright church, he said, " I would willingly lay myself in the grave, if, by so doing, I could accomplish this."

The freshness of the thoughts presented, the originality of illustrations, the suggestive character of the discourse, the general information conveyed, the importance of the subjects treated, the clear, rich tones of his voice, and his unstudied manner, all combined to render Mr. Judd a very attractive and popular preacher. His words made an impression that was carried away by the hearer, and which attended him through the week, and prompted to right-doing in the daily affairs of the shop, the office, the factory, and the farm.

CHAPTER VIII.

RELATION TO PROGRESS AND REFORMS.

————

GENERAL POSITION.

In this department of his character, Mr. Judd had no one-sided view to which he was wedded ; no one form of human interest on which he concentrated all his powers, and for which alone he labored. His desires for human welfare were all-embracing, comprehending every form of moral and intellectual improvement. No one more than he was sensible of the many existing evils, and the need of reformations. But, in his labors, he strove rather to lay the axe at the root of the tree than to spend his strength upon the branches. He regarded the spirit of Christ and his precepts as infallible specifics for the cure of every type of moral evil, and sought rather to imbue the heart with these than to enlist the feelings in opposition to any one description of wrong ; believing that, if the fountain was made pure, the streams could not fail to be pure also. "I hardly expect," he says, " to see freedom granted to the slave, or justice to the Indian, until Christian doctrine and principle become a living conscience with the mass of the people."

But, while this was the foundation of his labors,

and the most prominent mode of his exertions, he did not fail to proclaim against particular forms of evil, and to use his most earnest efforts for their suppression. Yet, in this, he pursued mainly an individual course. He could not, in general, unite with organized bodies, because he disapproved their measures. He did not believe in denunciation as a means of bringing people to a sense of duty; he did not believe in reforming people by coercion. "The moral reformer," he says, "must combine beauty in his manner, motives, and deeds, or he cannot persuade men. The moment one, in his spirit or expression, becomes ugly, though he be engaged in the best work in the world, he will enlist no sympathy, kindle no love, and, of course, accomplish nothing."

He relied on enlightening, convincing, and persuading. The spirit of love, persistently exercised in winning the offender from wrong, he believed to be omnipotent. He held to overcoming evil with good. "Instruction," he says, "reaches the intellect; love engages the affections; but denunciation, overpowering both these, convulses the passions, either quickening them into resistance or paralyzing them with fear."

He had nothing of the spirit of party; and, when he had opponents, he did not care to spend breath in disputing with them. He, indeed, would in silence leave his own cause to defend itself by its inherent merits, rather than contend. "Love and honor," he says, "and all gentleness and amenity springing therefrom, must rule in parties, govern

25*

opposites, and qualify antagonisms, such as are inevitable to a free land. Our politicians and reformers, our conservatists and radicals, our woman's-rights men and man's-rights women, our orthodox and our heterodox, rum men and anti-rum men, slaveholders and abolitionists, have got to come to this, — the recognition of the reasonable soul ; the observance of the sovereignty of ideas ; the creed and covenant of our higher nature ; or, in plainer words, to the simple letter of Scripture, which says, ' Provoke not, love one another, overcome evil with good ; ' or, however we may have truth and right on our side, we shall find we are perpetually degenerating to the plane of bestiality and barbarism, and that the disintegration of those moral bonds that should for ever unite us is rapidly hastening." The only reformatory societies he ever joined were " The Sons of Temperance," whose basis of operation, by moral suasion, corresponded with his own views; and "The League of Human Brotherhood."

It was a grievous thing to him to see men of noble mind and heart falling out with each other, and assuming the attitude of antagonists. Touching this point, he has these words : " There is something sublime in the rencontre between Webster and Hayne ; but, let me aver, there is something more sublime, more affecting, bordering more nearly on the deepest pathos we know of, — so touching as, I imagine, to draw tears from those serene orbs of Hope and Love that from the heavens look down on the centuries and us, — in the *parting* of two such men as Buckingham and Webster ; their total sepa-

ration, never more by ingle-side or country's altar to
meet, in heart or hand never more to meet on all
this round globe."

He was not at all radical in his tendencies. In
1841, he writes, " I am, in all valuable and essential
respects, an old-fashioned Unitarian. I would be
an evangelical Christian. I am in theology somewhat of a conservative." At a later period, he says
to his people, " I am sometimes called an innovator.
Your minister is charged with seeking after what is
unique and novel; he has even been classed with
those who would break up existing things, and
demolish the groundwork of existing society. I do
not believe there are half a dozen persons in the
parish, or in the town, who have more reverence
than I have — a cordial, hearty reverence — for old
people, old forms, old houses, old families, old cus-
toms, old churches. There is not one who would
give more to go back half a century, and spend an
evening, a day, a week, with our ancestors."

Again : " We hear talk of being behind the age,
or before the age. For one, I wish to be precisely
at that point where God and my own conscience will
approve of what I am, whether it is behind or before
the age. I think it possible to be very near the
true and the right, on whichever side of the popular
line we may chance to fall; and that I take to be
the identical position of the departed ones, comparing earthly things with heavenly." He further
remarks on this point : " Before the majesty of the
Christian law, if asked where I am, I feel as a noted
character did when they called him out after Jenny

Lind's singing, and can only say, 'I am nowhere.' I mean, there is something better than a side. There must be sides, indeed; but, as to the matter of absolute truth, it is rather a circle than a side,—like the sphere of Hermes, whose centre was everywhere, and whose circumference was nowhere. In questions of policy, there may be sides; but one need not be slab-sided; neither need there be so many sharp edges and barbed points."

He held to the utmost freedom of thought, and the fullest expression of it. While he did not at all sympathize in the ultra-views of some clergymen of the Unitarian body, he did not approve of excluding them from the fellowship of the denomination, because, in the exercise of their own conscientious convictions, they could not look at every thing just as he did. So, in regard to those who differed from him in the means of reform so far that he could not act with them, he was most tolerant and charitable.

The doctrine which in his mind formed the foundation of every species of duty to our fellow-men, was that of universal human brotherhood; embracing all of every color and nation, rich or poor, bond or free, Jew or Mahomedan, Heathen or Christian. He strove to lead men to love their neighbor as themselves; to do to others as they would that others should do unto them; to consider themselves children of one common Father, brethren of Christ, and, in love to each other, to be harmonious followers of the Prince of Peace.

WAR.

The most wide-spreading violation of this principle, and that which he regarded as most hindering the universal spread of the gospel of Christ, was war. This giant evil, whose name to him was Legion, penetrated his soul more than any other; and upon this he inclined to dwell more than upon other forms of human wrong. " Taking country with country, age with age," he says, " war is an infinitely greater evil than intemperance. While the latter has slain its tens of thousands, the former has slain its tens of millions." His early preaching upon this subject, and its consequences upon his chaplaincy to the Legislature of Maine, have already been narrated.

In a lyceum lecture upon " Non-resistance," which he delivered in Augusta, Dec. 1852, are the following passages : " It is said that force and war have aided civilization. I must deny this *in toto*. Almost the whole of ancient civilization, buried by the tide of violence, has been lost to the world. Arts have disappeared, perhaps never to be recovered. The cities of the East, once beautiful and prosperous as our own, are in desolation. The traveller everywhere wanders amid the sepulchres of departed virtues, or traces the footprints of lost attainments. Wherever we turn in the history of nations, says a recent writer, we are met by indisputable evidence of the former existence of ancient chronicles throughout the world, accumulated during countless centuries, now utterly annihilated. The ancient archives in

Greece, Asia Minor, and Syria, the Ptolemaic Library, the Alexandrian Library, which it had taken six hundred years to gather, the literary collections of Indian and Central Asia, the Tyrian annals, the Punic chronicles, the writings of the Arian fathers, the Hebrew Hagiography, the Roman public registers, are all gone. Egypt, possibly the nurse and founder of human civilization ; the productions of her priests and philosophers, the wisdom whence Moses and Plato drew ; the twenty thousand volumes in common use among her people, — are all dust and ashes, or silent, widowed monuments of a glory that was. The memorials of the ancient Britons met the same fate. After the Saxon invasion of England from east to west, Gildas informs us, nothing was to be seen but churches and other edifices, public and private, noble structures, burnt and demolished. The Danes committed to the flames the chief cities of England, where the chief wealth and intelligence of the country, in the arts, in literature, and manufactures, were collected. The Romans have been called the civilizers of mankind. Their first great exploit, says Mr. Taylor, in his 'History of the Fine Arts in England,' was the demolishing of the arts and civilizations of the Etrurians, who, it is well known, were so superior to the Romans in learning, arts, and manners, that the latter were mere savages as compared with that ingenious and interesting people. Mexico has been rendered tenfold more disorderly by our recent attack on her.

"I do not deny that civilization has advanced, yet not by means of, but in spite of, war. . . .

" Christendom expends more in one year on the means and instruments of human slaughter, than has been given to the promulgation of the gospel since Jesus Christ died upon the cross. The American Bible Society congratulates itself on receiving in a certain year $166,000. The same year, the American government expended on its army and navy $20,000,000. . . .

" If that Japan expedition would fling all its cannon and its powder into the middle of the Pacific Ocean, and say to those people, ' We come to you as brothers, from a great, growing, fraternal land ; help us and we will help you ; ' then they would give us the shelter of their harbors, and the facilities of their coal-mines ; nay, help us build warehouses in their streets, and erect telegraph-posts on their hills. Then those children of the evening and these of the morning would rejoice under a common sun, whose beams are an eternal noon to all, — the fatherhood of God and brotherhood of Christ. . . .

" There arises the question of intervention. We want to accomplish certain results, and we mistake the means ; we are in haste, and are not willing to wait the slower movements of God and time. Violence is a quicker remedy than persuasion. The sort of materialistic philosophy in which we are more or less educated, inclines us to draw the sword of steel rather than that of the Spirit. Our object is commendable : we would suppress some evil, or advance some good ; and, instead of asking Jesus Christ how he would have us do, we take counsel of our coarsest instincts, of the traditions of the elders, and dash like Caribs at the end proposed.

" The power of ideas, the force of truth, the omnipotence of example, the consuming energy of love, — these are not popular principles. Even the true force of Christ has been for ages lost to the world, in that his great work in this world has been supposed to be the baring of his naked breast to the keen, vindictive sword of Heaven's violated law.

" Well, we want to help Hungary. And what is the first thought that offers itself to the popular instinct? Why, pour in between the invader and the patriots a score of our gallant troops; shoot down the Austrian, beat back the Russian. The spirit evoked is that of the ramrod.

" The end proposed is commendable; but are we not wholly mistaken in the means? Do we not wholly overlook the power there is in moral force? Are we not more anxious to do something striking, than what is sure? Do we not in this betray the materialism, the grossness, the savageness of our philosophy? Where is our faith in the spiritual, even if it be invisible; in Christ, even if we see him not?

" Intervention! The most solid, enduring, effective intervention America can give, is summarily that of her example. A great and good republic, prosperous, stable, happy, and pure, on these western shores, is the most formidable and terrible thing to tyrants that can be conceived. The despotisms of the old world have as heavy cannon-balls, as sharp swords, as experienced gunners, as we have, and in the end stand as good a chance to come out best in the conflict as we do. They have not free schools; they have not universal suffrage; they have not a free press; they have not an equalization of ranks; they have not a voluntary religion. Here they cannot meet us. Here is our strength. These are our weapons of warfare. If we undertake to fight the devil with his own weapons, we shall find he can use them better than we.

"Intervention! Every day that America lives, tells on the destinies of Europe. Every day the sun passes over us in its progress round the globe, it scatters some bright hint from us to other lands. Every American ship that ascends the Thames, or penetrates the Baltic, practically interferes; every flourishing town, every new school-house, every railroad we build, interferes; our annual statistics interfere; all wholesome laws we pass interfere; humanity, thriving and advancing, interferes. Our not having a standing army is, if I may so say, a most violent interference. This little negative circumstance strikes dread and alarm to the bottom of the heart of the governments of the old world. Cities here without walls, highways without guards, travel without passports, a press without censorship, — these are the things that agitate Europe. . . .

"God once interfered on behalf of oppressed, degraded humanity, on behalf of sin and sinners, in favor of liberty, and against tyrants. How did he do it? He sent his beloved Son into the world to love us, to labor and pray for us, to teach us, and, if need were, to die for us. The mission of Christ to the world is precisely the mission of every Christian man; the mission of Christ to the world is precisely the mission of every Christian nation. If you can understand what Christ's mission was, so can you understand what the proper mission of America is among the nations of the earth."

On the point of Non-resistance, Mr. Judd says: " He whose birth determined the dispensation of history in which our lines have fallen, who founded the *cultus* to which we are attached, in whose name we are baptized, left precepts like the following: ' Resist not evil; render not strife for strife, but, if one cheek be struck, rather turn the other to the smiter; overcome evil with good; pray for your enemies: so shall ye be children of your Father which is in heaven.'

" From this language I educe a certain law of life; a law regulating the relations of the injured and the injurious, of truth and error, virtue and vice; the course of those who would do good, and the conditions of the loving and acting soul; a law applicable indiscriminately to individuals and communities, to families, schools, governments.

" I say the law is indiscriminately applicable to all communities of human beings. I see no cause or color of distinction. In the nature of the case, it refers to human beings in their social relation; and who shall dare limit the extent of these relations? Who shall interpret this language of Christ as belonging to church-matters, and not to state-matters; or as defining the duties of a dozen men, and not of a dozen million?

"It had been said, An eye for an eye, a tooth for a tooth. Christ replies, Nay, that was neither wisely, nor humanly, nor divinely said. There is a better way. Do not injure those that injure you. Benefit them, as the universal Father treats good and evil with rain and sunshine alike.

"I am supremely a Christian, being neither pagan nor Jew, unbeliever nor transcendentalist. I do not presume to vindicate Christ's doctrine; I dare not qualify it; I trust I have too much Christian honor to blink it. I accept it. As a Christian disciple, I would study it; as a Christian teacher, I would enforce it.

"Yet, while I receive it directly from Christ, I have no doubt that he, guided by the holy spirit that was in him, in proposing his system, embodied the accumulative wisdom of ages, condensed the results of the highest rationality, and reflected, in the clear mirror of his own heavenly thought, the fundamental principles of universal human nature."

Applicable also to this subject are the remarks subjoined from an oration before the fire-clubs of Augusta and the neighboring towns, delivered July 4, 1850, in the Court-house Square, Augusta, upon the subject of "Heroism:" —

"There is that heroism which appeals strongly to our sensibilities, which captivates the imagination, and takes with the popular heart. But what is heroism? What is it in its noblest, most divine, most pure exercise? The kings of the earth would make their subjects believe it is physical, military daring. So they have employed bards to sing and historians to record such exploits, and perpetuated the memory thereof in marble and in oil. So, if a man killed one man, it might indeed be murder; but, when he had killed a million, he was a hero. . . .

"Peace, we are told, is unheroic; it is stagnant, tame, corrupting. 'A subtle poison,' in the language of Mr. Alison, 'debases the public mind at such a time. Peace exhibits, indeed, an enchanting prospect; but beneath that smiling surface are to be found the rankest and most dangerous passions of the human heart.' The convulsions of war shake up and renovate this state of things; war is a sort of subsoil ploughing; it is the refiner's fire and fuller's soap; it is the thunderstorm that settles the dust, and clears the sultriness of a hot day.

I am obliged to say there is more heroism, more gallant daring, more generosity and manliness, in one year of peace, than in whole ages of war. I mean that there is more strict, undoubted, legitimate heroism in our steamship and railroad enterprises, in our cotton-mills and saw-mills, in our scythe-factories and starch-factories, in our scouring the ocean for whales, and excavating the earth for its ores, and similar things, than in all the battles of a century. There was more heroism in John Jacob Astor's attempt to found a colony in Oregon in 1812, than in the war that broke it up; more in De Witt Clinton, who about the same time started the project of the Erie Canal, than in the same war that broke that up; more in Whitney, who would give us a railroad to the Pacific, more grappling with difficulties, more fortitude in peril, more coolness in the midst of

assault, than in Leonidas or Odin. I mean at least
to say, that the greatest qualities of the human mind,
which, it may be, war sometimes develops, exist in
full force in peace. . . .

"There is need of heroes at the present moment.
America has need of them, and the kingdom of God
has need of them ; heroes, not of brute force, but of
ideas ; not of waste and ruin, but of reconstruction ;
not of carnage and rapine, but of virtuous action.
The old race of heroes is becoming extinct, and a
new one is rising; old notions of strife and aggran-
disement are supplanted by new ones of peace and
prosperity ; outward excitement and passion yield
to inward enterprise and energy. We want not
heroes in epaulets, but in pepper-and-salt ; not those
of the sword, but of the plough, the loom, and the
anvil. We want heroes of the river and the forest,
of the field and the ocean, of the pulpit and the
forum, of the ballot-box and the senate-chamber. . . .

"Hang up the old musket and the kettle-drum.
The lightnings of heaven are arming for us ; and
recruits from the impalpable air, on the pathway of
the telegraph, are ready to run round the world
in behalf of the great cause of liberty and virtue.
Steam, with all its ponderous agencies, comes up
from the fountains of water, and asks to be enlisted
for God and the right. The press, like the rising
sun, waits to irradiate the whole earth with the
brightness of our thought, the gladness of our love,
the wonders of our genius.

" *Hang up* the musket and the kettle-drum. Take
the spade and the drill, and the mountains flee away

at your approach, the valleys are filled up, and a way, a highway, is made for our God, — a railway is made for our wives and children, for our mothers and fathers, our brothers and sisters, the world over.

"In ancient times, the French had a sacred banner, called the Oriflamme, or Golden Flame, which was used only on august occasions, and when the Christians went out to war with the Infidels. It was a great banner, wrought of silk and garnished with gold, and bearing in its centre a white cross; and, when it was unfurled to the breeze, it glistened like the auroral lights.

"The sacred Oriflamme of America, O ye young men, unfurl! — the banner of freedom, the banner of knowledge, the banner of progress, the banner of universal brotherhood! a golden flaming banner, a white-cross banner, a banner of beauty and delight! Unfurl it to the admiration of all people, gather your forces around it, carry it at the head of your ranks; go forth under it to the conquest of sin and error, vice and iniquity, oppression and injustice; let it stream above your civil processions; let its golden light gleam upon your homes and your fields; plant it upon the top of American destiny and the world's hope; let it irradiate the future, let it catch the eye of posterity; let it greet the heavens, let it bless the earth.

"Be heroes, and, if need be, martyrs under it, — the Oriflamme, the Golden Banner, the White-cross Banner; nail it to the mast of highest enterprise and holiest endeavor; and, if you must perish, perish with that waving triumphantly over you."

SLAVERY.

In consistency with his general principles, Mr. Judd had a deep sense of the wrongs of slavery, and of the foul blot it forms on our national escutcheon. He felt it to be totally in opposition to the great law of human brotherhood, which was his central idea. He often deplored it in his sermons and in his prayers. Yet it was not with him an all-absorbing form of evil, throwing every other into the background. It was covered by the general ground on which he took his position. As a specific evil, he speaks of it as " that gigantic subject of gigantic difficulties." He did not undertake to solve readily the problem of its immediate abandonment.

He was utterly opposed to severe treatment of the slaveholder, or to harsh denunciations. " I do not believe," he says, " slavery is going to be abolished by abusing the South, nor by cowing the North." In reference to the harsh measures of abolitionists, he says, " As regards slaveholders, we might as well hang them all, and done with it. We make them guilty of all possible crimes. Or, if we do not like that, we may adopt the other alternative, and love them into repentance and reformation." He did not think their means adapted to their end ; that slaveholders could be denounced into emancipation. He could not band himself with them.

In an address upon " The Idea of our Country," delivered at Portland, July 4, 1852, these remarks occur : " The positive and leading idea of our country, as distinguished from most others, is supposed to be liberty, the basis of which is reason and intelligence, virtue and religion, — liberty for all in all things; freedom of action, thought, conscience; freedom of the press and the pulpit; freedom in the choice of our rulers. I love this idea, and for this idea I love my country. It is a noble idea, generous, trustful, implying unbounded confidence in humanity, and replete with hope for the race.

" A fact, a certain fact, that offsets this idea, that militates against it, that confronts it with a terrific scowl, — shall I name it? shall I suffer its shadow to rise in the beauty of this our pleasant prospect? shall I suffer its harsh clangor or its melancholy wail to mingle with the bird-like tone and the sweet sensations of this our Independence-hour? The last census informs us, that there are three million one hundred and ninety-eight thousand three hundred and twenty-four slaves in the United States; not rhetorical slaves, I take it, not slaves in fancy or by construction, but real veritable slaves, merchandise, wares, chattels.

" Well, here we are, on this Fourth of July, with our parade and paradox of freedom and equality. So we will be, so we must be, if for no other motive, that slavery may come to an end. The more we love liberty, the more we shall hate slavery. We dote on liberty, and hail it, and celebrate it, because slavery is so dreadful a thing. The clearer and stronger are our conceptions of liberty, the more wisely and the more earnestly shall we labor against slavery. . I am not sorry slavery seems hideous to us to-day; I am not sorry that you can scarcely bear to hear the subject mentioned, nor that it grates on the harmonies and pleasures that belong to the occasion and the multitude. It is so evil a thing, so discordant with every true American sentiment, that the pain the mention of it gives us shows how we abhor it, and that even our silence rebukes it.

"Slavery, I shall insist, is not an idea of our country. No. It may be legally, it is not logically, here; it is no correlative or deduction, no branch or offspring, of republicanism. The Declaration of Independence, the Federal Constitution, did not introduce it: they found it here. How much they are implicated I shall not undertake to say. The year 1620 united two remarkable events, — the arrival of a Dutch ship, laden with marketable negroes, in James River; and the arrival of the Mayflower, laden with the Pilgrim fathers, in the harbor of Plymouth. The Virginians welcomed slavery. The General Court of Massachusetts, 1646, returned to Africa a cargo of slaves brought into Boston, declaring themselves 'bound by the first opportunity to bear witness against the heinous and crying sin of man-stealing.' They were so scrupulous as to send and fetch back a slave who had been smuggled down into Maine. This was the sort of Fugitive Slave Law of our forefathers.

"No. The idea of our country is liberty. To this idea we consecrate this day; in it we will live and work; through it we hope ultimately to displace the terrible fact to which I have referred. For one, notwithstanding this opposing circumstance, I worship liberty as purely as any one; I will devote myself as earnestly to it as any one ; neither the stain of slavery is in my skirts, nor are its clogs about my feet."

"The foundation of all right politics," he remarks, "is the will of God ; that will as revealed in Scripture, in nature, or in reason and conscience. A regard to God's will — latent perhaps, yet actual — underlies all worthy legislative action. You may say you are guided by the will of the people ; so perhaps you are. But what is the idea of the will of the people ? That idea is expressed in the old maxim, *Vox populi vox Dei* ; that is, God is supposed, by his providence or his grace, by his spirit or his truth, to act in the will of the people. He who attempts to govern men, if he would govern them rightly, must govern them as God would govern them. That men have inalienable rights is an annunciation of a certain fact ; which fact originates with God. It is a truth based upon the harmony of certain ideas ; which harmony is a divine creation. It is a formula in which is set God's will to man."

THE INDIANS.

The wrongs done to the aborigines of our country also was a subject over which Mr. Judd's heart bled, and to which he often feelingly alluded. In the address just quoted from is found the following passage : "Another idea of our country is equity, justice to all. The most glaring defection here appears in our treatment of the Indians. I think we have dealt worse by the Indians than by the Africans. We exterminate the former; we domesticate the latter. We find the black man a peck of corn a week; we curse the red man with whiskey. I am sometimes astonished, that, in the varied philanthropies of the age, no advocate of the aboriginal population arises; that, where there is so much fervid denunciation of the wrongs of slaveholding, there are none to execrate that greater villany, Indian-driving.

"A few years since, it used to be our impression that the Indians, having passed the Mississippi, and fleeing before our rapacity beyond the Rocky Mountains, would at least find repose beside the blue waters of the Pacific. But this boon is denied them.

"These native Americans have not had justice: justice has not been rendered to their characters or virtues, to their capabilities or promise, far less to their rights and immunities. 'Tis in destiny that they must perish, some say. Destiny is a very convenient thing; it works just about as our passions dictate; it is a very agreeable thing, since it favors our particular plans and devices. I wonder what the Indian thinks of it, or of the white man's God, or the white man's religion. . . . Who knows what, if we would rightly interpret it, and conscientiously adjust ourselves to it, might be written in the destiny of the Indian?

"Away with this doctrine of manifest destiny, which, on our lips and in this connection, means nothing more than consummate selfishness!"

INTEMPERANCE.

The prevailing intemperance of our country came in for a large share of Mr. Judd's attention and labor. But this again he considered a form of evil which needed for its eradication, above all, a pure Christianity.

"Intemperance," he says, "after all, is only a branch of a larger tree of evil; a heavily-laden branch, I own. There are also avarice, and oppression of all sorts, much hurtful ambition, much general injustice to humanity; all cousins-german of the same stock. That tree is a corrupted heart, if you will, or a corrupt state of society, if you had rather. I wish to see the tree upturned from its roots."

In this, as in other reforms, he believed the appropriate and most effectual instrumentality is love, and not force. He did not approve of legal action in the case; thought it involved in labyrinthine difficulties, and not a means adapted to the end. He "could not consent that the constable should do the appropriate work of a minister of the gospel." Of the Maine law touching this subject he said, "I cannot avoid feeling it has a tendency to nourish the evil it deplores. It does not address the affections of those whose business it touches; it ignores the fact that man has a reasonable soul; it wins no love; it converts no man's will." He saw great objections to it in "its incentives to public corruption in the form of perjury, concealment, tergiversation, pretence, bribery, barratry; in the

operations of a dread resilience ; in the leadings on
to that something worse, an exacerbated collision of
public sentiment, where force shall be repelled by
force." But, while he had no confidence in the
adequacy or adaptedness of this law for the end
designed, and felt it to be entirely averse to the true
principle of moral reform, he contented himself with
defining his position, and passively awaited the result
of a fair trial of its efficacy by those who had faith in
its remedial power.

In Washingtonianism he recognized the germ,
which, if fully developed, would have banished
intemperance ; and its mode of operation he embraced heart and soul. He lamented that with most
it proved to be an impulse rather than a principle,
and that it was so soon abandoned and overruled by
the devotees of force. "Washingtonianism," he
says, "ceasing to rely on God, leaned upon an arm
of flesh, and has fallen to the ground. Formerly,
they loved one another ; they loved the beastly
drunkard ; they spoke kindly to the guilty rum-
seller. Brotherly feelings were in their hearts ; a
smile was on all faces, and a softness in all manners.
Good times were those, — a season of genial excitement, delightful recreation, exuberant gratitude.
Nobody wanted to drink then, so much was enjoyed
in other ways. Poor, broken-hearted mothers began
to sweep up the floor, wash the dirt from the faces
of their children, make the old house seem tidy and
neat, and look cheerfully out from their clouted
windows, because the father had signed the pledge.
The frown fell from the brow of Intolerance ; the

27

purse of Avarice was open ; Degradation creeped up from the kennel ; the hand of Fellowship was reached forth from the churches : Profanity spoke with miraculous reverence of God ; everybody congratulated everybody ; and everybody expected glad words from everybody. The single touch of Love thrilled and electrified the whole town. When we wrote letters, we made mention of it ; it was remembered in sermons and prayers. Those days are gone. And oh ! it is enough to make a strong man weep — darkness has come over the town ; we are repulsed by a cold expediency ; there is plotting and counter-plotting, crimination and recrimination ; the poor, broken-hearted mother shivers over her scant fire ; the Levite goes by on the other side, and the good Samaritan has been himself waylaid ; nobody congratulates anybody ; everybody believes everybody tells lies ; we have grown hypocritical and double-faced ; a brooding suspicion closes all hearts ; the work of temperance is carried on by whispers and secret manœuvring ; Christ has been cast out, and sent headlong down the hill ; the common enemy cries, 'Aha ! aha !' over our ruin. God send back the good old times !"

Again he says : " In the promotion of temperance, eminently and peculiarly a moral reform, moral and Christian means have had the go-by. Nothing is now heard of but force and violence. All the phrases and tactics and spirit of war are brought into the work. Moral suasion, they tell us, was good for nothing. I say moral suasion, in any proper sense of the word, has not been tried. I mean systematic, organized, continuous, untiring application of light and love. As a people, we do not know how to use moral suasion. The education of the people for ages has been that of legal suasion. The popular theology, which covers the whole life, touches every sphere of action, penetrates to the deepest springs of feeling, at the breasts of which the infancy of each generation is nursed, — the popular theology, I say, of this land, of all lands, is, to a great extent, that of legal suasion."

He traced the course of intemperance in New England, in a large degree, to the fact that our worthy Puritan fathers *made no provision for the recreative wants of the people.* "The Puritans," he says, "shocked by the profane recreation in England, instituted nothing in its place. They practised no sports themselves; they offered none to their children. To establish a system of recreation that would be at once satisfying and pure, enlivening and innocent, seems never to have entered their minds. They studiously refrained in their own persons from all kinds of agreeable diversion. Yet perhaps there never was a people in the world who stood in greater need of recreation than the Puritan colonists; none upon whom the cares of life pressed so heavily. But recreation in some sort, man will have; the laws of nature could not turn aside for Puritanism; the necessities which God has implanted in our constitution could not be satisfied by the sternness of these Anti-Jacobites; they were not stifled, they took a new turn, they broke out somewhere else. Our fathers, having discarded every thing else, *betook*

themselves for recreation to the cup. Denying themselves what was healthful and innocent, they made
ample amends in what was ruinous and criminal.
Here, then, we have laid bare one great secret of New
England intemperance. Our fathers had no dances,
no bowling-alleys, no sleigh-rides, no games of goose
or backgammon, no promenades, no systematic holidays, no musical entertainments, no literary or scien-
tific amusements, no pleasures of art, no ladies' fairs,
no tea-parties, no Sunday-school celebrations, no rural festivals ; they never went to Niagara ; Saratoga
was unknown ; their labors were arduous, their cares
incessant ; and their only recreation consisted in the
use of intoxicating drinks. Ministers, who denounced
sports, drank rum ; magistrates, who inflicted penalties for light conduct, drank rum ; parents, who
whipped their children for playing Saturday nights,
drank rum. To take a glass of liquor was a cheap,
summary, expeditious, unobtrusive way of self-re-
creation ; it gave offence to no one, it answered the
demands of nature, it imparted a glow to the spirits,
it relieved the sense of burden and fatigue, and lu-
bricated all the joints of action ; its ulterior effects
were not anticipated ; and those people seemed to
themselves to have accomplished all recreative ends,
when they had satisfactorily drank. Rum thus became the recreative element to our ancestors. If a
man was tired, he drank rum ; if he was disappointed,
he drank rum ; if he required excitement, he drank
rum ; the elders drank when they prayed, the minister when he preached. Rum sustained the patriotism of the soldier and the fatigue of the ploughman ;

it kindled alike the flames of devotion and the fires of revelry.

"Thus, as I conceive, were laid the foundations for that enormous extension of intemperance which our own times have witnessed, and we have been called so often to lament."

Therefore, in promoting the temperance-reform, in cutting off the means of gratification in this quarter, Mr. Judd maintained the necessity of supplying something to take its place. He says, "The friends of temperance and humanity have not fairly won the field, until the morbid thirst of the inebriate is diverted from objects of low sense to those of a more spiritual character, his self-respect and self-balance perfectly restored, his powers engaged in agreeable and salutary ways, his heart succored and blest, and his whole nature regenerated." He recommended, "as a preliminary good, that they should open coffee-shops, furnish them with books and newspapers, render them every way attractive, visit them frequently themselves," &c. He insisted that the intemperate should be furnished with the means of innocent pleasure, relaxations, and agreeable excitements ; that a general cheerfulness should be diffused ; that music should be cultivated; that dancing, unexceptionably regulated, should be practised.

The following is the concluding paragraph of a sermon upon "Intemperance," from which most of the extracts on this subject have been made : —

"Finally, my brethren, if we cannot afford to love one another : if we will give no encouragement to the charities of life ; if we refuse to be exemplifiers

27*

of the truth as it is in Jesus; if we will not aid in a universal dispensation of health and peace; if we will cultivate no sensibility to what is beautiful in sight, and sound, and motion; if we will not facilitate the entrance of the Spirit of God into the human heart, by every form of address; if we will make of the journey of life only a pilgrimage to the temple of Mammon; if we will prostitute every sentiment of virtue to the lust of office; if we will resist the inspiration of a more exalted philanthropy; if we will not descend to the depth of human affairs, and apply ourselves to the springs of action, and labor on a scale commensurate with our farthest-reaching hopes; if we will offer no replenishment to the waste, or succor to the wants, of humanity; if the rigors of our ancestral theology are never to be softened; if we will do nothing; if society will do nothing; if the church will do nothing, — then, as of old, the rum-bottle will continue to be the solace of New Englanders; not pledges, not societies, not laws, will save us from plunging into that horrible vortex, — so deep, no light from heaven will reach us; so deep, heathenism shall shine as the brightness of the sun seven times, in comparison with us; so deep, nought but the thunders of doom will awaken us to a sense of our condition."

TREATMENT OF CRIMINALS.

The proper treatment of criminals was another subject that engaged Mr. Judd's deep interest. He held that this should be reformatory rather than punitive. He had so much faith in human nature as to believe, that, however depraved the course of life may have been, there is still some uncalloused spot in the heart that may be touched by kind deeds and gentle words. He adopted in full the spirit of the old proverb, "Beneath every jacket there lives a man." He believed the testimony of the New York judge, who said, " I have never yet had a criminal before me for sentence, but whose feelings I could touch, and whose heart I could subdue, by allusions to his mother;" and remarks, "There is a mother-heart in all children, as well as a child-heart in all mothers."

He traced much of the persistence in crime to the practice of making the guilty one an outcast from society; one in whom no confidence can be placed, of whom no good thing can be expected. And, in this relation, he would quote another old proverb, "You may as well hang a dog as give him a bad name." With the Saviour, he would say to the offending one, "Neither do I condemn thee, — go, sin no more;" and maintained that a helping hand should be extended, a readiness to forget the past manifested, and encouragements for regaining self-respect offered. He urged that our prisons should become general schools of reform, and not abodes of punishment.

"I know it is a received maxim," he says, "that not the severity, but the certainty, of punishment prevents crime. I have little confidence in either mode. We must seek to reform the criminal. The most dangerous men, the dark prowlers through our community, are those whom we have punished in our prisons."

As to Capital Punishment, he believed it interdicted by the whole spirit of the New Testament, and totally inexpedient as a means of preventing crime; and he was filled with horror at the thought of judicially slaying a fellow-man.

MISCELLANEOUS REFORMS.

He wished the distinctions between the rich and the poor might be narrowed down to the simple basis of Christian relationship; that the poor should not indulge in envyings and jealousies of the rich; that the rich should not despise the poor, but honor humble merit, and aid and encourage honest efforts to rise. He would bring Victoria Square and Kunckle Lane together at the Assembly-room of the Griped Hand; have them shake hands and converse together like Christians, though certain people might not know where it would stop, though it might perchance go on through this world into the next. He maintained the dignity of labor, and that true honor arises not from condition, but from acting well one's part, whatever it may be.

"As regards Woman, and her grievances and aspirations," he says, "if she is not king, she is queen of home; she is mistress of a peculiar sphere; she is the head of a wonderful empire; and allow me to add, that, in proportion as home is made attractive, men will stay at home, and women can in this way come to rule the men. Let me add this also, that much of the vice of the world results from the practice of going from home in pursuit of excitement or pleasure ; and, if woman will make home pleasant and genial, she will do not a little towards uprooting vice and redeeming the world."

And in " Philo," in answer to the question, " What is woman's mission ? " he says : —

> " Her effect
> Lies not in voting, warring, clerical oil,
> But germinating grace, forth putting virtue,
> The Demosthenic force of secret worth,
> And Pantheism of truth and holiness.
> . . . . Need she push, when through all crowds
> She melts like quicksilver? . . . .
> Her action is not running, nor her forte
> To nod like Jove, and set the earth a shaking.
> Silent, she speaks; and motionless, she moves;
> As rocks are split by wedges of froze water.
> . . . .
> If woman feels the sacred fire of genius,
> Give her the liberty to genius owed.
> But the world's greatness is diminutive,
> And what is small the true magnificence,
> And a good mother greater than a queen.
> . . . .
> There's work enough for any woman, great
> In character and consequence as man's."

Mr. Judd's ideas in regard to Foreign Missions were in consonance with the same general philosophy of beginning with the roots rather than with the branches. While preparing for the ministry, he writes in his Journal : " As to foreign missions, I would go ; but there is war among Christian nations, slavery in our own, Christian sailors intemperate, licentious. Christian nations must first be converted. I am oppressed." The same views he always had, that, as long as the example of Christian nations was so ill a recommendation of their religion, so long as such great and glaring evils existed in connection with it, the Christian missionary had very little encouragement for attempting to Christianize the heathen. His sympathies were therefore much more in the direction of home-reforms, of bringing our own people up to the standard and spirit of pure Christianity, than in that of efforts abroad. He believed the heathen much better off as they are, than the great mass of people in professedly Christian countries.

Mr. Judd's treatment of the subject of Death — though not essentially differing from that of other clergymen of his faith — might perhaps not inappropriately find a place under the head of reforms. Instead of dwelling mostly on the shroud, the pall, and, by a preponderance of lugubrious expressions, seeming almost to leave the spirit as well as its temporary, its earth-garment, in the dark night of the tomb, — in the true spirit of our Christian faith, he gave chief prominence to the fact, that, in what we name death, the soul is only making an important stride in its existence; that then indeed commences its truest life, and from that point might well be dated its real birth. In the fulness of his belief in God, in heaven, in the soul's immortality, his funeral services tended to draw aside the veil between us and the invisible, and let in a flood of cheerful confidence upon the bereaved ones, that it is but a temporary separation, and that the departed one is in no very just sense lost to those that survive. He thus caused light to emanate from the apparent darkness, and fill the heart with buoyant, Christian hope.

Instead of shutting out the light of day, and shrouding in darkness and gloom the dwelling from which an enfranchised soul had sped its flight, he would allow the cheering sunbeams to penetrate, and the blue sky, with its serene depths and soft clouds, like angel-attendants, to look in. Flowers, and whatever art could furnish of appropriate beauty and suggestiveness, he thought the fitting garniture of the chamber of death. He did not approve of draping the whole person in weeds, and spreading an air of hopelessness and melancholy over every thing. At the same time, he felt there was something fitting and in unison with our natural sensibilities, in the wearing of some simple badge, some outward symbol of love and remembrance of those taken from our sight and our palpable communion.

Here are his own words in relation to the subject : —

"We get the somberest hues of the dye-house, and bury our persons and our griefs deep in night. Why is black the chosen color of death? Some people wear blue, some white, in token of mourning. I shall not enter into the question whether weeds shall be entirely discarded. Undoubtedly some outward symbol has its congeniality and appropriateness. But why should we make our mourning so mournful? But the reasonableness of black has not occurred. It is, indeed, suited to certain views of death and the grave, but only to the darkest, atheistic side of the case. It strikes me that some lighter color would as well become the Christian and the Christian death. We talk of the heathen, of their dark views of death ; but what impression of darkness could be greater than that of one of our own funeral scenes ? How black the hearse is, and the pall, and the procession ! Can it be, a Heathen might ask, that those persons have hope in death ? I do not say, my hearers, that black should be dispensed with. I cannot say, if God, in his providence, should remove by death those I love, but I should like to wear it. But, at least, let us illuminate this darkness of our vestments by some cheer, some hope, some serenity in our hearts."

COMMON SCHOOLS.

In the elevation and improvement of common schools, Mr. Judd was much concerned. For several years, as has been stated, he was a member of the Superintending School Committee in Augusta. He urged the importance of improvements in schoolhouses and their appendages. " Many schoolhouses," he says in one of his annual reports, " are badly placed ; crowded upon the street, half afloat in mud in the spring, smothered in dust in summer ; without trees, without blinds, without suitable outbuildings, without a yard for the children to play in. The edge of a public street is the worst possible site for a school-house. Is land so valuable, that the house cannot be withdrawn four or five rods further from the highway ? One would imagine there was a conspiracy on the part of the landowners to drive the school-house just as far into the road as possible ; as if the school-house were a wild animal that no one could tolerate on his premises."

He strove to effect a reform in the relations of parents to schools. It struck him as a deplorable insensibility on the part of parents, that, year after year, they should send their children where they were receiving impressions lasting as their lives, without even *seeing* the person to whom was entrusted the moulding of their characters, or scarcely the place and its appointments which were to give a coloring to their growing years. " The great defect under which the schools suffer, the leading, crowning defect," he writes, in his report, " is the *lack of interest on the part of parents*. Of the thousands in the town who sustain the most interesting relation to the children, *hardly one, during the past year, has visited a school*. It is a culpable, an unpardonable negligence ; a negligence well nigh fatal to the well-being of the school ; one that does more evil than any efforts of the committee can do good, that neutralizes the exertions of the most skilful teacher, and operates sadly to defeat the great ends of our educational system. Those who will not hire a bog-digger without superintending his labors do not go near one whom they employ to cultivate, develop, and form the mind and morals of their children.

" The occasional, informal, kind, and cordial presence of the fathers and mothers in the school would animate and encourage both teacher and scholar. It would promote good order, repress insubordination, anticipate and nip in the bud those troubles that are

28

liable at any moment to break out. It is due to the school, due to the expense lavished upon it, to the hopes founded upon it, to the hazard that evermore attends it, that it be visited by parents. It might be intimated, that, as a general thing, the parents in a district have no right, no moral right, to prefer complaints against a teacher on the *ex parte* statements of the children. Their first duty is to go to the school, examine for themselves, confront teacher with scholar, observe the routine of instruction and discipline, and see if there be sufficient ground of complaint.

" Parents sometimes complain of their children being rudely beaten in school : if they would visit the school occasionally, such instances of severity would not occur. They complain that their children are neglected : these visits would prevent such neglect. They complain that the teacher has a bad spirit : these visits would tend to rectify and repress this spirit.

" Let the committee do what it can, there will be a large field for parental exertion, vigilance, and oversight. Let the fathers go into the school as they have opportunity. Let the mothers, two or three of them together, take their knitting or their sewing, and sit an hour or two in the school."

He sought to have the practice of flagellation, or any mode of corporal punishment, done away with, and believed that moral government might, with infinite advantages, be substituted in its place.

He regarded it a great defect, that, while almost every art and science was simplified, and brought down to the comprehension of the young, so that they could easily become acquainted with its general principles, the science of morals, in familiar illustrations of its principles, and ready application to the common, daily intercourse of man with man, of child with child, had not a prominent place in schools ; and, through his urgency of this need, his suggestions and encouragement, the " Manual of Morals " was prepared, to supply, as best it might, this deficiency in popular school-books.

In his sense of the vast importance of right culture and general improvement to the young, as already alluded to, he met classes of young ladies for literary, as well as moral, advancement.   The boys and girls, of whatever denomination, with whom he became acquainted in the schools and other ways, he invited to his study, and offered to lend them books, on the single condition that they should be well treated and punctually returned.   And often might be seen one and another, with bright, grateful face, returning a volume that had given some new interest, or awakened a thirst for further knowledge, and receiving another chosen with reference to his mental condition, and dismissed with some pertinent and suggestive remark which would fix itself in his memory.   And thus Mr. Judd caused his private library to circulate to a considerable extent around the town.

PUBLIC IMPROVEMENTS.

All the great internal improvements of the country he watched with close attention.   In the subject of railroads and plank-roads no man took a greater interest, and few probably were better informed. But it was chiefly in relation to their influence in binding together the great human family in bonds of brotherly fellowship that he rejoiced to see them extended. He believed, that, if people could be brought to know each other, there would be less narrowness of views, fewer party-strifes ; that sectional jealousies would diminish, and the interests of the race be advanced. He thus beheld, in railways and their attendant wires for the transmission of thought, the engines of a higher civilization, and, in the end, of a more extensive promulgation of Christianity. Indeed, he was never known to avail himself of the electoral franchise, except in carrying forward an enterprise of this kind, which was to some extent involved in the pending election.

Nothing in the progress of the local interests of the town escaped his attention. The costly experiment of its dam for facilitating various mechanical operations, its factories, its foundries, its ship-building, and all sorts of machinery, received his careful notice. And, when Augusta assumed the attitude of a city, he deemed the event of sufficient importance and seriousness to demand a sermon upon the regulations requisite for promoting the physical and moral welfare of cities, — in the provision for an abundance of wholesome air, for the free inflowing of the light of heaven, for the bordering of streets with trees, the affording of ample space for gardens, and the securing of large, well-laid-out parks, where something of nature's sweet influences might be enjoyed by those whose means limit them to the confines of the city.

Improvements in house-building, as to taste, economy, and convenience, he sought to promote. He was thankful for Downing's contributions to this purpose, and was one among the many who mourned his untimely loss as that of a beloved benefactor. His own pleasing cottage, the first of an improved style of building in the town, gave an impetus to ornamental architecture, which quite changed the appearance of its neighborhood. He studied carefully and philosophically the best principles on which to construct hot-air furnaces. He took great pains to obtain for himself, and to recommend to his neighbors, improved kinds of apples and other fruits, and garden vegetables.

HOLIDAYS AND RECREATION.

Mr. Judd believed in the salutary influence of holidays, in their tendency to promote peace and good-will; to bring the poor, in some sort, on a level with the rich. He believed that Christianity has regard to this festive, recreative element of our nature; that recreation, in some form, is a God-ordained means of uniting, harmonizing, and equalizing mankind; and traced many of the evils existing in our country to the want of provision for the recreative element of our nature. He endeavored to make the most of the few national festivals we have, and would gladly have had their number increased. The rural sabbath-school festivals, which he did so much to

encourage, have been spoken of.   The observance of
birth-days, marriage-days, and other family-anniver-
saries, he thought, had a happy tendency.   He was
careful to have his church trimmed for the Christmas
season, and held a public service on Christmas eve,
and always provided some pleasant home-entertain-
ment to make a merry Christmas for his children.

While he honored our Puritan fathers in the main,
he could not but see and regret some errors into
which their sterling principles led them.   " I think,"
he says, " they committed a radical error in abolish-
ing all the papal holidays, or in not substituting
something therefor.   We have Thanksgiving, and
the Fourth of July, and Fast-day when the young
men play ball.   We need three times as many festivals ; or the least that may be asked is, that our
sabbaths be rendered more cheerful, more social,
more liberal.   The Puritans rejected saints' days ;
but, in the glorious gospel of the Son of God, in
this new, varied, majestic world to which they mi-
grated, was there nothing, in the infinite conditions
of the soul, out of which they might derive occasions
for public delight ?

" Man has a recreative want ; a want that keeps
its place side by side with every volition and every
action ; a want importunate in its demands, and
invincible in its efforts.   This necessity, moreover,
if it be not answered in ways healthful and harmless,
is wont to betake itself to what is injurious and
unlawful.   Nature always vindicates herself; and,
if we maltreat her in any way, she is sure to punish
us.   Man's recreative want belongs not to one part

of him, but to all parts; not to his body alone, but to his mind also. Every faculty of the soul, every function of the brain, every muscle of the flesh, is subject to the laws of action and reaction; must bend and unbend; requires recreation, relaxation. Man has also a higher need than mere physical rest; a moral need of gladness, enlivenment, peace, joy; a need of sympathy, kindness, love. He has need of humane influences that shall infuse themselves through the centre of his being; of a warm friendship that shall embrace him fraternally; of an inspiration that shall vivify and exalt his powers; of friendly voices to cheer him in all the pilgrimage of life; of aids in his endeavors, strength in his weakness, compassion for his distress, approbation of his honest thought. Agreeably to these laws, if such needs are not supplied, man becomes cold, hard, insensible, selfish, reckless, desperate. These are laws psychological and physiological, spiritual and material. They are natural and divine laws; they are of God's creating, and binding as any precept of the decalogue, punitive as any statute of the universe.

" Recreations, it will not be questioned, have been abused; they have been perverted to sinister ends by those who devised them; they have waxed gross in the hands of those who employ them. All this may be true, and yet the general principles for which we contend remain unaltered. The origin of this perversion is traceable to the early age of New England. Restriction, that should have directed the course of the stream, laid a curb-stone on the fountain, and the waters broke forth madly, destructively. Recreation took the form of pillage, and, while it glutted itself, wasted withal. Young men, tearing themselves from the coercive grasp of parents, magistrates, ministers, celebrated the achievement in a profusion of drunkenness. Then arose a species of excess, the vestiges of which remain in our day, known in common parlance as bursts, bouts, sprees.

"By recreation — need I say it ? — I do not mean merely children's plays ; nor do I me n circuses or theatres or negro-songs or jugglery. The entire idea includes many things : a gentler spi it pervading the whole constitution of society ; a gathering together of the scattered fragments of the human family ; a recognizance in all of brotherhood, the divine image, and immortality : it implies, especially, a ministry of refreshment, agreeableness, light and truth, kindness and love, to man's whole nature, physical and social, moral, intellectual, religious. As regards particular forms of recreative action, you will hardly oblige me to say, that you are to engage in nothing on which you cannot ask the blessing of God ; nothing that does not so fulfil his will as to promote his glory. And most deeply do I feel it to be the duty of the wise and good to do, what our fathers did not, — provide for the recreative wants of the people.

"Society owes it to itself and to its members, first to give recreation, then to regulate it ; what is given freely can be regulated with ease ; sanctity attaches to the munificence of the generous mind ; what is wrung from the miser, we squander without remorse.

Let society make of recreation a friend, and it will cease to be its enemy; let us overcome its evil with good. Let your children grow up with the idea that they may practise no recreation in which their parents, if not participants, shall at least be present as observers and wardens. The extremes of society ought to suspend hostilities, and compromise their dissensions; the sinful gaiety on one side should be abandoned, and the equally sinful severity on the other; there is the common ground of health and innocence, friendship and peace, purity and virtue, which, for a few moments at least of life, they might occupy together. We ought to strive for a pious happiness and a happy piety.

"Our people thirst for happiness, for recreation, for something festive; and, when a man is not sustained by religion, or fed by literature, when there is no genial, pleasant occasion to call him out on the common in company with his fellow-citizens, he betakes himself to his bottle. I believe happiness, on a large and general scale, is not unfavorable to morality; and for this reason, when all are happy, and all are united in their happiness, there is no opportunity for individual passion and selfish desire to be very active.

"There is something unitary in our pleasures; more than there is in our passions or our speculations, more than in politics or commerce.

"At these times, the human heart is mellow; it opens, it embraces. Everybody feels as everybody else does, and all love to have others feel as they do. You not only want to enjoy yourself, but you want others to enjoy themselves too.   As a merchant, you want to do more business than your neighbor, and sometimes you contrive to get away some of his business; but, when people come together on festive occasions, then they want everybody else to be as happy as they are: then, indeed, the only fear is, that others are not having a good time.

" A holiday is equally for the poor man and the rich.   I like the Fourth of July, for this reason, the poor can enjoy it; and I love to see them thus rising to a level, from which no one can drive them."

Mr. Judd makes " Margaret " speak thus in regard to dancing : " Another distinct and stringent law of God and nature is recreation.   Of the many kinds that are afloat, we have been obliged to use care in our choice.   What would Christ approve, what is best, we ask ?   In what can all ages and conditions unite ?   What relaxes without weakening, is cheerful without frivolity, and offers attraction without danger ?   Not to the exclusion of other things, our election has fallen on the dance ; a species of recreation enjoined in the Old Testament, and recognized in the New ; one practised in every age and country, and recommended by the sanction of the best and greatest of men.   It has music and beauty for its garniture and strength.   Its intrinsic value has won for it the approval of all.   We sometimes dance on the green, sometimes in our hall.   It is enjoyed in all families.   Parents dance with their children, husbands with wives.   It has supplanted many ridiculous games, and extirpated cruel sports.   It has broken up drunken carousals, and neutralized

the temptations to ardent spirits. Whatever grace
is needed in person, or courtesy in manners, it operates to perfect. It brings the people together, interests strangers, and diffuses a serene, whole-souled
harmony over the town. It has no boisterousness
and much life. It embodies the recreative element
in the healthiest and holiest forms. Where all unite,
there is no excess. We praise God in the dance:
it is a hymn written with our feet. I would dance
as I would pray, for its own sake, and because it is
well-pleasing to God."

Of Christmas he writes elsewhere: " Could it be
really felt in all its power, as that which signalizes
the advent of Christ into the world, it would help
to break up our miserable sects ; could it fall upon
the world in all its divine weight, it would be ' as
the stone cut out of the mountain without hands,'
that should become a great mountain to crush the
sins and follies, the abuses and oppressions, of the
nations. . . .

" I long for the festival of peace, for the jubilee
of freedom. I long to see the time when the whole
race might be summoned to celebrate some great
gala-day of brotherhood.

" Would that the song of the angels were more
often echoed by our Linds and Parodis! Would that
the key-note struck up among the stars might be
taken up by every organ and every choir on the
globe! Peace on earth, good-will among men, —
think of that as breaking out in the stillness of
night ; think of it as uttered by beings from another
world ; think of it as a voice poured into the atmo-

sphere of this our earth, and as floating unceasingly
in all winds, in all storms; a voice that shall never
die, till men really come to love one another."

IMPROVED STATE OF SOCIETY.

Mr. Judd yearned for a generally improved state
of society, for a millennium; such, in its spirit, as
has been long expected by the great mass of Christians, but the preliminaries of which they so incon-
sistently reject.

In the imaginary picture of an advanced state of
society, drawn in "Margaret," among other features
is the following, touching this subject: "Our festivals are twelve in number, one for each month in the
year. Three of them are such as have already become national, or, at least, New England: the Spring
Fast, Independence, and the Autumnal Thanksgiving. Three more are founded on the Beatitudes,
and are named as follows: the Festival of the Poor
in Spirit, that of the Peacemakers, and of the Pure
in Heart. There is the festival of Charity, or Christian Love, from 1 Cor. xiii. Then, from the life of
Christ, are Christmas, drawn from his birth; Childmas, which refers to his holy boyhood and youth;
the Festival of the Crucifixion, which comprises his
strong crying and tears in the flesh, his temptation,
his bearing his cross, his agony in the garden, and
his death; that of the Resurrection, which includes
his transfiguration, his spiritual anastasis, his being
the life of the soul, and his rising from the dead.
Then we have the Festival of the Universal Brother-

hood, taken from Christ's interview with the Samaritan woman; and the declaration of Paul, that in Christ all are one. We have also twelve other festivals in the monthly recurrence of the Holy Communion. Our bishop has also proposed a system of sabbaths, which he pursues with tolerable regularity. He has given us Baptismal Sunday, founded on Christ's baptism; Children's Sunday, his blessing the little children; Unity Sunday; Atonement Sunday, ' that they may be one in us;' Regeneration Sunday, 'except a man be born again;' Repentance Sunday, &c., &c.

"In most of our festivals, there is a short religious exercise in the church. The Poor in Spirit is a season of sober introspection, humility, and prayer. The Crucifixion has for its object to effect within us a crucification to the world, and of the world to us. Childmas, in May, gives several holidays to the children. They have a May-pole, May-dances, and a Queen of May. They go into the woods for evergreens and flowers. In the evening the band play for them, and they dance with their parents on the green. The Resurrection seeks to realize for us that spiritual resurrection from sin which St. Paul strove to attain, and which Christ so perfectly enjoyed. It also looks to the final elimination of the soul from the body. The Festival of Love would advance us in that love which thinketh no evil, beareth all things, is the bond of perfection, the seal of our being born of God, and fulfils the law. The Pure in Heart, among other things, is devoted to a general school-visitation. The school-houses are

filled with parents and friends; the scholars examined, and addresses made.   The election of the May
Queen is made to turn somewhat on these examinations.   On Peacemaker's-day, we decorate the church
with evergreens, have the lion and lamb symbolized,
and make our endeavors for private and universal
peace, seek forgiveness, and proffer restitution.   Our
festivals are not put by for `Sunday; but when they
fall on that day, which not infrequently happens,
the bishop prepares discourses accordingly.

" Thus is the whole year interwoven and girded
about by our beautiful festivals; some of them
exceedingly joyous and gay, others more sedate and
reflective.   What Herbert says of them, I dare
not : —

> ' Who loves not you, doth in vain profess
> That he loves God or heaven or happiness.'

Yet we do love them; and that, *because* we love God
and Christ and happiness."

So also in " Philo," with reference to the same
ideally regenerated state of society, he writes : —

> " Their swords
> To ploughshares, spears to pruning-hooks, they beat;
> Nor ever blacksmiths gave such lusty blows.
> They rend the forts, and whoop down citadels.
> The slaves are frolicking; to-morrow they,
> With freeman's will, a freeman's work will do.
> The alcoholic fire in fire goes out;
> A mob of advocates the gallows touse;
> See bands of exiles singing to their homes;
> Scrimp jails to airy hospitals arise;
> Cities exude their poisons as a fog;
> The mephitism is banished by the winds.
> The Cumberland road, with many wagon-loads
> Of reparations for the Indians,

A mirthful rabble crowd.   There is a town
In phalansteric change; the houses move,
As trees of old, to sweet synergic pipes.
See gardens multiply, and bulbs increase;
See tasteful cottages adorn the plains.
Our senators eventful progress feel,
And meet to Christianize the Constitution.
The epoch deepens, wide our God hath rule;
Beyond the seas prophetic crises thrill.
Love balances their power, and soothes their fears;
Their ships of war convey millennial rapture
Around the earth; the serf to burgher mounts;
The lazzaroni weave in factories;
The Moslem is agape, and opes his mosque
To gospel-preachers.   The glad news spins on
To Ispahan, and shakes the Chinese wall.
Enough for one day: let us homeward wend,
And in our hearts the solemn lessons tend."

CHAPTER IX.

AS AN AUTHOR.

GENERAL CRITICISMS.

FEW authors have probably undergone such discordant criticisms as Mr. Judd. It is not a little amusing to compare the diverse epithets and expressions bestowed upon his works.

In the various observations upon " Margaret," we find, that it is "a real book, the buyer whereof receives something more than paper and printer's ink in exchange for his money," and that it is " sheer nonsense, from beginning to end ; " it is " a true poem, though in prose," and " too stupid to waste time upon ; " " a true prophetic instinct animates the book," and, again, " it is a weak and silly book ; " " a full conception of the essence of Christianity," " rank blasphemy ; " that it is " no jest, but the sincere utterance of a sincere man," and that " the author is making a joke of his readers ; " it is called " a *real presence*," " transcendental," " a puzzle ; " " full of genius, profound in meaning," " nothing but a dull attempt at joke ; " it is characterized as " a remarkable book," " that strange production," " an extraordinary book," " a wonder of the age,"

" an evidence that an American literature is possible."

We find also that " it is a book not likely to be dismissed ; that the author evidently has stuff in him, sterling metal, that rings as well as shines ; " that it is " the only American book that has ever been written ; " that " its descriptions are perfect as the paintings of Claude, the plot full of dramatic interest, the characters drawn with a master's hand ; " that it is " an original book, full of beauty and power, with admirable fidelity to nature, having pages striking as Carlyle, quaint as Lamb, graphic as Washington Irving."

A friend writes the author in reference to " Margaret : " " The rivers and the forests were made for you ; nature loves you with a peculiar love, and unlocks her golden treasures for your own hand ; the clouds, the streams, the pines, all live in your words ; and, more than all that, I feel in them the beatings of the great heart of humanity. I read it first in the country, where I could hear the murmur of the bees as I read, and the whir of the humming-bird's wing, and the chatter and whistle of birds ; I have read it since in the city by my own fireside ; part I have read in silence, part aloud ; part my wife has read to me, and part I have read to her ; part I have kindled over, part I have wept over, part I have laughed over ; part I have wished blotted out, and part I have wished written in letters of gold."

A young, unsophisticated girl says : " ' Margaret ' herself, it seems to me, represents the power of the innate virtue, the *unborn* religion of the soul, in forming a pure and beautiful life. She is a bright, clear rainbow, spanning the volume, — one end planted where, in his death-chamber, 'Gottfried Brückman' heard 'the echoes louder from the shadowy shore,' the other resting where the flower-wreathed cross points heavenward from 'Mons Christi.'

"'Chillion' is a high-strung, sweet-toned harp, with the 'music frozen' into the strings, and no earthly breath warm enough to loosen it."

In regard to "Philo" we find the same striking contrasts. One says: "We have read this dramatic poem through, giving ourselves up to it, and carried on by it from beginning to end; and, if we can trust at all the impressions left on our mind, it is a poem of uncommon power and genius. After being wrapt in it as in a vision, we come away feeling that it has been good for us to be there. There are images of remarkable beauty, on which the soul may feed in its quiet hours, and passages of such boldness, that no writer among us would dare venture upon them, or, daring, would succeed as the author has. Its philanthropy is large, discriminating, and without a sting. The poem is a rich mine for those who love minute criticism, and will, doubtless, shock some good people, as the book of Job would, if it were not one of our sacred books. There is an energy of expression, a Titanic play of humor, a strength, and, with all its roughness, a delicacy of religious feeling and earnestness of purpose, a vigor of imagination, and a reverential, loving, living faith in Christ and his religion, which may more than compensate for many and great faults."

From another we have these comments : " What an *Evangeliad* is we have not yet learned ; but we suppose it to be something bran new. There may be those who will understand this book : we cannot. The lines have ' ragged edges,' from which we suppose it was meant for poetry. Passages which we have lighted upon, in opening the book at random, read like very gross burlesque, though we are not sure the author meant them for such, or whether he meant any thing at all. The work seems to us a crazy jumble of Tom Moore, John Bunyan, Don Quixote, Goethe's Faust, the Westminster Assembly's Shorter Catechism, the law of Moses, Theodore Parker upon stilts, and a Kilby-street auctioneer's catalogue. What with bad English, broken-backed lines, crazy metaphors, and rhetoric run mad, the whole thing is about as grotesque a Mumbo Jumbo as we have ever seen dressed up for the amusement and amazement of the public. It may be all meant for joke, for aught we know ; but it is certainly very poor fun."

On the one side we hear said to the author : " Its plan is original, its flow melodious, its scenes graphic, its thoughts often profound ; and the force of genius is felt through it, bearing one up, and hurrying one forward from beginning to end. Your children and your children's children may be proud of it, to the fourth and fifth generation. There are immortal things in it which the world will not let die." On the other it is remarked : " Why the author has seen

fit to string together so much commonplace verse
we cannot divine. The poem is not only not beautiful, nor at all fascinating in any part of it, but is
full of violations of good taste, in the verse and the
sentiments. We are sorry we have so little to say
in commendation."

So of "Richard Edney." In the judgment of
one, "It is written with that power which belongs
only to one who has power and intellectual energy
the most ample. Through the whole of it, there
runs a deep vein of thought, pure as virgin silver,
which is brought out with a wealth of illustration
in characters, in incidents, in the descriptive, and in
the narrative. We read it with the interest with
which we read 'Jane Eyre,' but with a thousand
times the more satisfaction. There are delineations
of character, almost without number, that are ex-
quisite blendings of light and shade in human being.
The volume is written in an unostentatious style ;
yet it abounds with passages of force and beauty."
Another says, "We found the reading of it a task,
— a very prosy tale, described in a most execrable
manner. There are few good things in the book,
and innumerable pages of prolixity, commonplace,
twaddle, and jargon. . . . If it were not for the high
moral tone of the work, we should be tempted to
think it was written under the inspiration of gin and
water."

But enough of all this contradictory testimony,
serving as well for curious specimens of the diversity of individual taste, modes of thought, and moral

appreciation, as for the purpose of its introduction here.

In an unpublished review of the poems of Jones Very, written by Mr. Judd before he became an author himself, and while yet in the Theological Seminary, is found the following passage: "We shall terminate these remarks by a single word on the nature of criticism, which is, that it should be akin to the subject of which it treats. What springs from the intellect merely, may be treated by the intellect. What has its origin in the soul must be treated by the soul. A genuine production of the soul, whether it be great or small, deserves a reverential consideration. It should be examined by its own standards. It should be judged for what it is, not for what it is not. This, it will be seen, allows little room for comparative criticism, that Procrustes of all authors and artists. A violet is a violet, and should be approved for what it is, not because it is not a rose. This rule of judgment also obliges us to collate and compare both the author and his work. What springs from the soul has a meaning agreeably to that soul. If it be a genuine production, there will be found to exist a correspondence, and a reflection of lights from one to the other. It is in vain that we seek to detach a work of genius from its author. Its design is alone appreciable through, and it can alone be understood by, knowing what he is. There is, in all minds, an instinctive propensity, an insatiable longing, to trace back a production to its source. If a man be false to what he has written, all voices condemn him, and his work even fades from public estimation."

And further, he says : "Why should a man who speaks from the impersonal, boundless, authoritative depths of his own nature trim and palaver to public taste ? What is public taste to him ? If there be souls like his own, they will appreciate what he says. If not, how vain the task of accommodation to shallow and partial intellects ! No power of criticism can make a piece of clay lustrous as a flower : the flower, though it be but the humblest, shows its own colors, exhales its own fragrance."

It would seem that these lines might have been penned with a self-justificatory reference to the criticisms passed upon his own writings.

It is not the object of this chapter to go into a critical examination of the literary merits or demerits of Mr. Judd's works. The aim is rather to show his own true stand-point in them ; the heart-promptings from which they originated ; his truth to himself in them ; and, instead of aspirations for personal fame, the burning purpose of elevating and spiritualizing the race, which inspired him at the outset, and led him on through all.

Never, from his earliest student-life, had Mr. Judd that inkling, often existing in the youthful brain, of seeing himself in print. His ambition never led at all in the direction of notoriety ; but, on the contrary, his natural sensitiveness and diffidence impelled him to shrink from it. He was far from having any tendency to loquacity, either with his lips or with his pen. He always thought industriously, but uttered comparatively little. He spoke when he had something within to say. He never went through an apprenticeship of newspaper paragraphs and poetry, or of magazine-essays and tales. Any impulse of the kind which he ever felt was stimulated by the sense of a moral or religious demand, or of some irrepressible feeling of his own heart.

His very first thought of authorship was that of a little volume, prompted, during his early religious experience, by a sense of his own derelictions from duty, and intended as a warning to young Christians to beware of the incipient temptations to worldliness and sin. But this was never carried into effect.

At a later period, when suffering so keenly from mental despondency and nervous wretchedness, he conceived the idea of a tale, chiefly illustrative of " The Philosophy of the Affections," — the deep things of the heart, its yearnings and disappointments, its aspirations and its sufferings. Towards carrying out this plan, he wrote quite a number of pages ; but, on regaining a more healthful tone of feeling, and entering upon the duties and interests of his profession, he abandoned the further execution of it.

While he continued to appreciate the wants of the individual heart, to take interest in their varying phases, and to sympathize deeply with the suffering spirit, these had taken a minor place in comparison with the great interests, wrongs, and oppressions of humanity in general. There came flooding into his mind an increasing sense of the errors of the day of mistaken views of practical religion, arising from falsity of creed; of unchristian practices, supported by legal sanctions; and of a state of society falling far short of the Christian standard. He had the pulpit, to be sure, from which to speak; but the narrow limits of his own church were to him a sphere too limited for urging truths of such universal importance. The fire in his bones must have an outburst in some way.

" MARGARET."

To meet this necessity, he laid the plan of a story, which should exhibit the errors of a false theology, mistaken zeal, narrow-minded religious views, and hypocritical professions; one that should set forth the evils of intemperance, its causes and cure; the mischiefs of the war-system; the unjust treatment of the red men of our country; one furnishing considerations for the more humane treatment of prisoners, the reform of criminals, the abolition of legalized life-taking. He wished to hold up avarice to view in its true guise and its legitimate results. Errors in the training of children he would expose. To nature, with her countless voices, her soothing influence, her pure and holy teachings, her infinity of beauties, to whose inspiration his own soul responded in every variety of joyous note or mournful tone, he would give a large place. Of New England, as it was in olden times, in its primitive, country simplicity, its modes of dress and rustic sports, its training-days, its huskings, its Thanksgiving-festivals, its stern, Puritanical faith, and its natural scenery, he would preserve a memoir. To a pure, noble, refined, and gentle affection, he would give place. He would encourage faith in humanity, and confidence in its advancement, from its beautiful developments, even under the most unfavorable circumstances. The omnipotence of goodness he would unfold. The possible improvements in the organization of society he would have believed in. The fond hope of the world of a coming day for the full triumph of Christianity, he would fain have realized. In the chief character herself, he would develop something of his own experience in the spirit's power to solve for itself its own mysteries. The descriptive and reflective he would blend in attractive harmony. " Material enough," as has often been said of his works, " to furnish the capital stock of half a dozen respectable volumes."

His idea, in the outset, undoubtedly was to utter himself, once for all, on these subjects which lay with such importance on his heart. And " Margaret, a Tale of the Real and the Ideal," was the result.

He began with modest self-distrust of his own powers for such a work, and with the full intention of remaining *incognito*. He took no one for a model ; for he was so constituted that he must of necessity work out his own. He proceeded industriously and *con amore* with the work, so far as his other duties would allow him time. He made diligent research into antiquities, overhauling the antiquarian lore of his father, searching old newspapers, and looking into old school-books, and the early pamphlets of the country.

July 4, 1847, he writes to his father: " I want very much that you should get for me any books published in this country during the last century, particularly after the close of the war ; school-books, reading-books, primers, books of devotion, &c. &c. If you cannot get the books, get their names. I want to come at what may be styled an illustration of that period of the country, — 1783–1800. Dress, literature, &c. &c., the general costume of the time, what influences were upon it, its architecture, &c. The books that I want are mostly those that have perished, hence a difficulty. Also, if you could lay hands on any old arms, or bits of dresses, any old furniture, &c. &c."

He visited Westhampton, his birthplace, revived his early reminiscences of relics of earlier times, and drew what he could from the older inhabitants. Its *store*, its noon-house, its horse-sheds, and its meeting-house, furnished him material. From its formerly stern sabbath-keeping, he drew somewhat. The church-catechising, and the hurrahing on the setting of the sabbath sun, was the childish experience of himself, his brothers, and playmates. To Norwich " Pond " and " Hollow " he went ; got what information he could of an old herb-doctress formerly living there ; found some relics of a peculiarly marked people that used to inhabit the place, and took notes of peculiar expressions made use of by them. He questioned his mother and other elder relatives as to all the lore that was handed down to their early days, — the cut of old garments, with their names, and the kind of stuff of which they were made.

With nature he held deep communion ; and anew she revealed to him her secrets, resplendent with her own dewy freshness. He made ornithological excursions into " Malta Woods," and took notes from their own mouths of the joyous wild birds that had just returned to tell of their winter retreats, their gladness at revisiting their old haunts, and their hopes for the coming summer-time. Not the humblest floweret escaped his notice, and he was on terms of close acquaintance with every tree of the forest.

" Margaret " was begun about 1841, and completed near the close of 1844. The next thing was to obtain a publisher. The manuscript was submitted to several publishing-houses in Boston for examination ; but, from its being quite out of the general course of productions of the kind, they were slow to take the risk of bringing it out. At length, Munroe agreed to publish it ; but, before putting it to press, he suffered a loss by fire, which forced him to give it up. Fortunately, the manuscript escaped destruction ; and, soon after, Jordan and Wiley undertook the publication of it, the author being responsible for one-half of the expense. In August, 1845, an edition, in one volume, of a thousand copies, was issued.

It was published anonymously, without note or preface, and, from its strongly marked characteristics, elicited no little comment from the leading journals and magazines of the day. It was reviewed at length in the "North American Review" and the "Southern Quarterly." The "London Athenæum" devoted its pages to the consideration of it. Through a personal friend of Mary Howitt, the author learned that she was so much pleased with it as to wish to republish it in England.

The author's *incognito* did not serve him long. In a familiar letter concerning it, he says : "The secret of the book is somewhat destroyed. It has been tossed about so, and passed from hand to hand, that, like a kitten in a basket, it must needs *mew*, and make itself known."

To the stern Calvinist it was offensive from its liberal theology. Those whose hearts had been untouched by the interests of a common humanity, and who had no sympathy with the movements of reform in any of its branches, found nothing in its spirit to interest ; and to them it was merely dull. Those deaf to nature's voices, and blind to her beauties, in fault of all else, could not find, even in the sweet delineations of her charms, a redeeming element. The regular novel-reader, who looks only for a story of thrilling incident, and who never dreams that an author can have any other aim than to help him to kill time, after culling out the brief story of Gottfried Brückman and Jane Girardean, threw it aside as too tedious to finish. Readers of sensibilities so fine as to think *manner* every thing, and *matter* of little account, were shocked, here and there, with something new and strange to them, and gave it up in disgust. Those but partially acquainted with the riches of their own mother-tongue found the study in getting at the sense a trouble too great to recompense the benefit of perusal. And the professional reviewer, possessing no glimmerings of genius himself, or the faculty of perceiving it in others, but well skilled in applying his views to the Procrustes-bed of an established criticism, however little adapted to all times and countries, and however effete some of its rules may have become, found his subject exceeding the just limits so much here, and falling short so much there, that he was forced to give it up in despair, as a nondescript, totally unmanageable. And those who cannot admit that a proper "style is the man himself," but would have it rounded off by other models, till very little force or individuality remains, found it highly unclassical. In short, those inviolably wedded to the old and time-worn, and frightened at the advancement of any thing new, though it were a preliminary even of millennial glory; who have no faith in progress, in the regeneration of our race, in the sufficiency of Christianity to effect a final triumph to itself, — to all such, the work was a dead letter, a thing with which they could have no sympathy.

Mr. Judd's idea of the work will be seen in the passages following, extracted from a letter —

To the Rev. E. B. H.

"Augusta, July 15, 1845.

. . . "The book designs to promote the cause of liberal Christianity, or, in other words, of a pure Christianity: it would give body and soul to the

30*

divine elements of the gospel. It aims to subject bigotry, cant, pharisaism, and all intolerance. Its basis is Christ: him it would restore to the church, him it would develop in the soul, him it would enthrone in the world. It designs also, in judicious and healthful ways, to aid the cause of peace, temperance, and universal freedom. In its retrospective aspect, it seeks to preserve some reminiscences of the age of our immediate fathers, thereby describing a period of which we have no enduring monuments, and one the traces of which are fast evanescing. The book makes a large account of nature, the birds and flowers, for the sake of giving greater individuality to, and bringing into stronger relief, that which the religious mind passes over too loosely and vaguely. It is a New England book, and is designed to embody the features and improve the character of our own favored region.

"But more particularly, let me say, the book seems fitted partially to fill a gap, long left open in Unitarian literature, — that of imaginative writings. The Orthodox enjoy the works of Bunyan, Hannah More, Charlotte Elizabeth, the Abbotts, &c., &c. But what have we in their place? The original design of the book was almost solely to occupy this niche; although, I fancy, you may think it has somewhat passed these limits. It seems to me, that this book is fitted for a pretty general Unitarian circulation; that it might be of some use in the hands of the clergy, in our families, Sunday-school libraries, &c. My own personal education in, and acquaintance with, 'Orthodoxy,' as well as my idea of the prevalent errors of the age, lead me to think such a book is needed. Will your judgment, sir, sustain mine? or am I mistaken? That another should approve the whole of 'Margaret,' is more than its author flatters himself to believe; yet he hopes there is that in it which will recommend it to a pretty general perusal. You will read and judge for yourself. The book furnishes rather a hint at important principles, than any distinct statement; and, out of what purports to be a history of men and things, it is in the power of the reader to make his own conclusions. The author wishes to hasten what are believed to be the peculiar triumphs of Christianity.

" With sincere regards, I am yours, &c.

"SYLVESTER JUDD, JR."

The most appreciative review of "Margaret," and that which approached most nearly to Mr. Judd's own idea in it, was the one contained in the "Southern Quarterly." It was a curious coincidence, and one of no little interest to Mr. Judd, that this article was written by the Rev. Dexter Clapp, then residing at New Orleans, but a native of the same town with him, and an early schoolmate; though, at the time the review was written, the author's name was unknown to the reviewer. A few of Mr. Clapp's remarks, containing a general summary of the scope of the work, are subjoined. "As a romance," he says, "we regard it as very imperfect, little more than respectable; but, as a record of great ideas and sentiments, we place it among the few good books of the age. 'Margaret' is a happy illustration of the

progress of the actual and natural to the ideal and
spiritual. The author has a true and open heart,
and has felt the power of genuine love. He seems
to us a deeply earnest man, really anxious to serve
his race. He speaks of Christianity like a Christian,
with eloquence, power, and truth. Pious cant, mere
ecclesiastical formalities, he treats with the scorn
they deserve. He makes them appear the very de-
formities they are, and a real service to religion every
man does who exposes any of the forms of hypo-
cracy. We believe he will win men to truth and
faith, by his beautiful and striking contrast of religious pretensions and pharisaism, with simple and
unaffected goodness. He is a teacher of sincerity.
He would break down and remove all those forms
that tend to oppress, and limit within material
bounds, the free and loving human heart. With
him, forms of faith are nothing, while faith is every
thing. He here strikes at a truth which the world
is slow to learn, but one which lies at the centre of
all moral progress. He goes deeper than the partial,
varying human letter, into the deep and universal
spirit of Christ.

"The work contemplates social advancement and
reform. Herein is its immediate and chief practical
worth. We recognize a higher truth in it than in
any other writings that have come under our notice,
which advocate the reorganization of society. He
pleads for religion. He looks to it as the only agency existing in the world, great enough to work out
its regeneration; and carefully does he distinguish
between the substance and the form, between the

dead letter and the living spirit. His faith in Christianity is sincere and deep. He believes in it as a
growing, ever-working force. To its keeping he
would entrust all human interests."

James Russell Lowell, in his "Fable for Critics,"
paid tribute to it in this wise : —

> "*Margaritas*, for him you have verified gratis;
> What matters his name? Why, it may be Sylvester
> Judd, Junior or Junius, Ulysses or Nestor,
> For aught I know or care; 'tis enough that I look
> On the author of ' Margaret,' the first Yankee book,
> With the *soul* of Down East in't, and things further east,
> As far as the threshold of morning at least,
> Where awaits the fair dawn of the simple and true,
> Of the day that comes slowly to make all things new."

A very gratifying circumstance to the author
was the fact, that Mr. Darley, a young artist, also
residing at the South, who knew nothing of the
author's name or residence, was so much struck with
the graphic delineations of the book, and their truly
American character, that he devoted his pencil, in
the spirit of an amateur, to a series of outline illustrations, which testify alike to the skill of the artist
and the genius of the author.

In 1851, after undergoing a careful revision,
" Margaret " was stereotyped ; and a new edition,
much improved in external appearance, was published in two volumes.

To this edition Mr. Judd prefixed the following
"Note," dated Riverside, Augusta, May 12, 1851 : —

" It is now more than ten years since ' Margaret '
was commenced. To-day is the revision of the work
ended. Not without sensibility has such a retrospect

been gone through with. Old acquaintances and familiar scenes of the imagination are not less impressive than those of the actual world. The author cannot retrace the ground of these pages, without being reminded of some things he would forget, and others that he is too fearful of losing. The book was written out of his heart and hope. Has a decade of years and experience vitiated or overset aught of that heart and hope? Going over the book at this time is not precisely like a call on old friends: it becomes a species of self-examination.

"In the result, as to the general character and drift of the work, the author finds little to alter. Not that he could write just such a book again: he could not. But he cleaves to the ideas according to which, and the objects for which, this was written.

"In the revision, sentences have been changed, not sentiments; and the expunging process has respected words more than things.

"'Margaret' was never designed for railroads: it might peradventure suit a canal-boat. Rather is it like an old-fashioned ride on horseback, where one may be supposed to enjoy leisure for climbing hills, and to possess curiosity for the trifles of the way.

"It is proper that some answer be given to observations that have been freely, and, it will not be doubted, kindly bestowed on the author and his labors: —

"'He is too minute; he seems to be making out a ship's manifest, instead of telling a plain story.' — The book was written for the love of the thing; and each item has been introduced with a love of it.

Every bird has been watched, every flower pursued, every foot-path traversed. No author can, indeed, expect the public to share his tastes, or join his recreations : he does solicit a charitable construction of his spirit and purpose.

" ' He is vulgar.' — A popular tradition declares tastes to be indisputable, and imparts to them an authority which belongs only to revelation. We are inclined to think there is a dispute about them ; and the issue may as well be made up first as last. Is what we call common life, are those who pass for illiterate, uncultivated, ignorant people, their properties and reminiscences, here in New England, to be regarded as vulgar ? — using the word in a certain odious sense. To take an instance from the following pages, — and that is where the question is carried, — is Obed vulgar ? We aver that he is not. He is an unrefined, rude, simple youth ; but in all his relations to Margaret, — in all the little part he acts in the scene, he is courteous, gentle, delicate, disinterested, pure. At least, he seems so to us. We may have failed to report him fairly. But, allowing him to be such, are we justified in pronouncing him vulgar ? Is Nimrod to be accounted a vulgar-spoken youth ?

" ' He is unequal, grotesque, mermaiden, abrupt.' — Here are involved the same questions as before, What is vulgar, and what refined ; what noble, what mean ? There are standards of taste valid and needful. But is not the range of their application too limited ? May not rough rocks have a place in the fairest landscapes of nature or art ? May not a dark pool of water in the forest, with its vegetable and animal adjuncts, mirror the stars? Have we not seen or heard of a cascade that starts, say, from the blue of the skies, pours down a precipice of rusty rock, and terminates in drift-wood and bog? Is that water *bathetic*? These are questions we do not care to argue here and now. Are they not worthy of consideration? Have they no pertinence to the subject in hand?

" ' He is no artist.' — If what everybody says be true, and what almost everybody says be almost true, to this iterated charge we ought to gasp out a *peccavi*, and be silent. But, good friends all, a moment's indulgence. May there not be a moral, as well as a material, plot? a plot of ideas, as well as of incidents? ' Margaret ' is a tale, not of outward movement, but of internal development. An obvious part of its plan is the three epochs of the life of its principal personage. Another part is the times in which the scene lies. Rose belongs to the plot of the book; so does the Indian. Master Elliman has been called a sort of diluted imitation of Dominie Sampson. The plot of the book involved this; that, while Margaret grew up in, or contiguous to, a religious and civilized community, she should remain, for the most part, unaffected by these influences; yet that she should not mature in ignorance, but should receive quite an amount of a species of erudition. To effect this, the master is introduced. The management of this part of the tale, it need not be said, was one of the most difficult problems the author had to encounter. To the general thread of the drama a variety of things are attached, not one of which, in the main, is not conceived to be tributary to the gradual evolution of the whole. The purely material accessories of the story, being deemed quite insubordinate, are thrown in corners by themselves.

"The book takes our country as it emerges from the Revolution, and does not bring it down to what now is, but carries it up, or a portion of it, to what it is conceived should be; and the final *dénouement* may be found in the last part. In all this is system, arrangement, precedent, effect, and due relation of things. We have wished herein to be artistical: certainly our feelings are not whimsical, neither is our method governed by any conscious caprice. How far we have succeeded, it is not for us to say. We would thank certain ones, assayers of literature, at least to consider what we have attempted to do.

"To those who have been glad at what the author has written, he extends the hope that they may never regret their gladness.

"Those who disrelish his publications, he knows, can find things in the book-stores to their liking; and he is sufficiently generous to wish them joy in whatever line of reading their fancies or feelings may adopt."

With the author's interpretation of himself just given, we will lay aside "Margaret," and turn to his second intellectual offspring.

31

" PHILO."

After finishing his first work, Mr. Judd found
that he had still certain moral ideas floating in his
brain, to which he had not given all the prominence
and definiteness he wished. He did not care to put
them forth in the form of essays : he did not wish to
discuss them in a formal manner in any way. He
had never accustomed himself to write in verse,
and had no ambition to set himself up as a poet.
But, in casting about for some mode of utterance for
his thoughts, he felt that the laws of verse would
offer many facilities, especially in not requiring a set
form of discussion, and in allowing a style sufficiently desultory to admit the variety of topics he
wished to introduce.

So he thought, at least, he would try the experiment of versifying. And, seated in the kitchen,
with his feet upon the stove-hearth, near the close
of 1845, his wife discovered him, greatly to her
surprise, and with a little fear as to his sanity, per-
petrating the first lines of " Philo," in pencil, on a
scrap of paper he held in his hand. Thus he made
a beginning. And from time to time, when variously employed, and sometimes in the most homely
ways, he might be seen taking a slip of paper from
his pocket, and with pencil writing down lines as
they came to mind. But these sibylline leaves at
length began to take the form of a systematic work.
Several scenes were written. And by and by the
author got courage to read them to a few of his
closest personal friends, with the consciousness with-

in himself that he was not a native-born poet, as expressed in the lines, —

> "Our minister is a new hand at rhymes;
> He rolls them off as teamsters bales of cotton;
> Waits Art's more perfect day for the fine tissue!"

Many a hearty laugh had the select family-group of listeners at these sittings, in which he himself was not loth to join, as some rude measures or unique expressions fell upon the ear. Yet from them he received encouragement to proceed, and his own power of versification increased as he went on. The work grew to its destined size. It embodied the ideas he wished to send forth on their mission of love. He revised the manuscript with care, and gave it completion in the commencement of 1848. Phillips and Sampson, of Boston, issued it in one volume in a handsome stereotype edition.

It was noticed by the papers and periodicals, much after the fashion of the criticisms upon " Margaret," — hailed by many as a true *Evangeliad;* but by those who did not even understand the meaning of the word, or sympathize in the idea which it expressed, it was of course condemned.

At the time this poem was composed, the Mexican War was in progress, regrets for and lamentations over which seemed to penetrate the author, even to the marrow of his bones. Among other moral evils that were made the theme of caustic satire and bitter mourning, this was the most prominent burden of the song.

The name of the work, " Philo," was given with reference to its character and mission. The grand design was, in the spirit of love, to hold up in their true light the glaring inconsistencies between the practices of this professedly Christian country, and the spirit of the gospel of Christ. It shows this in the want of love among different denominations bearing the Christian name; in the sufferance of man's enslaving his fellow-man; in the hideousness and heart-sickening horrors of war, that "hybrid of sin and death;" in the doctrine of expediency; in the rejection of the spirit of love, faith, and hope; and other kindred points. It closes with a vision of the general righting of all wrongs, of the spiritual regeneration of the world, and the commencement of a reign of peace and blessedness on earth; an age when seraphs shall chant anew —

> "Glory to God in the highest,
> On earth peace and good-will to man!"

with a chorus of people chiming in, —

> "Ages burst their silent tomb,
> Years of God begin their round;
> Prophecy fulfils its moans,
> Earth in Christ transfigured lies.'

Mr. Judd's own key to the aim of this work will be found in the letter following, —

To Rev. E. E. H.

"AUGUSTA, Dec. 21, 1849.

"My dear Sir, — Will you accept a copy of 'Philo,' and a brief claviary?

"First, the book is an 'attempt.'

"Second, it is an epical or heroic attempt.

"Third, it would see if in liberal and rational

Christianity, and there is no other, and that is Unitarianism, are epic and heroic elements.

"Fourth, it remembers that Calvinism has its 'Course of Time;' and it asks if Unitarianism, that is, the innermost of reason and divinity, will have any thing; or rather, approaching, humbly of course, the altar of Great Thought and Feeling, it would like to know if it would be agreeable to that altar to receive a little gift, a turtle-dove and a small pigeon, of Unitarian faith and hope.

"Fifth, and correlatively, it asks if, in this very sensible and sound age of ours, imagination must needs be inactive, and awed by philosophy, utility, steam.

"Sixth, and more especially, if any of the foregoing points are admitted, the book seeks through the medium of poetry to interpret prophecy. It is conceived that prophecy, the Apocalypse for example, was once poetry; and moreover that we shall fail to understand prophecy, until it is recast in its original form.

"This observation applies particularly to that most interesting, yet most enigmatical matter, the second coming of Christ, &c. &c.

"What may be the fortune of 'Philo,' I am neither prophet nor poet enough to tell.

"I am not a beggar of applause, as I would not be the pensioner of dulness.

"With sincere regards, I am yours, &c.
"SYLVESTER JUDD."

To another person he writes : —
"It is not a collection of poems, but a treatment
31*

of elevated Christian topics in blank verse. It is designed to be full of hope to mankind; it looks on the brighter side of nature, man, death; it is reformatory and improving in its spirit; it is (believed to be) pervaded with love and good-will.

" I chose this way, rather than prose, because I thought I could better express certain topics, feelings, interests, in a poetical form than any other. It belongs to the times.

" It is a book of liberal and progressive ideas; it is adapted to all who wish well to their country, the church, or the world."

Again he writes to the Rev. E. E. H. : —

"AUGUSTA, Jan. 11, 1850.

" My dear E. E. H. — I thank you for your letter, and for all you say and think and feel about 'Philo,' and about any thing else, now and ever.

" But to the book : is the drift of it, or of any portions of it, not sufficiently obvious ? Perhaps it is not, and of course I am sorry. What is a luminous road to me may be a heap of odious stumbling-blocks to some others. By dwelling upon certain sentiments, ideas, things, we get far into them, and forget at what a distance we have left the world behind us ; we may even close the entrance after us, and the world has no other notion of our whereabouts than by certain subterranean hollowings, the precise place of which it is always difficult to identify. We are innocently guilty of a species of intellectual ventriloquism.

" This applies to the topic, scriptural or metrical, of the Advent, or a second coming of Christ. Thanks possibly to Elder Miller, my attention some years since was called to this subject. I examined the New Testament with care and candor. This is the sum of my conclusions, — that Christ would come into the world again, that he expected to come, and promised to come. But how? *In the person of his followers:* in their virtues his would be reproduced, in their moral beauty his would be pronounced; they would walk in his steps, bear his cross, die his death, illustrate his life, and so personate him. The *coming* of Christ, and his *revelation*, are terms used interchangeably by the evangelists, and by the Saviour himself. So we read, 1 Cor. i. 7, ' Waiting for the coming of our Lord " (m. r. *revelation, ἀποκάλυψιν*). So our Lord, Luke xvii. 30, speaking of his coming, alludes to it as the day when the Son of man shall be *revealed*.

"This coming, revelation, or advent, is moreover a glorious event. ' He shall come with clouds and great glory.' Here commences the Orientalism, or, as we should now say, the poetry, of the thing. ' The trump shall sound,' — a poetical allusion to the jubilee fanfares of the Jews. ' The dead shall be raised; even now,' adds Christ, while he was then speaking, ' they shall come forth from their graves ;' the dead in sin, the carnally deceased. The theme is taken up by Paul, who expressly says, ' Christ is *revealed in us* ;' Peter energetically echoes the same idea, and speaks of the new heaven and new earth, *wherein dwelleth righteousness;* and John, in Patmos, finally throws the whole into a sublime poem, prophecy, or what you will.

" On this subject I have preached; for this coming I have prayed; on it I have meditated; and now, finally, have made it a sort of thread on which to string some pages of a book.

" Well, all this, this view of Scripture, this matter of hermeneutics, is familiar to you, and to many others. I cannot suppose it is familiar to everybody. How far ought I to suppose it familiar to critics in general?

" I did think of appending an explanatory note; but hoped, after all, that the text of the work would explain itself. I do still think a *careful* reading will make the thing plain. But ought we to presume on careful readers among the mass of those to whom Phillips and Sampson may distribute copies? I know not if there be any danger of mistake; I only wish *my friends*, whoever they may be, that shall undertake to review the book, may be set right. . . .

" I am so little acquainted with the machinery of the literary world, that, on matters of this sort, I hardly know what to say, or what not to say.

" I do not speak of uncandid minds, if there are such, but of candid; and should be sorry to have such stumble, not perhaps at the threshold, but at the postern, of the book.

" ' Margaret ' was a Christian consummation in a single neighborhood; 'Philo' is the same for the land at large, and the whole world. It is a sort of Christian estimate of the world; its ultimate idea is redemption by Christ. It admits of (poetical) supernatural agencies in Gabriel, &c. It looks, from the Christian or Christ's point of view, at men and things in the world. The fancy of 'the devil' is designed to drive the theological devil from the world and from the universe. The doctrine of the book is that no foreign, infernal, super-human agency is allowed in the world. It teaches, moreover, that the hope of the world lies in itself; in its men and women, its wood and iron, and in the blessed gospel of the Son of God, which also it has. It alludes to the evils, and more particularly to that culminating one, war. In Charles is expressed the sceptical, profane, dark side of things, &c. &c. It winds up with a poetical account of that which I believe to be the consummation of the wish, purpose, and plan of Jesus, — the Advent; that which Christ most literally, truthfully, and earnestly conceived; which was to his eye the grandest of all visions, and which he — and how could he do otherwise? — spoke of in terms borrowed from the imagination; borrowed, too, from the imagination of the sacred books of his people; borrowed from, and belonging to, the imagination of all times.

"Is this apparent, or is it closed to the common reader of the book?

"You allude to the Arians. Their history ought to be written. Materials, I know, are scant, and difficult of access; but such a work would be an admirable contribution to our theological literature, to say nothing of the claims which the abused, worthy dead have on the justice of the living. Wont you bestir yourself in this behalf?

"Yours, very truly."

And, with reference to the criticisms passed upon

it, he says, in a letter to a brother: "While the book has been gladly welcomed in some quarters, it has been shamefully abused in others. It has been trivially looked at, and trivially noticed. It has been treated as a joke, while really it is one of the most serious works ever written. Think of what the 'Literary World' charged upon 'Philo,' — 'an undisguised infidelity'! Compare that with the language of our sainted brother, 'that it was full of Jesus.' Are there no minds, are there not many minds, to whom it might come as a book 'full of Jesus'?"

"RICHARD EDNEY."

"Richard Edney and the Governor's Family" was written mostly in the interval between the finishing of "Philo" and its publication. A stereotype edition of it, in one volume, was published by Phillips and Sampson, the last part of the same year in which "Philo" was issued, 1850. This work underwent the same general course of remark as the two previous ones; some giving it a higher place than "Margaret," others regarding it as falling below that in merit.

In its general scope and design, this work is kindred with the other two, and animated by the same kindling spirit of love for humanity and desires for its elevation. It differs from "Margaret," in representing our own times. A prominent aim is to show that a man is what he makes himself; and that he can, by his own inherent energies, make himself what he chooses. Its bearing is to elevate the working classes; to bring together, in kindly intercourse and the interchange of good offices, the rich and the poor; and to confer on human labor the honor and dignity which is its due.

Another idea, which entered largely into the construction of the work, was to "catch the manners living as they rise;" or rather, instead of creating characters and scenes purely ideal, to take them ready formed at his hand, as he found them in daily life, in social intercourse, in his walks about town, in his rural excursions. At the time of writing this, his mind dwelt much on the fitness of thus drawing from the actual and real. Augusta, the bridge across the Kennebec, its dam, its factories, its freshets, were laid largely under contribution in the composition of the work, although any one would do wrong to suppose that "Woodylyn" was intended as a representation of that town, or, on the whole, answered to it. So, also, individual families and persons formed the *basis* of many delineations, though of no one could it be said that he sat for the picture. Still there are hints enough of local bearing and interest to give a peculiar zest to those who are in the secret and acquainted with the place. The truth to nature of the description of the snow-storm with which the book is ushered in, and the graphic portraiture of the Stage-driver, have universally found admirers. The children Memmy and Bebby have secured friends among all the lovers of juveniles. The "hard parting" of friends has received a sigh from every mourner's breast; to the "Athanatopsis" has been sent back a heavily tolling knell from the deep recesses of the suffering heart.

The last chapter, entitled "Parting Words," giving quite an insight into the genial humor and benevolent spirit of the book, as well as an intimation of the objects of all the author's works, and his explanation of himself in them, shall have some place here.

"To those authors," he says, "from whom, in the composition of this tale, we have borrowed, we return sincere thanks. If our publishers, who are obliging gentlemen, consent, we would like to forward a copy of the book to each of them. If they dislike any thing of theirs in this connection, they will of course withdraw it; should they chance to like any thing of ours, they have full permission to use it. This would seem to be fair.

"Pope Gregory VII. burned the works of Varro, from whom Augustine had largely drawn, that the saint might not be accused of plagiarism. We have no such extreme intention. First, it would be an endless task. What consternation in the literary world, should even the humblest author undertake such a thing! And such authors are the ones who would be most inclined to cancel their obligations in this way. We might fire the Cambridge Library; but, alas! the assistant librarian, whose pleasant face has beguiled for us so much weary research in those alcoves, and, as it were, illuminated the black letter of so many recondite volumes, — to see him shedding tears over their ashes would undo us! We are weak there. Secondly, it comports at once with manliness and humility to confess one's indebtedness. Thirdly, as a matter of expediency, it is better to avail one's self of a favorable wind and general convoy to fame, than run the risk of being becalmed, and perhaps devoured, on some private and unknown route. But, lastly and chiefly, let it be recorded, there is a social feeling among authors, — they cherish convivial sentiments, — they are never envious of a fellow ; there is not probably a great author living but that, like a certain great king, would gladly throw a chicken or a chicken's wing from his feathered abundance to any poor author, and enjoy its effect in lighting up the countenances of the poor fellow's wife and children. Wherefore is it that plagiarism, after all, is to be considered rather in the light of good cheer and kindly intercourse, than as evidence of meanness of disposition, or paucity of ideas. To the tourist, who, with guide-book in hand, and curious pains-taking, seeks to recover scenes and places, fleetingly commemorated in these pages, we are obliged to say, he will be disappointed. This tale, in the language of art, is a composition, not a sketch. There is no such city as Woodylin ; or, more truly, we might affirm, the materials of it exist throughout the country. Its population and its pursuits are confined to no single locality, but are scattered everywhere. Its elements of good, hope, progress, may be developed everywhere. Would, too, that whatever it contains prejudicial to human weal might be depressed in all regions of the earth !

"To the book itself —

' VADE, LIBER,'

(GO, LITTLE BOOK,)

'Qualis, non ausim dicere, felix.'
(What will be your fortune, I cannot tell.)

'Vade tamen quocunque lubet, quascunque per oras,
I blandas inter charites, mystamque saluta
Musarum quemvis, si tibi lector erit.
Rura colas, urbemque.'

(Yet go wherever you like, — go everywhere, — go among kind people;
you may even venture to introduce yourself to the severer sort, if they
will admit you. Visit the city and the country.)

'Si criticus lector, tumidus censorque molestus,
Zoilus et Momus, si rabiosa cohors,' — approach,
'Fac fugias,' — fly.
'Læto omnes accipe vultu,
Quos, quas, vel quales, inde vel unde viros.'

(Look cheerfully upon all, men and women, and all of every condition.)

"Go into farm-houses and rustic workshops; call
at the homes of the opulent and the powerful; visit
schools; say to the minister you have a word for
the church. I know you will love the family: you
may stay in the kitchen; and, as you are so neatly
dressed, and behave so prettily, they will let you
sit in the parlor. Let the hard hand of the laboring
classes hold you; nor need you shrink from the soft
hand of fair maiden. Speak pleasantly to the little
children; — I need not fear on that score; — speak
wisely and respectfully to parents; you may enter
the haunts of iniquity, and preach repentance there;
you may show your cheerful face in sordid abodes,
and inspire a love for piety and blessedness. Go
West — go South: you need not fear to utter a true
word anywhere. Especially, and these are your private instructions, speak to our young men, and tell

them not to be so anxious to exchange the sure results of labor for the shifting promise of calculation ; tell them that the hoe is better than the yard-stick. Instruct them that the farmer's frock and the mechanic's apron are as honorable as the merchant's clerk's paletot, or the student's cap. Show them how to rise *in* their calling, not out of it ; and that intelligence, industry, and virtue are the only decent way to honor and emolument. Help them to bear sorrow, disappointment, and trial, which are wont to be the lot of humanity. And, more especially, demonstrate to them, and to all, how they may BE GOOD AND DO GOOD.

" Should inquiries arise touching your parentage and connections, — a natural and laudable curiosity, which, as a stranger in the world, you will be expected to enlighten, — you may say that you are one of three, believed to be a worthy family, comprising two brothers and one sister ; that, a few years since, your author published the history of a young woman, entitled ' Margaret, a Tale of the Real and the Ideal ; ' and that at the same time, and as a sort of counterpart and sequel to this, he embraced the design of writing the history of a young man, and you are the result. The first shows what, in given circumstances, a woman can do ; the last indicates what may be expected of a man : the first is more antique ; the last, modern. Both are local in action, but diffusive in spirit. In the meantime, he has written ' Philo, an Evangeliad ; ' cosmopolitan, œcu-menical, sempiternal, in its scope ; embodying ideas rather than facts, and uniting times and places ; and cast in the only form in which such subjects could be disposed of, — the allegoric and symbolical; or, as it is sometimes termed, the poetic. The two first are individual workers; the last is a representative life. 'Philo' is as an angel of the everlasting gospel; you and 'Margaret,' one in the shop, and the other on the farm, are practical Christians. However different your sphere or your manners, you may say you all originate, on the part of your author, in a single desire to glorify God and bless his fellow-men. 'Philo' has been called prosy; 'Margaret' was accounted tedious. You, 'Richard,' I know, will appear as well as you can, and be what you are, — honest certainly, pleasing if possible.

"God bless thee, little book, and anoint thee for thy work, and make thee a savor of good to many! We shall meet again in other years or worlds. May we meet for good, and not for evil! If there is any evil in thy heart or thy ways, God purge it from thee."

"THE WHITE HILLS, AN AMERICAN TRAGEDY."

Another work of Mr. Judd's, in unpublished manuscript, is denominated "The White Hills, an American Tragedy." Its titlepage bears date, Sept. 8, 1851; 3, p.m. Ther. 90°.

A "Note" on the first page reads thus: "This Drama contains an allusion to the following passage, which may be found in Sullivan's History of Maine: 'The White Mountains have a singular appearance, when viewed from a distance: their tops are white like snow. There was an early expectation of finding a gem, of immense size and value, on this mountain: it was conjectured, and it is yet believed by some, that a carbuncle is suspended from a rock over a pond of water there. While many, in the early days of the country's settlement, believed this report, each one was afraid that his neighbor should become the fortunate proprietor of the prize, by right of prior possession. To prevent this, credit was given to the tale of the natives, that the place was guarded by an evil spirit, who troubled the waters, and raised a dark mist, on the approach of human footsteps.

" 'There was another tradition, that three hills of rocks were situated up Saco River, about forty miles from the sea, as full of silver as the mines of Peru. Fully persuaded of this, William Phillips, of Saco, purchased these mountains of Captain Sunday, a Sachem, in the year 1660; but he or his posterity have never been able to possess the expected wealth from these hills.' "

The drama is in five acts. It is written mainly in blank verse, and is allegorical in character. Its aim, like that of his other works, is chiefly moral; its object being to mirror the consequences of a man's devoting himself to an all-absorbing love of gain, — to the supreme worship of Mammon. The basis of the idea was suggested by the general rage for California gold, which, for a year or two before its commencement, had been so rife amongst almost all classes of the community. The Dramatis Personæ are —

NORMAND, a Student.
LEIRION, the Betrothed of Normand.
THE MOTHER OF NORMAND.
MAMMON.
VAFER, the Witch-mother.
TURPIS, the Witch-daughter.
PERNIX, } The Witch-relatives.
SKLEROTE,
THE GIANT OF THE HILLS.
A CHILD.
SUNDRY CASUAL PERSONS.

THE SCENE — *America*.   TIME — *The Present Time.*

In Normand, the principal character, is shown
how one who makes money-getting the great object
of life is led on, step by step, to sacrifice affection,
integrity, conscience; to barter soul and body in the
pursuit.   He is a young student, of noble mind and
aspiring aims, who suffers in his soul a sense of the
curse and sting of pinching poverty.   He cares not
for wealth in itself considered, but for the valuable
gratifications which it brings, and the respect and
consideration which he regards unattainable without
it.   He is attached, in fervent love, to Leirion, a
pure and heavenly-minded girl; but poverty will
not allow him to endow her as he feels she merits.
His boyhood's years were near to heaven in their
gentleness and love.   On him centre the earnest
prayers of his blind old mother.   He wears a cross,
a dying gift of a dear brother.   To nature's kind
and holy voice, his heart is tenderly attuned.   All
good influences encircle him around, and sacred
associations bind him to the path of duty.   But this
is the burden of his heart: —

"Alas! I'm poor. What is it to
Be poor? Is it to lack bread, credit, smiles,
Attendance? To be hungry, cold? 'Tis not
To want, but not to be. 'Tis that one's wants
Become one's being, and his hates his masters.
'Tis to feel mean, before some meaner clay
That one would spit upon. 'Tis not to suffer,
But to be pitied; it is not to need,
But not to dare to ask. 'Tis not that men
Neglect me: it is that I shrink from them,
Abjure the sun, and hide me from the street,
And hesitate at gentle courtesies
Of woman. This is to be poor. I could
Endure, defy perdition, kiss despair;
But let me be respected. With a proud
And lofty mind, I'm no man's peer; down, down,
Abject, dependent. I am not a slave:
I wish I were. I hate the poor: of all
That God hath made, they are the vilest thing."

While thus giving way to these maddening
thoughts, Mammon, in the guise of a modern gentleman, enters, learns his trouble, and leads him to a
spot from which the White Hills are visible in the
distance. Mammon waves a wand, and bids him look;
and at length gives him a glass, through which he
sees the immense size and radiance of the pearl.
His soul is fired with the view, and he determines
to snatch the prize; but he is warned by Mammon
of the peril of attacking the guarding genius, and
the hopelessness of attempting to do it in the condition in which he then was. Mammon, however,
directs him to the witch Vafer, who will "rake the
peril from his path." He also bids him abjure her

he loves, and the cross he bears about him; and Normand, in the wild excitement of the moment, is ready to surrender every thing for the gratification of this one over-mastering passion. He enters into compact with Mammon, commits himself to the clutches of the god of riches. Then come the re-action, the misgivings, the loss of inward peace, the remembrance of his innocent childhood, of his blind mother's prayers, of his beloved Leirion, of his dead brother's pious influences; and he is wretched. But he is fairly entangled: he has consented that gold shall be his god, and he cannot escape. He is led further and further into a mesh of sin and guilt, from which he has not power to extricate himself.

But ever and anon return upon him tender memories of earlier days, and the gentle influences of nature, from the power of which he cannot escape, and yet to which he will not yield. And thus goes on, through his whole career, a terrible conflict with his better nature; striking contrasts and struggles of feeling, with a fearful apprehensive foreboding as to the final result. The several phases of his state furnish some most striking scenes, in which the light and shade are blended with great effect.

Vafer, Turpis, Pernix, and Sklerote, the witch-family, are personifications of the qualities their names import; and the chief thread of the drama is a succession of scenes formed in accomplishing their requirements. The interviews with the witches are managed very much after the Shaksperian manner. All weird elements are made to bear their part in the charm Normand is to weave, by which to palsy the power of the guardian of the pearl, and thus to overcome him.

The accompanying scenery is varied, rich, and striking, including views of the White Hills, the Notch, the Old Man of the Mountain, the Basin, the Flume ; also of Lake George with its many islands, Saratoga, a city Exchange, the humble cottage of Leirion, &c., &c.

It will not be attempted here to go into a minute analysis of the whole piece, or to do any thing like justice to its merits. As has been shown, the scenes are laid in spots familiar and endeared to the traveller for pleasure ; and, in the preparation of the work, Mr. Judd made successive journeys to the White Hills, and also visited in person the seat of other scenes, and hence he was able to give to his representations a remarkable freshness and truth of coloring.

Specimens of the work will be given, in random extracts, here and there. The first which follows is from Normand's strugglings with himself in sight of the hills, the day after entering into compact with Mammon : —

" Was it some spiritual trance, a scene evoked
  In fever's fitful change, or history
  Of natural things ? Bright to the uttermost,
  It weighs on me like gloomy death, or sigh
  Disastrous, 'splendent death, auroral grave,
  Down which, with all my better life, I plunged.
  Reflection, like a tempest, sweeps my heart
  Of every trace of pleasure ; sadness reigns.
      The hills, in their calm fires, — they mock
  Me not. The sumptuousness of rest is theirs,
  As holy sabbath-time, white as a bride.

Behind me, Mammon ; 'neath, above, around,
Is God, my better self, my childhood dreams,
And ah ! my Leirion.   Which most inclines ?
What am I ?   Changed from what I was, or such
Self-questioning had never passed these lips.
Conscience is dead, stone dead ; the bent and aim
I cherished of a higher good in life,
More consonant with virtue, of deserved
Renown, and benefit to human kind,
If living, burns like a forgotten lamp.   I dare
Not think of what I was, I am so changed. —
Normand ! a voice calls Normand.   Normand is
Not here.   If I look like myself, it is
As frozen pippins that keep up the blush
And general transcript of a life that's fled.

 The hills gleam, blazing to their crystal core.
The pale pearl like a globed rainbow burns ;
And my ambition takes a gayer hue.
Ambition ?   'Tis revenge and trick
Heroic on the temper of the times,
That makes of gold a god, and penury
A crime.   I will be rich : I'll have estates,
A seal, blood, quality, and living ;
Some right of way along this crowded world ;
The smiles of art, and thanks of charity.
Had I the means, I'd do extensive good
As any man.   I'll rise, and so un-god
The age, and purge this odium from man.

 Abjure the cross !   The latchet of my dress —
A little thing, my brother gave it me,
A parting gift, and, with his parting breath,
Hoped I would wear it for his sake, not *its*.
One hung on it, and bore our sins.   He chid
Temptation, and, when Mammon tendered him
The pearl, refused it.   Empire, glory, all

The world can offer, more than it contains,
Were not a flexure in his even course
Of holiness and truth.   The cross this saith,
And more than speech, the rhetoric of form
Uttering a world of things in two straight lines.
I must away with it, as erst they did
With him.   Why hesitate?   It doth denote
What I have thought about, and sometimes loved.
Is that of consequence?   What sediment
Of pain is at the bottom of my nature,
And makes me all a turbid deep of woe?
I'll none of it.   Up, covetous design,
And dash to earth the cross!"

He seeks a parting interview with Leirion.   The
spot is a cottage, embowered in woodbine and shrubbery.   In a room, with open windows, set with
books, a harpsichord, ornaments of rustic art, and
furniture of simple use, Leirion is seen embroidering
a cross.   Normand, undiscovered, looks in at the
window, and retires.

NORMAND.

I cannot enter.   Nook of paradise,
With a bright angel in it!   It is no place
For me.   I'm lost, not callous or malign;
And contrast makes me lonely, dreadfully
Alone.   Back of the cottage is the sky,
And back of this is heaven.   And she's in heaven,
Whose awful azure glories her with heart
Of maiden innocence and holy peace;
While I retreat to what I am, to gaze
Across a pathless gulf on what I was.

Leirion, perceiving Normand, calls to him, and
he goes into the house.

LEIRION.

Art thou well ?   Sit here; let me see thine eye.

NORMAND, *pacing the room.*

I love to try the air as swallows do,
Where thou hast breathed.

LEIRION.

                Does thy head ache of work,
Or brain of thought, or heart of any thing ?

NORMAND.

I wish I were a bird, and I would sing
To thee ; a brook, and I would babble thee ;
A woman, I would be thee ; or a man,
And I would wed thee.

LEIRION.

         Thou art a man.

NORMAND.

                     A poor one.

LEIRION.

That is a circumstance quite out of time ;
I would not touch it ; I'll sing thee a song.

NORMAND, *earnestly.*

Tell me, why do you love me, Leirion ?

LEIRION, *smiling.*

Because 'tis natural to love.   For love
Of thee, I love thee.

NORMAND.

         Has't no obvious ground
Of prudence or reserve, or some delight
Of private feeling ?

LEIRION.

         To tell thee what thou knowest, —
That thou wert good and true, and aimed at greatness ;
And more, thou wouldst ennoble all thy means ;
True honor decked the spring-time of thy deeds ;
Thou sparkledst in sincerity as dew ;

Like youth of Athens, who with torches ran,
So thou, nor wouldst in darkness win the race.
Does that content thee?

NORMAND.
Ay, well, very well.

LEIRION.
But something frets content, and as a moth
About the lustre of thy gladness plays.
Thy eye is seared as there were drought upon't,
Thy look not cheerful as it used to be;
Abstraction seals thy lips, like funeral-time,
Or fearfulness, or what they say is sin.
Thy hand is cold; so cold, I should be sad
Enough, save that thy heart is warm. Do not
Withdraw it; it will freeze away from me.

NORMAND.
And with thee burn, burn a consuming fire.

LEIRION.
Fond, foolish twattler!

NORMAND.
'Twill be poor to thee, —
Poor as ingratitude, despite, and scorn.

LEIRION.
We will be poor together.

NORMAND.
'Twill be accursed.

LEIRION.
I could bear want or any thing with thee.

NORMAND.
And I with thee and for thee; to thee I'll
Not bring the bitter load.

LEIRION.
We shall be free
With moderate desires, rich from content,
And passing happy in each other's love.

33

NORMAND.

Whence fertile ease, illustrious action whence,
The charms of culture, or e'en nature's joys?

LEIRION.

From our good souls, love, worth a mint a year.

NORMAND, *looking from the window, agitated.*

The hills, — e'en here they lift to view, and force
This traitorous passion into dread relief.
Soft you, my love. Hast note of distant wealth?

LEIRION.

Too far for empire, and too vain for thought.

NORMAND.

A gem-capped mountain, Alpine opulence.

LEIRION.

I've seen the milkmaids whisper of the tale;
And every one did seem to tread on graves.
An evil spirit hath possession there!

NORMAND.

Let not thy fears so on thy knowledge tread,
And I will body out the simple facts.

LEIRION.

And evils every way encompass it!

NORMAND.

It can be compassed by this single arm.

LEIRION.

Which must endue itself in sorcery!

NORMAND.

We need it.

LEIRION.

Here's a pretty pattern wrought
With my poor cunning. [*Shows the cross.*]

NORMAND.

That alarum here!

LEIRION.

Thou usedst to peruse the sacred page ;
Let this thy progress tally and thy life ;
At turn of every day, make it a Mentor.
If e'er temptation seize thy inward thought,
Or thy uprightness bend before the stress
Of ills that try us all, this thy support.
Where is thy brother's gift ?   Thou didst forget
To wear it.   Or if, by accident,
'Tis lost, keep this in memory of that.

NORMAND.

I must away.

LEIRION, *aside.*

Ah ! deeper than I deemed
Is his distress.   His natural faculty
Is hurt, and nerves distraught.

NORMAND, *aside.*

Ne'er of myself
Be I the master, if not now.

LEIRION.

My Normand !   [*holding the cross to him.*]

NORMAND.

No more of that.   Kiss me, my Leirion ;
And fare thee well !

LEIRION.

Going, and so ?   No more
My Normand ?   Nor can I add a fare-thee-well !

NORMAND.

Take heart.

LEIRION.

This heart bursts on the cross it made.

NORMAND, *turning back as he goes.*

Dearest, I will return with goodly spoil,
To deck reunion, and to crown our love.

LEIRION.

This slight is fatal both to him and me.

NORMAND.

One gentle look !

LEIRION.

I ne'er shall see him more.

NORMAND.

Wilt pray for me ?

LEIRION.

He does a prayerless thing.

NORMAND.

O heavenly Leirion !

LEIRION.

Ah, lost, lost Normand !

At midnight, in a lonely place of rock, wood, and water, Normand, awaiting the appearance of the witch-mother, Vafer, thus speaks : —

Stars, glittering sentinels of sleeping space ;
Thou moon, whose silver lustre blesses earth ;
Ye deep and vaulted mysteries of nature,
In hill or glade, that keep your hoarded wealth ;
Silence, that hushes up the universe, —
Ye are but parts of what I am, or types
Of what I shall be.   Life and hope exalt
My venturous step, and crown the lonesome hour.
Ah, Leirion, too timid, too precise,
Almost unjust, so exquisitely pure !
Thou wouldst forgive and sympathize in this,
And let these joys thrill thy severer heart.
The vapors rise amain, and veil — ah ! yes,
Diffusive lustre — veil in brilliancy
The dubious moon.   So I, in shadows merged,
Shall pour on them my light, and through them shine.

The fogs increase, and darkness shuts me in ;
Yon moon declines ; the sorcerer's moment comes.
This humid lowland air is chilly.   On !
Good courage ! girt in genial hope, go on.
  An unseen nook breathes sassafras and mint,
And scent of fern ; and here are phosphor-sticks,
Gleaming like fiery reptiles in my path.
I used, a boy, to gather them, and loved
The woods, and tangled crevices, and dark
And wizard ravines, when others feared.
I'll not fear now.   Toss a pebble down this chasm ;
See if 'twill waken her, and haste my hour.

The witch-mother, Vafer, rises from the rocks,
with hair of bramble-roots, and vesture of skins of
earth-worms ; in her hand a piece of punk on fire.

Hail, powers of earth !   Hail, mother of all craft !
VAFER.
No time for ceremony; let us work.
The pearl thy aim ? the giant and the lake
Thy dread ?   Dost seek our aid ?   Wilt do as bid ?
Thou art a ready, docile fellow, meet
For fortune, fame, and all conceptive good.

NORMAND.
Most gracious and potential minister !

VAFER.
First, thou must get thy mother's blessing.

NORMAND.
     My mother ?

VAFER.
        Thy mother.

NORMAND.
Her pure and pious hand would light a curse
On what I do.

33*

VAFER.

Her blessing.   Dost thou hear?
What she, but most uncertain dam?

NORMAND.

Enough;
I'll kill thee, witch.

VAFER.

Of that most dubious thing,
Called Normand, littered chance, another form
That might have taken, and been surnamed a dunce.
Her blessing get, as thou wert bastarded;
A miser's curse, and put them in a bag;
A cat, wherein a dead man's soul inhabits;
A cricket from the hearth of a burnt house,
In whose deserted chimney thou shalt sit
The night; where, o'er a bright and verdant brook,
A roofless saw-mill, struck by ruin, hangs,
Some dust; feed cat and cricket with the dust;
In feted beer-shop get a drunkard's penny;
From some good smith one beaded drop of sweat;
A sprig of sorrel from thy brother's grave.
Our art is chemical: from wondrous sorts,
And test of stubborn things, the charm is wrought.
. . . . A wise word get
From the old mountain-man; the flume shall yield
A bubble, and the basin's sparkling bed
An emerald; a rainbow fetch that spans
The silver cascade; bring from Echo Pond
One cheering note; on Kearsage's breezy top
A willow basket weave, and put therein
Seven crow-berries.

NORMAND.

This spurs attempt,
And lures my spirit on.

VAFER.

Thou dost perchance
On doting maiden dotingly incline, —
A common thing, and, in its way, quite well.

NORMAND.

Too well to be discussed at this late hour.

VAFER.

As Hagar to that ancient saint, be she
To thee!

NORMAND.

Thou askest what, if given, were more
Ten thousand times than thou canst recompense.

VAFER.

Our Turpis cheerless waits the happy hour
To wed with thee.   Pernix and Sklerote,
Our cousins twain, will groom the festive scene.

NORMAND.

Is there no second thought?

VAFER.

A dozen, so
You will.   Let them not loiter.

NORMAND.

To thy wish,
Mother, and prudent counsel, I'm beholden.

The scene with his poor, blind, old mother, whom
he finds in her lowly farm-house knitting for him,
as he goes to seek her blessing, and also that in
which he seeks the sorrel on the grass-covered grave
of his dead brother, are full of tenderest pathos,
mixed with keen remorse. His watching for the
cricket in darkness, wind, and storm, in a solitary
place, amid the ashes on the hearth-stone of a burnt
dwelling, and his musings as he sits, send a shudder

through one's frame. So on he goes, from scene to scene, accomplishing the demands of the witch, which are to form the potent charm. Interesting dialogues, on various themes, ensue between him and those with whom he comes in contact.

To the Exchange he resorts for the miser's curse. There is a gathering of merchants on the walk; and at the foot of the columns that form the front of the building, crouched in corners, sit huckster-women. Normand surveys the scene from the platform above.

NORMAND.

My dreams are here transactions;
My choicest fancies reckon dividends.
No vulgar sweat, or boorish ruddiness,
A richer paleness thrones the countenance, —
The color of old gold, of long-enjoyed
Inheritance, and undisturbed resource.
That man is thin: a railroad has gone out
Of him. This, plump — tokay and stalled beef.
That snaps his fingers, lightnings bear the hint
Away. Here one marks with his cane the pave,
New cities rise. Another folds his vacant arms
As only wealth knows how. How rich a lip!
It hangs a liquid ruby on the face.
The President this style of men consults;
Reporters pet, and empire heeds their words.
What wives and daughters, ministers and grounds,
What winter operas, what summer tours,
Gleam in those eyes, and gladden all routine!
I shall not find the " curse " in such a spot.
'Tis blessings mart, and bourse of happiness.
But I am poor, and meaner than the dirt
The scavenger collects beneath their feet.

Let me go down, and with the hucksters idle.
I'll buy an apple ; dare as much as that
Beneath these columns, and before these gods.
Haply, the curse is squat behind a stall.

He talks with a huckstress, who, in reply to a
remark of his, answers, —

The air is well enough, if they would allow a poor
woman to raise a screen against the sun.

NORMAND.

They are generous men.

THE HUCKSTRESS.

To their dogs and horses.

NORMAND.

How infatuated is poverty ; how unjust! [*aside.*] They
are golden men.

THE HUCKSTRESS.

And alack have no coppers for me.

He goes back, and talks with one of the men on
'Change, and finally obtains the " curse," in consequence of asking of him a penny which is due the
poor woman for the apple he just had.

A very touching scene occurs between **Normand**
and the young, innocent boy of the smith, from
whom he seeks the drop of sweat, and who happens
to bear his name, thus reviving tender reminiscences
of his own childhood.

A cavern in a small, wooded island in Lake
George is the abode of the witches, to which he
resorts. In front of the cavern is a portico of skeletons, garnished with serpents and poisonous skins.
Within is a fire of drift-wood, tended by dwarfs.

The attendants of the witch family are swine, owls, wasps, bull-beggars, Simon Magi, Pick-thanks, Mesmerizers, Rappers, and other strange beings.

As the marriage-ceremony between Normand and Turpis is about to be performed by Simon Magus, a dimly luminous shadow of Leirion, with the cross, appears, and causes the witch-party to vanish.

At Saratoga, amid the noise of revelry in the various pavilions, and promenaders walking under the trees, he falls in with Narcissa, a young lady of great wealth, who, tired of gayety and frivolity, is glad to hold earnest discourse with him, although his poverty-stricken appearance makes him the butt of ridicule with others.

At length, after many adventures, wedded to Turpis, and equipped with the proper charm, he sets out for the hills, strong in belief that the prize is just within his grasp. Overtaken by night in the wilderness, travel-sore and faint, he applies at a solitary house for admittance, but is refused on account of his suspicious appearance. A raven, the metamorphosis of Vafer, alights on a stump near him. He pushes on, the raven flying before, and finally perching on the steps of a rustic church, standing alone by the wayside. The church is lighted, and appears to contain an assembly of people. He drives the bird from the steps, and sits thereon himself. He hears singing within : —

> Return, my roving heart, return,
>   And chase these shadowy forms no more ;
> Look out some solitude to mourn,
>   And thy forsaken God implore.

PREACHER, *within.*

What if you gain the world, and lose your soul, &c.

This is a highly wrought scene. Finding himself, as he says, —

"By ingle and by altar equal banned," —

he rises hastily and departs. A procession of fairies, bearing a dead soul, crosses his path, chanting, —

> Follow we along,
> Withouten bell or song.
> Who left it thus to die?
> Who sinned so wofully?
> By the murmuring water's side,
> Where flowery voices glide,
>> Bear it gently,
>> Bury it tenderly.

He looks upon this as the obsequies of his own soul.

In the beginning of the fifth, the last act of the drama, Normand is found at the White Hills. It is night: he is at the Notch, alone. He gazes upon the towering heights which hem him in, and thus utters his emotion : —

Ye hills! ye dumb and rayless attributes
And forms of all of the Eterne, we know
Or feel of mystery! that crowd, sublime,
My horizon, and my very vision blind,
To swell within me pathos, grandeur, awe!
That lift and calm, subdue and aggrandize,
That overwhelm, yet as in silent rhythm
The soul of darkness giving; terrible,

Still down these cheeks distilling sweetest tears.
. . . .
How still the mountains! as if God were all
In all; whose calm and bright beneficence,
Softly diffused in silvern, silent moon,
Doth so englory soul and place, and shade
And height, as we were in eternity,
And sight were bliss, and consciousness a worship.

He falls in with various parties of pleasure. Narcissa and her companions join him; and they go on to Echo Lake. He meets a poor artist, who is excited by the grandeur of the scenery, and complains that, —

These days, there is so little love of art,
That bread stands bailiff at the doors of genius.

A cannon is fired. They hear the echo, then another. In the boat, Aonida, a favorite artiste, sings : —

Wake, glorious heart; wake at our call!
          Oaoo, oaoo!
A merry band, in rapturous thrall,
To joy in Grandeur's silent home,
With lyre and song, afar, we come,
          Aha, aha!
Mid fountains, mid the evergreen,
In paths that eye hath never seen,
With rose-bay crowned, and winds at play,
Oh, beautiful, and maiden gay, —
          La la, la la!

Scene II. finds Normand on the top of Profile Rock, where sits, as —

> In a world
> Of summer blue, serene as adamant,
> A tough old man, who thinks much, and says less.

All that he can draw from him, by his most earnest conjurations to speak, are the oracular words, —

> Patience, the sun will rise;
> Silence, fate makes no noise;
> Courage, the world works well.

Scene III. is at the Basin, where, on thrusting his arm into the water, the Spirit of the Basin rises, talks with him, finally gives him a chrysoprase, and disappears. The artist approaches, and they again discuss his art.

Scene IV. At the Saco Notch, Normand engages a guide. They traverse the mountains together; and Normand seeks from him something of his family history in early times among these mountains, and of the legend of the pearl. Normand proposes he should sell to him the hills. The guide replies, —

> In all these haunts
> And pleasant things, yield me the right of way,
> I should not mind who held the fee. Like trees,
> We are rooted beings, growing to our birthplace.
> I've roamed these woods, and clambered every height,
> The roe-buck tamed, and wrestled with the lynx;
> The lowly coons, and mighty dome of rock,
> That shrubless, wintry, crowns the whole, are dear.
> There yet are unknown crypts and mystic caves,
> And nameless things that never saw the light.
>
> . . . .
>
> I wake with cascades for my morning psalm;

My sleep is soothed with murmuring forest-winds ;
And thunder, terrible beyond conceit
Of lowland dwellers, is my Sunday organ.

NORMAND.

Shade of Bach ! what effect !   These ancient towers,
And long-drawn aisles, and tinted lights, with such
A pipe to roll cathedral harmonies !
To worship here some summer afternoon,
With maidens holy in the solemn underwood,
Their hands together pressed, and on their hair
A glory from the saintly fountain streaming,
And on their silver cross —— Go on, good friend ;
I hang upon thy words as on a brink.

THE GUIDE.

So I have hung on fancies of my own.
I've known the darkness last till afternoon.
When all is still, one sometimes hears a moan
Running along the ridges ; there are trees
That shriek like corporal suffering.   Lost men
Are wandering, bodiless, for what we know,
In the ravines ; a lake, brimful in draught,
From yonder Eagle Cliff, discharges, clear
And cool, and blue as heaven.   What holds it there ?
A heavenly force ?   Thou art a scholar, tell.
Once, on Deception, not a stone's throw off,
And ne'er a cloud, I saw a circled rainbow,
And in the flaming rim a human face.

Night overtakes them ; and, beneath the shelter
of a rock, they prepare to sleep. But Normand
watches : he cannot sleep so near the goal of all his
wanderings. The moon lights up the summit of
the mountain ; and he sees the giant's profile, the
aspect of whose countenance, he says, a week shall
change.

We next find him traversing the woods ; and he approaches an undiscovered lake in the sides of the mountain, which he thus apostrophizes : —

Sable and glassy wave, where swan-fleets ride,
The beryl goblet of the monarch-bird,
Where cougar's harbor and the bittern shrieks,
Untouched by sunbeam and by storms o'erpassed !
O Mountain Tarn ! the pure and amber glass,
In secret chambers, dim and holy, where
Daughter of God, ideal Beauty, fits
And renovates immortal radiance,
Whenas she visits the fond dreams of youth, —
A sumptuous drop from nectared urns of heaven, —
I drink of it.

Scene V. With sling in hand, Normand is pursuing an unfrequented path in the neighborhood of the Glen House. He comes to Glen Ellis Fall, where the artist is sketching, to whom he again addresses himself : —

Friend, dash thy subject ; fear not to be bold ;
Let startled waters down the canvass pitch.
. . . .
Take Nature as she is : paint what you see, —
The foreground, and the mysterious source ;
Retreating, vague, and dreamy distances ;
The ever and forever ; and the leaf
Upon it ; wonder, tenderness, remorse ; —
These are eternal.

THE ARTIST.
Did you say remorse ?
I do not find it in these elements.

NORMAND, *pausing.*

He said remorse !   [*Looking at the cascade.*]
   So, arrowy, we fall,
In all the bliss of being, rippling on ;
And the recoil, with dark and icy eye,
And vengeful appetence, doth prey upon
The fundamental frame that holds our life.

A thunder-storm passes over ; lightning strikes the spot, and a rift of rock tumbles into the abyss.

NORMAND.

Paint it, oh ! though it crush the soul of beauty,
And unearthed apparitions swarm aghast.

The artist adjusts himself to the task.

NORMAND, *walking slowly away.*

It works ! he dares sublimely, yields to fame ;
With me subscribes the golden covenant ;
To me devotes his sum of lustihood.
The dread resolve of grandeur stirs within,
Nor medium flights shall tempt his vigor more.

Here fell the author's pen : his hand — *was stilled.*

PROMINENT CHARACTERISTICS OF STYLE.

In comments upon one of Mr. Judd's works, this remark is found : " Our own spirit must advance, we must plant ourselves on high and holy ground, before we can fully enter into the application and merits of the book." An observation more just and sensible, it is believed, is not to be found in all the criticisms upon his writings. He wrote with an object far beyond the price of his volumes. Pecuniary advantage, though a thing not to be despised in connection with his small income, was a thing that entered into his calculations only as an incidental accessory. He wrote from the love of it, and from the feeling that he had within him something to say, which he must utter.

Neither was a desire for fame a prompting motive. At one time, when a friend gently remonstrated with him against continuing a mode of writing which called forth so much severity of criticism, and rather urged his aiming a little more at suiting himself to the public taste, — " I *cannot,*" said he. " It is with me a sacred conviction; there is to me a *truthfulness* which I must follow out; I am willing to *wait* for approval."

One leading feature of his writings, the bringing together of the high and the low, — what some have deemed the sublime and the ridiculous, — grew out of that sense, with which his being was permeated, of the unity of all things with all, and of the oneness of all with the Supreme Unity from which they spring. To him, in this light, there was no great, no small; the one great Father acting through, encircling, vivifying all. Humanity, in its many-sided elements, in its every condition, he honored as the creation of God in his own image; degraded, indeed, from its pristine purity, but still bearing deeply the divine impress, retaining much of the divine likeness. In this view, the workshop and the farm were on a level with the drawing-room and the palace. " The kitchen and the clouds, the

34*

clouds and the gutter," were not to his mind so incongruous, nor in his groupings did he see such grotesqueness and irrelevancy, as those of his readers who took a less elevated point of view. His stand seemed, indeed, to be on some serene mount of God, far above the mists and vapors which befog the ordinary mind; and one from which, instead of partial, detached parts, he could take in the relations of the whole great system.

With Wordsworth, he loved to draw illustrations from the common and familiar, the humble and unpretending. He advocated this on principle. That near at hand and well-known, he contended, if aptly applied, would naturally produce a stronger impression than the far-off and less familiar. He could not see why man and nature, lying in the clear sunlight all around us, should be neglected, and even excluded, for what is dim in the distance and less impressive. The following comparisons based upon this principle, probably no one would object to: Margaret says of Rose, "She has at times a most mysterious spiritual look, like the moon shining through *white window-curtains.*" In " Philo," Charlotte says to the Spirit of Love : —

> " My habits, *as a pot of flowers*, I set
> In the warm rain of thy correction."

He has been charged with affectation. But he was the last man in the world to whom this would apply. It is that from the least shade of which his natural truthfulness revolted. What might seem like this, was really in him perfect naturalness. He knew no other modes. He could make use of no other. His mind, from a child, always operated in a way peculiar to itself. His own thoughts, comparisons, and illustrations were natural to himself, when they appeared strange to others; they were clear and connected, when to another they might seem obscure and abrupt. There was no *attempt* at originality: it *was* originality in him. When in a public lecture he caused a smile by the remark, " Never did I understand the great brooding heart of Jesus, till this very summer, when I had a hen of my own, and saw her gather her chickens under her wings," he did not know he was saying any thing to affect the risibles of any one : it was a simple utterance of a perfectly simple feeling, quite natural to his heart.

When asked, in regard to some of his characters, why he had them do and say so or so, he would reply : " Oh! well, I don't know any thing about it, only that was *their way*," in a manner that really seemed as though he had to do with existences out of himself. So in " Margaret," he says: " *Seems*, we say ; for the compiler of this memoir professes to know no more of the matter than any of its readers."

The use of uncommon words, which strikes one in his compositions, arose not from a desire to make a show of learning, nor from any oddity or love of a startling novelty. The habit sprung from principle. He considered words as the working instruments of thought. He sought those best fitted to express, in the most forcible manner, the very idea. He believed there was great wealth in our language

unappropriated.   He wished to draw from the deep
wells of his mother-tongue.   He had a strong, an
almost sacred, sense of the *truth* in words ; and it
seemed to rest on him with the force of a moral
obligation, to use them in their true sense.   If he
discovered a word more *pat* to his purpose than
any other, he could not see why he should abandon
it, because it had been suffered by others to fall into
disuse.

Trenck, in his admirable little work, entitled
" The Study of Words," thus justifies the revival of
old words.   "One of the most legitimate methods
by which a language may increase in wealth," says
he, " is through the reviving of old words, such as
are worthy to be revived ; which yet, through care-
lessness or ill-placed fastidiousness, or unacquaint-
ance on the part of a later generation with the older
worthies of the language, or some other causes, have
been suffered to drop."

In Mr. Judd's lecture upon " Language," delivered before a number of lyceums, occurs this passage: " Once no words were vulgar ; all were common, all divine.   Now, disagreeable associations
belong to some words, and we discard them ; not
for any vice in themselves, but because, like the
dog in the spelling-book, they are found in bad
company.   Adam and Eve saw no vulgarity in any
thing.   The ' London Quarterly,' before quoted,
alluding to what are called slang phrases, adds, ' Let
no dainty objector whisper that such words are common, vulgar, familiar, and cannot be poetical.   Daisies
are common, the sea is common, women and chil-

dren are exceedingly common; and yet we believe they are allowed by the best judges to be not only poetical, but the very stuff and matter of all poetry.'"

He was always a close student of words. It was almost a passion with him. His dictionary, next to his Bible, might be said to be his most familiar acquaintance among books.

An author from whom Trenck quotes, in his little work just alluded to, says: "Hardly any original thoughts, on mental or moral subjects, ever make their way among mankind, or assume their proper importance in the minds even of their inventors, until aptly-selected words or phrases have, as it were, nailed them down, and held them fast." A similar sense had Mr. Judd of the most fitting use of words.

He did not feel bound, of necessity, to old forms, to petrified modes, to say things just as everybody else had said them. In his review of Jones Very, before referred to, he says: "Invention, originality, the life, the world, the soul, nature and God, are not yet exhausted. Things have new phases. New minds have new thoughts. All that man hath been is not all that man may be. Tastes change, fashions wear out, systems decay, modes of thinking and of writing pass away. Yet ever is nature at work; ever is something. We look for that something *to be*, now to be. Fancy, imagination, thought, exist. Why should they not work, work for themselves, in their own way? Nature is ever new. No year is just like another. No spring is just like the present.

No elm, since the trees were planted in Paradise, is just like the one that overhangs my window. No sun-setting is just like the one we saw last night."

.... "We have considered these poems simply as an illustration of the soul of man. But it is the soul in one exercise, that of acting upon itself. The great poem of our day shall be that which starts from this point, which receives here its baptism and its inspiration, and elevates the soul out of itself, and brings it into connection with what is without, — nature, the world, the universe. All things that constitute proper subjects for poetry demand to be re-viewed. They must be looked at with the soul. The visions of external things which have so long floated before the eyes of poets are something more than visions. They are charged with an unperceived meaning; they have relations to the spirit, which the spirit alone can comprehend and interpret. We are no advocates of mysticism, or 'airy nothings,' but are assured there are realities which the poetic mind has yet to understand. There are depths into which no plumb has yet descended. There is a fidelity which few are willing to cultivate. The intrinsic difficulties of such an undertaking are neither few nor small. Genius, and perhaps a genius of the highest grade, is alone competent to the task. One of the chief difficulties, as we conceive, lies in the relation of words to ideas. Our phraseology is already hackneyed. If any one, warmed by a fresh impulse, undertakes to write poetry, he insensibly, and almost ncessarily, falls into the poetic diction. Garments that were worn by the ancients, and have been handed down from generation to generation, he must fit on to his thoughts; and thought itself appears old. Who will break from these leading-strings? Who can strike out a new path? Who will give to the soul what it needs?"

In support of the same ideas, we quote again from Trenck. He says: "It is not merely that the old and familiar will become new in the hands of the poet, or man of imagination; that will give the stamp of allowance, as to him it will be free to do, to words, should he count them worthy, — to words which have hitherto lived only on the lips of the multitude, or been confined to some single dialect or province; but he will enrich his native tongue with words unknown and non-existent before, — non-existent, that is, save in their elements." And thus Mr. Judd reasoned in regard to the use of words; upon these principles he practised; and from this followed a prominent feature of his style.

The question may be asked, "Was Mr. Judd a man of genius?" If it is the office of genius to combine and reproduce, as a new creation, forms and characters all its own, from various elements, the common property of all, infusing into them life, and an independent, individual existence, and that, too, with the ease and quietness of accomplishing the most common things of every-day life, then, with great significance, may this be predicated of him. He borrowed from no one. His ideas are his own, except so far as all ideas may, in a sense, be considered public property. He was original in his plans, original in his combinations and structures. And there was no labor apparent in the production of his literary works, no note of bustle or preparation; but, seemingly, he simply willed them, and they came forth.

CHAPTER X.

AS A LECTURER.

——

THE history of Mr. Judd's life, already given, shows the general esteem in which he was held as a lecturer. Among his most popular and most often repeated lectures were "The Beautiful," "The Dramatic Element in the Bible," and "Language."

This chapter will be composed of passages taken from his lectures, which will serve as specimens of this department of his literary efforts. The first which follows is from an address delivered before the Northampton Lyceum, in 1838, entitled —

"CHILDREN."

"My subject is one not too often introduced into the exercises of literary associations; yet I can think of none more worthy to engage the interest of this hour. It is a subject at all times about us, yet not noticed, — ever familiar, yet ever forgotten. You, the members of this lyceum; you, the adult and the aged, have convened this evening for purposes of intellectual improvement. But where is the child? What is the child? What you have

35

been, the child is.   What you are, the child shall
be, and even already is.   What you will be in the
lapse of time, or in the revolutions of eternity, that
shall also the child be.   My subject is 'The Child.'"

After depicting, in a graphic manner, the influences for good or ill that the child is constantly
receiving from those about him, he says: " I turn to
influences *from* the child.   The relation of childhood to age is a topic deserving our attention.
Association is the term that expresses all which
interests us here.   It is that which connects youth,
manhood, and old age.   As our associations are
through life, so will be our happiness or our misery.
Adam lived in Paradise.   Eve, heaven-moulded
and heavenly-beautiful, bloomed at his side.   The
uncursed earth expanded before him with a luxuriance that regaled every sense.   The sun shone out
upon him in the undimmed effulgence of its new
creation.   Yet Adam had no childhood.   No associations of childhood came rushing upon his thoughts,
and throwing their rapture of emotions over the
beautiful world he dwelt in.   With Eve, in bright-
eyed girlhood, he had never revelled among those
flowers, or sauntered on Pison's banks.   No father
had taught him how to rear the vine.   On no mother's
lap had he reclined his weary head.   No morning
sun awakened a thought of his youth.   No voices
echoed the past, — no images reflected the past.   Yet
we envy Adam his Paradise.   Childhood is every
good man's paradise, — a perpetual paradise from
which he shall never be driven, to the entrance of
which no swords of fire shall be interposed.   Man-

hood has its cares ; age, its infirmities ; youth blooms
ever. Then he was happy, then he was free. Dark
days intervene between childhood and age ; but no
darkness is so great that we do not look over to the
sun-lighted spot of boyhood. Ills accumulate and
weigh down the spirits ; but no pressure is so overwhelming, that every fibre of our hearts does not
thrill at the sounds of childhood."

He thus refers to the home of his boyhood :
" What resources for coming years are the children
of our village now treasuring up ? This is the practical consideration to which I invite your attention.
Northampton, of all places, is one of the most desirable for recollection. As your home, it is the only
place to which your thoughts can recur for childhood's scenes. Hither let them come. Here let
them be cherished. It is necessary to give our attention to the objects in which we would become
interested. President Dwight bluntly charged a
young man with whom he was riding in the country,
to open his eyes. Not that he was asleep, but that
he did not see what he ought to see. How many
travel the whole journey from the cradle to the grave
asleep! Strange perversion of the powers within
us! Strange neglect of the objects around us! Our
direction to the child and the youth is, — Open your
eyes ! Pick up the next pebble your feet trip upon
It is a portion of granite-rock, remote from any
granite-formation. How came it where you found
it ? What force detached it from its parent-stone ?
It is hard, yet round and smooth. In what beating
of waters did it receive its abrasions ? The sand

you tread upon, the soil your ploughshare turns, is all rocks, fragmentary rocks, broken down in unknown ages, when oceans swept over our dry lands, and all that the corn might grow, and the waters run. That pebble is a token of mysterious agencies, a tradition from past generations, a monument of the power and goodness of God.

"Our village in its character is rural, but the ideal of rural life is hardly realized here. As in the Switzer's home, no young men and maidens, no old men and matrons, collect on our greensward, to join the circles of the dance, to merry-make or crown the queen of May. We retire into our houses from the rich landscapes around us, that we may look upon them from our windows. We talk of them to the stranger, rather than enjoy them ourselves. Yet the elements of the beautiful and picturesque are here. Rivers and rivulets, hills and hillocks, slopes and levels, woodland and lawn, elm-trees and rose-bushes, are grouped, contrasted, variegated, in forms and colors that captivate every beholder. But nature, inanimate nature, is never superlatively beautiful. It is man, living man, that makes all God's works beautiful. Here you are, and here is your youthful home! Here are your play-grounds, your fishing-streams, and your skating-ponds! A winter evening's party, with its cakes and plums, with its nicety of dress and manner, is not half so well fitted to your nature as a summer's Saturday afternoon, when the blithe air calls you forth, and with baskets for berries and nuts, in groups of two and three and four, you turn your footsteps and hearts to the greenwood and the plains. Our young girls are forbidden the free sports that are the delight and health of boys. They practise callisthenic gesticulations for exercise. Nature, methinks, would lead them into the open sunshine, send them for nosegays on the hill-side, and teach them to sport freely on the healthful bosom of the earth.

"Independence-day comes, and brings with it something of rural life, in its lawn festivities, with their green arbors, flower-wreaths, and tree-shaded seats. There are smiles of the beautiful, and there is intercourse of the friendly. But childhood pours not its full heart into those scenes. Day after Independence comes ; and you may see, or might see (I hope the practice is continued), companies of boys and girls toiling, or rather, I should say, sporting, their way up the steep path that conducts to the summit of our Holyoke. Holyoke, — what subterranean fires threw up that observatory ? What unseen power rolled back the hills, and spread out this beautiful valley ? What river-nymph, with her white waters, lingers in these meadows, embalming the scene in beauty, and pouring fertility over the soil ? Holyoke is our own and our loved. Gaze, my boy, upon the scene at your feet. You may never behold a fairer. Look at your own town, with its straggling streets and pretty houses. Let your eye follow the declivity that comes from the far western clouds, and terminates by the river's margin. You see the villages and the woodland. You know what hearts are there, and what homes. Let your eye travel to the northward and the south-

ward. Treasure up the objects you witness. They
are the pride of New England; they are scenes
of your home. In the far south, the Connecticut
seems to have mounted upwards towards the skies;
and there it rests in the light of the sun, pure and
white as the rivers of heaven. Angels might step
down and float in pastime on that surface. Recollect,
my boy, our spirits must tend upward, upward, till,
in the full illumination of heaven, they shine spotless
and pure. On the verge of the rock that forms the
precipitous part of the mountain, you will find a
little flower, — the blue-bell. Examine it. Remember its shaping and its hue. It is a simple, blue
flower. But in coming years, in zones and meridians
far removed from hence, you may meet that same
blue-bell. I need not tell you it will be pleasant
then to have brought to your mind the view from
Holyoke, the valley of the Connecticut, and the
home of your childhood."

EXTRACTS FROM THE LECTURE ENTITLED
" THE BEAUTIFUL."

" I will instance this, the light of day, as that
which is beautiful to everybody. Take this in the
bland, Madonna-like blush of morning, the unfa-
thomable blue of noon, with its islands of opal and
snow, and at sunset, when the sky thrills with color
and flame; take it as it appears on the plains of the
tropics, where it inspires the traveller with a certain
majestic tranquillity, and where it seems to wrap all
objects in a harmonious and dream-like vapor; take

it nearer the poles, where its oblique rays, striking across the inequalities of glacier-land, portray castles and caves, and where, with fairy power, it weaves above the spectator crowns of glory and splendor ; take it in its Attican softness or Italian purity ; take it as it is refracted in the rainbow, or concentrated in the dew-drop ; take it as it beams in the eye of health, or as it reposes on the face of the dead, — take it where you will, and it is beautiful ; and all acknowledge it to be so. As it touches the wretched kraal of the Hottentot, his susceptibility kindles to it ; the Green-lander, from his subterranean abode, amid lubber and foulness, blesses it ; the North American Indian, whose fashion was paint, whose art was a bow, whose pride has ever been the rejection of what we call civilization and refinement, hailed its glimmer in the greenwood ; the Turkish female, notwithstanding the unpardonable mistake she has made in her trowsers, never mistakes the beauty of sunlight.

" Furthermore, God, the God and Father of our Lord Jesus Christ, has sought to make that same Jesus, our Saviour, beautiful, pleasing, attractive to the human mind. How did Christ appear ? Was there any thing in him fitted to arouse repugnance, suggest suspicion ; any thing to displease or affront a rational being ? He says, ' I am come a light into the world,' and again, ' I am the light of the world,' — morning, noontide, the clearing off of night and storm, the blue-break into the sin and sorrow that were as clouds over our anxious day ; light, the light of the world, blended, confluent, choir-like, sun, moon, and stars, that Christ was.

" Moreover, Christ would commend his person and mission to mankind by this superadded enrichment of beautiful ideas. He calls himself a vine, a shepherd, a well of water, — touching images of the East. He is not merely a shepherd, but a good, καλὸς, the beautiful shepherd. Sylvan pictures appear in his teachings : a marriage-festival adds a certain liveliness to the sacred drama ; he embroiders, if I may so say, the lily on his great ideas ; birds spring up from the ground where he treads, and carol his faith and love. Never did I understand the great, brooding heart of Jesus, or the tenderness of his tears, till this very summer, when I had a hen of my own, and saw her gather her chickens under her wings ; nor shall we ever understand the glory, the beauty, the loveliness of his second coming, till we study more the glory, beauty, and loveliness of the clouds in which that coming is symbolized.

" There must be beauty in religion, or we cannot cordially embrace it; in prayer, or we cannot take pleasure in it ; in repentance, or we shall never sincerely exercise it ; in duty, or we shall not cheerfully go forward in it.

" There is beauty in consistency of character, and for this we admire it ; beauty in a well-spent life, coming in like a shock of corn fully ripe, and for this it awes us ; beauty in well-regulated domestic affairs, and therefore we rejoice in it. There must be beauty in our own deepest being, or there will be none to love us.

" There is beauty even in sadness and sorrow, in tears and grief ; beauty in the memory that inurns the dead ; in the fidelity that bears flowers to the grave-side ; in the vigils that bereavement keeps through the long night of its anguish.

" There is in the human mind, I think, an undying desire for the beautiful. It is an unquenchable thirst, an innate instinct. The slovenliness and brutality of the ages have not wholly stifled it. Like the good and the true, so is it an aspiration. It is a species of rest to the soul, as it is a consummation of endeavor. No character, no deed, no work, ever yet satisfied us, that did not rise above mere utility into those harmonies and unities and sweetnesses that we call the beautiful. No smirched iron-worker ever yet drove a rivet, that did not, after the useful was done, add a few more blows for the beautiful. There is no word that so expresses the whole of deepest human feeling, that so outshadows what can only be felt, and not expressed, as *beautiful.*

" While we cannot define the nature of the beautiful, nor enumerate all its types, it may be we have some clear glimpse of its final cause. Why did God make all things beautiful ? Out of the exceeding beauty of his own nature. Out of the beauty of his own nature, he would that all his offspring, the animate and inanimate world, rational intelligences, and the busy spheres, should be beautiful too. Every thing of God's that we look upon, — the stellary worlds, the feathered tribes, the floral realms, snow and rain ; so also patience, heroism, faith, love, — all reflect the brightness of the glory, and bear marks of the express image of the person, of the Almighty.

" I have read of a temple of alabaster so clear as to be always full of light, without doors or windows. We are in such a temple, the universe, ever shining with the light of the beautiful. Darkness is beautiful, so is the storm ; winter is beautiful in its high brilliancy, its wavy drifts, its starry flakes, in the moonlight flooding down the enamelled slopes, — beautiful in this, that, as a robe of ermine, the snow warms and cherishes the bosom of our mother-earth, with all her fountains and streams, all her seeds and roots.

" By all that God hath made, — by the glittering dew, by the soft gliding of water, by the notes of birds, by the curved line, by Corinthian proportions, by the endless purposes of utility, by the tenacious charm of association, by the vine that shall festoon the communion of nations, by the firmamental brightness of wisdom, by the resplendent immensity of his own attributes, by his own glorious image seen in Jesus, by the fathomless depths of human sentiment, — God is calling us to adoration and to duty, to repentance and to love.

" And heaven itself — what is it but the starry dome that overhangs our little faith and hope here ; the bud and blossom of these germinant, terrestrial years ; the Infinite, with white arms and golden crowns, welcoming the finite to a higher birth, into still higher realms of truth, goodness, and beauty ? "

FROM THE LECTURE ENTITLED
" LANGUAGE."

In this lecture, Mr. Judd maintains the position
that language was of divine origin, and thus he discourses : —

" The original, divine words filled the great reser-
voir of human speech, which has been flowing down
all the mountains and through all the valleys of
human society ; now throwing itself off in beautiful,
many-tinted, belles-lettres vapor ; here taught by
the poet to leap in jets, or pour in cascades ; sometimes distilled by philosophers, sometimes muddied
by boys ; and in which, at last, Christianity itself is
embodied, and descends as the dew and the rain
upon the earth.

" There is something sublime, perhaps awful, in
words. The ἔπεα πτερόεντα, the winged words, the
utterances of the fireside and the market-place,
the confidential whisper, the fleeting gossip, the eloquence of the forum, the talk of the table, go up, on
the one hand, to the judgment-seat ; they go down,
on the other, to the creation ; they connect us with
men and ages past, they connect us with God, the
infinite Father of all ; the original, indestructible
media of human intercourse, descending from generation to generation, passing through the lips of this
present time, and surviving to the latest period of
man's existence on the earth. . . .

" Time was when there were no words ; when
the universe, the sun and the stars, the shadowy
grove, the whistling wind, the glancing brook, the

playful fawn, the swift-winged bird, had no name;
when all things were, in a sense, blank, devoid of
interest; when, too, man, with all his powers, was,
as I think, utterly impotent to bestow these names.
Divine love interposes, and not only sets man out
on his journey of life, but gives him wherewithal to
make the journey pleasant and prosperous. . . .

"Language is, in a sense, eternal. It survived
the first pair to whom it was communicated; it survives the generations through whom it is transmitted;
it survives the vicissitudes of empire and the decline
of nations; it lives on when marble columns and
brazen statues crumble. How could such a thing be
left to the mere winds of chance to blow together?
It must, in the nature of things, have possessed considerable perfection, even in its incipiency and primitive use. Man could not invent it; God alone could
give it. . . .

"What marks of a divine hand, what glorious
traces of an Almighty, benign interference, what
beams of supernatural light, cluster about the first
epoch of our world! Is it not almost literally true,
that the morning stars sang together, and all the
sons of God shouted for joy? Then, when man
required still further the guiding care of heaven,
God spake to the fathers by the prophets, and now
speaks to us by his Son. Oh! I can believe it all: I
can feel it. One is led to exclaim, Oh the height,
the depth, of the goodness of God!"

"IDEA OF OUR COUNTRY."

In this address Mr. Judd shows the leading *ideas* of our country, in contrast with existing *facts*. He closes as follows : —

"We have great and goodly ideas. To these I would recur ; in the light of these, I would this brief moment might be passed. God only knows what is before us ; yet God has put it in our power to make every thing bright along our way.

"Like shadows on our hill-sides, the spirits of past ages assemble around us ; they unfold the dread panorama of history ; they say, Read and learn, ponder and be wise. The Genius of America, too, rises to view, youthful but collected, fair and sad ; the words of all time beat his sunny locks ; his foot stands on a mountain, the verdure of which is the decay of dynasties and the dissolution of empires. Around him are empty mausolea, crumbling arches ; temples, once gorgeous in worship, peopled by moles and bats ; palaces, once fraught with luxury and humming with gladness, buried in the sand ; commerce, such as your promising town never dreamed of, stranded on black and silent shores ; on the stream of years that rushes by, float the wrecks of upturned grandeur, and a turbid medley of art, wealth, and power. Battle-fields and conflagrations pour lurid horror on the sky, whithersoever he turns. 'Great God!' methinks I hear him say, 'What is the hope of my country ?' From the upper heavens, clear and blue, a voice replies, — a voice as of the Son of God, 'Let Americans love one another, let them be at

36

peace with all men; if their enemy hunger, feed him; fling away the sword, arm yourselves in virtue, free the slave, affiliate the Indian, enact the highest laws, negociate by eternal rectitude, conquer by kindness, annex by sympathy, obey God, and he will dwell with you, and ye shall be his people.'

"Bright-winged cherubim take the Genius to a still higher mountain, and show him a far and glorious futurity, where are pleasant vales and limpid streams, and many a goodly village, and many a forest-city, and railroads, and mills, and spires of churches, and cupolas of school-houses, and white pennons streaming, and bands of music playing; and, above all, is the dome of the sanctuary where everlasting love abides, — and that is America."

A few passages follow from Mr. Judd's lecture on

"THE PURITANS."

"Their (the Puritans') vision in some respects was very distinct, in others obscure. That the privilege of sinning could be purchased by money, that kings were the appropriate head of the church, that any sanctity lay in the color of a gown, were things which they saw to be enormities. Yet they believed in witches, in portents, in apparitions. Still, when I reflect on the myriad superstitions of all sorts and on all subjects that prevailed in the old world, I am rather astonished that our fathers brought so few of them to the new. They left behind, not only holy-days, but hosts of unlucky days. In England, the clergy were wont to repeat the creed, looking towards the East : the Puritans thought holy aspirations could be uttered towards any point of the compass.

" They were earnest men, with souls in their bosoms, and desires which nothing but an eternal life could satisfy. They were earnest in their religion ; they wanted to be near to God, and have God near to them ; kneeling, vestments, neat and proper as they may be, the rites that had accumulated in the church, were all dark bodies between them and the sun, a constraint on their spirits. For myself, I must say, I love to turn my mind towards them, though perhaps I should not enjoy being among them. They seem to me stern and awful men, like those described by Isaiah, who thresh the mountains and beat them small, and make the hills of vanity as chaff. Their heavy tread is as the tramp of doom to innumerable vices and follies of the world. They appear to me rather just than loving men ; more inflexible than comprehensive : few smiles play among the perpetual rigors of their faces. Their justice seems not always to have been tempered with mercy or with wisdom. They would make admirable groups of statuary : they are not such men as the women of our time would be apt to choose in marriage. The epithet *blue* has been applied to them and their doings ; not blue, I should say, but rather bronze.

" The most interesting light in which I can view the Puritans of New England is their progressive character. They were, in the providence of God, the ordained missionaries of progress to the world. That they fully realized the extent of their charge, cannot be asserted; yet they had some most palpable consciousness of what they were to accomplish. In the covenant I read, this appears: they promise obedience to whatever truth they had, and to *all that should be made known to them.* They could not shut themselves in articles and confessions; they did not feel that they possessed all truth; they would reverently wait on those divine oracles that are ever uttering their voice to mankind. . . .

"Puritanism, or, as I might say, Congregationalism in New England, has made progress, and been the means of progress, — in science, in religion, in liberty, both at home and abroad, far beyond any other system that has existed. Other systems have flourished under its shadow, or attached themselves, misletoe-like, to its trunk; but this is the mighty tree that sustains the whole. In their own simple language, they were " stepping-stones unto others ; " lowlily, resolutely bending, that, as it were, from their necks the genius of America might mount to its sublime elevation. To quote their own words, they ' *broke the ice for others.*' They were needed men, with their coarse iron shoes, to break the ice of usurpation and nonsense, beneath which lay the floods of everlasting beauty. . . .

"Their principles were better than their practice. Their principles, which recognized God and his word as the supreme arbiter, and men as equals, must needs lead to great issues; their principles were regenerative and progressive; they were higher than they were, and rose like the sun upon their own mists and darkness, and dispersed them. . . .

"With some trembling anticipations, with some flutter of hope, I think they saw what was before them; their eyes, penetrating the forests and the gloom in which they were embayed, got some glimpses of the illustrious future that lay in the distance. They would not always preach under a great tree, nor send to England for peas and oatmeal; nor would Boston be always infested with wolves and rattlesnakes. That their vista embraced what now meets the eye of the beholder, this empire, these states, cities, towns, may hardly be imagined."

EXTRACTS FROM THE LECTURE DENOMINATED "THE DRAMATIC ELEMENT IN THE BIBLE."

"In the commencement of the Old Testament, after a brief prologue, the curtain rises, and we, as spectators, look in upon a process of interlocution. The scene is the sunny garden of Eden. The *dramatis personæ* are three individuals, Adam, Eve, and the Serpent. There are the mysterious tree, with its wonderful fruit; the beautiful but inquisitive woman; the thoughtful but too compliant man; and the insinuating reptile. The plot thickens, the passions are displayed, and the tragedy hastens to its sorrowful end. The voice of the Lord God, walking in the garden in the cool of the day, is heard; the impersonal presence of Jehovah is, as it were, felt in the passing breeze, and a shadow like an eclipse falls upon the earth.

"But, leaving these scenes, let us turn to others
36*

more grateful.   In the light of our subject, we will approach the New Testament.   How different do all things appear !   We seem to stand on some new realm of being.

"Through the tempest and storm, the brutality and lust of the Greek tragedians, and even of the barbarous times on which Shakspeare builds many of his plays; through the night of Judaical back-sliding, idolatry, and carnal commandments, we patiently wait, and gladly hail the morning of the Sun of Righteousness.   The New Testament is a green, calm island in this heaving, fearful ocean of dramatic interest.

"But how shall we describe what is before us ? The events open, if we may draw a term from our subject, with a prologue spoken by angels, — ' Peace on earth, and good-will among men.'   There had been Jezebels and Lady Macbeths enough ; ·the memory of David still smelt of blood; the Roman eagles were gorging their beaks on human flesh ; and the Samaritan everywhere felt the gnawing, shuddering sense of hatred and scorn.   No chorus appears answering to chorus, praising the God of battles, or exulting in the achievement of arms ; but the sympathies of Him who was touched with the feeling of our infirmities answer to the wants and woes of the race, and every thoughtful mind ecstatically encores. The inexorable fate of the Greeks does not appear ; but a good Providence interferes, and Heaven smiles graciously upon the scene.   There is passion indeed, grief and sorow, sin and suffering ; but the Tempest-stiller is here, who breathes tranquillity upon the waters, and pours serenity into the troubled deep. The Niobe of humanity, stiff and speechless, with her enmarbled children, that used sometimes to be introduced on the Athenian stage for purposes of terror or pity, is here restored to life; and she renders thanks for her deliverance, and participates in the general joy to which the peace gives birth. No murderers of the prophets are hewn in pieces before the Lord; but, from the agonies of the cross and the depths of a preternatural darkness, on behalf of the murderers of the Son of God, the tender cry is heard, 'Father, forgive them: they know not what they do.' No Alcestis is exhibited, doomed to destruction, to save the life of her husband; but One appears, moving cheerfully, voluntarily forwards, to what may be termed the funeral-pile of the world; from which, phœnix-like, he rises and gloriously ascends, drawing after him the hearts, the love, the worship of millions of spectators.

"The key to the whole piece is redemption: the spirit that actuates it is love. The chief actors, indeed, are Christ and man; but innumerable subsidiary personages are the charities. The elements of a spiritualized existence act their part. Humanity is not changed in its substance, but, in its tendencies, the sensibilities exist, but under a divine culture. Stephen is as heroic as Agamemnon; Mary, as energetic as Medea. Little children are no longer dashed in pieces: they are embraced and blessed.

"But I wish to select for your attention, and for a conclusion to these remarks, a particular scene. It shall be from Luke. This evangelist has been fabled a painter; and, in the apotheosis of the old church, he was made the tutelar patron of that form of art. If the individuality of his conceptions, the skill of his groupings, and the graphicness of his touch, gave rise to such an idea, it would seem to have its foundation as well in nature as in super-stition. . . .

"The event is Christ's dining at the house of Simon the Pharisee, and, while they were reclining at meat, the entrance of a woman, which was a sinner, who bathes the feet of Jesus with tears, and wipes them with the hair of her head. The place is the city of Nain; the hour, noon. The *dramatis personæ* are three, — Jesus, Simon, and the woman; and, if we choose to add, the other guests, who are silent spectators of what transpires.

"Let us consider, first, the woman. 'She was a sinner.' This is all, in fact, we know of her; but this is enough. The poetry of sin and shame calls her the Magdalen; and there may be a convenience in permitting this name to stand.

"She was condemned to wear a dress different from other people; she was liable, at any moment, to be stoned for her conduct; she was one whom it was a ritual impurity to touch.

"She was wretched beyond measure; but, while so corrupt, she was not utterly hardened. Incapable of virtue, she was not incapable of gratitude. Wel-tering in grossness, she could still be touched by the sight of purity.

"The vision of Jesus had alighted upon her. She had seen him speeding on his errands of mercy; she hung about the crowd that followed his steps ; his tender look of pity may have sometimes gleamed into her soul. Stricken, smitten, confounded, her yearnings for peace gush forth afresh.

"But how shall she see Jesus ? Wherewithal shall she approach him ? 'She has nothing to pay.' She has tears enough, and sorrows enough ; but these are derided by the vain, and suspected by the wise. She has an alabaster-box of ointment, which, shut out as she is from honorable gain, must be the product and the concomitant of her guilt. But with this she must go. We see her threading her lonely way through the streets, learning by hints, since she would not dare to learn by questions, where Jesus is ; and she stops before the vestibule of the elegant mansion of Simon the Pharisee. Who was Simon the Pharisee ? He could not have been an unprincipled, villainous man, or he would never have tendered to Jesus the hospitalities of his house. He was probably a rich man, which might appear from the generous entertainment he made. He was a respectable man. The sect to which he belonged was the most celebrated and influential among the Jews. He had some interest in Christ, either in his mission or his character, — an interest beyond mere curiosity, — or he would not have desired him to dine with him. He betrays a sincere friendliness also in his apprehension lest Christ should suffer any religious contamination.

"The third person in the scene is Christ, who, to speak of him, not as theology has interpreted him to us, but as he appeared to the eyes of his contemporaries, was the reputed son of Joseph and Mary, the Bethlehemites ; who, by his words and deeds, had attracted much attention, and made some converts ; now accused of breaking the Jewish sabbath, now of plotting against the Roman sovereignty ; one who, in his own person, had felt the full power of temptation, and who had been raised to the grandeur of a transfiguration ; so tender, he would not bruise the broken reed ; so gentle, his yoke was rest ; raying out with compassion and love wherever he went ; healing alike the pangs of grief and the languor of disease ; whom some believed to be the Messiah, and others thought a prophet ; whom the masses followed, and the priests feared. This is the third member of the company.

" The two last, with the other guests, are engaged at their meal, and in conversation.

" The door is darkened by a strange figure ; all eyes are riveted on the apparition ; the Magdalen enters with long dishevelled hair. She has no introduction, she says nothing ; indeed, in all this remarkable scene, she never speaks ; her silence is as significant as it is profound. She goes behind the couch where Jesus, according to Oriental custom, is reclining. She drops at his feet ; then her tears stream ; then the speechless agony of her soul bursts.

" Observe the workings of the moment. See how those people are affected. Surprise on the part of Simon and his friends turns to scorn, and this shades into indignation. Jesus is calm, collected, and intently thoughtful. The woman is overwhelmed by her situation. The lip of Simon curls, his eye flashes with fire of outraged virtue; Jesus meets his gaze with equal fire, but it is all of pure heavenly feeling. Simon moves to have the vagabond expelled; Christ interrupts the attempt. But the honor of the house is insulted. Yes, but the undying interests of the soul are at stake. But the breath of the woman is poison, and her touch will bring down the curses of the law. But the look of Christ indicates that depth of spirituality, before which the institutions of Moses flee away as chaff before the wind. Simon has some esteem for Jesus, and in this juncture his sensations take a turn of pity, spiced, perhaps, with a little contempt; and he says with himself, ' Surely this man cannot be a prophet, as is pretended, or he would know who and what sort of woman it is that touches him; for she is a sinner, she is unclean and reprobate.' ' Simon!' says Jesus, with a tone that pierced to the worthy host's heart, and arrested the force of his pious alarm, — ' Simon!' ' Sir, say on,' is the reply of the Pharisee, who is awed by this appeal into a humble listener. Whereupon Jesus relates the story of the two debtors, and, with irresistible strength of illustration and delicacy of application, breaks the prejudice and wins the composure of the Jew. ' If then,' he continues, ' he loves much to whom much is forgiven, what shall we say of one who loves so much? See,' he goes on, pointing to the woman, — ' see this woman, this wretch : I entered thine house, thou gavest me no water for my feet; but she has washed my feet with her tears, and wiped them with her hair. She kisses

my feet, she anoints them with ointment. Wherefore, I say unto thee, her sins, which are many, are
forgiven ; for she loved much.'

"This scene, however inadequately it may be set
forth, contains all that is sublime in tragedy, terrible
in guilt, or intense in pathos. The woman represents humanity, or the soul of human nature ; Simon,
the world, or worldly wisdom ; Christ, divinity,
or the divine purposes of good to us-ward. Simon
is an incarnation of what St. Paul calls the beggarly
elements ; Christ, of spirituality ; the woman, of sin.
It is not the woman alone, but in her there cluster
upon the stage all want and woe, all calamity and
disappointment, all shame and guilt ; in Christ, there
come forward to meet her, love, hope, truth, light,
salvation ; in Simon are acted out, doting conserva-
tism, mean expediency, purblind calculation, carnal
insensibility. Generosity, in this scene, is con-
fronted with meanness in the attempt to shelter
misfortune. The woman is a tragedy herself, such
as Æschylus never dreamed of. The scourging Fu-
ries, dread Fate, and burning Hell, unite in her ; and,
borne on by the new impulse of the new dispensation,
they come towards the light ; they ask for peace ;
they throng to the heaven that opens in Jesus. Simon embodies that vast array of influences that stand
between humanity and its redemption. He is a very
excellent, a very estimable man ; but he is not
shocked at intemperance ; he would not have slavery
disturbed ; he sees a necessity for war. Does Christ
know who, and what sort of a woman, it is that
touches him ? Will he degrade himself by such a

contact? Can he expect to accomplish any thing by familiarity with such a person? Why is he not satisfied with a good dinner? 'Simon!' 'Simon!'

"The woman could not speak, and so she wept, like the raw, chilling, hard atmosphere, which is only relieved by a shower of snow. How could she speak, guilty, remorseful wretch, without excuse, without extenuation, in the presence of divine virtue, at the tribunal of judgment! She could only weep; she could only love. But, blessed be Jesus, he can forgive her, — he can forgive all!

"The woman departs in peace; Simon is satisfied; Jesus triumphs. We almost hear the applauses with which the ages and generations of earth greet the closing scene. From the serene, celestial immensity that opens above the spot, we can distinguish a voice saying, 'This is my beloved Son, hear ye him.'

"I speak of those things as dramatic; but, after all, they are the only great realities. Every thing else is mimetic, phantasmal, tinkling. Deeply do the masters of the drama move us; but the gospel cleaves, inworks, regenerates. In the theatre, the leading characters go off in death and despair, or with empty conceits and a forced frivolity; in the gospel, tranquilly, grandly, they are dismised to a serener life and a nobler probation. Who has not pitied the ravings of Lear, and the agonies of Othello? The gospel pities; but, by a magnificence of plot altogether its own, — by preserving, if I may so say, the unities of heaven and earth, — it also saves.

"Of all common tragedy, we may exclaim in the words of the old play, —

'How like a silent stream shaded with night,
  And gliding softly, with our windy sighs,
  Moves the whole frame of this solemnity!'

The gospel moves by, as a pure river of water of life,
clear as crystal, from out the throne of God and the
Lamb; on its surface play the sunbeams of hope; in
its valleys rise the trees of life, beneath the shadows
of which the weary years of human passion repose,
and from the leaves of the branches of which is
exhaled to the passing breeze, healing for the nations."

CHAPTER XI.

HABITS OF STUDY.

———

WHILE yet a little boy, Mr. Judd gave evidence of possessing an active, inquiring mind, and great facility in the acquisition of knowledge. His early unconquerable desire for a student's life has been already portrayed. He always had a habit of constantly adding to his stock of information, one scarcely knew how. He was always *thinking*, even when he seemed only to be amusing himself; and had a way of educing, by some alchemy best known to himself, something valuable in thought from the most trifling and insignificant things. There was scarcely any thing he looked upon that did not furnish some hint, some suggestion that he found means of turning to good account.

An early habit of his was making use of little note-books, or a piece of paper folded up small, which he had always about him, on which he jotted down, as it came before his mind, any thing he wished particularly to retain. It was one of the most common things, day by day, to see him quietly take from his pocket one of these bits of paper, and, with pencil, briefly note down some talismanic words, as it seemed; for rarely any eye but his own ever lighted on these scraps of thought or items of knowledge. From some little specimens, it appears that they were sometimes pithy remarks of individuals, put down verbatim; sometimes a peculiar development of human nature, or something illustrating the philosophy of mind; sometimes a broad truth, uttered by his father; often something by way of self-inspection; perhaps an unusual word that he chanced to hear; a valuable reflection upon something that had fallen under his notice; a question for consideration; an historical fact; critical distinctions; or an expression of wit or humor.

He read much, and his reading embraced an extensive range; yet he *thought* more than he read. He digested well whatever he perused. He never read for mere amusement, but as a study. He never perused books *literatim;* but had the power, by glances here and there, of catching at the contents, pausing on the points material to his purpose sufficiently to make them his own. *Truth* was always to him the great thing sought after, " the pearl of great price." He wished to find out the views of others, and their arguments for them; but he made up his conclusions independently, according to the dictates of his own reason and conscience.

He commenced a private journal on his eighteenth birthday, July 23, 1831, which he continued for about seventeen years; his last date being August, 1848. In this, he did not write daily, as a matter of form; but from the spontaneity of his feelings, whenever they prompted. This was sometimes every day, sometimes at longer intervals; but so frequent as to leave no important gaps. It was not a record of events, but of emotions; not of outward occurrences, but of his inner life, — his heart, his soul, religiously and emotively. With deep sensibility, he regarded this as a sacred deposit, a duplicate self, the inner temple of his own spirit, into whose secret chambers none might enter. Scarcely a passage was ever looked upon by any eye but his own, until he found his spirit's mate, to whose inspection and keeping this, together with his whole being, was entrusted. From this source, it is found that the journal contains his early religious experience, while receiving the doctrines of Calvinism; the commencement of his difficulties regarding adherence to that faith; the distressing doubts and almost confirmed infidelity to which they led; the depression of his troubled spirit during those years of nervous debility, of darkness and loneliness, which ensued; and the record of domestic life, the last few years the journal was continued. As they are of a nature so private, and abundant material on all-important points has been found elsewhere, these records have been drawn from but very sparingly in the preparation of this history.

His first child he made a close study, and watched all her unfoldings in the spirit and purpose of systematic investigation. As an aid in this, and also as furnishing memoranda of interest to her in after-years, he immediately commenced a journal of the child, which contains much curious matter relating to her babyhood, her incipient mental development, and her moral emotions. The same course, though in a less minute degree, he pursued with his second child ; and, as soon as they were able to use a pen, he endeavored to lead them to journalize for themselves.

Mr. Judd's study of his dictionary is well worthy of notice here. In 1832, he obtained a copy of Webster's royal octavo dictionary. In a little time, there were observed to be, here and there, numerals placed in the margin against a word. These went on increasing from time to time, and at length amounted to some thousands, attracting the attention of any one who chanced to look into the volume, though they were as mystical as Egyptian hieroglyphics to any eye but his own. After nearly twenty years' use, and the great multiplication of these figures, in 1850 he had this dictionary rebound in two volumes, with the insertion of blank leaves alternating with the printed ones. On these blank leaves began to appear, opposite some particular word, a succession of synonyms, or words of similar import, of every sort and kind, found either on other pages of the dictionary, or gathered up from some occasional sources. On a careful examination of this dictionary within the last few months, for he ever kept the clew to its apparent mysteries in his own hand, it has been discovered that the figures referred to were made to subserve a kindred purpose with the blank leaves, — that of collating and comparing words of like meaning, by indicating the pages on which they were to be found. Thus did Mr. Judd commence the critical and systematic study of his own language with his regular college pursuits ; a rare instance, as it is believed, of a student's feeling the supreme importance, among the acquisition of various arts and sciences, and many other languages, ancient and modern, of making himself perfect master of his own tongue.

To this course of study may be attributed Mr. Judd's power over language, the richness and variety of his expressions, and his use of so many terms, to him familiar as household words, though to many of his readers unknown and seemingly strange and far-fetched.

This plan of introducing blank pages was rather a favorite one with him.   He had a copy of the first edition of " Margaret " and of " Philo " rebound in this way for revision.   In his sermons and lectures, not only pages, but leaves, were often left blank, for the purpose of additions and the rewriting of passages ; and on these pages may be found sometimes a scrap of newspaper pinned on, containing an item bearing upon a given point, or some additional illustration, reference, or argument, — all showing that the discourse was not written to subserve a particular temporary purpose, and then to be thrown aside as a thing he had no more concern about, but that it was based on truths and principles which were his constant study, and in regard to which his mind was perpetually advancing.

Of the " Index Rerum " he availed himself ; and two volumes — the first commenced in 1834, and the second in 1845 — are found filled with important matter, references, and so forth.

Mr. Judd's study exhibits striking evidence of the

intellectual progress he was continually making, of the multitude of diverse materials he was garnering up for future use. From newspapers, of which he took a great many, he cut out items of every description, dates, speeches, statistics, various matters of fact, which he would paste into a large scrap-book prepared for the purpose, under their appropriate departments, so that they were easily referred to as occasion required. He had a large, folio blank-book, into which thin, impermanent sheet-maps were pasted.

In a blank-book, bearing date so late as Dec. 20, 1852, there is a commencement of copious references to Scripture on a great diversity of subjects, with an index, by means of which any one set of references could be turned to at once. For instance, there is the heading, " Nature : its goodness, beauty, and that it is to be enjoyed, — Gen. i. 29, 30 ; ii. 9, 16 ; ix. 1—3, 7 ; xxvii. 28." " Recreation, — Gen. ii. 9." " Music, — Gen. iv. 21." " Art, — Gen. iv. 22." " Agriculture, — Gen. ii. 5, 8, 15 ; iv. 2, 20 ; ix. 20." " Prayer, — Gen. xxiv. 63." Other subjects, with references in the same manner, are, " Universal Brotherhood," " The Church," " The Family," " Labor," " Providence," " Wealth," " Festivals," " That we must obey God, even if we displease man," " That we must do our duty, and leave the consequences to God," &c. Almost all the references are in the book of Genesis ; and it would seem that he had begun to take the Bible in the order of its contents, and thus form an index to all topics of prominent importance to his own mind.

Mr. Judd's immediate surroundings were of great consequence to him in his writing and studies. In fitting up his first study after commencing house-keeping in Augusta, the location affording nothing of particular interest to look out upon, he felt it a need that his windows should be hung with white drapery; and in its folds and curves, with a little patch of blue sky for a background, he found some-thing of the harmonizing influence essential to a ready flow of his thought. When he came to plan a dwelling of his own, the *study* was the starting-point. It occupies the whole southern wing of his cottage, having a large bay-window on the south; a window to the floor, opening upon a vine-covered veranda, on the west; and, opposite this, another window, looking towards the sun-rising and his garden. It commands many fine views, including a sight of the smoothly-flowing Kennebec just below his dwelling on the west, and again stretching off and disappearing towards the south. But this apartment, the most pleasant in the house, was not appropriated to himself exclusively. He never studied alone. It was another essential point in facilitating his intel-lectual pursuits, that he should have his wife and children about him; and therefore the study was also the sitting-room for the family.

He was always adding to his library as far as he was able. He accumulated quite a large number of well-chosen volumes, on a great variety of subjects, many of them rare and very valuable. In the strict economy he was obliged to observe in the increase of his library, he often resorted to stalls of old books, where, at reduced prices, he could find works essential to his purposes. In consequence of this, his library, to a considerable extent, presents an old and well-worn look.

A little compartment in one of the sets of book-cases was allotted to the children as a sort of baby-house and gathering-place for toys. The study-table was a unique contrivance of his own ingenuity, constructed with many curious little conveniences to suit his peculiar fancy.

He would gladly have adorned his study with busts, paintings, and statuary, and felt it a great deprivation that he had not the power to do so. A few handsomely bound and illustrated volumes and books of engravings, with here and there, on the walls, a framed engraving, a cross of moss, or a few plaster casts, was all the luxury with which he could indulge his taste. The study was a delightful place of resort, with its beautiful out-lookings in summer, its bay-window plants and sunniness in winter, together with the bright wood-fire upon the hearth, which was kindled chiefly for the pleasure of its cheerfulness.

Mr. Judd never was accustomed to study late at night, neither was he an early riser. And yet his nights were often sleepless; and in summer he always depended on getting a nap after dinner. He took exercise, more or less, every day, working in his garden and about his grounds, or walking to different places about the town. He had a habit at one time of feeling that he could write only in his shirt-sleeves, without any sort of over-garment, even in winter ; but this he at length gave up, and disciplined himself to wear a study-gown.

In the preparation of his literary works, he made great use of little note-books, devoted exclusively to the purpose, in which he put down any thing that came under his observation, having a bearing upon his object. In one of these, the vocabulary of the saw-mill, for " Richard Edney," is taken down as the workmen actually used it ; many of the little doings of Memmy and Bebby, such as " taking off stockings, and running about with their feet in their mittens," " each with a chicken's leg in each hand, drumming on the tin oven," &c.

In fragmentary notes, apparently for the construction of the lecture on the " Dramatic Element in the Bible," the references are exceeding copious, embracing the " Edinburgh Review," the " North American Review," Horne, Aristotle, Hazlitt, Jameson, Hudson, Heeren, Terence, Noyes, Calmet, Pathi, Johnson, Lamb, Gillie, &c. &c., implying a wide range of research.

In notes for the " White Hills," there stand, under date, Lake George, Aug. 19, 1850, entries like the following : " Shadow of a mountain by moonlight in a lake, dark, cloudlike, dim ; " " Steamer John Jay in the white mist like a snow-field." And again, in notes for this work : " Dead hemlocks, covered with moss ; " " Chimney standing, of a house that had decayed years before ; " " Deserted saw-mill on a green brook ; " " Sand-piper on the margin of Lake George, feeding from the waves, following, retreating ; " " Little tow-headed boy makes a bow ; " " The basin, water emerald-green, green pebbles at the bottom ; " " Silver cascade ; sounds ; deep, hollow gurgle ; also a sound down the cascade as of rain, a sprinkling sound. Three dead, spectral hemlocks above it." " The Notch ; streak of moonlight in streaks." " Mount Washington ; smoke rising like vapor, blue and pink tinted, white at the bottom. Black shadows, grey and blue, — clouds in long bars, — smoke rises and droops like an elm-tree, purplish tinge." " Church in a pine-grove, near Bethel." " Glen Ellis, — parts of mountains casting a distinct shadow ; parts in distinct, well-defined shadow. Hollows in light, peaks in shade, long ridge in shade," &c. &c. Thus were these little note-books filled up, showing Mr. Judd the closest student of all the varied phenomena of nature. They also contain lists of the plants indigenous to the place, of the birds and other animals ; and observations on the spot of every sort and kind, showing his principle of truthfulness to nature and to New England in all his works. In the same connection also are copious references to histories, traditions, travels, and the like, proving with all the rest, that he was no off-hand writer, throwing before the public crude impressions of the moment ; but that every thing was well studied and matured in his own thought before being sent abroad. And it is believed that all this pains and research gives to his writings a value unperceived by the cursory reader ; but which, as time passes on, will cause them to be more and more appreciated by the discriminating student of nature and lover of truth.

Thus, with Mr. Judd, was intellectual, as well as moral and religious progress, an element in which he lived; at all times adding to his mental stores, and taking in knowledge with a readiness, an ease and quietness, that showed the capacity of his mind, and the breadth of his general culture.

CHAPTER XII.

TEMPERAMENT AND GENERAL CHARACTERISTICS.

MR. JUDD's physical organization was of quite a delicate texture, with very slight development of muscle. His temperament would class under the nervous-sanguine. His figure was well set, and of the middle size; his face between the oval and the round. His complexion was florid and clear; his eyes blue; his hair sandy. His head was proportionably very large; the forehead high and remarkably prominent, rather overshadowing the eyes. He had a highly intellectual and kindly expression; and, in various states of emotion and excitement, when his soul diffused itself over his countenance, it was radiant with a refined and spiritual beauty. The engraving represents his face in a state of thought and repose, and is more stern than his usual look. In conversation he had very great play of the features. He was never disposed to put forth much physical exertion: indeed, it appeared an almost painful effort for him to do so, and he had not much power of endurance. If even a slight illness assailed him, he seemed to have very little force of resistance, and experienced universal prostration from it. Yet his general health was always good, and there appeared to be no disease lurking in his system.

His feelings were enthusiastic, ardent, deep, strong; his susceptibilities quick and tender. He never felt any thing by halves, but with him almost every emotion was a passion. From this constitutional temperament, he was fitted for experiencing the most lively enjoyment and the keenest suffering. A nervous system so sensitive is very much at the mercy of outward circumstances. Feelings, that with those of a more phlegmatic temperament are calm and gentle, seizing upon delicately wrought nerves in an easily excitable state, become pangs and daggers, and fearful are the inward crucifixions from which the victim cannot escape. And then, to add to the intensity and poignancy of the sufferings of one so constituted, is the consciousness of the fact, that, by those around him who have never experienced the like susceptibility, he is misunderstood and misjudged; that being attributed to ill-humor or bad temper which is as purely physical and beyond control as the electric shock consequent upon seizing the poles of a voltaic battery.

This nervous phenomenon, Mr. Judd began to experience at an early age. The first very prominent exhibition of it arose from the crossing of his strong desire to go steadily on in a regular course of study. Then came his pecuniary embarrassments in the prosecution of his education; and last, and most weightily, the wearing conflict in his theological opinions, which for a long time alternated between Calvinism and Infidelity, and was ever attended by the anguished thought of the disappointed hopes and pious sorrow which the prospective termination of the contest would bring on those his heart most fondly cherished. The painful result of all this on his nervous system has been detailed. And although, after his settlement at Augusta, the effects, in a great measure, subsided, yet still not only did the original susceptibility remain, but the torture which the nerves had undergone so left its impress, that they ever readily suffered an excitement and irritation that was beyond his control. The diverse manifestations arising from this source were not generally understood or rightly appreciated even by his nearest friends, and much less by those who knew him not intimately.

One thing that added to the difficulty, not only so far as others were concerned, but with himself also, was his great natural reserve. This was a strongly marked family-trait, which his father and grandfather had before him. He could not explain himself; he could not even put into the hands of others the key of interpretation to outward appearances, which he knew were totally misunderstood and wrongly judged. He never spoke of his nervous excitability, or the sufferings attending it, unless it was wrung from him by very peculiar circumstances. From various incidental remarks in his note-books and journal, it is evident he understood what in himself seemed to his friends peculiarities, much better than they were aware. He says in one instance: "I have often been desirous to speak to a person generally on some subject that interested me, yet I could not for my life." Again: "If I ebb and flow, my deep internal essence is ever the same." But, whatever were the ebbings and flowings within, his natural tendency was to keep the tossings and heavings concealed in the depths of his own heart, and present to others only a tranquil, equable exterior. This, however, was often beyond his power; and some unexpected and unaccountable phase would present itself, that rendered him an unsolvable enigma, or called forth condemnatory remarks, according as the observer failed to have been somewhat initiated into the intricacies of human nature, or was uncharitably disposed. Not that Mr. Judd was in the way of manifesting that pettishness which is often an attendant on such a physical state, or that he exhibited ill temper except very rarely and in an excessively excitable condition. It was rather those appearances which are called odd, queer, strange, peculiar.

His disposition was kind and sympathizing. He wished to see all about him in a happy state of feeling. All deep *heart*-emotions were his familiar acquaintance; and with a penetrating sympathy he could instinctively detect and enter into all sorrows pertaining to the affections. In " Richard Edney " he speaks from personal experience when he says: " There is no trial so severe as that of the heart. There is no furnace of affliction so hot as that enkindled in the sensibilities. There is no temptation from which a man had better pray for quick deliverance than that addressed to the affections and sentiments."

For old acquaintances whom he had not met for years, and with whom he never enjoyed any particular intimacy, he entertained kindly feelings, though perhaps passed from their remembrance, and would gladly give them a genial greeting. An instance of the kind is that in "Richard Edney," where, humorously speaking of destroying the works from which he had borrowed, he refers so pleasantly to "the assistant-librarian." A similar reference is made in the same work to his "respected college rhetorical professor."

In his expansive benevolence, country, color, rank, all melted away into one universal brotherhood, with one loving God and Father over all. Yet, with this full tide of feeling, by some he was considered selfish in details; and it must be allowed, that to the observer who did not know him well, or who had not the philosophy to unravel the complicated secret motives of action, there were sometimes exhibitions that might bear such a construction. But, as the matter lay in his own heart, it is believed there was no ground for such an imputation.

He was a man of a remarkably cheerful temper. He inclined to look on the bright side of things; and, even if darkness seemed to close around, he would always, here and there, discover the illuminated, the silver lining of the clouds of life. In one of his letters occurs this remark: "I have often told you I am never disappointed. I am not in common things." His meaning was, not that things always turned out as he might wish or expect, but that he was not overconfident in his expectation, and cheerfully acquiesced in results. He had a lively sense of the ludicrous, and often discovered its elements where nothing of the kind was perceived by others. A vein of humor constantly made itself felt in his conversation and writings. His ideas often took a remarkable juxtaposition, producing unexpected resemblances quite exciting to the risibles of his hearers, when he himself had no intention of the kind. He often introduced the keenest satire; but it was generally with a gravity that showed his lamentation over the evil, rather than ill-will towards the perpetrator.

He was exceedingly hopeful, both as to individuals and to the race. He had great confidence in human nature, and believed the better elements prevailed by far over the unworthy ones. He always *expected* good, and not evil, from men; and, in regard to those who had been guilty of any wrong to himself or to others, he was ready to find excuse for it, — was lenient and forgiving to the last degree. Many and many a time, with a peculiar meekness of demeanor, has he been heard to say, in reference to some one from whom he had suffered an injury or a disadvantage, " Oh! well, he did not mean it, he did not intend to do any harm," or something to this effect. In some of his writings this passage is found, — speaking of man in general : " If there be an element of hope in his case, I catch at it; if I know nothing about him, I would still hope for him; if there be positively no ground for encouragement, I can but shut my eyes to the dark catastrophe. I know, too, how often in this world that passes for sin which is no sin, and otherwise." These expressions are a most faithful transcript of his practice, and his sense of the dignity of human nature, as partaking of the divine. He would be cut to the heart at any seeming unkindness from his near friends, or those he loved; but he never harbored ill-will, and was anxious to have it passed over and forgotten, as though nothing had happened, as soon as possible; and it pained him to have allusion made to any unpleasantness that had occurred. He had a great aversion to fault-finding, and could not bear to see people take pleasure in discussing the imperfections of others, or in retailing scandal.

Extreme simplicity was a decided characteristic of Mr. Judd; a trait which, perhaps, to those not in habits of familiarity with him, was one of his most striking features. This element was deeply inwrought in his nature; and, even in his mature years, he continued remarkably childlike and unsophisticated. Many of the conventionalities of life he could not understand; in many more he could see no fitness or propriety; and, in either case, he could not adopt them. The guilelessness of his own heart led him to suspect none in others. He was upright, straightforward, plain, sincere, well-intentioned; and he took others to be so too. If he had feelings that were right, in themselves considered, he saw no necessity for concealing them, or of suppressing actions that were based on good and honest motives. Indeed, it never occurred to him to do so. He never thought of it. It did not dawn upon his mind that it was important to govern himself by factitious rules ; to accord with established usages, by putting on appearances contrary to the reality of things. Truthfulness lay so deep in his nature, that he could not see that many of the forms of society, which in the letter were untrue, were not so in reality, because nobody was deceived, but all received them for just what they were worth. He had no art ; he detested policy ; he could not admit expediency as a rule of action ; he possessed not what is understood by tact. Consequently, in his intercourse with society, to those who did not understand him he sometimes gave offence when least suspecting it. Persons would perhaps consider themselves neglected, ill used, or possibly insulted, when he had no feelings but those of perfect cordiality and kindness. By some the developments to which this led were considered unaccountable strangeness. And thus, while, if sifted to the bottom, this feature would have been found to grow out of one of the most beautiful elements of his moral constitution, it often operated very unfavorably upon others, and was the cause of much mortification and chagrin to himself from the misunderstandings and wrong judgments to which it exposed him. It must be acknowledged, however, that Mr. Judd had a marked *individuality* of character, which was apparent in all he said and did, and which often gave the impression of oddness and eccentricity. But, by whatever term it may be designated, it certainly grew out of the greatest *fidelity to himself,* and did not arise from any desire, or even any consciousness, of being singular. It was full of a sweetness, simplicity, and *naïveté*, that gave interest and pungency to his whole demeanor.

While very social in his feelings, he was rather averse to mingling in general society. His usual range of thought was upon subjects of an elevated rank; and he had not that agreeable fund of small talk which finds the best currency in mixed companies. His extreme sensitiveness and nervous excitability were attended by their usual concomitants, — diffidence and want of self-possession. So that, take him all in all, he was quite the antipodes of what is generally understood by a man of the world. He did not possess the ready power of adapting himself at will to any circumstances in which he might be thrown. He writes in his Journal: "I can never be of the world. I must undo my nature first."

His circle of acquaintance with the literary world was much more limited than that of most persons who hold as high a rank in it as he did. This was partly due to his residing away from the prominent centres of literary reunion, without adequate time or means for seeking them; and partly from the naturally independent action of his own mind, which found abundant stimulus and food within itself. Yet no one better than he enjoyed free conversation in private with one whose views, feelings, mental calibre and attainments, corresponded with his own. Then, with his mind animated on some subject of interest, the rich imagery of his conversation, the fire and force of his far-reaching thought, his natural quaintness of manner, all mingled with the full tide of human kindness, — the ether in which floated all his most brilliant intellectual riches, — often charmed those of the favored circle. In many conversations of this kind, in his own house, with some visitor of high culture and refined taste, groups of willing listeners have thought it a privilege to sit by in silence ; or perhaps felt justified, in an unobtrusive way, in playing something of the eavesdropper in passages or veranda in connection with the apartment of conversation. His table-talk, under similar circumstances, would, it is believed, not suffer in comparison with some of the best of this kind that has been given to the world.

A travelling companion of Mr. Judd, on his return from the Baltimore Convention, writes : " It was our privilege to listen to his rich discourse for an hour or two ; and the memory of his racy talk, with its brilliant and apt illustrations, tender and loving spirit, engrossing sincerity, is like the memory of some scene full of fresh novelty, radiant with light, and vocal with wild, sweet music. There was a union of the ideal and the practical, the play of a poetic imagination over the solidity of good sense, the enthusiasm of the lofty-souled visionary flashing out amidst the sober counsels of a useful every-day wisdom, that made his conversation, on that calm, serene night, exceedingly beautiful, winning, and suggestive."

In his intellectual capacities, he had great quickness of perception, and a readiness and ease in receiving knowledge. He could take in a long range of thought without confusion ; and at unfamiliar or strange ideas he was not frightened. Though to others it seemed that his memory was faithful and ready, he himself complained that it did not serve him well. His associations were apt to be based upon delicate resemblances, unnoticed and unthought of by the common observer. Imagination in him was bold and strong, altogether prevailing over fancy. To him, almost every thing he looked upon was endowed with life; and his use of figurative language was abundant. Though often exercising wit, humor in general had the ascendancy.

He might be said to have equally exercised the subjective and objective powers of his mind. He was accustomed to much introversion. His private writings show close self-inspection. He grew from within, outward; and also, by the reverse process, from without, inward. If his observation was nice and continual, his self-reflection kept pace with it.

To him, the outer as well as his inner world was a living presence. Nature was to him the revelation and embodiment of Divinity itself. In her motherly arms she seemed to enfold him. On her kind bosom he could throw himself for solace and refreshment. If he was sick, she was his tender nurse; if saddened, her pure and gentle ministries would gladden and restore him to himself. He walked with her as with a friend; he wooed her as a lover; and no phase of her appearance, no feature of her forms, escaped his attention. Her many-tinted hues, her polyphonian voices, were all familiar to his eye and hear. He also studied nature as a science. But here he did not stop. This was not

an end, but only a means of introducing him into the
secrets of the natural world, revealing more fully its
latent beauties, and thus preparing him for those
minute, truthful, graphic descriptions for which he
was remarkable.

His own soul was delicately sensitive to the
beautiful; and, among its infinite forms in nature,
few escaped his notice. He discovered it in rich
abundance, where the ordinary observer perceived
nothing but simple form and color. "Something,"
he says, "like what we are pleased to term infinite
moment, hangs on this thing, — the beautiful. I
can say, happy indeed are they who have loved the
beautiful from childhood, clung to it with a devoted
will through after-life, and who prize it as a talismanic gem wherewith to open the gates of truth;
prize it, too, as a serene light from heaven on their
earthly pilgrimage." His mind naturally tended to
make each object accordant with its surroundings;
and thus, in his writings, he would group in harmonious blendings to his own eye, what, to another,
would sometimes seem harsh and incongruous.
Unable to see ugliness and deformity in the *natural*,
to him the picturesque was easily attainable. Resemblances and relations, far from obvious to the
common mind, were to him readily suggested. The
wintry appearance of the dark, leafless boughs and
twigs of the tall trees look to him "like bold, delicate netting or linear embroidery on the blue sky; or
as if the trees, interrupted in their usual method of
growth, were taking root in mid-winter up among the
warm transparent heavens." Every thing with him

39

was sentient. The snow " fell soft and even upon shrubs and flowers in the woods, as if it were tenderly burying its dead." The influences of nature seemed almost essential to his devotional feelings. He said of himself, when walking in the city at a certain time, under a hot sun, upon scorching pavements, brick walls on either side, and no tree or spire of grass for the eye to rest upon, that he " felt as though he had lost his religion," and must needs go out to Haerlem to see the grass and hear the birds.

To the readers of his works, and to those who have listened to his public discourses or his conversations, it is not necessary to enlarge on this element of his character. The balmy breath of nature is emitted from almost every page of his writings. The woods and wild flowers contribute their fragrance. Birds blend their carols with the joyous spring-notes of softly-murmuring streams and gurgling brooklets. Soft, snowy clouds move in still grandeur and beauty over the serene blue above, like convoys of the blest, in watchful guardianship over each human soul. And, to crown all, the great and good Father of the whole universe lives and reveals himself in every thing his power produces, the least as well as the most immense ; in the humblest flower and tiniest insect, as well as in the vast worlds and systems which gem and solemnize the skies of night.

He was fond of contemplating Christ as conversant and identified with nature ; as symbolizing himself and his cause under figures such as the vine and the mustard-seed ; drawing his illustrations from the lilies of the field, the birds of the air, fields ready for harvest, serpents, doves, water, stars, and light. A beautiful illustration of his view of Christ in connection with nature is found in a sermon upon the subject, from the text, " Consider the lilies of the field." In concluding the discourse he says : " Christ was a lover of nature ; he entered into its spirit, he reproduced its forms, he spoke in its language. There is no department he overlooked ; vegetables, animals, minerals, the wind and rains, lightning, the orbs above us, — into every domain of creation he entered.

" And how did he do this ? Not as an economist, or a speculator or surveyor ; but as a child of the infinite Father, communing with the works of his hand, in the love of beauty and the spirit of faith. He walked by the sea-side, he traversed woods, to derive lessons for the souls he was to save, and a method for that kingdom he came to establish."

Art, as well as nature, was to Mr. Judd a study and delight ; and the relations of the one to the other he loved to trace. " Trees," he says, in " Richard Edney," " considered as an avenue for the eye to traverse, enhance the beauty of objects at the end of it. The reader has looked through trees at water or the sky, and witnessed this effect. Nature, like art, seems to require a border in order to be finished. The dressmaker hems and ruffles ; the carpenter has his beads and pilasters ; the painter never rests till his piece is framed. . . . If we should say nature loves a bordering, as it used to be said she abhorred a vacuum, we might state the whole truth. An uninterrupted plane ; a continuity of

similar surface, vast, monotonous, silent, — is intolerable. So a column must have its cap, and a house
its cornice ; so along the highway spring innumerable
flowers, and on its margin the forest is lavish of its
foliage ; so the sea is terminated by the sky ; and
we look at the sky through vistas of embanked
and woofy cloud. Were you ever in a fine grove of
a bright moonlight night? How different from
standing upon a mountain at such a time ! We
recommend to any on an eminence to go back from
the brink thereof, and stand in the forest, and look
out through the breaks and crevices. A moss-rose
is an instance in point, beautiful because it is bordered : it is a landscape seen through trees. A
house in the midst of shrubbery is an instance ; so
are islands in a pond ; a view through half-raised
window-curtains, and distant scenery through a long
suite of rooms ; so are light on foregrounds, and
shadows on backgrounds, in all pictures. Glens,
valleys, a flower in the grass, a star in the sky, belong
to the same category. So did Memmy and Bebby,
at this present speaking ; they were bordered by
trees ; cedars and birches were about them, like
curls on the face of fair maiden. . . . Then, in this
case, the children were on the go, while the bordering kept still ; they were the picture, dancing up
and down in its frame ; they were the blue sky,
crisping and rippling behind the clouds.

" Lo !` now Bebby stands between, and partly
screened by, two little cedars, about as tall as she ;
and how beautiful she is ! She is a moss-rose ; a
rose mossed, bordered. Bebby runs away. Bebby

is the same Bebby; the trees are the same trees; but how different apart! The rose has lost its moss, the view its border. Run back, little additament! Throw yourself into the middle of the picture, or what will be a picture when you get there! Consent to be bordered. Those happy blue eyes, those flocculent, foamy locks, — were they ever so pretty? The pea-green, crinkly little cedars, — what enchantment they suddenly assume! How the beauty flashes from one to the other, and centres in the whole! How it vanishes when Bebby quits!"

For paintings and sculpture, Mr. Judd had great taste and appreciation, and a very well-cultivated judgment. He would study by the hour a single piece of real merit, and his criticisms were highly discriminating. In the tragedy of the "White Hills," before quoted from, among other remarks upon art, in conversation with the artist, he makes Normand say: —

"If spirit shrinks, as from a hand profane,
Paint depth, with breadth and distance too, the forms
Of universal, omnipresent life,
Nor wall up surfaces. Why ever work
In side-views, as if nature had no front,
And man were only lateral-jointed, like
A dancing-jack? Canst thou not handle night,
And shades as black as night, that lie
Along the wooded margin of a lake?
Or space project, and pebbles sink in water?
Ye study attitude, geometry,
The starts of tragedy, what warm, what cold;
You ilk have murdered men to see them die;
Spurning Dione smiling through the trees.
Hast seen the spirit, — make it felt
In what thou dost, the visible, invisible."

39*

He sometimes tried his own hand at modelling, in the clay about his house, grotesque busts for the amusement of his children. He had great sympathy with artists, and wished that, in this country, they might find more appreciation and encouragement. It was a matter of regret to him, that our Puritan fathers, in their zeal to do away with existing abuses, so entirely rejected all art, and laid no foundation for its cultivation in this country.

He sought as much as possible to encourage art among his people. In the construction of his own house, and the embellishing of his grounds, in which every tree was set with regard to effect, his own sense of beauty and art is embodied as far as his means would allow.

In mechanical operations he had considerable skill, and had a great fondness for getting up peculiar little contrivances that nobody else would think of.

For music Mr. Judd had a great love. He was very sensitive to its power. It affected him deeply. Yet he was unable to produce it himself. Musical tones coursed through him like wind through the trees; or, rather, his frame vibrated under their influence. It seemed to be pure musical tone mostly that affected him; for he did not always definitely distinguish one air from another. In a letter to his wife, dated October, 1852, he writes: "As to music, 'tis not all 'association,' 'tis partly the severe requisitions of my own mind, 'tis the despotism of a fine art within me, that moves me." Much of the soul of music is shadowed forth in Chilion, and the moral influence of his violin, with which also the poor boy said he had done all his praying.

Among all Mr. Judd's prominent characteristics, his religious tendency was the most striking. Religion was to him the first thing and the last; it pervaded his whole life; it was to him all in all. A sense of duty, a sense of right, was ever his governing motive. So strong was this feeling, he never seemed to have any temptation even to make compromises with his conscience; and conscience was the ever-ready arbiter in his decisions. His principle was to obey God at all earthly hazards; to perform duty, and leave the consequences to God. In the language of another, "The struggle of his heart was not to embrace heaven and earth by *turns,* and thus turn both to the ashes of despair; but, wherever earthly love came in conflict with the heavenly, the former was always sacrificed to the latter. He sought rather to *heavenize* earthly love; to make it a part of the spiritual perfection and joy of man's earthly state. Most touching was the sad music of his spirit, when the triumphing of the heavenly claim upon its powers was heard simultaneously with broken-hearted love and expiring passion." In the preceding narrative, there has often been occasion to refer to his reverence for truth, and his own corresponding truthfulness of character. Love to God and to man, as has often appeared in these pages, was the key-note of his being; it was the sum and substance, the foundation-stone, of his religion. He labored for the happiness, the elevation, the moral purity, of the race. This benevolent principle in him had no bounds. To the sorrowing and afflicted he had words of cheer, even when his own heart was sinking under some oppression.

Great earnestness was a quality for which he was conspicuous. It was seen in the prosecution of whatever he undertook; especially was it developed in carrying out his fond idea of the birthright church. At the association in Belfast, when that subject was under consideration, something was said about a want of earnestness in the ministry; he said he acknowledged no such want; and, as one who heard him says, "in a manner that took from his words all appearance of presumption," he added, "I have as much earnestness as I want; as much as I can carry." There was in him a constant vitality of thought, and a firmness and independence in acting up to his honest convictions.

He had great humility of mind; never manifested an undue estimate of himself, or made others feel that he claimed superiority over them, but, on the contrary, was exceedingly unpretending, unassuming, and innately modest in the highest degree. In a letter previously given, referring to his part in the movements of the Unitarian Church in Maine, and urging others to go forward, he says, "I am tired of so much personality."

His resignation under trial, the quiet submission with which he bowed to the dispensations of Providence, was one of the strongest and most beautifully marked features of his religious character. Christ was ever his pattern and guide; to be like Christ, the standard from which there was no appeal. His

life was far above the range of trivial, earthly things :
it seems not too much to say, with the apostle, that
it was " hid with Christ in God."   Not that it is
claimed that he was perfect, or free from faults ; yet
no one who comprehended him fully, or knew him
intimately, could fail to see that his governing principles were high and holy, and that they permeated
every department of life and of human interest.
He acted from principle in all things, even to the
patronizing of home-mechanics and artisans, though
perhaps a little at the expense of appearance.   Those
who knew him best, — his family-friends, the witnesses of his most unreserved daily life, — while by
no means blind to his imperfections, could not fail
to venerate the moral purity of his character ; to
feel that it was indeed Christ-like.

He lived near to God in the communion of his
spirit.   God was to him a loving Father, an ever-
present Friend.   Devotion was the habit of his
mind, the repose of his spirit.   It was deeper than
words ; it was higher than outward forms ; it was
not governed by times and seasons.   God was in
connection with all his thoughts.   As he walked by
the way, he worshipped.   He once let fall the remark to a young friend, on walking across the lot
from his house to that of his father-in-law, — " This
is my prayer-ground : there is Malta Woods on one
side, the river on the other, the heavens above."
He had not that high, ecstatic religious enjoyment
which some have experienced.   It was not so much
rejoicing as great inward trust, submission, peace.

It was, in short, the feeling of at-one-ment of him-self with God.

Such are some of the salient points of Mr. Judd's character. But, as manifest in him, they were so mixed and blended as to produce an indescribable uniqueness, which no one could fail to perceive from the briefest acquaintance with the man or his writings. With the most profound seriousness of thought was an easy play of natural humor. In his extreme rectitude of principle, there was nothing stern : his Christian graces melted into the common-est affairs of daily life. Firm and independent, he was neither self-consequent nor overbearing. Ever genial in his feelings, he was often reserved in out-ward manner. Refined in taste, and keenly alive to the beautiful, there was often something of gro-tesqueness in his combinations. Self-reliant, he was not presumptive. He did not display the different features of his character by turns, but, as it were, was each and all at the same moment ; bringing, by some secret sense of unity best understood by himself, seeming discrepancies to meet in the same thought and action. The lights and shades blended and flickered, and were lost in each other in in-tangibility in his actual existence ; yet every thing held its own, went on, attained its end. And thus naïve, unique, he stood out in bold relief in his own individuality, — himself, and no one else.

CHAPTER XIII.

DOMESTIC RELATIONS.

In the current history of Mr. Judd's life, which has already been given, much has appeared illustrative of his general tendencies of a domestic kind. But home, its relations, its affections, its manifold interests, held a place so vital in his heart, and had so much to do with the very essence of his life, that justice to the subject seems to require it should receive a separate notice.

The family-state held so high a place in his estimation as to prompt the following expression in one of his sermons: "I believe it is a greater sin to neglect the family than to neglect the church. Much as I love the church, and there are none who love it more, if either institution must, from any sad necessity suffer, let the blow fall upon the church rather than the family."

The homes of his childhood and youth were precious to him, even in their localities. The old place in Westhampton he always loved to revisit; and his fond childhood's associations invested even its barren hills with beauty and attractiveness. Northampton, his later home, had ever with him something paradisiacal in its charms; and a sight of its old, familiar objects never failed to swell his heart almost with rapture.

All along through his life at college and the divinity-school, home was the centre of his thoughts, and there his affections were garnered up. He looked forward to his vacations with longing desire to find himself again encircled by his own kindred. His letters were frequent in the intervals of separation, and were mostly addressed to his *mother*, who, though her health was always poor, was yet, by her energy and resolution, the secret spring and life of the family-arrangements and comforts. With the children, in their later as well as earlier years, nothing was deemed impossible with "mother." If the problem was to renovate the wardrobe, it was she who could make the "auld claes look amaist as weel's the new;" if to make the most of a little, she it was who could do it. No one was so untiring as she, in season and out of season, in attending to the needs of her children, and administering to their pleasure. Her taste and refinement of feeling were ever a stimulus to them to aspire after the best things. They were always sure of her disinterestedness and self-sacrifice in contributing to their happiness. They confided in her as a friend; they revered her as a mother; they venerated her as a Christian.

In no one of her children were these sentiments stronger than in Sylvester. They were indeed attended with a peculiar glow in his breast, and were connected with all that was most tender in his nature.

His father was always social, loving to discuss all

sorts of matters with his children. His study into men and things had been extensive; his judgments were usually well founded; and from his fund of knowledge and experience, useful and interesting lessons were always to be learned. And, on his part, he was glad to draw out from his children whatever they had acquired from study and observation in their wanderings from the paternal roof. For him his children entertained great respect and an honest pride; and between him and them existed a deep affection.

The children were bound to each other by the strongest ties. In the drama of the " White Hills," Sylvester says : —

> " It sometimes seems as all the milk
> Of human kindness went to brotherhood."

And no one but those who knew him intimately can understand how *truly* these lines express his own heart, his own experience. In 1838 he writes: " Every day adds to the strong interest that attaches me to my brothers." And in his Journal, March, 1840, stands this record: " A letter from brother C. P. How precious are ye to me, my brothers, one and all! May Heaven keep us holy!" Yet there were no peculiar outward demonstrations of affection, unless particular occasions drew them forth; and a stranger might not readily have detected any great warmth of fraternal sentiment.

Such were the elements which made up the home of Sylvester's younger years and his early manhood. It was in these home-gatherings that he always

longed to be one, when he was away pursuing his
studies.   It was hither his frequent epistles were
sent.   It was to those dwelling here that the injunction was so often penned, " Write," " *Write soon !* "
And, after completing his professional studies, the
prominent objection to settling in Augusta was its
remoteness from his kindred.   Established there,
and taking his place in the world as a man on his
own footing, as a child he sighed for a place at
his mother's table, on occasion of the time-honored
and tenderly associated festival of Thanksgiving, and
had the secret feeling that it was hard to stay and
make Thanksgiving for other people, and have none
himself; that is, none that anwered to his old, fond
ideas of a Thanksgiving, which are so well pictured
in the letter which follows, addressed —

To his Mother.

" Cambridge Theological Seminary, Nov. 28, 1837.

" Dear Mother, — This letter will find you in the
midst of the festivities of Thanksgiving.   I send it,
and it is all I can send.   I wish I could be at home
myself to participate in the delights of this, our
most joyful anniversary.   But I must be content to
remain here alone.   Yes, *alone ;* for almost all of
our students are going to their respective homes.
Our halls will be deserted ; and my joys will return
upon me in pain, and my thanks, I fear, will be
mingled with something of discontent.

" A. introduces quite a luscious break in A. H.'s
last letter, and presents a tempting account of *new
cider,* pumpkin-pies, &c.   She came upon the stage

before it was a sin to quaff the pure juice of the
apple. The man who *invented* the sin of a cider-
draught ought to be compelled to drink and feed on
bran-bread and water all his days. Who will write
the history of New England's cider? — or the tale
of the last cider-drinker? Thanksgiving was always
a favored time. Freegiving would be a better name.
Great times we used to have at Grandpa Judd's at
Thanksgiving. There were good eating, and good
drinking, and good feeling. There was the mug of
flip too. I remember it well. Father thinks I am
a little beset with a *spiritual* nature. Yet those
were glorious times. They are gone. Their vision
glimmers among the things that were. A. and
H——i and P——n have no remembrances of this
sort. Their recollections will only cluster about
their own father's festive board. May these ever
be to them cherished, sweet, pure, holy! . . . . A. H.
says the old carpet is on the parlor-floor. I would
give a thousand times more to see it next Thursday,
with the table full of papers, and the old trunk,
than to see the finest Brussels and the nicest maho-
gany of Boston. Home is home, you know, though
ever so homely. My home is decidedly characterized as respects its exterior. Yet I love you nor it
none the less.

"I want to be with you. Think a little of the
absent ones. C. P. and I must take our meals in
somewhat of sadness. Say a good word for us;
wish us well. Say you wish C. P. could have such
a piece at dinner, and I such a bit, and how you
wish we were there, and 'twill do us good.

"You will be thankful for blessings received, and ills prevented. I have hurried through this sheet at a galloping rate, which must account for incoherence. I felt as if I must say something. 'Twas 'like a fire shut up in my bones.' I feel as if it was almost a sin not to be at home Thanksgiving. But I must make the best of it. You know that I have not kept it at home but once for five years."

To a friend, about this time, he remarked that he trembled all over, every letter he got from home, and hardly dared to break the seal, lest it brought the news that to his father, his mother, or some one of the family, evil had happened. After he had a family of his own, the same fond desire for the parental home continued. Visits to it were looked forward to as a consummated happiness, and were repeated as frequently as circumstances would allow. In a Thanksgiving sermon, of which the subject is "Home," this passage occurs : — "We can be free there. We can throw off the dress of the street and the manners of society. A man is not obliged to conceal his headache, and he can give vent to his own feelings, when he enters his house. One is not a merchant or a doctor or a lawyer at home. There is one place in the world where even a clergyman can be a boy again ; and that is his father's house. His father calls him by his first name, and his mother asks him to bring in an armful of wood. There is throwing off of care, and rejection of conventionality, at home, and yielding one's self to nature, and slippers, and loose gown."

The first severing of the tie which bound Sylvester so closely with each and all the members of his father's family was the removal from tangible intercourse, in the year 1850, of his brother H——l, a man in the prime of life, of the greatest purity of character, of a singularly devout life, the utmost resignation to the will of Heaven, and with faith in the Father above, which may be said to have been lost in sight. He had, for many years, been an invalid; and his duties had confined him very much to his own little family. Sylvester had long been planning and wishing to secure a visit from him, and had counted largely on the pleasure it would afford, and the improvement it might effect in his health, to spend some time at the Augusta Parsonage. But, as the months drew near when he hoped to realize this long-cherished wish, this brother began to decline more and more. Hopes of his rallying grew less and less strong. The feared and dreaded message at last arrived, that he had approached the confines of the spirit-world. Sylvester's efforts to reach him in season for one more earthly interview, one parting exchange of the deep love of their hearts, were fruitless. Ere he arrived, with familiar discourse upon the subject, with the calmness of preparation for a short journey, and with sweet, child-like trust and composure, expressing a willingness at any moment to leave the world, his spirit had passed away : his body, as if in gentle sleep, alone remained. Sylvester's grief at this rending of the brotherly tie shall be given in his own words, in a letter addressed —

40*

To his Wife and Sister.

"Northampton, Feb. 27, 1850.

"My heart bleeds. Last night, I went into the parlor, where the body lay, and shut the doors to be alone. I must needs give way to the sadness of my feelings. Poor, dear, good H——l! poor, dear, good H——l! I kissed his forehead for myself, and for you all. Calm, composed, he looked; his forehead fair, smooth, beautiful, as ever. But dead, dead! Where was his accustomed sweet smile? where his gentle welcome? where some response to the bursting agony of my spirit?

"No voice, no eye, no cheerful interest! My brother, my best brother, dead! I sat down in silence, in deepest sorrow.

"There are the old pines in the neighborhood of his house, once enlivened by his presence; there are the fruit-trees that he took such interest in; there are the firs I had talked with him so much about. To-day I saw some old stalks of corn that he left, and, too, the neighbors' hens that used to perplex him so, and that he drove off in so quiet a way,— all things full of his sweet image. His old, living, good form comes up continually in all this desolation.

"So it is: he is gone for this world; but the other world gains a noble inhabitant. The other world must be enriched to our eyes and heart by a new interest. God prepare us all for our last end!"

In relation to the same bereavement are the following extracts: —

To his Brother J. W.

"Augusta, March 9, 1850.

" I cannot, I need not, express all that I, all that we all, feel about our great loss.　H——l was a very dear brother to me : the thought of him was dear ; the idea of visiting him was dear ; the expectation that he would visit us was dear.　What a melancholy reigned about his house, and over his garden, and under those green pines, and must for ever reign !　The maples and firs and peach-trees he set out, and watched so carefully, and watered so industriously, — they all seemed to be in mourning for him.　Think, too, of his dear wife, who mourns him because she knew him so well, and of the little children, who will never mourn him because they never knew him.　To me it was, as you may suppose, a sad office to be called to perform the funeral-service.

"But his end was serene, hopeful, bright ; and his consummation is now glorious.　Our sorrows are softened ; the very gloom of our hearts is uplifted to the light and the joy of heaven.　Dear spirit of our departed brother, we know thou art blest.　God prepare all of us to meet thee in peace !　Thy memory will ever be about us to cheer, admonish, guide, and save."

To his Father.

"Augusta, March 10, 1850.

" Dear Father, — I think a great deal about the dear departed.　His miniature is now open on my table.　His gentle eye, his tender feeling, are all there. His sudden decline deprived us of a deeply cherished hope, that he would visit us this summer, recreate his strength, see our houses, and enjoy a portion of our life. How lonely and sad must F. be! how seemingly unsheltered are the two orphans! But God's will be done!"

TO HIS SISTER-IN-LAW, F. J.

"AUGUSTA, March 24, 1850.

"Dear Sister, — P. writes that you are going to leave your house. It must be sad parting with the house, even as it was with him who was the life of it. I think a great deal of my dear brother. His daguerreotype stands continually open before me upon my desk. His pure spirit in the heavenly world blesses me. Yet I did wish — oh, how I wished! — to see him in the flesh a little longer. His death weighs upon my heart, yet without disturbing my faith.

"That house is endeared to you ; the garden, the shrubbery, the fruit-trees, even to the kitchen and the shed. How he watered those trees! how interested he was in their growth! what a variety of little plans he had for the future! All gone, all gone! God's blessed will be done!

"How we did calculate on a visit, a long visit, from H——l this summer, and hoped to give him that leisure and recreation which would favor his health!

"We are looking forward to a pleasant summer. I too have a garden and trees, — which H——l will never see.

" God's love, and good promises, and sustaining spirit, be in your heart ! "

To his sister P., April 7, 1850, he says : " Dear face, we shall see it no more. The blessedness of H——l, his virtues, his meekness, his quaint, good ways, — it makes me sigh every day when I think that, as to this world, they are lost to us for ever. I still see, in my mind's eye, his homely, benevolent form walking under those shadowy pines. Shall I greet it no more ? "

In a blank-book, apparently with the intention of writing a memorial of this dear brother, stands only this simple record : " Died, my dear, blessed brother Hall, Feb. 26, 1850."

The sermon on the " Affection of Brothers," which this event called forth, has been referred to.

Sylvester had great influence with his brothers and sisters, and was intellectually and spiritually a leading member of the band. In all their good fortune he participated ; and for their sorrows his sympathy was ever ready. To his brother J. W., who was mourning the loss of a dear little boy, he thus writes : —

" Oct. 23, 1845.

" My dear Brother, — I have been wishing to write you ever since I received yours, announcing the sickness of Channing, ' the sweet little one,' but have hardly found one collected moment ; and even now, just after getting your very full account of his death, and when I could most wish to write, I have hardly a spare moment. We do all most deeply sympathize with you and E., as we did all most deeply love the little boy. Channing's sweet smile, his soft voice, his winsome ways, his gentle spirit, we can never forget. It must have been a melancholy errand, that of going with him to H., and shutting the remains of so much innocence, so much loveliness, so much beauty, in the silent grave. God only knows the bitterness, the anguish, of your hearts; and may he sustain you in this severe trial!

"I preach that children go to heaven, that he who blessed them on earth blesses them there, that the dead little ones are treasures laid up in heaven; and what is preached, we would all practically believe. There is a reunion. There comes a time when we shall go to the loved and lost, — when parents shall meet again their children. Angels have charge over their pure souls, and will keep them until we go for them. In this hope let us rest; in this bright prospect let our tears be dry, and our afflicted hearts find repose. In the earth rests his body: let our souls rise with his to the skies. I will pray for you."

In November, 1845, he wrote as follows to his brother H——l and wife, who were then under like circumstances of bereavement : —

"My dear Brother and Sister, — We have received tidings of the death of your little boy. I know your hearts are pained by this sad event; that a strong parental hope is crushed, and a portion of your daily life, as it were, blotted out for ever. I believe you are sustained by those reflections that flow from our holy religion ; that you call to mind Jesus, the bosom-friend of little children ; that you anticipate a reunion with the loved and lost ; and that you acquiesce in the will of your heavenly Father.

" Notwithstanding our religion, our philosophy, our stoicism even, it is a sad thing to bury a child ; to shut it away from our arms, our sight, and our love, and consign it to the silent grave. To part with its voice, its face, its sweet eyes, its plays, afflicts us sorely. But its memory will abide in your soul ; and the prospect of again meeting it will brighten your lonely pilgrimage. W. too has been called to mourn : his Channing, mild, spiritual boy, is no more. Let us feel that we are all children of the universal Father, and that our children are his also ; and, when he calls them to himself, we will resign them without doubt or complaint.

" Our hold on things of earth is frail : let us therefore use them well ; let us love, and do good to, our children, and they will be better fitted to go, and we to spare them. Presently it must come our own turn to die. If any children are left to bury us, may it be with the feeling that we were good fathers, good mothers.

" Your brother very affectionately,

" SYLVESTER."

More deeply still was he affected by the loss of " Arthur Willie," as the little fellow called himself, the only child of his sister A. This endeared boy, of high promise, was doubly his nephew, and almost

twin in age with his own little girl. The two children had been associated together from their birth,
and, as they advanced in age, had been almost daily
together, sharing the same playthings, the same
attentions. The father and uncle had watched with
equal interest the developments of the two, marked
their contrasts, idiosyncracies, and intimations of
future character. The two households, indeed, were
somewhat one ; and the children seemed to be
shared almost in common. The blight of that noble
little form, the transit beyond the reach of sense of
that winning spirit, touched his heart with the most
tender grief, and drew forth unwonted sobs and
tears. In a little Journal in which he kept the
record of the childish sayings and doings of his little
girl, he writes : —

"*Dec.* 15, 1846. — Little Arthur died. At one
sudden stroke is thus swept away much attractiveness, the fairest promise of youth, and the strongest
joy of many. Arthur had a light complexion, blue
eyes, blond hair, red cheeks ; was agile, energetic,
talkative ; his limbs were hard, fat, and round ; his
step firm, his manner enthusiastic. He was developing fast, and that in a way that made each but the
presage of some still more beautiful attitude. He
won the good opinion of all, and retained the interest
of old friends. He was two years and four months
old ; two months older than Lizzie. These two children, contemporaneous and juxtaposed, seemed fitted
to grow up together, and were mutually intertwined
about the same parental hearts. They are separated,
and these hearts bleed."

" *Dec.* 18. — Arthur was buried. It snowed all night, rained all day. But four of us went with him to the tomb. His grandfather carried the coffin in his arms, from the house to the carriage. We laid him in silence to his last rest. God have mercy upon us ! "

He writes his parents and family-friends at Northampton, announcing this sorrow : —

"Dec. 16, 1846.

" You have heard of the sickness of little Arthur, and I have now to communicate the sad intelligence of his decease. This morning he lies in his little crib, near the bed, as he used to sleep. He is fair and lovely in death. At the head of the crib I have placed those two little plaster-casts, representing youth and innocence. A. has placed her little ' Samuel ' in the same room. Some flowers are on his breast.

" I need not say that we are greatly, very greatly afflicted, nor ask for your sympathies, which will flow so freely towards us. It seems as if *I*, as well as they, had lost a child, — as if half of our little one was gone. Arthur had grown exceedingly strong, active, and promising. He was full of life and spirits, and conveyed the gladdest impressions to all who beheld him. His healthful form is extended in death ; the ruddiness of his cheek, the brilliancy of his eye, have fled ; his sweet, exhilarating voice we shall hear no more. How great the blow ! Arthur has been a blessing to us, and we will not complain that that blessing is now restored to its Author, and to our Father in heaven."

And, under the same date, to his brother J. W. : —
" You, my dear brother, can sympathize with us in
this affliction ; you, who have had your fair and promising children cut down, can tell what is the deep
and bitter anguish of such a bereavement. You
know how Arthur had grown ; you have seen how
promising he was, and you can well understand how,
not only his parents, but all of us, had become
strongly attached to him. But he has gone ; a dark
veil has suddenly been drawn over all his bright
future ; into the heart of affection sinks an irrepressible anguish.

" We would not murmur at God's dealings ; we
would that all chastisement may work for our good."

Again, when the infant son of his brother H——l,
and the sole supporter of his name, followed that
sainted father to the skies, he thus wrote the bereaved wife and mother, —

His Sister-in-law F. J.

" Augusta, Nov. 17, 1851.

" Dear F. — We were not surprised to hear of
the death of your little boy. He has been a great
sufferer, and death is to him a release. To you it
is a sadness and bereavement. The good God support you under your manifold trials ! Though he
cause grief, yet will he have compassion according
to the multitude of his mercies. I do not presume
to penetrate all the mysteries of Divine Providence ;
but only of this am I assured, that Infinite and
unchanging Love rules the universe, and directs our

lot. On this will I rest; to this will I come; before this will I humbly and meekly bow. Let me be the child of this love; and my children, and all I love are its too.

"I was very sorry not to see you last summer. I rode by 'H———l's;' saw the great pines where he used to come up, the maples and peaches he watered, the garden he hoed, the house he built, — *he* was not there. Yet sweetly, serenely, his memory and the shadow of his spirit rest on all. He cannot come to us; we shall go to him."

Sylvester never let a very long period pass without writing his mother. Even when most pressed with the duties of his profession and his literary labors, with accustomed filial love and duty, he would from time to time jot down for her eye a few brief items connected with his daily life; a few words of affectionate remembrance. These letters were generally interspersed, here and there, with a little merry humor, to cheer and enliven the somewhat solitary old home, left nearly childless by the establishment of one after another of its early inmates, in business or households of their own. He often contrived to get up a little amusement at the expense of his youngest sister, the only child remaining with the parents. A few specimens of these familiar home-letters are here given: —

To his Sister P———n.

"Augusta, April 7, 1850.

"Dear P———n, — The days pass off without much that is novel or interesting. The ice has left the river; and last night a beautiful little steamboat came up to our wharves. I have set some new trees, and reset some old ones. We have had the window leading from the parlor to the veranda changed to a door. I have some early peas sprouted, which I shall sow to-morrow. J.'s roses and other flowers in the bay-window are looking splendidly. The children play about the house, jam their noses, bring in mud, run off to Mr. F.'s, &c., &c. Birds are beginning to be quite merry in the morning. A. was here to tea; J. at his mother's; J. C. has sent me a patent bee-house, and I think some of purchasing some inmates for it.

"We rest in the strong hope of seeing you all here this summer.

"With much love," ———

To his Mother.

"Augusta, Dec. 21, 1851.

"Dear Mother, — I preached yesterday on 'Poverty : its various remedies.' I conclude that industry is the only effectual cure.

"I have no great confidence in our liquor-law.

"We have had pretty cold weather. —12°, however, is, I think, our lowest.

"F. and K. seem to enjoy themselves pretty well.

"Gravel-cars run on our railroad daily. It will open for passengers next Monday.

"I go to Bangor next Saturday ; preach, and lecture on Monday.

"J.'s hens do not begin to lay.

"Apples here are tolerably good and plenty. We get them for about fifty cents a bushel.

"The Cony Academy has twelve scholars.

"Our study is warm, sunny, and pleasant. I wish you could be here.

"I hope P——n will have a good time in S. She need not visit the Armory unless she wishes to.

"Tell her the latest fashions are red and blue folly, laced with corn-colored nonsense. She will see plenty of it in the street every day. Face exposed, nose a good deal stuck out, and, if it is cold, crimson. Legs surrounded by mud and taffeta.

"Your son, affectionately,

"SYLVESTER."

If, in P——n's letters to her sister in Augusta, Sylvester chanced to discover any little references to dress or fashions, he was very likely to take the matter up in a letter to his mother, and discuss it, as in this wise: "She asks, 'How do you dress your hair?' Now, 'dress' implies clothing, something put on; and she would not say, how do you *clothe* your hair? To be sure, we sometimes speak of dressing down a horse, or giving a boy a good dressing, that is, thrashing; we dress flax, that is, break it in pieces, get out the chives. But you would not apply this to a lady's hair. It would be proper to say, How do you fix, or comb, or curl, or frizz, or fantasticate your hair?"

Again: "There were some things in P——n's letter I could not understand. Is she losing her mind? There was a whole page about patterns and turning in (one turns in when he takes his

41*

berth in a steamboat), and edges, and Julias, and what not!"

And to P——n herself: "You ask about 'tight waists.' They are the worst things in the world, stop the breathing, crook the ribs, deform the shape, and bring on death or a premature old age. I would not have one."

A frequent close of his letters to his family-friends was like the following to his brother C. P.: "God keep us alive in his own good love. It will be a long time before we all shall meet. Let us hold together, by pen and ink at least; and may the great God bless and watch over us in all our ways!" And to his mother: "Warmer days will come, and softer airs. The good God have us all in his keeping, summer and winter, for time and eternity!"

Thus were Sylvester's relations to the home of his youth. Strong and tender were his affections for his parents, his brothers and sisters.

But with a nature so sensitive, with a soul craving for continual and perfect sympathy, it may well be supposed that some still deeper, more exclusive individual love was necessary to satisfy his needs. And, without intruding too far into the secret chambers of his heart, much, it is believed, may be revealed of what to him was the light of life, the holiest of his earthly relations.

In a letter to a friend, written in 1840, he says: "The secret, the weakness, the essential self of my character, is a *desire of sympathy*. These are my Sampson's locks. Strange that I should confess it to you. But you have it. On this point I am weak, weak as water. This gate entered, you are sure of the citadel. Only take care in falling it does not crush you. When I came to Augusta, it was with the fixed determination to repair, to wall up, this weak spot; to destroy this tendency of my heart; to make war upon myself, till this part of myself was subdued and extinguished. Alas, how foolish are ourselves, are we! How impotent the arm we lift against our natures! My desire of sympathy, or rather, I should say, the compass of my being, has a threefold aspect, — sentiment, philosophy, religion. In each of these I live; in each I have suffered: each is by turns or together the sunlight or the shade of my existence."

The entire fulfilment and consummation of this desire of sympathy was not enjoyed until after Mr. Judd's entrance upon professional life. To her with whom this long and earnestly desired spirit-alliance was at length formed, delicacy forbids any thing more than the indirect allusions which occur in unfolding whatever of this part of his nature may be developed.

Sacred as are the precincts to which we now approach, it seems almost a duty somewhat to draw aside the veil, and reveal his pure, beautiful ideal of the wedding of souls; the fresh coloring it gave to the tissue of his existence, and its blendings with what was most sacred to him in time and for ever.

And here especially must he be allowed to speak for himself. In his Journal he writes : —

"*Augusta, Feb.* 11, 1841. — My new life takes its date. I am born to-day. I may well open a new book, adopt a new caption, write a new style, indulge a new strain. Time is past. Eternity commences. My probation is over; my reward imposed. My travels are at an end; my home is reached. My half-soul has found its mate. My tomb-life is broken; my real life enjoyed. My heart is happy; my purposes free; my future certain; my aspirations are at rest. I am tranquil now. I fret not; I forbode nothing. Chiefly, ever, and for ever, I thank thee, O my God! Every good and perfect gift cometh from thee; and J. thou hast given me. I give to thee my supreme gratitude, my overflowing thankfulness. I consecrate my love, myself, my all, to thee. From thee I received her, to thee I give her. From thee I received my heart, to thee I give it. All is thine! all is mine! From thee I would not for a moment be separated. In thee I would be united with all I love. Take us to thyself, to thy own bosom, to thy own love, unworthy, weak, and sinful as we are. In thee alone are we holy. Without thee we are lost. In thee alone do we dare to live. With thee our love is a holy flame. Bless us, we pray thee, now and evermore."

Thus did this great epoch of his life serve to restore him more perfectly to himself, to reinstate his *integrity of being*, and to make him more entirely one with God, with nature, with humanity. It was to him a new existence, a fresh birth of his soul. The tide of affection flowed forth higher than before towards his ever-cherished family-friends. All things seemed good to him. His love he felt to be a holy thing, that he could carry up to heaven, that would bear the light of eternity.

In communicating this intelligence to his mother, he writes: " This does not take me from you, my dear mother; and from all my own dear home. It multiplies my happiness, without dividing it. I shall love you all more and more. Do write me soon, my dear mother. Give me a mother's blessing, congratulations, prayers. You know I must be happy. You know I have needed some one to love me. . . . Write soon, my dear father, and confirm my own step by giving me a father's blessing and hopes. Give J. the seal of your adoption."

To a sister-in-law he says : " I have to write you this morning from a new life, in a new world, and yet one from which you have often wished to hear from me. It is the region of the affections, of the heart, and happiness. Do send me your congratulations. Send me a sister's blessing. Send to her a sister's love. All this also to your dear husband, to my, to our, dear brother."

And to his brother H——i : " In your letter of October 15, you say, 'The next thing to be done will be to take to yourself a wife from among the many daughters of earth.' Such a prospect is now fairly before me. What seemed to me a hint of the impossible becomes a prophecy of the true. I know you will share my happiness on this event, and I am pleased immediately to apprise you of it. Write me immediately ; write to *us*, and welcome your new sister to the household and to your own heart."

The interval before marriage, to use his own

words, he " passed in new soul-enjoyments, tranquil
progressions, serene anticipations."

April 15, his Journal says: "She read my book,
took a glance at my former self. *Quam mutatus ab
illo!* I can say in the best sense. The stream that
rustled and maddened down the mountain sleeps,
with a quiet surface, a serene depth, at the bottom."
To A. H. he writes, Aug. 28, just on the eve of
marriage: "We have few fears, few trepidations, few
movings of the spirit in any way. We are already
upon the sea. 'Tis only passing from latitude to
latitude. We sail on as goodly as possible. Heaven
bless us! Our friends pray for us. We glide into
all things so naturally, so easily, we hardly feel the
change. God is good to us. Our own souls strive
for virtue and holiness. We can but be trustful."

On the evening of Aug. 31, 1841, Mr. Judd was
married. The usual ceremony on such occasions
seeming to him altogether inadequate to his own
idea of the *true marriage,* he prepared for the purpose,
as the only medium of expression that could satisfy
his needs, the following form of words: —

"You, Sylvester Judd, jun., take Jane Elizabeth
Williams to be your lawful and wedded wife ; you,
Jane Elizabeth Williams, take Sylvester Judd, jun.,
to be your lawful and wedded husband, — a union
of the finite with the finite soul, under the embrace,
protection, presence, and love of the Infinite Soul ;
in deep humility of spirit, in solemn sense of respon-
sibleness, in supreme devotion to virtue and to
truth, to Christ and to God, in earnest prayer for
divine illumination and aid ; feeling in your own

consciousness an identity and affiliation of sentiment, faith, and purpose; pledging the strength and constancy, the assiduity and ministries, of your love; engaging to one another a mutual and reciprocal submissiveness and authority, deference and honor; subordinating each motive and wish, each action and feeling, to your common happiness and sustenance; resting your hopes for the future upon the good providence of God, and the sacred interests of your own hearts; — so you are, so you effect, so you covenant, so you are espoused for ever."

In the fulness of his happiness, on taking his wife to the old home, he thus puts forth his feelings in his Journal : —

" *Northampton, Sept.* 4, 1841. — J. is where I have been, walks my walks, sits my seats, sees my sights. How changed does it make me! or rather it brings me to myself."

" *Sept.* 8. — Last evening we went over Round Hill, through groves and scent and density of pines. How strange it seems to me to have one with me in these old scenes! To-day we have been upon Mount Holyoke. The river, the beauty, is there. I am changed. I am happier. I have a soul with me. Another being blends with mine. Another love loves with me. How I loved to see her moving on the road, under the trees, through the sunlight, in the scenes, a part of the beauty! I was so calm, so joyful. The world seemed fixed in beauty: the heavens were stable over my head. A shower of gentle influence came from the sky into my heart. I was almost afraid of my happiness. The big mountains, the broad vision, the white river, the meadows, the sweet love, the eternal God."

" *Sept.* 12. — At Westhampton, went over to the graveyard. Saw the monuments of our family. Old scenes, familiar hills and trees, and solitude and quietness. Some old crickets, some sand in the roads. Showed J. the room where I was born. Showed her the school-house where I learned my letters, the store where I tended, the meeting-house where I heard the old minister, &c.

" Westhampton is greatly changed in all' save its hills and its solitude. The people are changed. The boys and girls whom I knew are gone, some dead. S. J. is dead. I recited in philosophy with her. . . . My brothers are good. Perhaps I am not open enough to them. I will try to be more so."

He writes, during this visit, —

To his Mother-in-law.

" Northampton, Sept. 10, 1841.

" Our dear Mother, — You have heard of our journey, our arrival, our health and happiness. We are happy in ourselves, happy in our circumstances. Our friends are well, and happy in our being with them. God has blessed us in all our ways. We are joyful in his presence ; we are grateful for his mercies. We trust in his goodness ; we repose on the everlasting arms. We were sorry to anticipate the arrival of our father Williams, and glad to anticipate the departure of our father Judd. May God bless and love both our dear parents, and supply to them all that realization of hope, that fruition of labor, that reward of interest, which a parent has, does, and feels for a child! We are not insensible of our obligations or their claims. Whatever affects their happiness in the least penetrates our own hearts most deeply. My own father's hairs are white, white as your father Cony's. We are both reminded of the scriptural injunction to honor the hoary head.

"I think my mother likes her new daughter very well. Would that her son might make in all ways his new mother as happy! . . . J. is glad I have brought her to so beautiful a place. God is indeed good to us; good in creating such a world as this, good in giving us hearts to enjoy it. To his name be all the glory. We are not proud, if we are happy. We hope not to forget God, even if we are full ourselves. We should be very sinful, if we were not happy. Our trust is still in God. It is his providence that brought J. and me together. It is in his love that we have loved; it is in a consciousness of his approval that we are married. Our own happiness is complete only in the blessing of God. That we have sought; that we still seek; on that is our rest for ever. We have given ourselves to Christ and the church. Christ is God manifest in the flesh to us. He is our life, our light, the substance and the inspiration of our souls. Christ's first miracle was done at a marriage. We believe he was present at our espousals. We believe he, as an elder brother, loves us, a brother and sister in the Lord. His promise and his blessing are ours; and why should we fear? Life, indeed, is before us;

its duties, its trials, its hours of darkness, its scenes of adversity, sickness, and death. But there is no death to the righteous; there is no insupportable affliction to the pure in heart. Let us be righteous, let us be pure, and God will take care of us. . . . To our friends also we commend ourselves; to the kindness and love of our dear parents, our dear brothers and sisters, we commend ourselves. Our happiness and theirs is inseparably linked. We would be dutiful, and love for ever. May the good love of God protect and bless us all. For myself and J.,

" Your affectionate Son."

The planning and building of his cottage-residence, and the embellishment of his small grounds, was to Mr. Judd a very pleasant thing. But it was the idea of a *home*, — one constructed according to his own taste and convenience; one around which should cluster fondest memories, dearest associations, and which should become a cherished spot to his children, — it was this which gave him the chief delight. It was to him a very interesting problem, with given means and essential comforts, to produce the most pleasing effects.

The site of the cottage is an acclivity on the eastern bank of the Kennebec, forming a grassy slope in front. From its proximity to the river, the view of whose waters was to him an abiding pleasure, he adopted the name Riverside, as the family and social designation of his residence; while, in relation to his church, he always called it Christ Church Parsonage. All the interior household appointments are cheerful, commodious, and tasteful. Its pointed roof with cross-sealed gable, its dormar windows and light verandas, together with the abundant foliage and vines of its summer costume, give it a very charming though modest appearance. It seems to nestle in greenery, coolness, and quiet. Almost every species of forest-tree is here represented; and every shade-tree, vine, or fruit-tree around, was planted, if not by Mr. Judd's own hand, at least under his particular supervision. All were arranged with regard to pleasant effect, and so as not to obstruct, when grown, any important view. Here is a little clump of maples or arbor vitæ; there, a solitary elm or pine. The avenue of entrance is formed of evergreens mixed with deciduous trees. On one side is a little arbor for the children's play-house, constituted of white birches set closely in a circle, their branches making the canopy; and on the other are young trees of all sorts, blended in native wildness, encircling a large, decaying, old red maple, and leaving quite an area around the central tree.

The house commands an unbroken view of the Kennebec for the distance of a mile in a southerly direction. The principal part of the town of Augusta lies in full view, amphitheatre-like, on the opposite or western side of the river, its various church-spires pointing upwards to the same heavens. There, too, are seen, on one hand, the capitol, and, on the other, the marble tablets of the cemetery for the dead; and, crowning all, the sun-setting horizon, with its undulating outline and woody summits.

And this was the home which to Mr. Judd was
so precious, to which he sent letters almost daily
when absent, and óf which he says : " My heart
turns to it with eagerness, and fondly settles on the
objects of my love there, — my wife and my children. . . . I shall leave for home, — blessed, longed-
for home, — to-morrow morning." It is this which
he looks out from, and, with as much truth as
beauty, paints in " Richard Edney," where he says :
" A tale is like this June morning when I am now
writing. I hear from my open windows the singing
of birds, the rumble of a stage-coach, and a blacksmith's anvil. The water glides prettily through
elms and willows. There are deep shadows in my
landscape ; and yonder hill-side, with its blossoming
apple-trees, glows in the sunlight, as if it belonged
to some other realm of being. On the right of my
house is a deep gorge, wet, weedy, where are toads
and snakes ; and fringing this, and growing up in
the midst of it, are all sorts of fresh, green shrubs,
and the flickering, glossy leaves of white birches.
Superb rock-maples overhang the roof of an iron-
foundery, down under the hill at my feet. The
dew, early this morning, covered the world with
topazes and rainbows, and my child got her feet wet
in the midst of the glory. Through gully and orchard, basement-windows and oriels, shade and sheen,
vibrates a delicious breeze. Over all hangs the sun ;
down upon the village looks that eye of infinite blessedness, and into the scene, that urn of exhaustless
beauty, pours beauty. The smoke from the foundery, and the darkness of the gorge, are beautiful ;

cows feeding in my neighbor's paddock are pleasant to look upon; Paddy, with pickaxe on his shoulder, is happy; Rusticus, in the cornfield, is a picture; and the granite, through the verdure of a distant mountain-side, gleams out like silver. This morning's sun idealizes every thing. Nature is not shocked at toads."

As may well be supposed, Mr. Judd was an exceedingly domestic man, seeking his happiness, no less than the performance of his duties, at home. He was always there, unless called away by important duties; and then, whether out of town or at a social tea-drinking in his own neighborhood, his arrangements were to return as soon as possible.

His sabbaths at home were always peculiarly serene and happy, whatever might exist calculated to disturb the tranquillity of his mind.

His impressions on becoming a father were of the deepest order. He regarded the new-born one as a fresh creation from the hand of God; and, from the first moment, it became his earnest study to discover what new revelations it might make to his mind of nature, of spirit. The day succeeding the birth of his first child, he writes in his Journal: —

"I hold it, and watch the expressions of its face. All passions and emotions are muscularly developed, — anger, derision, hope, fear, love, joy. It smiles, it weeps; it looks old, it looks young; it pouts its lips in derision, it contracts them most sagely; and all owing *to wind in the stomach!* Can that be? Is life a forgetting? . . . I notice the child, in crying,

very distinctly pronounces the syllable, Ma.   It
commences with bringing its lips together, and then
suddenly parting them."

And again, a few days after : " I brought the
baby into the study this afternoon, and lay down
with her upon the sofa.   Is she wholly insensible
of a father's love, of his arms about her ?   Why
gazes she so fixedly, so sharply, so dully ?   How
interesting these first few days !   She will soon awake
from them.   She will return no more to them.   She
will come to her consciousness ; she will laugh ; she
will understand.   I would see what she is of now,
so I love to hold her."   Again : " I set it upon a
pillow, where it can look out of the window.   What
sees it ?   It looks fixedly."

The extracts below, from a sermon on the Death
of Children, reveals still farther his own experience : —

" The birth of a child is an epoch in a family.   It
is the Annus Domini of every mother's chronicles.
She adjusts all dates by that event.   That nativity
has a creative power : it is genius incarnated in
infancy.   It moulds us into new forms, and directs
us into a new activity.   Every child resembles Jesus
in this, that his birth is an advent to the household ;
in every room a new light shines, and all give glory
to God, as the shepherds did.   Even the maid-ser-
vant smiles, as she meets you at the door.   A woman
is not herself, and knows not what she is, until she
becomes a mother.   One feels that his own life is
more valuable after the birth of his child : his honesty,
his industry, his piety, directly rise in his estima-

tion, while his vices assume a corresponding aspect of disgust. There is something, if it be not wholly a solecism so to say, something awful in a child. The child invests life with a new interest. In meteorology is the *dew-point,* that at which dew begins to be formed. The advent of the child is the dew-point of the world : a new crystal drop attaches to all things we look upon. It is as if colored stars and bright rays appeared on the chairs and tables. Whatever is beautiful appears more beautiful ; whatever is lovely, more lovely. Work is less hard, fatigue less oppressing, to one who is a parent than to one who is not. A child is never heavy to its parents. One tends his flowers or tills his garden with greater interest, when children are growing up to enjoy them. . . . Children create a strong sentiment of home. Men hasten to their homes where their children are. Many cords are upon men in the street ; but there is one cord stronger than all, that which draws them to their children and their homes. . . . The simple enjoyment of a child it is a luxury to behold. It attracts everybody's eyes. To see little children at play is a psalm of thanksgiving. It is God's way of showing us what happiness is, and we distinguish something of divinity in it. It is the chord on which great nature harps to us, and our hearts respond as to sweet music. . . . The first articulation of a child, the objects that arrest its attention, how it creeps, how it gets down stairs, what are its attractions and what its repulsions, whom it most loves, the way it uses its hands, all engage us sensibly. We never tire waiting for the unfolding

of that hidden spirit; we are often surprised at unexpected disclosures."

And such a study were Mr. Judd's own children
to him; so carefully did he watch all their developments. To educate them rightly, to render their
physical constitutions healthy, and to secure their
minds from prejudices, false ideas, and unworthy
conventionalities, was the subject of his morning,
noon-day, and evening thoughts. In their government, he never used force, never suffered any corporal punishment to be inflicted on them. In this,
as in other things, he believed in the final triumph of the omnipotent power of love. Though
leniency might, for the existing time, be attended
with some disadvantages, he believed in the end its
evils were far less than those of severity. One part
of his plan was, by furnishing his children with
healthful recreations and pleasant employments, to
promote their happiness, and thus prevent the risings
of ill-temper. He would, as far as possible, leave
them to their own will, even at the expense of a little trouble; and many of the scenes of "Memmy
and Bebby," at the bowl of Indian meal and otherwise, as well as the description of their persons,
stood very well for the portraiture of his real children.
He entered with them into their plays, encouraged
out-door sports, and got up many little devices for
their amusement. In their play-arbor, he prepared
a rude table, seats, and cupboard, and encouraged
them in going through the routine of childish
entertainments, washing their little dishes, and the
like. He was not willing his children should, while

yet in their tender years, suffer the confinement of school, or apply their minds to the study of books. He thought it enough that they should continually drink in knowledge from their observations upon nature and every thing around them. He would not that into their young minds should be thrust any theological dogmas, but only that they should imbibe the pure milk of gospel simplicity. Of the folly and sin of inculcating in the minds of children a passion for dress, a love of finery and fashion, or of fitting their garments in a manner prejudicial to health, he had a strong sense, and conscientiously insisted upon a severe simplicity, both as to cut and material. He wished there should be nothing in their clothes that should particularly attract their attention, or lead them to transfer a sense of the prettiness of their dress to themselves.

When from home, the father's heart was with his children ; and, before they were able to read a word, he commenced addressing them letters.

To his Eldest Daughter, when Three Years Old.

"Boston, Sept. 21, 1847.

"My dear Daughter, — How do you do this morning? and how is little Lullaboo? Do you not wish to see papa? and would you not like to kiss him? He wishes to see you, and go out in the garden with you, and get some potatoes. Tell Becca she must not let the horse eat papa's corn. You must go to bed at eleven o'clock, because mamma wishes you to. Little Charlie is well; he drives about the street at a great rate. Do you not wish

papa would come home, so you could see him in
the bed in the morning ?   Kiss mamma and Lullaboo twenty times for papa.   Papa misses you very
much.   Papa will come home by and by, and bring
his little ba*bee* some can*dee*.

"Your affectionate Father,

"S. Judd, Jun."

Other Letters to his Children.

"New York, July 11, 1851.

"My dear little Children, L. and F., — Your
mother will show you on the map where New York
is.   It is a great city, and full of people, and full of
nice things for children, which, if I had money, I
should like to buy for you.   But you must remember papa has not much money.   You must be good
children, and be kind to each other.   L. must not
speak sharp.   F. must do what her mother wishes.
L. must take good care of the hens, feed and water
them."

"Brooklyn, July 19, 1851.

"My dear little L. and F., — Papa has great love
for you, and thinks much about you.   He wants you
to be very nice children, and be very kind to your
mother, and not trouble H. [the servant].   You
must love one another very much, and let each
other have your playthings.

"I shall not bring you home any thing but books.
I have two or three little ones for you to read in.
You must not expect any toys.   How is 'Jenny
Lind' ?   Are her chickens alive, and doing well ?
How is the turkey ?   Does it grow any ?

" The little children here have no green grass to play on, as you have ; and no gardens, no hens, no wheelbarrows.   Your affectionate Papa,

" SYLVESTER JUDD."

" NORTHAMPTON, July 24, 1851.

" My dear little Children, — How much I wish you were here with papa, to see grandpa and grandma, to walk in the garden, and see the plum-trees, and the peach-trees, and the pear-trees ! Then there are chickens bigger than yours. Grandpa said, at dinner to-day, how glad he should be to see J. and L. and F. ; and grandma said so too.

" The trees and grounds and roads and walks and mountains and meadows in Northampton are very beautiful. Mamma will show you where the town is on the map. You are three hundred miles from papa ; yet he loves you very much, and longs to see you and kiss you, and longs to have you good children, and very kind to your mother, and very gentle to each other."

" BELFAST, Aug. 3, 1852.

" My dear Children, — I arrived here after a ride of ten hours. I saw bunch-berries and raspberries upon the road. Mr. P., at whose house I am staying, has four nice children.

" You will love one another, and not contradict, or dispute, or lay your hands quick on each other. Feed the hens twice a day, and water them once. Do not trouble Laura [the servant] ; help her all you can. Show uncle H——i where you keep the matches. You must do what aunt A. bids you. Look after that chicken of ' Norma's.' Say your

Pater-noster with Laura and aunt A. every morning.

"With great love, and God to bless you, I am
your loving father,

"SYLVESTER JUDD."

"NEW YORK, Oct. 18, 1852.

"Dear L., — Papa wants you to be a nice, good
girl. Do what mamma wants you to do. Be very
helpful, now papa is away. You were a very good
girl in Northampton. Aunt A. was very sorry you
did not come to Brooklyn. Dear little F., too,
papa often thinks of you, his bright-eyed little
wogin. He wants to see both of his darlings very
much. Cousin C. has a little black puppy, that
sleeps with him. You must both be kind to your
mother, and kind to Laura. Give papa's remembrances to Laura. Papa should be glad if his children would write to him about the chickens, or any
thing else. Uncle W.'s 'Beppo' is better."

A few passages, culled here and there from *other
letters,* despatched, when absent, to his home, will
close this chapter : —

"BOSTON, Dec. 5, 1849.

"Dear J., — . . . . Tell the children there was a
little boy in the cars, who, as night came on, began
to cry, 'Boo hoo, want some supper ; boo hoo, want
a drink of water, boo hoo.' And he kept this up
mile after mile. I gave him one of those lozenges
that F. put in my pocket Sunday afternoon. Another
little boy chimed in, and cried, 'Boo hoo, want to
see the baby, boo hoo, want to see the baby.' I

gave this one a lozenge, that quieted him. I thought of our own dear little ones; and these little ones pulled away at my heart-strings quite lustily, and rung the chords of feeling in a smart way.

" Is it cold at Riverside? Do you miss anybody? Would you be happier if this noon somebody sat opposite you at the table, and cut up the children's meat?

" Give a thousand of loves to the children, all you can spare from yourself. Tell L. papa wishes her to be very good, not to dispute with C., not to trouble F., always to mind her mother. Tell F. papa is in Boston, will be home pretty soon, wants to see his little children."

" *Bath, June* 5, 1848. — There is a little girl here who reminds me of L.; not that the resemblance is striking, but, in the absence of any thing of the sort, I am glad to take up with this. Ask L. if 'she is capable of judging' what this means.

" I went by a candy-store, and saw great bunches of red, blue, and white candy at the windows, and all sorts of sugar things in glasses. Could I help thinking about my children? could I help buying some for them? What single mitigation is there to absence, if one may not, in imagination, be affording those little pleasures to his family, and thinking how the little ones will come round him when he gets home, looking so wistful, and L. at length venturing to speak, and F. so moving in her dumbness, and the dear wife even willing to *eat some?* well, well."

" *New York, July,* 1851. — . . . . I hope you will have health and heart. There is no place to me like home. There are no persons whom I value as my wife and little ones."

"*The Parsonage, Aug.* 12, 1852. — I have written you three letters, one to Niagara, two to Saratoga, not one of which I suppose you will get; and now to sit down, and, as it were, re-write what I have written, is not the best way of doing the thing. Now in your letter dated last Sunday at Niagara, you say, direct to the Revere House, where you may be, Heaven knows when. So I must write, not to you, but to space and time and vague emptiness. And you will be almost home when you get there. What will you care then about the chickens or flowers; or of what use to tell you the children to-day are well, which is the fact nevertheless? What may happen between this and that time, I cannot tell.

"I suppose you are to-day in — Heaven knows where. I hope you enjoy yourself very much, — Montreal, Saratoga, Lake George, or whatever it be. At least, it is where I am not, but where I would like to be. . . . You will come home fresh and warm. There is no need of growing old. If we keep our hearts right, we are always fresh, always in summer-time. Our years will have a perpetual verdure. . . .

"The children have been good, quiet, docile, busy, happy. They have been so because I have *let them alone.* I would be about my children as a gentle influence, not as a special governor.

"Whether it shall ever be mine to see what you have seen, and to go any where without feeling each cent I spend, God only knows."

"*Northampton, Oct.* 4, 1852. — . . . This is Northampton, my old home. I have sat in the south-east
chamber; the mountains, the trees, the luxuriance
and beauty, spread before me as of old. There I
had my dreams of youth; there this warm, aspiring
heart indulged its early visions. These old dreams
and visions come clustering round me now, seeming
to ask, 'How is it with you?' My heart swells
within me. My soul is pervaded with the tenderest
emotion. Each tree-top waves a strange and almost
melancholy consonance to me. I wish you were
here. Into what was my world of the future, you
have come. You have flown down as the sweet
spirit that was to be the sister of my heart, and
sharer of my life. Many kisses to F. Her tears,
that ran when we left, long flowed in my soul.
She did not want to have us go. She is happy now."

"*Oct.* 5, 1852. — . . . The tendency of domestic
harmony is to make all other things harmonious.
The family is a certain root and source of all that
we are in this world. 'Tis the foundation, in an
important sense, of the church, of the state, and of
all right being. . . . We are one, not two; one in
life, one in emotion, one in property, one in our
children, one in God. There may be variety in unity,
individuality in communion. The idea advanced by
some, that marriage is only a mode in which man
and woman are to develop their individuality, and
confirm their independence, — that is, make themselves both as detached and independent of each
other as possible, — seems to me not right.

"I cannot look upon a landscape without wishing

you to look too, or sit at the Lord's table without
wishing you to sit too, or eat a peach without wishing you to eat too, or take a ride without wishing
you to ride. This is my nature; a social one, and
most social in what I feel most. Being at Northampton reminds me of the solitary years of my
being; of deep, consuming loneliness, and too of a
solitariness that became a pleasure, my food and
drink almost. You were the one who, as I said
yesterday, alighted on my path, — flew, as it seemed,
from heaven into my soul. There continue still.
There, dearest one, abide ever. God bless and keep
you, and F., and the unborn."

" *Northampton, Oct.* 8, 1852. — . . . I wish you
and F. were here; the walks are so pleasant, and all
things so beautiful. I tell L., ' Here I used to live
when a little boy; there is a tree I got chestnuts
under,' &c. &c. The atmosphere is almost oppressive with memories and sentiments, and the spirit of
our earlier life sings in all the trees. . . .

" Shall I not have a letter this afternoon? How
is it about the Parsonage? Is the place a holy one
to you? If sentiment and love ever went into a
place, they have gone into that. The walks, the
trees, each outlook, each of what artists call ' effect,'
are all results of our own hearts and minds. There
is *feeling* everywhere. Even the little open space
from our bedroom north-window has a meaning: it
was that we might look over to your mother's, and
she look on us. . . . I think of the Parsonage and its
inhabitants, of the church and its members, with
gratitude, love, and prayer. May our earthly life,

in all its forms, fit us for the heavenly! May sadness and sorrow be the ministers of our peace, of deep, eternal, mutual, and joyful reunion, embrace, harmony, love!"

"*Northampton, Oct.* 9, 1852. — I got your letter yesterday afternoon; went up into *that* chamber to read it. I took a cigar, sat and smoked; looked out upon the luxuriant world about me, — golden maples, elms lifting their majesty to the sun, apple-trees studded with high-colored fruit; all things soft, warm, deep, beautiful, soothing. I only wished, instead of your letter, I had yourself."

"*New York, Oct.* 15, 1852. — ... I am no monk, no ascetic, no solitaire; my being thrives and grows in the atmosphere of a most sympathetic love. ... Got one or two little French and German primers for L. and F. ... This will reach you, I hope, to-morrow afternoon. May it find you well, and be pleasant to your heart! You cannot imagine, or rather you can imagine, how much I think of you in this long absence. Every night I ejaculate a prayer to God for you and for the dear children. I think of you as the dear guardian angel, in my absence, of what is to me the most beautiful spot on earth, the Parsonage; as one who in spirit sympathizes with all I here see and enjoy."

"*New York, Oct.* 19, 1852. — ... I do not wonder at J. C.'s sadness. With none to love us, and care for us, and do for us, we are the wretchedest of beings. Religion cannot, and never was designed to, cure all the ills of life, — I mean, independently of life. It was designed *to make us lead a good*

43*

life, and so cure the ills we are subject to. It is a part of religion, that we love one another, and make one another happy. So I have always believed; so I have always preached. We have not any religion, so to say, when we neglect one another. This is the cardinal mistake of all the sects, as I view it: it makes of religion one thing, and life wholly another thing. We are most religious when we love one another most. We are most religious, in every sense of the word, both as to God and as to man, when we love one another most."

"*Baltimore, Oct.* 24, 1852. — . . . . Though I am a minister and a traveller, I can never forget that I am a man, a lover, a husband. The sentimental part of my nature is deep, strong, pervasive. It is to me almost religion. . . . Never did I feel more thankful than at the idea of being on my return home. What is there in the wide world like our little cot, our simple home, our children, ourselves, our love! — Your doting and devoted Husband,

"SYLVESTER."

CHAPTER XIV.

DEPARTURE FROM EARTH.

In the passing history of Mr. Judd's life, we left him, after his then recent return from the Baltimore Convention to the home so doated on, with high hope and vigor making successful efforts in carrying forward among his people his plan of the church; with a long list of lyceum-engagements for the winter and spring of 1853; and, in the full tide of life and activity, on the eve of departure for Boston to present at the Thursday Lecture his idea of the "Birthright Church."

But, ah! spontaneously float back upon us in mournful, chilling echoes, the prophetic tones of his own last lines in verse:—

> " So, arrowy, we fall,
> In all the bliss of being, rippling on ;
> . . . .
> Nor medium flights shall tempt his vigor more ! "

And brief the record that remains.

On the evening of Monday, January 3, 1853, after having been almost incessantly engaged during the day in condensing his cherished views into the Discourse to be delivered in Boston on the 6th, he left his home between eight and nine o'clock for an hotel near the railroad depot from which he was to take the cars very early the next morning. On arriving, he sat an hour or so in the private parlor of the proprietor, who was one of his parishioners, chatting pleasantly and appearing quite well. About ten he retired, without complaining of indisposition.

But the weather was severe, his room not so warm as the one to which he was accustomed, and his bed extremely cold. The nervous energy of his system was very much exhausted by his long-continued mental excitement. At tea with his family that evening, his mind seemed abstracted, and his taking of food quite mechanical. His wife, on parting with him, noticed looks of paleness and fatigue that left on her heart an impression of deep sadness. His physical system had never possessed much power of resistance against attacks tending to disorder it. Being thus in a condition which placed his bodily well-being at the mercy of any adverse circumstances on which he might chance to fall, immediately on going to bed he was seized with severe chills which precluded sleep, but which he endured until about three o'clock in the morning, when he was also attacked with violent pain. At five o'clock a physician was called, who considered his symptoms as indicating a slight inflammation of the bowels. The morning found him in a state of so great exhaustion as hardly to be able to open his eyes or utter a word. The most he could say to his wife, as she came in haste to see him, was, that he had

"had a dreadful night." "Poor papa, poor papa!" was all he could say to his little girl; and to his sister, he simply said, "I am *so disappointed.*" And this disappointment, of going on to deliver his sermon in Boston, and his lyceum-lectures in Salem and Gloucester, seemed, in the first hours of his illness, more bitter than the distress of body he suffered. Sick as he was, he could not give up the idea that the next day he might be able to proceed. He undoubtedly felt the detention all the more, as the winter previous he had been prevented, by an injury received from a fall, from meeting an engagement to lecture in Worcester.

The remedies applied that day and the following one gave him no particular relief. On Thursday, a second physician was called, who agreed with the first in thinking the attack one from which he would in a few days recover. Yet, on this and the next day, he had a recurrence of terrible chills, followed by stupor and profuse perspiration; and his own impression was that his disease was very deeply seated.

But on Saturday, Jan. 8, although his symptoms were not essentially better, the weather being mild and favorable, he was warmly enveloped, placed in a close carriage, and removed to his home. While being borne from the hotel, he was heard by an attendant lowly murmuring kindly adieus to the room he had occupied, and to his hospitable host and hostess, who had made many personal sacrifices for his accommodation, and rendered him every care and attention in their power. His pleasant study

had been fitted up for the reception of the poor
sufferer, with every comfort and convenience that
the most solicitous affection could devise. Changed,
indeed, was he from the condition in which he quitted
that spot a few days before ; but, looking around on
the old, fond, familiar objects, his countenance bright-
ened up with an expression of delight. The care
of his people was forcibly brought to mind. He
requested that the church should be opened the
next day, and gave some directions as to the sabbath-
school. From this removal, which had been under-
taken with much anxiety as to the result, he did not
apparently suffer any detriment.

The early part of the second week of his illness,
his physicians thought the crisis of his disease was
past, and used measures to restore his strength.
But, as day followed day, there was no decided
amendment. His system seemed to possess no re-
cuperative power. The dreaded chills frequently
returned ; and his prostration was excessive. In
sleep, the natural fertility of his imagination displayed itself in revels amid the most charming scenes
of physical and spiritual beauty. Those "visions,"
as he called them, left a deep impression on his
waking hours, which he sometimes strove to describe. At one time, he said he was introduced by
"a man in the eastern country," as he expressed it,
into all the glowing richness of oriental splendor ;
but he told him "all *he* wanted was *rest.*" A sister-
in-law thus records what he said to her of these
dreamy fancies : " ' O F. ! I have had such wonderful visitations since I have been sick, such glorious,

such transcendent visions, I have almost become a believer in spiritual communications in a moment. Do you know anybody that understands the philosophy of these things?' I told him no, and asked what was the form of his visions; if he saw persons. ' No ; not persons, but states of being. They seem to be *sub-local.* I have been on the tops of the mountains before ; but now I have been *under* the mountains. Oh! I would be willing to be sick a month for one such night as I have had.' " He seemed to labor in vain to set before the mind of another the pictures impressed upon his own ; and, not only in this, but in other connections, it was not a little amusing, while at the same time sad, to see him in his weakness, and in the paucity of language at his control, attempt, by words new-coined and newly combined, to body forth his thought.

Frequently a little of his natural humor would appear, as in addressing, in somewhat of a singing tone, one or two young ladies, his relatives, who were attending him, as "sweet sisters of charity," and another friend as "aunt Good-one." He often spoke jocosely to his physicians about their bad treatment of him ; and one morning, when one of them told him he looked better, he said, "I am like the dog which the boys beat, and then said he looked better."

He frequently took pains to send kind messages to his neighbors. He was very grateful for attentions, and considerate of the convenience of others. The barber came one time when he did not feel as though he could just then receive his services ; but, on being told he could wait, Mr. Judd replied, "Oh! no; he has so much to do; he is so busy." He said to his wife, one day, "I shall have a great deal to tell you when I get well, but cannot now, I am so weak, — how our whole life has been reproduced in such beautiful forms, the elm-trees, &c." She told him aunt H. thought he was better. He replied, "It is only because I am submissive now, and yesterday I was not. I'll tell you when I get well." His allusions to his brother H——l were frequent, and always with deep feeling.

One evening he asked to have something read from Dante or Milton; then a hymn from Watts, and the twenty-third Psalm, both of which he enjoyed extremely, and frequently uttered ejaculations while hearing them.

The first part of the third week brought no material change, and his physicians did not consider his situation alarming. Yet he could take no nourishment; his chills were again and again repeated; his sleep was disturbed, and his mind sometimes a little wandered on waking. His excessive weakness continued; nothing raised him, nothing made him any better. In reply to the remark that he looked tired, "Yes," said he, "that is it, *tired to death*." He said also, "I can hardly pray; but there is one passage of Scripture I think of a great deal, — 'Ye shall neither at this mountain nor yet at Jerusalem worship the Father; . . . but the true worshippers shall worship him in spirit and in truth.'" The last of the week, more unfavorable symptoms appeared.

On sabbath, January 23, he expressed regret that

he was not able to take his accustomed seat at his sister's tea-table on that day. He conversed with a friend who called in the afternoon, and said many rational and many incoherent things. He had seemed all through his illness to study the probabilities of its termination, and to have many thoughts of his departure, but had not directly alluded to it. Referring to the subject at this time, he said: "It is not that I am afraid of death and the solemn hereafter; it is that life has so much for us to do. People tell me I have been doing too much; but you know how it is, there is no such thing as stopping." His friend, Mr. Waterston, who had supplied his desk that day, called in the evening; but he was too weak to see him. "It is one of the miseries of my condition," said he, "that I am not able to see my brother-minister."

On Monday, the 24th, his strength somewhat revived, and he seemed more like himself. He sat up in bed for an hour, desired the window-blinds to be opened that he might look out, and expressed something of his usual interest about the coming in of the railroad-cars. He also saw Mr. Waterston for a moment this forenoon; he took his hand, looked up in his eyes earnestly, and said, "I am sorry I cannot say much to you; you see how it is; but next summer you must come again, and go to Moosehead. I am *very* sick, but hope I shall be better." He was very much agitated by this interview. The latter part of the day, his bad symptoms returned, and continued, with no abatement, through the night.

44

Tuesday morning, the 25th, found him in a very alarming condition; his breathing labored, his features sharpened, and he scarcely recognizing his most familiar friends.   He, however, awoke to more consciousness in the course of the forenoon, and seemed himself very solicitous concerning his state. About noon, he sent an urgent request to his father-in-law, that he would come to him directly; and on his arrival, with difficulty of articulation, but great earnestness of manner, he said, "Did you ever know any one as low as I am to get well?   I want some one candidly to tell me how I am.   It is not that I am afraid to die.   I bow in perfect submission to the Infinite Will."   On Mr. W.'s replying he had known persons as ill recover, but did not know how it would be with him, "Oh! I understand it," said he: "if I can get well, I shall be glad; but if not, why, let it go."   He spoke tenderly of his wife and little children; and seemed happy that he could say, in regard to the latter, that he had "never struck them a blow."   In the afternoon, he asked for the little orphan-daughter of his brother; and she, with his own little girls, all rosy and fresh, came and stood by his bedside.   He looked at them a few moments with satisfaction; said, "Healthy children, nice little children;" and, too weak to bear their presence but a few moments, soon added, "Now you may run out."

Knowing that Mr. F., one of his church, was in the house, he expressed the wish that he should come into his room, and pray with him; but implied that he was too weak to speak with him.   As Mr.

F. knelt by his side in devout supplication, he joined in it with manifest feeling and satisfaction, ejaculating "amen." Through the night, he slept some; and his mind was in a natural state, though it was difficult for him to speak, and he said but little.

And now, all that remains to tell may be given in the words of one who watched these last night-hours beside him. "I sat a little while," she writes, "in the rocking-chair, by the parlor-fire, and heard sweet sounds like music in the distance. Probably this was the wind; yet I could not but connect it with the music of heaven, feeling how near we were to the spiritual world. When daylight came, the morning of the 26th, we saw that our dear brother was evidently very near his spirit's home. I felt that he could not stay with us through the day; yet was he quite unconscious of it. Mrs. J. had tried to lead him to speak of his feelings, and asked whether he was resigned to his departure. He replied 'yes,' but said nothing more. How she longed for some parting words! how much he would have had to say to her, if strength had been given him in those last hours! She wished him to know he was going to leave this, his earthly abode, and requested a physician to communicate to him distinctly the intelligence. It came upon him, at that moment, like an unexpected, an overpowering stroke, rudely sundering all his tenderest ties to earth, and causing the death-struggle of his affection's heart. Bound as he was by deathless love to the particular objects of his attachment, and enlisted as was his soul in carrying out his great idea for making more life-giving and extensive the holy principles of a true Christianity, it was indeed to him 'hard parting.' He broke out in piercing tones of anguish, 'Oh, my God! I love thee, — I love heaven, — I love its glories! — but my dear brothers and sisters, — my parents, — my *wife* and *children*, — *I love you, — how can I! how can I!*' But he soon became quiet, as he had been before the announcement, although much exhausted by his emotions and his efforts to speak. I sang 'Majestic sweetness sits enthroned,' and 'All is well.' J. read passages from the New Testament. His children were referred to; but, too much overcome to bear more then, he said, 'Let the dear children come to-morrow, — little children come to-morrow,' evidently not thinking his hour so near. He said to us who were about him, 'Cover me up warm, keep my utterance clear.' He afterwards added, '*I'm doing well*,' — and, in a few moments, with but a slight indication of the transition, his spirit passed away."

And who shall say that convoys of loving spirits had not been circling that couch with heavenly music, while waiting the moment of his release; and were at hand to receive a kindred spirit, and conduct it to a realm of fresh existence, where all its powers might unfold and bloom for ever under the full light of Infinite Love, — that Love on which it had ever fed, and to which it was so fully assimilated; to that heaven it had ever contemplated as so glorious, and to which its highest aspirations had ever risen? And, though lost to human sight, who shall affirm, that, with the eye of the spirit unsealed, we might not behold our dear departed ones hovering round us on ministries of love, and, with tranquil look, gently soothing our grief, as their enlarged vision descries the final blessed issue, even to ourselves, of the afflictive blow; and perceives that "what to us, at the moment, seems nothing but privation will, somewhat later, assume the aspect of a guide or genius;" that "we only let our angels go, that archangels may come in"?

Although weakness and suffering did not allow Mr. Judd to speak much of this great era of existence when upon its immediate confines, it was a theme on which his mind had ever dwelt with familiarity, through all the years of his earthly life. His sermons were full of allusions to it, and always of a kind to cheer the mourning heart, and light up the apparent darkness. To his own removal, he often adverted in them. In one he says: "I am not pretending to conceal the fact, that often, in dying, there is something painful, and even mournful: I only wish to lighten the mind in respect of that apprehension. I think I am in the way of duty, if I seek to disarm even the physical part of death of as much of its terror as I can. I would pronounce, if it may be, a benedicite on all this grief and gloom. I know, among other things, it is sad to think of dying, when we feel that we have so much to live for. I experience this sensation as strongly as any one of you. I feel sometimes as if I had hardly begun to live. Duties and accomplishments dilate before my eye like new universes. Yet when I think how many have died, just at this stage of things, I see

44*

that I am not alone.   Warren died at the first battle of the Revolution.   Summerfield died in the midst of souls, whom, so to say, he had just begun to convert."   He often referred to this great change in his letters, and for it his mind always seemed in habitual preparation.   In a state of illness, he made the following entry in his Journal : —

" *May* 13, 1838. — This may be my last record here.   I fear not death, — can cheerfully commend my soul to God.   World, — I can bid it farewell. The beautiful in it, I can behold for the last time. Friends, I meet you in a better world.   My soul is at peace.   God is good to me."

And it was in the very last discourse he ever preached, that occur these words, so remarkable in their coincidence : " Will it be you that shall next perform the last sad duties to the cold remains of your pastor ? " — words whose resonance still seemed to linger among the Christmas evergreens that first received them, when, a few brief days afterwards, mingled with mourning weeds, was verified a sad response.

The Pastor, in " Philo," too, utters the poet's own heart-felt words, in saying : —

> " Above the gloomy grave our hope ascends,
>   E'en as the moon above the silent mountains.
>   These partings are reunions in the skies;
>   To that great company of holy ones
>   We go;   .   .   .   .
>   In shadowy void, betwixt two worlds, we stand;
>   The distant All-Light opes its wicker gate,
>   The future beams auroral, flesh expires,
>   The soul begins its perfect day."

But earth was now left behind. Tender friends arranged for its last rest the cherished form that alone remained, and placed it in *apparent* comfort upon his couch, as if in quiet, natural slumber. A winter rose lay by his side ; a simple circlet, twined by loving hands from his own fresh evergreens and house-geraniums, was the symbol of his pillow. No sound of preparation of funeral weeds disturbed the quiet scene ; no air of gloominess and dread was thrown around. Freely as when their father was ever ready to greet their entrance to that study with a welcome smile, the children passed in and out, but with a wistful gaze, a chastened cheerfulness, and tender foot-fall, that told their little hearts had saddened comprehension of the change. Mourning parishioners came in groups to look on that dear pastor's tranquil face, — on that pale brow, still noble in its amplitude.

When the hour arrived to prepare for burial that lifeless form, no stranger-hands were permitted to share the service ; but only those to whom in life it had been dearest now took part in this last sad office. With tenderest care, they wrapped it in the folds of that same silken robe in which he always stood before his people, now, alas ! in preparation for that silent service in which he was to appear before them. Placed in easy guise upon a simple lounge, the burial-case received within its snowy folds that gentle form. Sympathizing friends from his own and distant cities sent fresh, fragrant flowers he loved so well ; and these were placed upon his breast and pillow. And there he lay, well-nigh as lovely and attractive as in life. The children, as they came around, involuntarily exclaimed, "How beautifully father looks!"

And thus was carried out his own idea, that, even in the house of deepest mourning, cheering symbols should bear witness that life goes not out in eternal darkness.

One by one, there gathered to this scene of sorrow — but all too late for even a parting recognition — each living member of his childhood's home, save the devoted mother, whose feeble health precluded so long a journey at that inclement season.

The time fixed for the solemn obsequies was the sabbath morning, the hour on which he was always seen quitting his home, and so meekly wending his way to minister to his people. But now, after brief, fitting service, that unconscious form was borne along the avenue of pines and cedars which had grown up amid his companionship, adown the gravel walk familiar with his footstep, and through the gate of that tasteful, rustic fence enclosing his domicil, — the last work for its improvement he ever planned. The most ethereal of snow-flakes, at this moment, began slowly and solemnly to fall, on all its way to the house of God, curtaining around that funeral carriage with an emblem of heaven's own purity. At church, the profusion of Christmas greens still lent their decoration in strange yet pleasing contrast with the black drapery that had everywhere been blended. In front of that hallowed desk there hung a cedarn cross, that favorite sign ; and the communion-table beneath received its precious burden.

Immediately around were grouped the children of the sabbath-school. The church was densely filled, all denominations testifying to the value of the *man,* the *citizen;* and the *stillness felt* telling how deep the sense of loss. In touching tones, and with tender manner, the Rev. Mr. Waterston performed the funeral service, and, in beautiful yet discriminating remarks, showed forth his appreciation of his early friend. The choir chanted in plaintive notes those stanzas sung by the children in " Philo : " —

"A SONG THEIR PASTOR TEACHES THEM.

" O Love of God ! we seek to dwell
In love and God and thee;
The end of woes, the end of sins,
Shall love's perfection be.

" O Crucified ! we share thy cross;
Thy passion, too, sustain;
We die thy death, to live thy life,
And rise with thee again.

" O Glorified ! thy glory breaks;
Our new-born spirits sing;
Salvation cometh with the morn;
Hope spreads an heavenward wing."

And then, with bearers from the different churches of the city, the mournful train, augmented by a long procession, recrossed the river beneath the arches of that old bridge so humorously set forth in " Richard Edney," and moved onward to that beautifully secluded family-tomb to which the pale sleeper's first rural excursion on the eastern bank of the river had been made. Gathered beneath the funereal firs around, the mourning congregation and afflicted relatives took their last, sad, parting look at that dear face. At that moment, the clouds, which all day till then had shrouded the heavens, suddenly parted, and bright rays of sunlight, penetrating that open vault, illuminated its dark, mouldering depths; or, — to close this history, penned with love, delight, and sorrow, mingled in varying hues, in his own beautiful words, descriptive of a like occasion, and striking in their coincidence with the present scene, —

"As the relics were conveyed into the tomb, the clouds broke away in the heavens; a bland light diffused itself over the severities of the season; there seemed something of bloom, or warmth of coloring, in that blue break of the skies. How fair an induction to the final rest!"

IT may be of interest to some readers to know what was the fate, among Mr. Judd's own people, of those cherished views for which he so earnestly labored during the last two or three years of his sojourn with them, and to which, it may almost be said, he sacrificed his earthly life.

On the afternoon of the sabbath whose morning hours had been consecrated to the performance of the last sad duties to their lamented pastor, his bereaved people again gathered in sorrow to that church whose walls were never again to resound to his *living* voice, but which was still alive with the echoes of his fervent teachings mingled with those of the mournful service which had there just taken place. The following account of the doings of this meeting was prepared by its chairman, Mr. J. Burton : —

"On the afternoon of Sunday, January 30, a meeting of the Society of Christ Church, Augusta, was held at the church, for the purpose of mutual condolence and Christian sympathy, under their heavy affliction, in the loss of their beloved pastor, Rev. Sylvester Judd. Devotional exercises were conducted by Rev. Mr. Waterston, of Boston, who had, with such appropriate eloquence, truthfulness, and justice to the character of the deceased, so acceptably officiated at the funeral ceremonies in the forenoon. Remarks of a deeply touching and solemn character were made by Mr. Waterston, and several gentlemen of the Society.

"The following preamble and resolutions were presented by a committee previously appointed, and unanimously adopted; and copies directed to be transmitted to Mrs. Judd, and furnished for publication in our city papers, and in the "Christian Register," Boston, and "Christian Inquirer," New York.

" ' WHEREAS, in the mysterious providence of God, we have been called upon to mourn the loss of our beloved pastor and friend, in the prime of his life and in the midst of his usefulness, — we, the members of his society, deeply sensible of our loss, and living witnesses of his worth, of his untiring devotion to the great interests of Christianity, and of his benevolent exertions for the welfare of his race, being desirous of giving a public expression to our feelings, and a living form to our sentiments, that those who come after us may learn to appreciate his real character, —

" ' *Therefore, unanimously Resolved,* That, in the decease of the Rev. Sylvester Judd, his society have lost an able and faithful teacher, an exemplary Christian, a warm and devoted friend, an upright citizen, and a good man.

" ' *Resolved,* That his idea of a Christian church, as recently promulgated, and for the establishment of which his best energies were expended, is, in our opinion, the embodiment of one of the vital principles of Christianity, and, as such, demands our serious consideration.

" ' *Resolved,* That we ought, as the best testimony we can give of our appreciation of the labors and teachings of our lamented pastor, to carry out the plans which he had matured for our spiritual good ; and, to this end, we will cause the paper lately drawn up by him, embodying what he regarded as the true idea of a Christian church, to be recorded according to his expressed intention, and that the names of his parishioners be subscribed thereto.

" ' *Resolved,* That we tender our heartfelt sympathy to the widow and other relatives of the deceased, in this hour of their deep affliction, and recommend the religion which he preached, as their only effectual source of consolation and support under this great bereavement.'

" Some lines offered by a lady of the church were read with much feeling by Mr. Waterston, and the occasion was one of deep and solemn interest.

" The work which it was the ardent wish of his soul to consummate is now being perfected by us according to his desire, and an answer is thus accorded to his many prayers to that effect.

" Attest,   J. BURTON."

In the blank-book selected by Mr. Judd for the purpose, was recorded, as above resolved, the Declaration embracing his idea of a true Christian church, which, before his illness, he had had printed on single sheets, and circulated among all his people. This was now offered to them for signature; and it was affecting to see them, almost without exception, come up by families, and enroll their names, parents and children, as born under that "new covenant" established by Christ, alike subject to its obligations and entitled to all its privileges; a scene on which that beatified pastor might look down from his glorified sphere of new existence with ecstatic delight. Great warmth of Christian feeling has since prevailed in Christ Church; and active energy has been displayed, not only in establishing Mr. Judd's views among themselves, but in making their value, as witnessed by their own experience, known and appreciated by the entire Unitarian body. Together with his more immediately responsible family-friends, they have felt it a sacred trust left in their hands to see that views deemed by him of so vital importance to the welfare, if not, indeed, to the *permanence*, of the Christian church, should be submitted to the consideration of the public; an end which has been secured by the efficient exertions of Joseph H. Williams, Esq., a parishioner and brother-in-law of Mr. Judd, in the publication, under the title of "The Birthright Church," of the discourse prepared for the Thursday Lecture, and also of a volume of sermons relating to the same subject, entitled "The Church." Not only have they testified their conviction of the worth of Mr. Judd's teachings, but they have also evinced their high appreciation of his genius as a preacher, by the fact, that, a great part of the time since his removal, they have desired nothing better, in their public sabbath services, than to listen to the reading of manuscript sermons which he had perhaps more than once delivered in their hearing ; a rare instance, it is believed, of the life-giving elements embodied in the common round of weekly discourses.

It may, perhaps, not improperly be added, that the sense of loss occasioned by Mr. Judd's removal was not limited to his own people and his own particular friends. It drew forth expressions of regret extensively from the public prints ; and several discourses with reference to it were delivered the following sabbath. The Rev. Dr. Gannett, in a sermon preached in Bangor, alluding to the event, paid the following kindly tribute to Mr. Judd : " If the loss were confined to that sister-church in Augusta, it would be a fit occasion for us to remember the counsel which directs us ' to weep with those that weep.' But the church to which our friend sustained the relation of pastor are not the only mourners who feel a sense of personal bereavement. From one and another I hear the exclamation, ' His death is a loss to the whole State.' Let me give to the conviction that prompts these words a still wider reach. His death is a loss to the whole country ; for, by his writings and his character, he has made himself known far beyond the sphere of his personal influence. Even in European countries, an American literature would be incomplete which did not notice his works."

On the May-day succeeding Mr. Judd's departure, the lambs of the church, as they had been for so many years in the habit of doing, assembled in the morning around Christ Church Parsonage ; but the accustomed shepherd was not there to conduct them forth over the green hills, and amid the forest-shade. Yet did another kind leader attend them ; and, in their ramble, they twined green wreaths, with which they approached the pastor's resting-place, and garlanded his tomb with these fit emblems of immortality ; thus unconsciously responding to these words, incidentally let fall in one of his earlier discourses to his people : —

"I sometimes ask myself the question, If I were to die to-day, should I, too, be forgotten to-morrow? Am I enriching no soul with those treasures of goodness which form the only desirable memorial? Am I leading no one in the path to heaven, so that my guiding hand will not be missed when I am gone? Am I creating life and joy, beauty and purity, in no one's heart and life, so that no one would regret my absence? Shall the summer air visit my grave, and will not you?"

It was ever a matter of sentiment with Mr. Judd, that our mother-earth should receive into her very bosom the remnant of mortality left behind, so that, above the cherished form so closely connected with our identity, the grass might green, flowers bloom and diffuse their fragrance on the gentle breeze; that birds might warble forth their gushing songs from waving, impendent branches; that all the kindly and suggestive ministries of nature might serve to soothe and cheer fond friends who should gather there, and divest of gloom the little mound of earth indicating that henceforth the "corruptible *has* put on incorruption." Particular circumstances have as yet prevented such sepulture; but it is designed that, at an early day, this pleasing idea shall be consummated, and that a symbolic monument, bearing appropriate emblems, shall mark the spot.